M000104155

Creating the New Egyptian Woman

Creating the New Egyptian Woman

Consumerism, Education, and National Identity, 1863–1922

Mona L. Russell

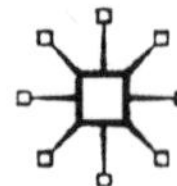

CREATING THE NEW EGYPTIAN WOMAN
© Mona L. Russell, 2004.

All rights reserved. No part of this book may be used or reproduced in any manner whatsoever without written permission except in the case of brief quotations embodied in critical articles or reviews.

First published in 2004 by
PALGRAVE MACMILLAN™
175 Fifth Avenue, New York, N.Y. 10010 and
Houndmills, Basingstoke, Hampshire, England RG21 6XS
Companies and representatives throughout the world

PALGRAVE MACMILLAN is the global academic imprint of the Palgrave Macmillan division of St. Martin's Press, LLC and of Palgrave Macmillan Ltd. Macmillan® is a registered trademark in the United States, United Kingdom and other countries. Palgrave is a registered trademark in the European Union and other countries.

ISBN 1–4039–6262–6 hardback

Library of Congress Cataloging-in-Publication Data

Russell, Mona L.
Creating the new Egyptian woman: consumerism, education, and national identity, 1863–1922 / Mona L. Russell.
p. cm.
Includes bibliographical references and index.
ISBN 1–4039–6262–6 (alk. paper)
1. Women—Egypt—Social conditions. 2. Women consumers—Egypt. 3. Women—Education—Egypt. 4. Women's rights—Egypt. I. Title.

HQ1793.R87 2004
305.42′0962—dc22 2004041687

A catalogue record for this book is available from the British Library.

Design by Newgen Imaging Systems (P) Ltd., Chennai, India.

First edition: October 2004

10 9 8 7 6 5 4 3 2 1

Printed in the United States of America.

To my loving parents

Contents

List of Illustrations

Acknowledgments

My first debt of gratitude must go to my parents, Drs. George and Laila Russell. Throughout my life they have provided me with an unending stream of emotional support. Their example of integrity, honesty, and excellence in their personal and professional lives has set a standard that I strive to meet daily. They have always encouraged my work, and they are always willing to read anything that I have written. For that reason, I should also thank them for helping me to make my research accessible to those outside the field.

This work grows from the doctoral research that I carried out under the mentorship of Judith Tucker, who continues to provide me with support and encouragement. The other members of my doctoral committee, Amira Sonbol and Peter Gran, have been incredible sources of knowledge on the Egyptian archives specifically, as well as getting things done in Cairo, generally. Carrying out the research would have been near impossible had it not been for the year that I spent in language study on a fellowship from the Center for Arabic Studies Abroad (CASA) in 1991–92. I would especially like to thank Mona Kamel, Nadia Harb, and Nabil Abdelfattah for honing my basic skills in Arabic, and Nawal el-Saadawi, Ayman Fuad Sayyed, and Raouf Abbas for their classes in Women's Studies, Paleography, and Social History, respectively. Raouf Abbas deserves another round of praise for having served as my advisor in Egypt during the period of my doctoral research.

I would like to thank the American Research Center in Egypt for its generous support during my initial period of research in 1994–95, as well as on my return to Egypt in the summer of 2002. I appreciate the assistance that I received from the staffs at the periodicals division of *Dar al-Kutub*, the research division of *Dar al-Watha'iq*, the documents office at the Museum of Education, and *L'Institut d'Egypte*. Their patience with my unending stream of questions and requests will not soon be forgotten. As well, the staffs at the Jesuit Library at the *Collège de la Sainte Famille*, the Creswell and regular libraries of the American University in Cairo, the Geographic Society, and the Huda Shaarawi Association deserve acknowledgment. Additionally, I would like to thank Hossam Abbas M. Sadek for his assistance in locating articles of interest and Maha Abbas M. Sadek for hand-copying sketches from textbooks that could not be photocopied. My life in Cairo was immeasurably improved by the presence of my extended family there. I am grateful for all the Friday lunches, birthday parties, other special gatherings, and more recently, for introducing my children to Egyptian family life.

I owe a special thanks to Lisa Pollard. We first met at the time that we began our doctoral research and have remained close friends since then. Our collaboration on research, panels, and endeavors completely unrelated to history has meant a great deal to me. Another long-standing friendship that helped me along this path has been that of Mine Ener, who just recently passed away. Mine helped me with everything from my first entrance into *Dar al-Kutub* to feedback on conference papers, and I will miss her dearly.

I value the three years that I spent working at the Massachusetts Institute of Technology. Having the opportunity to reshape the "Nationalism in the Middle East" course into "The Politics of Identity in the Middle East" has enhanced my understanding of both gender and national identity. I owe a great deal to the students who took this class and continued to prod me with difficult questions. Indeed, all of the students that I taught at MIT helped me to think in new directions, places that the historian might not generally go. MIT supported my numerous trips to conferences and workshops, which also facilitated the writing of this book. My colleagues there provided me with warmth, support, constructive criticism, and an understanding ear. Finally, having the Technology Children's Center across from my office made working motherhood a joy for both me and for my children. My sincere gratitude goes to the staff there for their loving care, their open door (for my midday visit), and for knowing when a call to Mommy was needed (or not needed).

My acknowledgments would not be complete without a special thanks to my husband Pete Allen Boyer. Without his support, commitment, and encouragement the undertaking of this project would not have been possible. There are no words that can describe or measure what he has added to my life. His ability to divide the day between regular exercise, diligent work, and quality family time has been both an example and a comfort to me. Last, but certainly not least, I would like to thank my daughters, Hailey and Jasmine, for bringing such happiness to my life. Their bright eyes, beautiful smiles, and inquisitive minds make each day better than the previous one. Before having experienced motherhood myself, there was always an aspect of the New Woman that I did not fully appreciate.

Note on Transliteration and Translation

My aim has been to make this work accessible to the nonspecialist, while also acknowledging the needs of the specialist in the field. Thus, the entire text appears in English without diacritical marks, even for Arabic names. The exceptions to this rule are places in which Arabic words or titles appear in the text for emphasis or clarity. I have opted for the common English rendering of certain words, for example, Cairo and Zamalek. In the endnotes, I have translated the titles of articles for the sake of non-Arabic readers, but in the interest of the Arabic-reading audience, I have adopted a modified *International Journal of Middle East Studies (IJMES)* system of transliteration for authors, periodical titles, and book titles. The Egyptian letter *gim* has been transliterated as j, except in cases where the Egyptian rendering of g is more familiar, for example, Giza or Darb al-Gamamiz. Since Arabic does not utilize capitalization, I have not capitalized any part of titles, with the exception of names of people and places. I have eliminated diacritical marks for long vowels and initial *hamzas* because they are largely unnecessary for Arabic readers. I utilize a dot beneath the letter for emphatic consonants, ^{c} for the letter ^{c}*ayn*, and ʿ for the *hamza*. In both the text and the endnotes, I have anglicized names according to two basic rules: preference for the individual's rendering of his/her own name and the modified *IJMES* system. Every effort has been made for consistency, but complete uniformity is near impossible.

Many of the documents that I examined appear in both Arabic and French, with some appearing in one language or the other. I have read both the Arabic and French versions, where they exist, and I have translated titles of such documents into English. As well, Arabic document titles have been rendered in English. Certain documents appear in French alone, in which case I have left the title in French.

All translations are mine, unless otherwise indicated. In places where translations needed additional English words for clarity, I have indicated such additions in brackets.

Chapter 1

Introduction

In his work by the same title, Qasim Amin described the New Woman as "one of the fruits of modern civilization" and connected her rise in the West to "scientific discoveries that freed the human mind from the powers of delusion, suspicion, and superstition." This process allowed the woman to move from a frivolous state into one in which she could be "a sister to man, a companion to her husband, [and] a tutor to her children—a refined individual." Amin hoped that "this transformation" would take place in his own country, arguing that it would be "the most significant development in Egypt's history."[1] Implicit, and even explicit, in Amin's description are comparison to the West and the notion that the New Woman is an improved, superior woman.

Amin was, in Arland Thornton's words, reading history "sideways." He was confusing variations across geographic space for those across developmental time, assuming northwest Europe to be at the apogee; and further, he assumed that transformation of societies would take place based upon key changes in familial life, notably the status of the woman.[2] He wholeheartedly embraced this paradigm of developmental idealism, viewing such changes with optimism and enthusiasm.

Nevertheless, while broadening horizons may have characterized the life of New Women in Egypt at the turn of the century, new forms of oppression, domination, and patriarchy also characterize such change, for "old" and "new" women alike. The reader should not view the New Woman depicted in this work as either good/bad or desirable/undesirable; but rather (s)he should view the evolution of the New Woman as shaping a range of both positive and negative possibilities for the New Woman and the people with whom she had contact. One remarkable example would be the training of women as *ḥakimas* [female doctors]. While on the one hand, education, opportunity, and the spread of modern medicine to the population at large had immeasurable positive potentiality; on the other hand, as the work of Khaled Fahmy, Mervat Hatem, Hibba Abugideiri, and Mario Ruiz demonstrates, the state utilized *ḥakimas* as a means of controlling, surveying, and regulating women's bodies in nineteenth-century Egypt.[3] Although this work tends to focus on the positive aspects of these changes, we cannot ignore the other possibilities nor view history in a teleological sense.

The *Oxford English Dictionary* defines the New Woman, in a series of definitions of "woman" relating to "qualities denoting status, occupation, or character." She is "a woman of 'advanced' views advocating the independence of her sex and defying convention."[4] The New Woman, who arrived in Egypt in the late nineteenth century, was neither new nor alone. She appeared worldwide between 1850 and 1950. As the previous definition indicates, she would come to be connected with citizenship, nationalism, and women's rights in a wide variety of states, while still displaying characteristics unique to her individual history. While much of the research on the New Woman has focused on her role in feminism and feminist movements, more recent work has connected her to various aspects of consumerism and material culture.[5] Since I first began this research in the mid–1990s, there has been an abundance of innovative research on her various regional incarnations.[6]

Who was the New Egyptian Woman? In order to define, categorize, and characterize her, we must come to an understanding of the "old" Egyptian woman; yet, no such construct exists. There is no "baseline" standard from which a New Woman can emerge. Gender and nationality are but two components in a much more complex network of relationships, including race, class, region, and religion. In examining the historical experience of "old" Egyptian women, class is by far the most significant of these factors. Recent work on eighteenth-century elite women suggests that despite seclusion, women were active in the social, cultural, and economic realms of society. They visited friends and family, enjoyed regular trips to the bathhouse and the cemeteries, and were present at religious and secular festivals. Furthermore, they exercised power in society through their membership in ruling households, which was buttressed by their economic rights to property and inheritance, as well as their role in strategic marriage alliances.[7] At the other end of the economic spectrum, Judith Tucker's *Women in Nineteenth Century Egypt* documents changes in the lives of rural and urban lower class women with the growth of the Egyptian state. Traditionally, women were involved in agricultural and non-agricultural production, as well as in trade. The spread of capitalism and increased state control of the economy worked against many women, who lost access to previous sources of wealth, status, and power.[8]

Thus, two vastly different pictures emerge of the "old" Egyptian woman: the secluded, privileged upper-class woman and the woman who worked alongside her husband in agriculture, craft production, or trade. By the turn of the twentieth century, images in the media, advertisements, and textbooks depicted a "New Woman" who embodied traditional values, yet superseded her grandmother in her ability to run her home, educate her children, serve as her husband's partner in life, and in turn, serve her country by fulfilling all of these duties. The mainstream and women's presses clearly defined the roles of the "New Woman" with numerous articles on her education, her duties in the home, her responsibilities in marriage and motherhood, and the importance of all these activities in the creation of the Egyptian nation. Advertisements depicted how she could carry out these roles more easily and effectively with the help of new products and services. Curricula in the growing number of state and private educational facilities reinforced these images.

The new Egyptian woman was neither ubiquitous nor homogenous, nor did she reside outside the large cities of the delta.[9] She was an urban phenomenon found mainly in Cairo and Alexandria. Not only were these cities at the cutting edge of Egyptian society, they served as socio-cultural "magnets" of the *Mashriq*, attracting journalists, entrepreneurs, and their families.[10] These cities were important centers of trade in both intellectual and material commodities; and given their cosmopolitan make-up, they combined Ottoman, European, Ladino, and indigenous trends.

The "New Woman" was not synonymous with the Westernized woman, nor was her appearance unveiled a litmus test for this label. The type of veil, the clothing underneath, the accessories that complemented the outfit, were also significant factors. The construct of new womanhood that emerged in Egypt at the turn of the century represented the infiltration of new ideas, fashions, and goods, tempered by a cultural authenticity and burgeoning nationalism, both of which encouraged indigenous concepts of morality and virtue. The New Woman would glean the best from Eastern and Western cultural worlds, avoiding "the Frankensteinian combination of the worst of both [worlds]."[11]

The process by which the "New Woman" was created was tied to new patterns of consumption and greater educational opportunities for both women and men. Indeed, the story of the "New Woman" is the counterpart to the story of the "New Man." Furthermore, the creation of these new individuals played a role in the formation of a national identity. The "New Woman" was part of the new household, whose members all had important roles in the creation of the Egyptian nation. The father-provider headed the household, and he worked diligently outside the home in order to materially support his family. He was aided by his partner, the mother-educator, who attended to the emotional and material needs of the household. The children were to be clean, responsible, and obedient, absorbing the virtues of their parents. By advancing the moral and material level of the household, Egyptians could advance the nation.

Although the rhetoric of national reform carried the underpinnings of Victorian domesticity and separate spheres, these concepts evolved from completely different structures. In western Europe, the ideology of domesticity and separate spheres arose as industrial capitalism moved work outside the home, giving rise to waged labor. While women did not gain access to better-paying jobs, their importance as household managers increased.[12] In her study of the rise of the bourgeoisie in the Ottoman Empire, Göçek argues that this process in western Europe created new concepts of civilization, space, and fashion that resulted in changes in the home regarding allocation of public and private space, in addition to its decoration with appropriate furnishings and artifacts.[13] Although upper-class households in the Ottoman Empire, in general, and in Egypt, in particular, adopted these divisions of space by the late nineteenth century, their application does not represent an evolution from a similar historical experience. As Göçek argues, "[t]he household as the Ottoman unit of analysis . . . united public and private spheres, family and government, rulers and ruled . . . cut[ting] across various social functions and social groups to structurally unite the sultan and his officials with their families, slaves, administrators, and laborers."[14] While Fay similarly argues that eighteenth-century elite mamluk households served such a function harkening back to a "resurgent" mamluk system, Hathaway emphasizes the specifically Ottoman nature of these households given the important role they played as a nexus between center and province, as concubines, slaves, and clients moved between the poles.[15]

The interplay between household and power is a key theme in this work. The household of Muhammad Ali, like the Ottoman-mamluk households of the eighteenth century, united public and private functions. We examine the process by which the creation of a centralized state and bureaucracy altered the role of the ruler's home and resulted in the creation a network of households with vested interests in that state. Much of the story involves how Egyptian rulers conceptualized themselves and their authority. Muhammad Ali viewed himself as a vassal of the Ottoman state, seeking a greater share of autonomy, similar to mamluk beys of the eighteenth century. He in no form or fashion envisioned himself as an Egyptian. He was part of an Ottoman-Egyptian elite, which expressed itself in Turkish. Among his successors up through Ismail there was a progressive movement to further Egyptian autonomy and preference their own hereditary line of succession.

The reign of Ismail (r. 1863–79) in many ways continued some of these trends and inaugurated others. Ismail envisioned Egypt as joining the ranks of Europe and tried to remap his home and capital to fit this vision. While Turkish remained the language of the ruling elite, Ismail also encouraged the use of both French and Arabic, as a means of Europeanizing and separating Egypt. Identity serves to define as well as to exclude, and in attempting to create a European Egypt, Ismail laid the foundation for an Egyptian Egypt. Nevertheless, as will be addressed in chapter 2, Ismail's extravagance set in motion the process that inaugurated the British occupation.

The arrival of the British during the reign of Tawfiq complicated the situation by again creating an oppositional other. As the work of Eve Troutt Powell demonstrates, Egypt's continued occupation of the Sudan facilitated this process. While she sees the Ottoman-Egyptian elite as defining itself, she maintains that Muhammad Ali and his successors "did not identify themselves as Egyptians."[16] Perhaps a more careful look at the rulers, their languages, and their households helps to paint a somewhat different picture. The recent editing/translating of Abbas Hilmi II's (r. 1892–1914) memoirs is useful in this respect. He portrays himself as a ruler whose mother tongue is Turkish, yet he dramatically emphasizes the importance of the Arabic language (from the time of Ismail). Furthermore he identifies himself as an Egyptian ruler during whose reign "national spirit became defined and consolidated."[17] In the span of a 100 years, the dynasty evolved from viewing itself as leading a vassal state of the Ottoman Empire to reigning over an Egyptian nation. This change in perception was possible because of the diffusion of power from a handful of military/political fortresses to a middle class of bureaucrats and professionals, as well as their families, who believed in the idea of an Egyptian nation and saw their home as a crucial building block.

Another aspect of this development was related to changes in education for men and women.[18] Much of the existing historiography on the topic of women and education, while connecting it to nationalism, tends to view it through the prism of feminism or the feminist movement.[19] In *Feminists, Islam, and Nation*, Margot Badran seeks to reconcile the fact that women were at the forefront of the 1919 Revolution, yet they remained unliberated in the years after independence. She asserts that male nationalists appropriated the feminist movement as a means of articulating their nationalist demands, but after 1922, these same men were too busy competing for political power to set forth on a feminist agenda.[20] In contrast, Beth Baron argues that female intellectuals appropriated the rhetoric of nationalism in order to achieve their aims in women's rights, education, and philanthropy.[21] More recently, Lisa Pollard has eschewed these frameworks of appropriation in favor of examining the gendered discourse of nationalism in the post–World War I era, examining male and female education.[22]

The importance of the press, advertising, and consumption has received greater attention in recent years, particularly its role in inspiring nationalism and bringing about revolt or revolution.[23] As Heather Sharkey argues in her study of nationalism and culture in Sudan, "[n]ationalism was . . . a literary undertaking . . . reliant on the power of the written word to affirm and eventually popularize its values."[24] The fact that such a nationalism was both elite and exclusive does not remove its power as an ideational force in society. This study views the reign of Ismail as a watershed moment for this process. In part it was by chance that he came to power as the revolutions in transportation and communication were at a critical juncture in Egypt, and his program of education and development inspired both awe and criticism. His support of various intellectual societies and the press created a forum, albeit somewhat limited, for discussing the issues of the day.

By focusing on the issues of consumerism, education, and identity I hope to build on this body of work, examining other significant issues in the historiography of Egypt, for example, the rise of capitalism, the development of an indigenous bureaucracy, the creation of a modern educational system, and the evolution of the nationalist movement. Trends in consumption provide a window into more than what people are, but rather what they aim to be.[25] According to Göçek, "[g]oods make and maintain social relationships and fix public meaning . . . social groups utilize consumption to reinforce or undermine existing social boundaries." She goes on to describe how the goods amassed by an individual represent his/her "hierarchy of values" thus "attach[ing] meaning to the goods."[26]

While the history of consumption and its meanings are relatively new to the historiography of the Middle East,[27] the subject in the American context has been well studied. With respect to the role of women as consumers, opinion is divided between those who see consumption as a form of empowerment for women and those who view it as an extension of male authority. The former optimistically argue that women exercise power in both the quantity and range of decisions encountered in the consumer experience.[28] Critics, such as John Kenneth Galbraith, contend that consumption extends male authority by providing a veneer of free choice over a reality of unremunerated work for women.[29] Furthermore, critics claim that media images encouraging consumption reinforce the economic and sexual subordination of women to men.[30] Viewing the role of consumption in either of these extremes overlooks both the opportunities and challenges that it provided for women. For example, in his study of women and turn-of-the-century department stores, William Leach examines how consumption created new definitions of womanhood:

> [P]articipation in the consumer experience challenged and subverted that complex of qualities traditionally known as feminine-dependence, passivity, religious piety, domestic inwardness, sexual purity, and maternal nurture. Mass consumer culture presented to women a new definition of gender that carved out a space for individual expression similar to men's and that stood in tension with the older definition passed on to them by their mothers and grandmothers.[31]

In the Egyptian context, consumption allowed women of the middle and upper classes to similarly challenge old definitions of womanhood. Consumerism was by no means a nineteenth-century invention, nor was it necessarily a consequence of capitalism. In the eighteenth century, consumerism among women was limited to the upper classes, and it took place within the home. While women had the choice to buy or not buy and the ability to make requests, the quantity, quality, and variety of goods was determined by female traders [*dallalas*]. The spread of capitalism in Egypt and the subsequent growth of the infrastructure of consumption led to both an increase in the quantity of goods available and the number of people with access to those goods. As was the case in western Europe, new patterns of consumption led to new conceptions of individualism, fashion, and decency.[32] Nevertheless, the Egyptian context was neither a small-scale imitation of the West, nor was it merely a building block in the colonialist project. The Mrs. Consumer who arose in Egypt differed from her American counterparts by her class, education, and taste, as evidenced by the products and services that were repeatedly advertised for women. The shopping experience, whether in the home, in specialized departments for women, or in stores without gender segregation, allowed women to experiment and challenge old forms of identity as well as to confront the British occupation through their consumption (or non-consumption) of goods. Thus, this study sees the spread of capitalism as more than just the replacement of indigenous goods with Western ones, it examines the creation of a new lifestyle and ideology based upon new patterns of consumption.[33]

These new patterns of consumption involved more than products and services, but also ideas as articulated in the new educational system. This work attempts to situate female education in a larger struggle for cultural and intellectual hegemony. State sponsorship of education is a key aspect of hegemonic leadership. The creation of the modern Egyptian state necessitated the training of individuals to serve as workers for the state. The expansion of educational and career opportunities for men helped to build the ranks of the urban middle class, a class distinguished by its patterns of consumption, sources of income, and participation in public life. The state also had a vested interest in expanding professional opportunities for women in medicine, education, and social work. Nevertheless, the aim of public education did not mesh with the emerging ideal of "New Womanhood." How could a woman serve as the emotional pillar of her family if she worked outside the home? At the same time, the new ideal necessitated education for women; but how could women be educated without female teachers? This study examines governmental attempts to alleviate these inconsistencies by emphasizing a domestic curriculum. Although articles on female education in the mainstream and women's presses emphasized the importance of women's role in the home, views on the nature and practicality of domestic education differed along class and gender lines.

The existence of a two-track educational system only complicated matters with respect to girls' education. Since the system established by Muhammad Ali worked from the top to the base, initially, it was necessary to recruit and maintain students from traditional schools. Furthermore, Muhammad Ali had no need to dismantle these structures, for they still served important socio-cultural functions in the community. The existence of this parallel system of education later allowed the British to extend hegemonic control by providing an inexpensive form of mass education, while simultaneously limiting access to the Westernized educational system. Both the British and the Egyptian ruling elite found this system to be effective in restricting government employment and the liberal professions to men of the upper classes. This strategy did not work, however, in the girls' schools. The vocational emphasis of the upper track discouraged matriculation by girls of the upper classes. A vast array of alternatives to state-run schools for girls existed in the form of governesses/tutors, as well as mission, private, and community schools. Mission schools sought to advance Christianity and Western education, while the foreign/minority schools sought to preserve the language, culture, and heritage of the individual community. Both types of schools served to spur the Muslim majority into creating alternative forms of private education for girls. Despite benefits gained in European languages, boys preferred the passport to public service that state education provided.

Education was a means for articulating a nascent national identity. The emergence or existence of a national identity does not and did not erase other forms of identity, such as religion, class, locale, or occupation.[34] The emergence of an Egyptian identity often overlapped with a larger Ottoman or Eastern identity, and many of the journalists and textbook authors, who helped to convey these notions, were Levantine in origin. Furthermore, it is ironic that the "Westernized" educational system served to forge an Egyptian identity. Both Western advisors and indigenous bureaucrats helped to shape this identity.[35] In particular, I discuss Rifaat Tahtawi and Ali Mubarak, both of whom made significant contributions through their long tenures of service, their writings, and the legacy created in the school system itself. These men were profoundly influenced by their experiences in Europe and with European states. Moreover, as Powell highlights, both of these men were shaped by another oppositional other, the Sudan, which helped to create "an idealized, burgeoning nationalist sense."[36]

While both Tahtawi and Mubarak acknowledged serious differences between the Egyptian and European contexts, they sought to apply European models to their own milieu, as well as to Egypt's rule over Sudan. Tahtawi believed in the use of curriculum to advance new models of citizenship, and thus he emphasized the study of national history, geography, and politics.[37] In contrast, Mubarak focused on applying Western models of organization, structure, and discipline. As the system graduated and employed more men exposed to these views, they, in turn helped to further shape the system by adjusting the curriculum to socio-cultural needs and political realities. For example, by the 1890s, Turkish became optional in government schools, and it was eventually phased out completely.[38] Meanwhile, mathematics textbooks omitted Turkish currency from conversion charts by the turn of the century.[39]

Although British occupiers sought to reshape curriculum in language, history, and geography to suit the colonialist project, debate in the press advanced growing nationalist views. As a result, more classes were taught in Arabic, and the number of lessons in religion increased, reinforcing the study of both Islamic history and the Arabic language.[40] Furthermore, a new course of study emerged: *al-tarbiya al-qawmiyya* [national education/morals].[41] It subsumed an old course in manners and morals, adding a civic dimension. In other words, its structure indicated that one's personal behavior had greater implications for society. Meanwhile, in schools for girls, these lessons were reinforced in the home economics classroom. Although these developments in curriculum took place slowly over the course of several decades, they are nonetheless significant in the formation of identity. Furthermore, they challenge recent studies on nationalism that view the period between World War I and the 1919 Revolution as the pivotal, explosive era in which territorial Egyptian nationalism emerges.[42]

A significant theme throughout this work is the issue of contact and confrontation with European thought and culture. In seeking to address this issue, the historian runs the risk of falling into the old modernization paradigm for the study of Middle East history. In this study, I have attempted to demonstrate that Western thought, processes, products, and structures do not, in fact, displace indigenous ones. In the first place, there is rarely wholesale imitation or adoption of Western ways, even amongst the upper class. There is always some level of accommodation and adaptation. Second, in some cases, there were already indigenous precedents, for example, the increasing interest in French luxury products in the eighteenth century or the existence of the *daya* [midwife] historically. Neither the growth of the department stores nor the training of women to be *ḥakimas* can be fully understood without looking back to these precedents. Third, it is important to realize that traditional structures continued to exist, and in some instances, to thrive. Modern shops do not replace bazaars, nor does the higher primary school replace the *kuttab*. Thus, the persistence of parallel structures is a theme throughout this work.[43] Since my focus is on the urban middle and upper classes, more attention is necessarily given to the new structures; but in no way is this emphasis a value judgment. Finally, I have included indigenous critiques of both the new patterns of consumption and the new education system in order to highlight the lack of acceptance of Western ways amongst certain segments of the population.

Part I

The Household, Consumerism, and the New Woman

Chapter 2

The House, City, and Nation that Ismail Built

The House that Ismail Built

When Muhammad Ali first got official word that he would be viceroy of Egypt in 1805, neither he nor the Ottoman Sultan who conferred the title had any idea that his family would continue to rule Egypt until the mid-twentieth century. Indeed, both probably approached the venture with a "make the best out of it" attitude. Egypt had been largely out of central Ottoman control for more than a century, and someone who could restore order and remit taxes would serve a beneficial function. From the point of view of a merchant-sailor, namely Muhammad Ali, Egypt held great potential for the person able to navigate the difficult waters between local potentates, interfering European powers, and the central Ottoman administration.

Muhammad Ali did not introduce a completely new system, rather he built upon the foundations laid by the mamluks. He learned their techniques of centralization and the establishment of law and order, yet he departed from his mamluk forbears with his policies on industry, agriculture, education, and the Egyptianization of the bureaucracy.[1] It was not until after his infamous soirée at the Citadel in 1811 that he put into place the features of his reign that made him unique, and embarked upon sponsorship of royal architecture.[2] Since Umayyad times, perhaps earlier, architecture has played an important role as an emblem of Islamic rule. Through the sponsorship of residences, mosques, fountains, schools, hospitals, and the like, Muslim rulers have symbolized their power and created institutions to sustain the community.

Before building his own palace, Muhammad Ali first resided at the former home of Muhammad Bey al-Alfi. In 1812 Muhammad Ali demolished an old palace at the Citadel and the *diwan* of Qaytbey to build the first in a series of *Rumi*-styled kiosks and palaces. By adopting architectural styles from his native Albania and its environs, he brought his own imprint to Egypt, while simultaneously banning certain elements of mamluk architecture. In addition to new palace buildings at the Citadel, he built a palace in Alexandria, one in Shubra, one for his daughter Zaynab in Azbakiyya, and one for his daughter Nazli on the Nile.[3]

British intervention put an end to Muhammad Ali's expansion (beyond Sudan) and industrialization plans; however, many of his other policies remained, and the *Rumi* architectural style continued to be popular with the local population throughout the rest of the century. Although he lost significant commercial and industrial power in the Treaty of Balta Liman (1838), through the Treaty of London (1841) Muhammad Ali's family received the right to rule Egypt as a hereditary *pashalik*, following Ottoman succession practice (eldest male of ruling family). Muhammad Ali's successors, Abbas and Said, lacked his creativity and political *savoir-faire*. Under their rule, many of his programs were reduced or dismantled. Nevertheless, they continued efforts at modernization of transportation and communication with the development of railroad and telegraph networks in Egypt. They continued to sponsor various royal architectural projects, particularly Abbas.[4]

Despite the fact that the *firman* granting the dynasty succession specifically placed Egypt under Ottoman practice, even in the lifetime of Muhammad Ali there was some effort at primogeniture by his eldest son. Ibrahim ruled in his father's name for seven and a half months in 1848, but preceded his father to the grave. According to Toledano, Ibrahim was too ill and had such poor relations with Istanbul that he was unable to carry out this goal. Once succession went to Abbas (r. 1848–54), he too began to maneuver a change in the law of succession to primogeniture. The first step in this process was to marry his son Ilhami to Sultan Abdul Majid's daughter. Nevertheless, Abbas died before his plan could come to fruition.[5]

The ascension of Ismail marks a transition to a new architectural and ruling style, as well as the reimplementation of some of Muhammad Ali's practices.[6] Foreigners present in Egypt at the time, saw his rise to power as the inauguration of a new and promising era in Egyptian history.[7] Ismail, like his grandfather, sought to revitalize Egypt by imposing order and improving education. Additionally, he desired further investment and settlement by sponsoring new forms of consumption in an Egypt that he viewed as being part of Europe. These changes began at the level of his household, continued in his capital, and spread throughout the country as a whole. Where Ibrahim and Abbas had failed to inaugurate a system of primogeniture, Ismail succeeded. He was able to utilize an important link to the Ottoman Sultan Abdul Aziz—they were maternal cousins. His mother laid the groundwork for the plan during a state visit in 1865, and although she was not given any encouragement, the law was changed a year later. Ismail also obtained the title Khedive, a Persian word for ruler, and a title that his father and grandfather had used unofficially.[8]

Another way in which Ismail heralded his reign as an era of change, was through the initiation of a large number of palace-building projects. In 1863 Ismail began work on his new official residence. He felt that his grandfather's palace in Shubra was too far from the seat of action. Instead, he wanted to make Abdin palace a political and social center, easily accessible to the (soon to be) chic neighborhoods of Ismailiyya and Azbakiyya. After buying the home of Abdin Bey, Ismail purchased and/or expropriated the surrounding land and buildings. He then replaced Abdin Bey's home with an enormous palace, constructed by Italian architect Di Corel Wel Rousseau. The outside was neo-Classisical, while the interior blended a series of diverse and contrasting styles. Intricate gardens surrounded the palace, including an aquarium, where Ismail collected rare fish. The total cost of the project was close to

£700,000, and it took eleven years to complete. The Abdin project was but one aspect of his larger Haussmanization of Cairo, and given its long-term implications, Ismail began work on the Gezira and Giza palaces as well. Tamraz points out that these palaces are important intermediaries between the earlier *Rumi* style and the European style characterized by his later constructions, such as Abdin.[9]

The new palace and gardens at Gezira incorporated the palace and kiosk of Muhammad Ali. Construction was completed in 1868, in plenty of time for it to serve as the temporary home for the Empress Eugénie during the Suez Canal festivities in the fall of 1869. Apparently Ismail went so far as to order that her private apartments be an exact replica of her suite at the Tuilleries. The Gezira Palace was situated on 60 *feddans* (roughly acres) and comprised a palace for the female quarters, the *ḥarim*, and two areas for the reception of guests (*salamliks*), the latter designed by the Austrian architect Franz Pasha. The palace combined "oriental"-style furnishings and "magnificent" interior decoration with imported Western wrought-iron balconies fashioned in Islamic style. The surrounding gardens were enclosed with a fence to keep Ismail's collection of animals. The garden was illuminated by gas lamps, which helped to create the image of a "fairy land."[10]

According to Ali Mubarak, the cost of the Gezira palace approached £900,000; however, relative to the cost of the Giza palace, he considered it a nominal amount. Ismail spent nearly £1,400,000 on the Giza palace, which had formerly belonged to Said. He purchased it from Said's son, expanded the existing palace, and increased the number of buildings on the 30–*feddan* tract of land. He brought Western engineers to construct a *salamlik* of sculptured stone. The original gardens were expanded, and the old walkways demolished and repaved. Ismail appointed Barillet-Deschamps to landscape the area now known as Orman gardens. This area later provided the nucleus for the zoological gardens and Cairo University. The current *majlis al-dawla* building in Giza was likely part of these same renovations.[11]

In the words of Ismail's minister of public works, the Khedive was absolutely "enamored of building." Ismail sustained numerous projects for both himself and his family, including the 400-room al-Qubba palace near Heliopolis built for his son Tawfiq and al-Zaafran palace in Abbasiyya originally built for himself but later given as a present to his mother. He renovated a number of older palaces and established new ones in Minya, Mansura, and the island of Roda. Finally, the Khedive invested a good deal of money in his home away from home, the *Mahrussa*. The accommodations on the yacht were no less luxurious than in the palaces, including fine porcelain tiles, inlaid banisters, and silver-cased staterooms.[12]

By the time of Ismail, court culture in Egypt was thoroughly enmeshed in both Ottoman and European modes of consumption.[13] Even his predecessor Said (r. 1854–63) had engaged in European-style conspicuous consumption with his French chef, fine wines, and splendid *fêtes*.[14] What made Ismail different was both the extent of his consumerism and his desire to develop the nation in the same way that he developed his home and his capital. According to Pierre Bourdieu, "[t]he effect of mode of acquisition is most marked in the ordinary choices of everyday existence, such as furniture, clothing or cooking . . . " Furthermore, Ismail's choice in clothes, toiletries, and grooming habits exemplifies the use of his body as a "materialization of class taste." The Western luxury items that he chose for his home served to inscribe and reactivate distinction in each act of consumption by means of economic and cultural appropriation. Not only does one have to consider what Ismail imported, but how and why he used those items. For example, his eating habits cannot be considered independently of his lifestyle. The preparation, presentation, and manner of consumption were as important as the *haute cuisine* that he served.[15] By examining the records of the *Période Ismail* series relating to Ismail's purchases for the home and visitors' accounts, one can see the distinction Ismail sought for his homes. Although the records are obviously incomplete, they give the reader a sense of Ismail's taste.

In provisioning his home, Ismail sought catalogs and designs for the most magnificent furnishings. A piece of correspondence from 1875 indicates that any of the drawings could be tailored to meet Ismail's individual needs. While the Khedive hired Egyptian, Italian, French, and Turkish decorators, he also liked to provide input on the decoration process. Visitors to his palaces were universally impressed by the luxury of the interiors. Many even go so far as to mention the cost; however, they do not divulge the source of their information. Ismail sought furnishings that would reinforce his place among the European aristocracy. Not only was the style and cost of furnishings important, but also the activities linked to these furnishings. For example, in early 1876, Ismail sent word to his favorite European merchant that he wanted a billiard table of high quality.[16]

Ismail's distinction was manifested in the foods, beverages, and tobaccos that he selected for consumption in his homes. He ordered expensive meats such as leg of lamb and smoked tongue, as well as specialty items like *foies gras* and smoked salmon. Ismail had a taste for fine imported cheeses, and he ordered items not easily found in Egypt, for example, artichokes and asparagus. More surprisingly, he imported fruits, vegetables, and legumes widely available in Egypt, including onions, beans, carrots, peas, and tomatoes. Finally, he complemented his selections with items such as tarragon vinegar, vermicelli, bread, chocolate, candied fruit, and fruit-flavored syrups. The food served in the palace was beyond compare. Princess Emine Foat Tugay relates an anecdote that is telling of Ismail's extravagance. A former slave in Ismail's *ḥarim* was apparently unable to eat the food provided by her new bridegroom. Her indulgent husband visited the palace kitchen to learn the secrets of the head chef, who showed him the large storerooms of meat used for preparing all dishes, including rice and vegetables. The husband returned home and informed his wife that he would be bankrupted in a month were he to provide her with food prepared as in the palace.[17] Ismail could not possibly have served such rich, gourmet foods without the appropriate beverages. Thus, he ordered the finest wines, champagnes, liquors, beers, and mineral waters in cases by the dozen.[18]

Lavish meals require proper implements for both cooking and serving. Therefore, Ismail ordered special pots, pans, casseroles, grills, sieves, and grinders for the imperial kitchen, as well as jewel-encrusted plates and fine silver place settings.[19] Guests frequently commented upon the splendor of both the meal and its presentation. According to Mrs. Grey, "[t]he dinner was excellent, with every luxury that a true French cuisine and French taste could produce; the table beautifully arranged and decorated . . . " Nevertheless, not all of the European innovations in eating had made their way into the *ḥarim*. The same visitor reports eating Turkish-style in the *ḥarim*, where the women ate with their hands (off of a gold tray and plates of gold with precious stones), and she was given only a tortoiseshell spoon for the soup. All of the women dipped from the same tureen. Mrs. Grey was so horrified that she found herself unable to eat. The third wife of the Khedive mistook her disgust for bashfulness, dipping an onion in gravy for her and putting it in her hand. Unfortunately, Mrs. Grey was unaware that such an act was an honor.[20]

Ismail topped off his lavish meals with fine tobacco. He preferred cigars over Oriental water pipes. He enjoyed cigars both for his own pleasure and to present as elegant gifts. In the existing records of the *Période Ismail,* cigars were among the most frequently recurring expenses.[21] According to a European diplomat, Ismail "always carried two kinds with him in two of his pockets, one kind of an ordinary good brand, but the other was supreme . . . I don't think I ever smoked a better." Apparently, Ismail enjoyed impressing his guests and offered varying qualities according to both the occasion and the recipient.[22] Relli Shechter credits Ismail for switching from pipes to cigarettes at official functions. Furthermore he views the move to cigarettes as "embod[ying] and symboliz[ing] the acceleration of the pace of life in Egypt resulting from reforms."[23]

Ismail sought the latest technology for his home, and he was particularly enamored of photography and related gadgets. He bought expensive equipment, photographs from around the world, and portraits of himself and his family. For example, in 1867 he purchased a stereoscope with views of Paris, four albums of Russian photographs, other assorted albums, plus thousands of pounds worth of photographs and proofs of his formal portraits.[24] According to Sarah Graham-Brown, items such as the albums and stereoscopic slides had become "the rage in Europe."[25] Aside from Ismail's desire to immortalize himself and his family through pictures, his interest in both Paris and Russia are telling of his concerns. Paris represented the model he wished to follow for Cairo, and he could not help but be interested in his suzerain's competitor, another land-based, agrarian, multi-ethnic, multi-religious empire.[26]

Ismail extended his rampant consumerism to personal items such as clothing, jewelry, pharmaceuticals, and even toys. The Khedive's bill from one French company, covering a three-month period in 1877, totaled almost 600 francs. His order included a dressing gown, a dozen pairs of woolen socks, seven pairs of pants, twenty-four ties, three nightshirts, and assorted colognes.[27] He made frequent purchases of colognes, perfumes and jewelry for himself, his mother, the princesses, and his mistresses.[28] Ismail was even part of the latest Western trends in health and beauty products. He patronized the same company used by the Queen of England, the Prince of Wales, and Napoleon III. Ismail must have been pleased by the fact that his name appeared with theirs in the company's logo.[29] European contemporaries give accounts of his "child-like" love for a variety of consumer goods, including toy trains.[30]

The royal *ḥarim* sought the same distinction by purchasing these European luxuries. Emmeline Lott, who resided in the *ḥarim* in the mid-1860s, recounts the large quantity of fabrics from around the world and cases full of the latest French footware.[31] Documents from the *Période Ismail* series confirm Lott's observations. Dresses, blouses, jackets, nightshirts, pantaloons, corsets, and socks were ordered by the dozen.[32] Estimates of the *ḥarim* population vary from 150 to 900 (women only).[33] Even taking the most conservative estimate, keeping these women dressed to the hilt must have cost a small fortune, given what might be spent for a single formal function. Mrs. William Grey described the clothing at a state function as "ridiculous and tasteless . . . in a European fashion . . . [with] hideous round hats with bright flowers and feathers . . . diamond ornaments, earrings, and brooches and a few had the Viceroy's picture set in stones on their shoulder."[34] What seemed to disturb her most was that their appearance defied the "Eastern" look of the *ḥarim*.

Although official functions were more likely to cost a fortune, even the day to day whims of an individual princess could strain the royal coffers. According to Clara Boyle, wife of a British diplomat, Ismail's beloved daughter Zeinab had an account with a Paris dressmaker, and "in a single year she spent £10,000 on black velvet alone."[35] Ellen Chennells, Zeinab's governess, confirms the princess's love for clothes, which often took preference over her lessons.[36]

The ladies of the *ḥarim* did not always dress in high fashion, nor did all of them dress in European clothing. Mrs. Cromwell Rhodes reports that she once went to a private reception at the palace and was shocked to find all the court ladies in flannelette dressing gowns. This form of dressing was in sharp contrast to the "lovely brocade dresses" that all the ladies had worn at a state reception. It appears that the more formal the function, the more likely that women were to dress and eat in a European manner.[37] At another party, Mrs. Rhodes notes that the ladies all wore European dress, but at the end of the evening, they changed into their "shabby pink flannel gowns" after an evening of drinking "beer mixed with champagne, whiskey, etc."[38] Mrs. Rhodes, like Mrs. Grey, expressed disappointment that Eastern royalty did not adhere to her romanticized ideal.

Not only did the princesses share Ismail's love for clothing and fine beverages, they too admired elegant jewelry and jewel-encrusted objects. Just as imperial cuisine required the proper presentation, so too did jewelry. Many items were so ornate as to sometimes require special instructions for placement in hair or brooches.[39] The ladies of the *ḥarim* were also consumers of the new health and beauty products, ordering items such as *Crème Impératrice* and *Lubin* cold cream. Between 1874 and 1876, at the Khedive's pharmacy alone, they spent almost 50,000 francs.[40] What better way to show off their new clothing, sophisticated hair-styles, elegant jewelry, and fine make-up than by recording their images with photographs. According to Margot Badran, male photographers entered Ismail's *ḥarim* and took pictures of the women in their Western-style clothing.[41]

It appears that the princesses and women of the *ḥarim* enjoyed using European clothing, jewelry, and beauty products. They seemed to have a fondness for all things European. Emmeline Lott reports that "they abandon[ed] any habits which . . . were repugnant to delicacy, especially when I told them that such were not *à la Franca*, 'European.' "[42] Hanafi al-Mahalawi, author of a book on the royal *ḥarim*, points out that it was during the age of Ismail when the official consorts of the ruler took the title "*princessa*" as opposed to the old title of "*hanum*."[43] The term did not displace *hanum*, but it occurred more frequently with reference to his official wives in particular. Despite the adoption of these Europeanisms, the *ḥarim* was still furnished in the traditional Eastern manner. According to Mrs. Grey, the only furnishings were *divans*. She points out that there were no tables and no European-style washing materials, even in the bedroom of the Grand Princess.[44]

The Queen Mother often dictated style and functions of the *ḥarim*, and in her own home, al-Zaafran palace, she favored the traditional in both clothing and furnishings.[45] Like the palace as a whole, the *ḥarim* did its share of entertaining, following elaborate rituals for both foreign and native guests. A visit would begin with the *Agha* helping the visitors descend from their carriage and walking them to the door of the *ḥarim*. Here they would be met by servants, who would lead them to a salon on the ground floor where their *yashmak* and *faridji* (veil and cloak) and/or overcoat would be taken. Cloaks and veils would then be sent to the *tezrecis* to be pressed with an iron. Meanwhile, the visitors were guided to a special salon for the princesses on the second floor, where they were greeted by a (female) servant dressed in embroidered men's clothing. This servant, chosen for her grace and charm, would twirl a baton between her hands until the princesses, donning their fine European gowns, arrived. Foreign visitors were then presented with a special servant for the purpose of translation. When the visitors were ready to leave, they would find their cloaks, veils, and gloves placed inside the folds of satin or velvet brocade squares, which were laid out on tables or settees.[46]

Court entertaining and rituals provided the opportunity for Ismail and the *ḥarim* to engage in conspicuous consumption. Perhaps the most elaborate of these rituals were royal weddings. Between 1873 and 1874, five of Ismail's children were married, four of the weddings taking place in week-long ceremonies on consecutive Thursdays during January–February 1873. According to one observer, who attended three of the weddings, the celebrations cost at least 15 million dollars and eclipsed the festivities surrounding the opening of the Suez Canal, including "brilliant and profuse pyrotechnic displays," "dinner and feasting . . . in wanton luxuriance . . . music intermingled with salvos of artillery." He goes on to describe the wedding procession that consisted of "hundreds of harem carriages . . . horses gaily decorated . . . ladies in laces and gorgeous colored silks and satins . . . Pachas and Beys in tarboosh and showy uniforms, on prancing steeds . . . " During such festivities, the Khedive also distributed enormous quantities of food to the poor.[47]

Ellen Chennells recollects the excitement of this period. Apparently, the *ḥarim* was a flurry of activity with French *modistes* and great confusion over clothing bills.[48] Weddings necessitated intricate planning, and new outfits were required for each of the days of celebration. Mrs. Grey, who attended the wedding of Ismail's eldest daughter Tawhida several years earlier, describes the conspicuous consumption of that event as a "total disregard of expense" costing some "£40,000, half being given by the Viceroy, and half by the future husband." After elaborately describing their hair styles, clothing, and jewelry, she marveled, "I never saw anything equal to it."[49] It is clear from contemporary descriptions that these weddings allowed Ismail to bring the distinction of the court to the public eye.

What is even more notable about the 1873–74 weddings is their peculiarity as "new" marriages, that is, as Western-style bourgeois marriages in which the husband and wife are social equals.[50] It was not all that uncommon to marry royal women or even important slaves to socially significant men. Nevertheless, the idea of a male from the ruling family settling down with a single wife of equal status was rather odd, particularly for Ismail to impose upon his sons.[51] The first of these marriages was for Ismail's heir apparent Tawfiq, who married Amina, the daughter of Ilhami Pasha

(Abbas's son) and Sultan Abdul Majid's daughter. While imposing this woman of double royal lineage on Tawfiq, Ismail himself had fourteen official wives or consorts, as well as other concubines at his beck and call.[52] Despite the novelty of these marriages and the extravagance of celebrations, the form remained traditional, with separate functions for male and female guests.[53]

Like weddings, funerals too could be venues of conspicuous consumption; and the style and manner of consumption was traditional. The funeral procession for the Khedive's beloved daughter Zeinab numbered 100,000, had sacrificial buffalo and people hurling bread and dates to the crowds; and included Cairo's water carriers, the blind, and school children; the theologians of al-Azhar; members of the various Sufi orders; the princes; and members of the civil and military orders.[54]

Education in the Royal Household

Ismail's interest in things European was not limited to merely objects. He was interested in European ideas as well. He inherited this love of learning from his father. Although usually portrayed as a brutish military man, Ibrahim Pasha was a learned individual with an immense library. He took fastidious care of Ismail's early education, which included science, Arabic, Persian, Turkish, French, and mathematics. Marsot argues that Ibrahim had more of an Egyptian identity than an Ottoman one given his residency in Istanbul as a "guest" (hostage) of the Sultan early in Muhammad Ali's reign. Furthermore, she points out that he spoke Arabic with his men. Thus, it is not surprising that Arabic was included in his son's curriculum and that Abbas II remembers his father's and grandfather's stress on its importance.[55]

Ibrahim was concerned with all facets of Ismail's education. He even saw to it that his son continued his lessons when he suffered from opthalmia, and he rewarded Ismail's academic efforts with horseback-riding sessions.[56] As a youth, Ismail studied in Vienna and Paris, and it was during this stay in Europe that he gained proficiency in written and spoken French.[57] After his return, he tried to maintain his knowledge of European languages and world affairs by subscribing to 50 European newspapers and journals, as well as maintaining a subscription to the journal *la Turquie*. Even the *ḥarim* subscribed to the *Levant Times*.[58]

Like his own father, Ismail was particularly interested in the education of his children. Having studied in Europe, he was keen on providing his children with European governesses. According to Yacub Artin, European tutors first entered the royal *ḥarim* during the reign of Muhammad Ali.[59] At first the process for recruitment was somewhat haphazard. An educated foreigner might visit the *ḥarim*, and an elder would attempt to engage her for the benefit of the group.[60] By the reign of Ismail, however, the process for recruitment was more rigorous, and it sometimes involved the efforts of the Inspector-General of the schools and other government officials. Qualifications for such a position included descent from a good family; knowledge of English, French, and sometimes even German; facility in the fine arts; and, of course, a good general education.[61]

Ismail carefully monitored his children's education and commended their progress. His correspondence with his children is testimony to this interest. Writing to his son Hassan in 1867, Ismail commented:

> My dear son, it would make me happy to hear from you and know how you are applying yourself, and how you are progressing in your classes. Also, let me encourage you to be consistent in your efforts, and to take advantage of this education in order to develop your intellectual and physical abilities. In this way, you would know that I have devoted all my affection to you.[62]

This concern was not reserved for his male children alone, as the following correspondence between him and his daughter Zeinab demonstrates:

> Zeinab: We have received the letters which you were so good as to send to my brothers and to me, and we thank you many times for your kindness in writing to us. My mother thinks that you may perhaps like to have a little letter in English from me. I hope that you will be so kind as to excuse my faults as I have not (learnt or learns) English very long. We have been so glad to hear that Your Highness is quite well, and we shall be so happy when we will see you again. I have been helped with this letter which I hope will please you . . . .
>
> Ismail: [In French] Your short letter is delightful, and it has given me great pleasure. It is well written . . . It pleased me to know that you are working hard and behaving well. That is the best news that you could give me . . . [63]

Zeinab's letter also indicates her mother's interest in her studies. Indeed, the memoirs of governesses Ellen Chennells and Emmaline Lott demonstrate the great concern for education by both parents. The Queen Mother also supervised her granddaughters' education.[64]

Educating women of the *ḥarim* was not new to Ismail, Muhammad Ali, or to the Egyptian upper class. The royal family in Egypt, like many other upper-class families in the Middle East, had a tradition of educating women. Islam as a religion enjoins all believers to seek knowledge.[65] Educated women rank among the revered figures of the classical period. According to Jonathan Berkey, during the later Middle Ages, Cairene women were important contributors to and transmitters of Muslim learning.[66] In particular, women were key players in advancing their own education, the education of their children, and the education of other women. These trends continued right through the nineteenth century.

Despite the fact that it was not uncommon for women of the upper class to receive instruction, both the curriculum and the manner of instruction changed with Ismail. Previously, women learned to read Arabic, Turkish, and Persian, either from other family members or from elderly *shaykhs*.[67] Nevertheless, teaching them to write was rare. Princess Emine Foat Tugay reports that her grandmother, originally a slave from the Caucasus (and later a consort of Ismail), learned only to read because teaching her to write would have been an "inducement to pen love letters."[68] Emmaline Lott, governess to Ismail's son Ibrahim, confirms that during her tenure in the mid-1860s, women learned to read, but none could write.[69] Records in the *Période Ismail* series include letters written in the mid-late 1870s by Ismail's daughters Melek and Zeinab, as well as his niece Nazli. By the handwriting and mistakes, it appears that the letters were penned by the girls themselves, rather than a secretary.[70] By the time that Ellen Chennells arrived in the early 1870s, the *ḥarim* curriculum included writing. She instructed Zeinab in English, French, and music. The princess also received more traditional instruction in Turkish and Arabic from elderly *shaykhs*.

Nevertheless, the European instruction took precedence over the traditional curriculum. The royal family allowed Chennells first choice in scheduling, and the native masters were forced to work around her timetable. She continued to tutor Zeinab after marriage, and the princess convinced her to move into the *ḥarim*. Chennells even extended her lessons into the Opera House. The English governess's presence and influence upon the princess did not go unnoticed by the native masters, who refused to allow her to observe their lessons, nor by the slaves and eunuchs, who did not trust Europeans and resented the attention that Chennells received.[71]

The royal princesses were not the only residents of the *ḥarim* receiving an education. It was not uncommon for the royal household to provide slaves with an education for a number of reasons.[72] First, many women were educated as musicians, dancers, comedians, and mimes for the purpose of entertaining the residents of the *ḥarim*.[73] Second, young slaves, both male and female, received instruction alongside free children in order to stir up scholarly competition.[74] The most intelligent slaves received a higher education and became secretaries.[75] Finally, these slaves might later provide well-educated, upper class men with suitably educated brides. In addition to the jewels already in her possession, slaves wishing to marry were provided with a proper husband, a trousseau, more jewelry, furnishings for her home, and sometimes a house, as part of her dowry.[76] Marrying the slaves of the royal family was considered an honor, and according to Princess Nazli, they continued to be offered protection after their marriage.[77] As more elite men began to receive European-style educations, the gulf between them and the remainder of the populace widened. At least for some of these men, it perhaps became more important for their consorts/wives to receive a similar sort of education.[78]

This education not only made the women of the imperial *ḥarim* better suited to their husbands, but they also became more prepared to carry out their duties. Traditionally, Ottoman and Egyptian women of the upper class made significant contributions through their sponsorship of education, art, and architecture, as well as through their influence in politics.[79] Education undoubtedly made the women more aware of their contributions, and press coverage allowed literate men and women to follow their activities.[80]

Suez and the Spread of Western Consumption

The activities of the women of Ismail's *ḥarim* form but one aspect of consumption in his homes. They followed the Khedive's lead in adopting Western forms of consumption; however, they still maintained a number of traditional customs and styles. Similarly, though Ismail sought to impose new standards of consumption on the country as a whole, the transformation would remain incomplete. Although Ismail sought to separate Egypt from Africa and reattach it to Europe, his intent was never to completely Europeanize all of Egypt and all Egyptians. He merely aimed at Europeanizing the capital, a number of port cities, and the upper class. Furthermore, only certain areas of Cairo were "Westernized," and even within those districts certain traditions remained. Egypt's agricultural districts were modernized only to the extent that would enable them to produce the wealth necessary to support consumption in the urban oases of Western civilization. Despite infrastructural improvements, the countryside could not support Ismail's grandiose schemes. He continued his predecessor's borrowing from European creditors, and he believed that those creditors would be influenced by the new patterns of consumption adopted in the large cities of the delta.

Ismail sought not only a regal court and a majestic court life, he also desired a dazzling capital and a modern nation. He had visited Paris in 1867, attending the *Exposition Universelle*. Upon his return, he was eager to embark on a new crusade. In the short term he wanted to demonstrate Egypt's dignity and civilization during the inaugural festivities of the Suez Canal; and in the long term, he sought a "remake" of the whole country. The Suez Canal project had begun under his predecessor Said, and it had taken ten years and 100,000 Egyptian lives to complete. In November of 1869, the waters of the Red Sea met the waters of the Mediterranean, and Ismail invited luminaries from around the globe to participate in the unprecedented celebrations.[81] The festivities drew European royalty, as well as celebrated figures from the fields of diplomacy, business, science, academia, journalism, music, stage, art, and sports.[82] An invitation meant an all-expense paid (up to) two-month journey, including passage to Egypt, lodging and internal transportation, admission to all functions, translators, food, and even personal expenses.[83] al-Rafai estimates that Ismail spent about £1,400,000, although this estimate appears conservative.[84]

Visitors partook in a whirlwind of tours and scores of marvelous parties. Edward Dicey describes a ball at a specially constructed palace on Lake Timsah where the "champagne flowed like water" and open tables remained for three days amidst a background of fireworks and traditional Bedouin processions.[85] Ismail hoped his visitors would leave with positive memories of Egypt; however, they saw only the Egypt that Ismail desired them to see. All outings and diversions were carefully orchestrated to achieve this result.[86]

Ismail wanted visitors to see the condition of the new streets, the orderliness of the towns, and the cleanliness of the nation. According to Timothy Mitchell, such things were an expression of the "intellectual orderliness" fundamental to the "political requirements" of the country. A number of government officials had visited Paris with Ismail in 1867, and they were profoundly influenced by the newly renovated capital. Among the Egyptian entourage was Ali Mubarak, a member of the rural nobility who had advanced in the bureaucracy through his skill, determination, and modern education. In his long tenure of service to the government, he served as an engineer, teacher, and administrator. Mubarak extended his visit to Paris in order to study the new layout of the city and its educational system. Upon his return, he was appointed Minister of Schools and Minister of Public Works. His long-term plan was to bring the order of Haussman's Paris to Egypt. Nevertheless, the visitors for the inauguration of the Suez Canal would soon be arriving. Thus, it was necessary to expedite changes in the new port cities and in the most important quarters of the capital. A law for ordering the streets of Cairo was proclaimed in order to facilitate preparations for the opening of the canal. Special attention was to be paid to the quarters of Ismailiyya and Azbakiyya.[87]

Ismailiyya, the quarter running from Azbakiyya gardens westward toward the Ismailiyya canal, was to be completely Europeanized. Before 1865 there had been little settlement in this undeveloped wasteland. The Khedive's namesake was now to have streets laid out in grid fashion and illuminated by gas lamps, and its homes were to be served by running water. To expedite settlement, Ismail offered land to anyone who would build a suitable domicile, that is, one costing upwards of £2,000. The bigger and better the house and gardens, the larger the land grant. Ismail had two goals in mind with this plan: settle the area before visitors arrived and to attract new residents once the visitors arrived.[88]

Azbakiyya underwent a transformation as well, but rather than being an innovation, it was the continuation of a process underway since the time of the French invasion.[89] Azbakiyya was to be the hub of the new Cairo, the point from which the broad new streets radiated. Old buildings, structures, and alleys were demolished to make way for the new thoroughfares, mansions, and public buildings. The former home to the Ottoman aristocracy, the Egyptian religious bourgeoisie, and the Coptic community became a Europeanized quarter. Building owners and tenants were urged to sell and move out. As in Ismailiyya, some land was granted to those who would construct a suitable home. The neighborhood now boasted new shops and cafes, as well as a comedy theater and a rococo-styled Opera House. Azbakiyya square and its environs were leveled and rebuilt with gardens, grottoes, and fountains. The Azbakiyya renovations were not complete by the time of the Suez opening; however, older structures were whitewashed and the streets illuminated by gas lamps in preparation for the visitors.[90]

One of the grand events of the Suez inauguration was the opening, or rather preopening, of the Cairo Opera House. Ismail commissioned Italian architects Fasciotti and Rossi to build the new structure and Verdi, Europe's premier opera composer, to write a work befitting the festivities. The Opera-House director Draneht Bey passed a note from Ismail to Verdi in which he wrote:

> In choosing you, dear Maestro, to be the composer of an opera whose action revolves in my state, I have realized my wish to create a national production which may become one of the most glorious memories of my reign.[91]

Reluctant at first, Verdi finally agreed to compose the opera *Aida* in June of 1869. It served Ismail's purposes well. Its form was entirely European and its content glorified Egypt—the ruler even collaborated with Verdi on the project. Mariette, the curator of the Egyptian Museum had written the story, based upon his research. Nevertheless, neither the finishing touches on the Opera House nor the opera *Aida* were ready in time for the opening. The building was far enough along to house a performance, but *Rigoletto* was performed instead. The true grand opening of the Opera House did not take place until late 1871.[92]

Ismail wanted Egypt's visitors to view the country as a cultural and intellectual playground, of which the Opera House was just one part. The Egyptian Museum had also been sponsored by the Khedive and special arrangements were made to aid the canal visitors. Ismail presented himself as more cognizant of the value of Egypt's treasures than his predecessors, and early in his reign he commissioned a French Egyptologist, Mariette, to build an Egyptian Museum.[93] The original plan was to house the museum in Azbakiyya, a central and accessible location. However, to expedite the process for a rare 1863 visit from his cousin, the Sultan, the museum ended up in Bulaq. During the canal festivities, a special reception was held at the museum for the foreign dignitaries and visitors.[94]

By inviting Europe's "A list," carefully controlling the Egypt that they viewed, and bringing order to his country, Ismail hoped to raise world estimation of Egypt, glorify his reign, and attract further settlement and investment. Once the canal visitors left, the frenzied pace slowed, but the process did not stop. Ismail continued improvements in Cairo, applied the same method of organization to some of Egypt's other major cities, and sponsored further intellectual and cultural development. It was also during this post-Suez era that he inaugurated the "new" marriages for his children.

Ismail continued to bring order to Cairo by sustaining road construction and other public works, expanding public services and by extending the authority of the state into the lives of Cairo's citizens. In the same way that he developed Ismailiyya, Abdin, and Azbakiyya as hubs for the new thoroughfares, Ismail created such centers around the mosque of Sayyida Zeinab, Ataba al-Khadra, Sultan Hasan, and Qasr al-Nil. He also developed a series of open squares, smaller versions of these, in the squares surrounding Azbakiyya (Opera and Khazindar), Bab al-Futuh, Bab al-Luq, Muhammad Ali, al-Azhar (Falaki), and at Birka al-Fil. Traffic and sanitation were improved by the development of a new series of bridges and canals, as well as the installation of a special police force to regulate traffic. After completing work on the Gezira and Giza palaces, he developed these neighborhoods as well.[95] A reorganization of the police force, penal reform, and the creation of a fire brigade all brought more order and discipline to the capital city.[96]

Improvements in and around Azbakiyya continued. The renovated park was officially opened in 1872. Concessions included restaurants, cafes, music kiosks, a bar, a photographer, a theater, a shooting gallery, a Chinese pavilion, an aquarium, paddle boats, booths for tobacco and toys, as well as various food stands, all of which were regulated by explicit government standards. The park offered both European and Eastern music in establishments subject to *de facto* segregation. The khedivial orchestra, consisting of both Eastern and European members, performed military music each evening. The park was accessible to all, at least in the morning. Afternoon visitors over the age of six were charged one Egyptian piastre.[97]

Prior to the completion of the Azbakiyya project, speculators jumped at the opportunity to buy land in the surrounding area, the most expensive lots being in proximity to the Shepheard's hotel. Azbakiyya had long been an elite neighborhood and this location smacked of power. Since its erection in 1797 it had served as the home of Alfi Bey, Napoleon, Kléber, and Muhammad Ali, as well as the latter's School of Languages. The neighborhood came to include a number of European consulates, the Cairo Stock Exchange, the most exclusive hotels, fashionable stores, and fine dining establishments. Azbakiyya continued to thrive long after the deposition of Ismail. An 1896 guidebook describes the park as "well-kept . . . a very favorite place of resort" to which "the inhabitant and visitors to Cairo owe a debt of gratitude to Ismail Pasha for forming this tasteful pleasure-ground."[98]

Ismail may have created a small piece of paradise in the center of town, but it was accessible only to a few. The admission price, although not prohibitive, was not trifling either; and the masses probably could not afford the majority of activities, products, and services within the park. As for the surrounding neighborhoods, Ali Mubarak reports that by the end of Ismail's reign, only 200 houses/mansions were built in the Westernized zone between Shubra and Ismailiyya. Only Europeans and the Europeanized upper class could afford these districts. The emerging bourgeoisie moved to new quarters to the north (Faggala, Zahir, and Abbasiyya), where less expensive versions of the new housing could be found. When the British arrived in 1882, they created their colonial city within the grid pattern designed by Ismail.[99]

Cairo was not the only city to undergo municipal development. Other sizable delta towns and cities reorganized their streets, improved sanitation, increased public services, and created public parks. In particular, Alexandria with its large foreign contingent, underwent considerable change.[100] New streets and neighborhoods were planned, existing roads repaved and illuminated, its homes received running water, al-Nuzha park opened, and the port was renovated.[101] Nevertheless, these municipal improvements did not extend beyond the delta, nor did they extend beyond the largest cities within the delta. The *ṣa^{c}id* (upper Egypt) and the rural regions of lower Egypt served to produce the wealth that allowed the larger cities to engage in new patterns of consumption.[102]

Ismail placed a high priority on linking these sites of consumption and production. Thus, he improved transportation and communication by increasing the railroad and telegraph networks and by bringing the postal system under government control. Under Ismail, the railroad administration was overhauled and the length of Egypt's tracks increased from 245 to 1,085 miles. This increase reflected new lines both within the delta and from the delta to middle and upper Egypt. The patterns of development indicate an effort to move goods from the areas of production to the major ports, as well as an interest in connecting the urban centers of the delta.[103] As for the telegraph network, Ismail increased lines in both Egypt and the Sudan, concentrating mainly on the delta. At time of Said's death there were only six short lines, and by 1876, there were 36 lines spanning 5,500 miles with 10,400 miles of wire. An English company provided lines that linked Egypt to Europe, India, Australia, and the Far East.[104]

Up until 1865, the postal service in Egypt had operated as a private concession. In late 1864 the government purchased the concession for £46,000 and hired the former owner to continue running the service. By the end of Ismail's reign, the government had 210 post offices serving 67 towns and villages, including 15 in the Sudan, 5 on the Red Sea, and 7 outside offices in the Levant. The increased railroad network facilitated greater service. There was at least one daily delivery between Alexandria, Cairo, and all the principal towns of the delta. Nevertheless, house to house service proved too difficult, and private boxes were necessary. In her recent study of Sudanese nationalism, Heather Sharkey cites the postal system as an "important" means of "nationalist exchange" allowing for "the cheap and increasingly quick distribution of books, periodicals, and letters."[105] For women who were secluded, efficient postal service meant a much greater connection to larger intellectual and social currents.

Ismail continued to sponsor cultural and intellectual development. Egyptian historian Abd al-Rahman al-Rafai describes the age of Ismail as a musical renaissance, a time when more people listened to music and more forms of music were available for consumption. Ballet and opera were among the innovations of the period.[106]

Nevertheless, the impact of this musical renaissance on the population at large was really quite limited. Aside from the replacement of the *rababa* with the violin in urban musical groups, and the concert hall as a new context for performance, few innovations made their way into popular music at that time.[107]

The Opera House had its official grand opening in December of 1871. Verdi's *Aida* finally made it to the stage; and for the 750 fortunate individuals who garnered advanced tickets, it was an amazing event.[108] Samuel Selig De Kusel, a British official, attended the performance along with other European and Egyptian officials and the royal family, including women in latticed boxes. He noted that "[t]his premier performance of 'Aida' was simply perfect," and indeed the entire evening "had been divine."[109]

While the cost of the new opera house was relatively modest, the true expense came in the high salaries of the actors/actresses and the "unheard of magnificence" in scenery and costume design.[110] Other theatrical performances took place at the Azbakiyya comedy theater, as well as the Zizinia and Alfieri theaters in Alexandria.[111]

Ismail continued his work on museums, libraries, and other educational institutions. In addition to the museum of Egyptian antiquities, Ismail began planning an Islamic museum in 1869. He hoped to collect important Arab and Islamic artifacts in this new museum, which did not open until the reign of Tawfiq. Ismail also sought to gather and preserve important books and manuscripts in a national library. In 1870 he founded the Khedivial Library (later Dar al-Kutub) in Saray Darb al-Gamamiz to house this collection. Finally, Ismail's gaze reached to the stars with a new observatory in Abbasiyya.[112]

During the age of Ismail, intellectual, cultural, and scientific societies flourished. Many of these societies received royal patronage, including the Khedivial Geographic Society, founded in 1875 for the purpose of studying the geography of Egypt and Africa with respect to Egypt's industrial and commercial interests. While it met Ismail's economic and cultural goals, it was a "grand and imitative gesture" "on the model of European institutes similarly devoted to the study of other cultures." Few Egyptians participated in the lectures, either as speakers or listeners.[113] Similarly, Ismail provided financial support to *L'Institut d'Egypte*, the institution founded by Napoleon at the time of the French invasion.[114]

In this climate of cultural and artistic development, other institutions such as the press flourished. According to Abbas Kelidar,

> It became overtly politicised, giving expression to a ferment of new ideas in a style of Arabic prose which marked the introduction of modern journalism. The main preoccupations of writers and editors were political matters related to the movement of Islamic reform, the westernisation of Egyptian society and politics, as well as the question of Egyptian independence. Ismail's headlong drive for the modernisation of Egyptian culture, accompanied by the desire for the assertion of his independence from both the

> Ottoman state and his European creditors . . . provided fresh impetus for the growth and development of the press.[115]

Ismail offered both political and financial support for writers, encouraging many Arab writers to immigrate to Egypt. Furthermore, the ascension of Abdul Hamid II (r. 1876–1909) brought forth an era of repression and censorship in the Ottoman press, and many journalists relocated in Cairo or Alexandria. As Ismail took Egypt further down the road of Westernization and debt, the first opposition press developed, particularly after government funding for journals withered away.[116] Egypt's revolution in journalism arrived at the same time as those of communication and transportation, thereby increasing the magnitude of its significance. In his study of the socio-cultural origins of the Urabi movement, Juan Cole describes the change that took place over the course of Ismail's reign. When he first came to power in 1863, there were no Arabic language newspapers and in the span of about twenty years, circulation of various newspapers rose into the tens of thousands. Furthermore, it was not just an increase in the numbers of readers, but there were substantial qualitative changes in content. One need only compare the official gazette of 1863 to the more sophisticated publications of the late 1870s, which carried greater emphasis on foreign affairs, editorials, and cultural essays, as well as improved coverage of remote provinces.[117]

Ismail's Legacies and the Appearance of Monogamy

Ismail brought great developments to Egypt; however, these came at a great cost. The Khedive never did anything halfway, embarking upon enormously expensive ventures that had little hope for immediate profit.[118] His aim was to increase the productive and intellectual capacities of the country by investing in bridges, canals, railroads, refineries, telegraph lines, and ports, as well as schools, newspapers, and cultural institutions. His personal expenditure combined with these lavish public works projects sunk Egypt into a vortex of continued loans and indebtedness that ultimately brought Anglo-French financial control, Ismail's deposition, and the British occupation. The Khedive, who had been the darling of foreign dignitaries in 1863, had become the enemy of the bond-holding Europeans by the mid-1870s. By this point Ismail no longer had a blood relative as Sultan, nor was Abdul Hamid II sympathetic to Ismail's designs. As Egypt neared bankruptcy, Ismail authorized the creation of the *Caisse de la Dette Publique* in 1876 and Dual Financial control shortly thereafter. By 1879 Egypt could not even pay the interest on its sizable debt. Ismail refused to cooperate fully with the European controllers, and they engineered his deposition "without the slightest qualms on the part of the Sultan and his government."[119] Under the careful tutelage of the European powers, his son Tawfiq (r. 1879–92) took the reins of government.[120]

Despite Tawfiq's image as a puppet, one imprint of his father remained, his creation as a "New Man" with a "New Woman" at his side. Ironically, despite his desire to present himself as a "New Man," rumors regarding his origins tinged his reputation.

Even more humorous was the fact that his puppeteers were among those who continued to propagate the stories regarding his father's inability to control his passions in the presence of a nubile lower-order slave and having his way with her, resulting in the birth of Tawfiq. The fact that Ismail did not marry Tawfiq's mother until the Sultan compelled him to do so (when he changed succession to primogeniture), fed grist to the rumor mill.[121] Regardless of his parentage, Tawfiq presented himself publicly as a bourgeois sovereign, with his attractive, intelligent, and beloved wife Amina at his side (although they traveled in segregated entourages). The Khediva Amina appears to have had popularity with Europeans, who noted her intelligence, as well as Egyptians, who endowed her with the title Mother of the Charitable because of her devotion and beneficence.[122] Building upon the work of Yunan Labib Rizq, Pollard has argued that "[m]onogamy had become the showpiece of modernity, and the public display of Tewfiq's household very literally connected the shape and practices of his domicile to the building of the nation state."[123] A nation of reformed families must start at the top.

Tawfiq died unexpectedly in 1892, and he was succeeded by his teenaged son Abbas II (r. 1892–1914), named after his maternal great grandfather/paternal first cousin once removed. Where his father had been compliant and obsequious, Abbas II was exuberant and at times defiant. During his first meeting with Lord Cromer, the latter remarked that "the young Khedive is going to be very Egyptian."[124] Abbas II wanted to follow his grandfather's desire for independence and his father's example of monogamy, or at least he wanted to appear to do so. In his memoirs, while indirectly chastising his father's "errors," he notes that Tawfiq's great legacy was his monogamy, "in an ancient country with polygamous traditions."[125] At the time of his ascension to the throne, the young Khedive was unmarried. It was his mother's hope that he would marry a suitable Ottoman princess, and she worked to arrange the matter while vacationing in Istanbul. At the same time, she allowed him access to one of her slaves. Before an Ottoman marriage was brokered, he impregnated Iqbal Hanum and married her nine months after the birth of their first child (she would bear another five of his children). Abbas, however, being the New Man that he was, came to believe that Iqbal, a mere Circassian slave, was not a suitable companionate mate. Evidently, after a chance encounter with the sister of a schoolmate from the Theresianum (Countess) May Torok von Svendro, he experienced "real" love and married her. May changed her name to Djavidan Hanum, after her conversion to Islam. Nevertheless, it appears that Abbas was not divorced from Iqbal when he first married Djavidan Hanum and married her again more publicly after a legal divorce was secured. Ken Cuno suggests that these "unnecessary" efforts demonstrate the desire of the royal family to prove the soundness of their domestic lives to the "civilized" world.[126] Djavidan's upbringing did not mesh well with her restricted lifestyle. She was the "trophy wife" of the Khedive, yet it was not possible to appear in public at all venues with him. Thus, she was known to dress in men's clothing and pretend to be part of her husband's entourage.[127] Abbas's marriage to Djavidan Hanum lasted until 1913. Rumor has it that he had returned from Paris that summer with a new love interest. While vacationing in Istanbul in 1914, the British accused him of cavorting with the enemy and deposed him, in favor of his Uncle Husayn Kamil (r. 1914–17), a son of Ismail, thus breaking the line of primogeniture.[128] The British invested Husayn with the title Sultan, and he proved to be a more compliant ruler than his nephew. Like his predecessor, he too engaged in a veneer of monogamy, or what might be termed serial monogamy.[129] This pattern, followed by Fuad (r. 1917–36), involved a first marriage to a "royal" followed by marriage to a commoner—in addition to other liaisons. As the days of slavery waned, mistresses replaced concubines. Nevertheless, the ruling family desired to put forth the appearance of monogamy for the benefit of the British and the rest of the world.

Conclusion

It is indeed ironic that a man with fourteen wives/consorts would leave an imprint of monogamy on the ruling family. While he was unable to attach Egypt to Europe, he was able to convince his successors of the need to act like (or at least project the appearance of) European royalty. Many of Ismail's other projects were abandoned or scaled back; however, some advances remained, including the growth of Egyptian participation in the bureaucracy, which was fueled by the expansion of education and the increased use of the Arabic language in government.

Chapter 3

Patterns of Urban Consumption and Development, 1879–1922

The new ideas, products, gadgets, and services that Ismail brought to his home(s) spread to the upper classes over the course of the last decades of the nineteenth century. The foreign community in Egypt served as the channel and pacesetter for the new styles of consumption.[1] Large numbers of foreigners began to reside in Egypt during the reign of Said. About half were Greeks, who came to take advantage of the Capitulations established late in the reign of Muhammad Ali. Up till the British occupation, Italians and French dominated the remaining half of the foreign community. At the end of Muhammad Ali's reign, there were only about 3,000 European residents in Egypt. By the end of Ismail's reign the number had reached 70,000; and by the time of the British occupation, the foreign community numbered 90,000.[2] These residents were clustered mainly in Cairo and Alexandria, and to a lesser extent in other port cities of the delta. According to the census of 1907, the number of Europeans resident in Egypt had reached 147,000.[3]

Social Life in Cairo and Alexandria

There were two types of Europeans in Egypt: the permanent and the temporary. The (semi)permanent residents had business or government-related interests in Egypt. This group ranged from foreign diplomats and businessmen to school teachers and actresses. The second category of Europeans came as visitors, some of whom came annually for "the season" and others who merely stopped en route to adventures further to the south or the east.

Temporary visitors sought lodging in the collection of exclusive hotels centered around Azbakiyya gardens and Ismailiyya or in therapeutic accommodations at the spas and resorts of Cairo and Helwan. By the turn of the century, even second-class hotels in the capital had modern conveniences such as electric lights and baths. First-rate hotels, such as the Shepheard's, boasted these amenities and more, including steam laundry, elevators, telegraph service, billiard halls, libraries, restaurants, cafés, and taverns. Many visitors came to Egypt during the winter months to escape the cold and/or to seek therapy for illnesses such as tuberculosis. The leading hotels all advertised their cleanliness, the advantages of their location, and their modernity.[4]

Hotels served as the meeting ground between the temporary and permanent Europeans in Egypt, as well as between these two groups and the Egyptian elite. They housed three mainstays of the European community: drinking, fine dining, and dancing. All of the principal hotels held weekly balls throughout the season, each on a different night of the week. According to one British official, no other place brought "the art of hotel dances . . . to such perfection." Another described them as "the leading feature of our society . . ." Here the Italian explorer could exchange banter and drinks with the British official, the French actress flirt with the Greek merchant, and the young pasha dance with the visiting German heiress.[5]

Hotels were quite the center of fashion. A 1914 guidebook warns travelers that at "the leading hotels . . . evening dress is *de rigueur*," while a 1909 guide reminds visitors that "Cairo is quite as fashionable, from the point of view of dress as a European capital, and affords plenty of occasions for wearing smart clothes."[6] Additionally, these guides inform travelers of the availability of fine stores in Cairo. Earlier guides recommend that travelers bring more gear, while these later guides reflect Egypt's incorporation into an economic and cultural world economy. According to Nancy Mickelwright, foreign women played a key role in fashion transmission, providing journals, patterns, and stores.[7] It should be noted that in many areas of the Empire up through the seventeenth century, European visitors adopted Ottoman dress to "avoid offending Muslim sensibilities." In other words, up till the eighteenth century, opportunities for observing European dress were limited and varied according to location. During the nineteenth century such opportunities increased with the arrival of more foreigners, as well as the *Tanzimat* reforms, which encouraged changes in dress.[8] Furthermore, new technologies such as photography, the sewing machine, and the printing press helped spread these changes more rapidly.

As previously discussed, the royal family was quick to pick up on new fashion trends. The upper class rapidly followed suit. Bayard Taylor had visited Egypt in 1852 and returned in 1874. He was shocked to find unveiled ladies riding in open carriages, and veils that uncovered more of the face.[9] Turn-of-the-century women's magazines depict Western styles, ranging from the Victorian to the flapper.[10] Nevertheless, most pictures outside the home depict women of the lower classes in the *milaya* [sheet-like wrap] and the *burquᶜ* [long veil covering the face from the nose down], and women of the upper classes in the *ḥabara* [black wrap covering the hair, clothing, and hands] and *yashmak* [Turkish facial veil].[11] Only upper-class women could afford the new clothing, yet they still necessitated traditional garments of modesty when in public view.[12] Meanwhile, upper-class men abandoned their robes and turbans in favor of the frock coat and *tarbush*.[13] A British official described the clothing of an elite official: he was donning a *tarbush*, a "pink satin tie with a pearl pin, a brocade waistcoat, . . . braided frock coat, . . . grey . . . trousers, and yellow leather spring-side boots." Complementing his outfit were lavender kid gloves, a walking cane, a gold cigarette holder, and the strong scent of perfume.[14] Obviously, men of the upper class were as susceptible as women to new forms of fashion, even at the expense of comfort.

Notably he was seen smoking a cigarette, a symbolic acceptance of a new pace of life and era of reform in Egypt.[15]

European residents of Cairo and Alexandria set the social standard for the upper class. In addition to the attractions of the hotels, Europeans looked to their elite sporting clubs, the Opera House, theaters, cafés, bars, and gaming rooms for diversion. An 1867 guidebook lists no sporting clubs; however, by 1896 there were four in Cairo and four in Alexandria. By creating such institutions, the foreigners were able to distinguish themselves socially and create a European haven within their foreign surroundings. Like the clubs of Europe, they sought to preserve their homogeneity by subjecting aspirants to rigorous entrance procedures. Furthermore, through high membership fees and annual dues, the elite sought to keep outsiders and substandard members of their class out. Some clubs even allowed elite Egyptians to join.[16]

Club life punctuated the daily activities of the European community. In a single day, a member might go to the club for breakfast, return in the mid-afternoon for a game of golf, and come back a third time in the evening for pre-dinner cocktails. Even in the heat of summer and the winds of the *khamsin*, Europeans managed to play golf and tennis, for these activities linked different segments of the elite together. One British official marveled at the thought that any soldiering got done in the morning, given afternoon sports and the evening dances.[17]

Sporting clubs gave rise to a host of others: social, scientific, literary, and artistic. Eventually, these clubs spread to the Egyptian aristocracy. These organizations set standards for Egyptian members and sought out key foreigners who were admitted to enhance the status of the organization.[18] The notion of such organizations was so new to Egyptians, that in an 1894 announcement for a new club in Cairo, the transliterated word "club" appeared in parentheses after the word *nadin*.[19] As clubs and societies spread among upper-class and upper middle-class men, women began to see the utility of such organizations.[20]

The Cairo Opera House remained a mainstay of the elite social circuit, and it continued to receive government support.[21] It sponsored improvement projects, paid annual subventions, and sought out quality performers and directors.[22] During the high season, the Opera House usually engaged a French or Italian company. Its popularity meant that good seats were hard to obtain. In Alexandria, some of the theaters housed operatic performances during the winter.[23]

The number of theaters in Cairo and Alexandria continued to grow as the popularity of theatrical performances increased. Theaters sought to engage reputable French and Italian companies for the high season, whereas earlier, they settled for European amateurs.[24] Nevertheless, Europeans sometimes complained about the quality.[25] The better theaters also housed popular acts. For example, in 1897 the Azbakiyya theater rented space to a Mr. Richard who could heal the crippled, blind, and deaf by means of electricity.[26] The theaters also began to cater to Egyptians with theater troops from Syria and Lebanon.[27] By the early twentieth century there were theater choices for those on more modest budgets. Rud al-Farag in Shubra developed into an arena that even the aspiring *effendiyya* could afford. Similarly, performers who got their start in this district might move on to the more prestigious theaters clustered around the Imad al-Din and Azbakiyya districts.[28]

Egypt's European residents and the upper class created a demand for increasing numbers of restaurants, cafés, bars, and gaming halls with such establishments growing more than threefold in the last decade of the nineteenth century.[29] Europeans found other, seamy pleasures in the European prostitute quarter, the Fish Market, just north of Azbakiyya gardens.[30] The native quarter was located nearby in Midan al-Wasaa. It should be noted, however, that neither district was exclusive with respect to both patrons and clients.[31] In Alexandria, the brothels located on Seven Sisters Street serviced the needs of British soldiers.[32] While prostitution was certainly not new to Cairo or Alexandria, the increasing number of male foreigners helped to increase demand for male and female "dancers" (prostitutes).[33]

Museums and libraries remained a source of interest for the European community and greater numbers of Egyptians. The Egyptian Museum moved from its location in Bulaq to Ismail's Giza palace in 1889. Although the new building was more sumptuous, it made access more difficult. In an effort to attract more visitors to the Giza location, the museum allowed visitors to enter free of charge from April 18, 1896 to October 15, 1896. Nevertheless, by this point the government had received so many complaints that it had already decided to build a new museum in a more central location, next to Qasr al-Nil. Although the museum, which opened in 1902, catered mainly to foreigners/tourists, it did represent a national cause, and thus the desire to make it more accessible.[34]

In 1904, the Islamic Museum and the Khedivial Library were combined in a single building. The new building, costing £66,000, aroused condemnation by Egyptians due to the expense. Despite the initial criticism, the majority of the library's visitors were Egyptians. The library housed both Arabic and European language texts, which numbered over 70,000 volumes by 1909. There was also an attempt to create a patriotic library, exclusively for Egyptian authors. The library received little patronage, perhaps owing to its half a piastre admission price. The books were then donated to the Khedivial Library.[35]

The new parks, gardens, and grottoes common to Azbakiyya and Ismailiyya spread to the new middle-class suburbs in the last decades of the nineteenth century and the early decades of the twentieth century. Creating public parks was thought to bring harmony, order, and hygiene to the cities.[36] Moreover, for officials with ties to the countryside, gardens offered a respite from the rigors of urban life. The new parks were the sites of concerts, cafés, al-fresco theater, as well as traditional street performances. The fancier parks sought to capitalize on the modern, the unique, and the amazing. For example, the horned man came to Azbakiyya and received coverage in the press.[37] Nevertheless, more conventional activities took place at the parks as well: flower shows, photo exhibitions, and cultural expositions.[38]

Many of these activities still remained beyond the reach of the masses. The two-piastre admission price for the horned man in 1892 was as much as the admission to the zoo in 1904. The government deemed this fee too excessive, and in an effort to make the zoo more accessible, the price was reduced to half a piastre. The revenues from the zoo did not decline significantly because of the increased traffic. In 1908, the home economics section of *al-muqtaṭaf* ran an article about the utility of taking children to the zoo and other exhibitions, pointing out that the entrance fee was "trivial," at least for the readership of this publication.[39] Although the zoo opened to the public 12 years after his deposition, it was Ismail who was responsible for creating the landscaping, and his menagerie provided the initial inhabitants of the zoo. In 1878, Ismail's collection numbered about 600, and by 1909 the zoo collection had grown to almost 1,400 animals representing 387 species.[40]

New discoveries brought both technological developments and new pastimes to Egypt. The advent of electricity helped to bring about many changes, although the cost in Egypt was much higher than in other countries. The scientific press heralded electricity as the greatest new wonder, capable of heating homes, hunting fish, coloring cheeks, providing lighting for surgery, and creating a servant-less household.[41] Electricity also brought motion pictures to Egypt just before the turn of the twentieth century. The first cinema opened in 1906; however, movie theaters did not begin to spread until the 1920s, and the first truly Egyptian film enterprises did not begin until the 1930s. Film helped to disseminate many significant events in Egyptian nationalist history, for example, the funeral procession of Mustapha Kamil and Saad Zaghlul's return to Egypt.[42] The press praised the advances of cinematography in the West and described ways in which motion pictures could be used to enhance everyday life through newsreels, lessons, and stories.[43] Nevertheless, access to the masses remained limited. One barrier was language; however, translations began in 1912. By then cinemas had moved into middle-class suburbs, such as Zahir, Shubra, and al-Husayn. Prices, even for first-class theaters, were generally less than half of those for live performances.[44] Cheaper versions of the moving pictures could be found in inexpensive stereoscopes and the traveling "window on the world" (*ṣanduq al-dunya*).[45]

Egyptians of the middle and upper classes engaged in a lifestyle that was relatively sedentary compared to that of the peasant or the factory worker. Exercise became trendy as people became more aware of the dangers of a sedentary lifestyle. Both men and women were encouraged to exercise, and physical education became part of the curriculum in the primary and secondary schools at the turn of the century. New inventions like the bicycle offered Egyptians further means of exercise, though articles usually pointed out the simplicity and benefits of walking.[46]

Urban Developments: Municipal Improvements, Mass Transit, and the Suburbs

While the social and cultural activities sponsored by Ismail spread quickly, the pace of other advancements proceeded more slowly. Municipal improvements in the principal cities of the delta included the acquisition of land for public use, widening and paving streets, the expansion of public utilities, and the continued reform of the police, prisons, court system, and fire brigade. Greater order came to Cairo and Alexandria with a new system for numbering streets and homes.[47] Nevertheless, such developments remained limited to the large cities of the delta, with Cairo and Alexandria receiving the lion's share of the improvements. This process reinforced the notion of the city as the site of consumption and the countryside as the site of production.

The single most important transformation in Cairo at the turn of the century was its expansion to the north and northeast, made possible by the spread of public transportation. According to Abu-Lughod this development could not have taken place without the open squares and new thoroughfares laid out during the age of Ismail. During a period of about 20 years, from 1897–1917, Cairo was able to triple its area without increasing the time that it takes to travel from the most distant region to the center of town. An important step in this process was filling in the *khalij* [canal] and creating a centrally located north–south artery.[48] Cairo and Alexandria's first tramway lines opened in 1896 and 1897, respectively.[49]

Not surprisingly, the owner of the first tramline concession, Baron Empain, was also the founder of the suburb of Heliopolis. Speculation and development followed the path of the tramway, and land values soared.[50] The relatively barren suburb of Abbasiyya blossomed and the desert oasis of "New Egypt" (Heliopolis) flourished with the opening of the new tramlines. Abbasiyya was the namesake of the Abbas I, who facilitated the region's initial development by building a palace there, improving the road to Cairo, relocating military barracks there, and forcing *amirs* to construct villas in the district. Said, in an effort to discredit his predecessor, obstructed the development by moving the military barracks to Qasr al-Nil, on the site of his sister Nazli's palace.[51] Said's efforts were initially successful. An 1867 guidebook refers to Abbasiyya as a "miserable memorial of the wish . . . of its founder to ennoble his name . . . ."[52]

Ismail, like other nobles, had built a palace in Abbasiyya (Saray al-Hamra). He constructed another, al-Zaafaran where he initially intended to reside, but he decided to build a new palace (Abdin) that fit his developmental plans for Cairo. Another aspect of Ismail's plans for Cairo meant moving the military barracks back to Abbasiyya, which made sense given the area's isolation and utility for training exercises.[53] Thus, the quarter did not remain uninhabited. Furthermore, Ismail constructed al-Qubba palace for Tawfiq just north of Abbasiyya, which helped to sustain the district.

It was not until the tramway reached Abbasiyya in 1896 that the neighborhood became more desirable as a residential area. The tramway, which ran along Sharia al-Abbasiyya, served to separate the eastern district with upper-class villas and mansions and the western district with middle-class and upper-middle-class houses.[54] The tramway brought growth to Abbasiyya and beyond. Wealthy merchants moved from the Old City into new mansions in Abbasiyya, and speculators jumped at the opportunity to buy land at the end of the line for casinos and resorts. In 1905 a group of financiers created the Oasis Company to continue development beyond Abbasiyya into Heliopolis. The idea was to create a European-style garden satellite town in the middle of the desert. The company was able to purchase what was viewed as valueless land for one Egyptian pound per acre.[55] By 1909 Abbasiyya and Heliopolis were connected by both a modern road and an electric tram. The "oasis" already contained 80 villas and shops, a hotel, and a casino.

Within another five years further developments took place. A 1914 guidebook describes Heliopolis as a suburb for British officials and a health resort "laid out on an ambitious scale."[56] Foreign interests ran high in Heliopolis, although it could not be defined as a European town. While its European population by 1925 was considerable, it did not exceed 20 percent. Given these circumstances its foreignness was highlighted by its architecture and layout, including a large cathedral, the

Heliopolis Palace Hotel, the racecourse, and Luna Park. Furthermore its tramway lines received preferential treatment.[57] A 1922 cartoon in *al-laṭa'if al-muṣawwara* depicts the Minister of Transportation booting a female Helwan down a flight of steps and uttering a triple divorce oath while a coy Heliopolis looks on. The text of the cartoon implicates foreign interests by pointing out the "luck" of foreign companies in Egypt (see figure 3.1). Other targets for criticism of the tramway included crowding, safety, and planning.[58]

Another significant aspect of the growth of Cairo and its transportation system was the spread of bridges connecting eastern and western Cairo, allowing for the development of Gezira and Roda. Once again, the origins date back to the reign of Ismail and his construction of the Qasr al-Nil bridge. By 1914 there were three routes connecting eastern and western Cairo. Garden City, on the east bank of the Nile, was one of the areas to benefit from these changes. Ironically, it shared few characteristics with its European namesakes, which contained modest and affordable housing. In

Figure 3.1 Foreign interests and the tramway
Source: *al-laṭa'if al-muṣawwara.*

Egypt the area became the headquarters for the British occupation, filled with ornate villas and mansions.[59]

The new roads and bridges that allowed Cairo's tramway to expand also helped to improve other forms of transportation. Now there was room for horse-drawn carriages, the omnibus, and even a few automobiles. Carriages, in the early nineteenth century, had been a royal privilege; however, by the reign of Ismail, ownership filtered into the upper classes and private carriages were available for hire.[60] As Toledano points out, carriages offered the utility of "separation" from the noise, dust, dirt, and smell of the street. Horses, the traditional marker between the ruling elite and the masses, provided only distance.[61] By the turn of the century, donkeys, the traditional transportation for Cairenes, were being used less frequently, particularly by Europeans and the upper classes.[62] Omnibuses helped to supplement the new transit system. Although the car arrived in Egypt shortly after the turn of the century, the high cost of purchase and maintenance made it less accessible than other forms of transportation.

Cairo's expansive growth at the turn of the century and the development of mass transit allowed the emerging bourgeoisie to settle in the suburbs of Zahir, Faggala, Abbasiyya, and the like. Here they could create less expensive versions of the new housing styles and avail themselves of the new public services. According to Tamraz, "the design, foundation, and façade of the buildings [we]re in most respects European, but . . . the uncompromising steadfastness of the traditional screen [*mashrabiyya*]" served to preserve traditional standards of segregation and privacy.[63] The housing styles of Azbakiyya and Ismailiyya were slowly seeping into the middle class. Public utilities and improvements had spread to the new suburbs, although the process was often lengthy and incomplete.[64] Nevertheless, life in the suburbs approached the splendor of life in the chic neighborhoods relative to the remainder of the country.

The New Home

In the eighteenth century, the aristocratic mamluk home had great significance. It was both a symbol of conspicuous consumption and a seat of power.[65] Over the course of the nineteenth century, as the seat of power moved away from *amiral* households and into a centralized state, such residences became anachronistic. As discussed in chapter 2, Muhammad Ali promoted southern European architectural styles, eschewing the old mamluk style. Thus, the changes in architectural style reflect not only changing tastes, but also changing relations of power. Although the spread of these new styles took some time, by the mid–nineteenth century the *Constantinopolitan*, with its flat roof and high narrow windows, became the house of choice for Cairo's elite. Rather than employing the traditional *mashrabiyya*, these new homes utilized high walls and gates for privacy.[66] Furthermore, it was no longer necessary to house private armies of mamluks. Muhammad Ali and his top officials together held about 1,610 mamluks, of which 500 were the Viceroy's alone. In contrast, Ibrahim had only 300 and Abbas, 150. The latter did not allow his uncle and heir apparent Said to maintain mamluks.[67] Thus, where the great households of the Ottoman age emerged around such groupings, by the mid–nineteenth century, they had disappeared and new forms of housing represented these changes. At about the same time, legislation passed both in the Ottoman Empire and in Egypt to abolish the slave trade.[68] Furthermore, new types of marriages took place as the male, and later female, slave trade ended. The old (and new) Turkish-speaking Ottoman elite began marrying the sons and daughters of the landed Egyptian elite (see chapter 5).

The redistribution of power in Egypt, the expansion of new neighborhoods, the growth of the urban middle class, and the spread of the new architectural styles, allowed greater numbers of Egyptians to utilize their homes as a venue for conspicuous consumption. No longer would distinction come from imposing fortress-style homes owned by a handful of the elite. The new home would now gain its distinction from its location and façade, its proper divisions, and the furnishings chosen for its interior.[69]

Previously, the location, style, and materials of the home had been important factors; however, the idea of dividing the house and having rooms with fixed functions and furnishings was new. Aside from rooms set aside for visitors (male and female), as well as the kitchen and bath, rooms in a mamluk-style home had great permeability and flexibility. Any room could be used for sitting, sleeping, or dining by simply arranging or rearranging cushions, mattresses, and trays.[70]

With respect to the role of the woman in the home, it is clear that women were not the slovenly *odalisques* portrayed by Western travelers. Nevertheless, evidence as to what role they played in buying for the home has been extrapolated backwards from the nineteenth century.[71] Even if the role were not new for elite women, growing numbers of middle-class women began to serve as the arbiters of taste and function in their new homes. Whereas individual *amiral* households had previously been the seats of power, now urban homes were building blocks of the nation. To furnish their homes and to make life easier, Egyptians were exposed to new stores, products, and services. Department stores offered a wide variety of goods, including standardized textiles, shoes, furniture, appliances, and even foods.[72]

Wealthy urban women, who had formerly been at the mercy of *dallalas* and tailors, could now embark on a whole new world of comparison shopping.[73] The *dallala* was a female trader who supplied secluded women with textiles, jewelry, and other personal items.[74] These women, who continued to function in the early twentieth century, were either independent traders or brokers for male traders, some of whom worked for their husbands. While *dallalas* were active in introducing women to new (imported) luxury goods, the selection was bound to be limited.[75] Furthermore, prices were likely to be high.[76]

Linking the Sites of Production and Consumption

Just as Cairo had become a smaller place with reference to the length of time needed to traverse the city, so too had Egypt become a smaller nation. The expansion of railroad and telegraph networks and the advent of the telephone brought Egyptians closer together. By 1914, Egypt had 1,634 miles of state-controlled railroad. In particular, links between agricultural centers in the delta and Middle Egypt grew. According to Robert Tignor, the primary aim was "to enable Egypt to move goods easily within the country and ultimately to export some of the products overseas," and secondarily, to allow for the "movement of populations on a vaster scale than had existed previously." These changes linked the peasant to his district capital, enabling him to take advantages of modern services.[77] Nevertheless, Tignor offers no evidence as to what percentage of the new lines were used for freight, passengers, or both.

The postal system advanced, and telegraph and telephone lines multiplied. By the outbreak of World War I, Egypt had nearly 2,000 post offices, and the government had initiated service to more remote areas. The telephone arrived in Egypt in 1884; and by 1898, the telephone company had agents in Cairo, Alexandria, Port Said, Suez, Assiut, and Mansura.[78] By 1900, advertisements for stores, companies, and even doctors, began to list their phone number in addition to their address. The areas of mass production were now easily linked to the areas of mass consumption. With these changes in networks of communication, the "New Woman" did not necessarily have to reside in Cairo or Alexandria.

Critique of the New Patterns of Consumption

The response by both Egyptians and foreigners to these changing patterns in consumption was not wholeheartedly positive, particularly for Egyptians with vested interests in traditional patterns of consumption and Westerners seeking an exotic oasis. Although Western guidebooks touted the developments that had taken place, many European travelers and officials lamented the changes, particularly in Cairo.[79] Edwin de Leon bemoaned the fact that by the mid–1870s it was not just Azbakiyya that had European-style homes. Throughout Cairo he saw "square, formal, uniform, hideous-looking imitations of the ugliest architecture in the world replacing the most picturesque if not the most comfortable . . . ."[80] The new Egypt no longer fit the stereotypical exotic image.

Egyptians themselves were often quite disparaging of the changes that took place over the course of the last four decades of the nineteenth century. Perhaps one of the most interesting critiques comes to us in the form of a story. Muhammad al-Muwaylihi's *ḥadith ᶜIsa ibn Ḥisham* is an amusing Rip Van Winklesque story of a Pasha from the days of Muhammad Ali who rises from the dead in the last years of the nineteenth century. The Pasha emerges from his grave and finds a writer, Isa Ibn Hisham, wandering through the tombs in order to get inspiration for his writing. Once Isa recovers from the shock of seeing a man rise from the dead, he attempts to help the Pasha. The Pasha does not understand why Isa does not know the exact location of his house, given the prominence of his family. Isa explains that "houses are not identified by their owner, rather [they are known] by their streets, alleys, and addresses."[81] This interaction is the first in a series of disturbing revelations for the revived Pasha. The two protagonists have a series of adventures that lead them through the revamped police system, the new courts, the new neighborhoods, the new professions, and even the new clubs. Muwaylihi uses the Pasha's astonishment over the changes and Isa's explanations as a mechanism for criticizing the adoption of Western clothing, habits, and customs. Nevertheless, sometimes Muwaylihi takes a neutral or positive stance with respect to the adoption of certain Westernisms, for example, newspapers, which he explains are a Western importation that has been adapted to the needs of the country.[82]

Muwaylihi came from a family of wealthy Hejazi textile traders, who had benefited from the Red Sea trading boom of the eighteenth century. His branch of the family moved to Egypt in the early nineteenth century and established ties with the ruling family. The fortunes of the Muwaylihis waned as European economic dominance grew, and his family actively opposed European financial control.[83] Thus, it is not surprising that Muwaylihi would be such a vehement critic of the changing patterns of consumption.

The nationalist, scientific, popular, and women's press also contained articles critiquing the new patterns of consumption in general, and women's relationship to these changing patterns, in particular. The thrust of these critiques was not to avoid imitating the West altogether, but rather that Easterners should adopt only that which is in harmony with their morals and disposition. The targets for criticism included clothing, health/beauty products, foods and beverages, transportation, amusements, the home, stores, and the moral order (or lack thereof) resulting from the adoption of these habits. Interestingly enough, the critics sometimes even translated articles from the West in order to critique Western habits.

Critics of the changing patterns disliked Western clothing because of its inappropriateness for the East, its health hazards, and its lack of modesty. Numerous articles appeared regarding the dangers of the corset and other articles of Western clothing. In an article from *Nineteenth Century*, reprinted in the home economics section of *al-muqtaṭaf*, the author critiqued the practice of wearing clothes that restrict the body, for example, corsets and gloves, and other dangerous practices, such as the braiding of hair, which restrict growth and movement.[84]

Others argued that Egyptian women do not get to show off their clothing, and they lack the finances to follow the fashions of the West: "Those who educate the daughters of the wealthy and the middle class must firmly establish in their minds that they cannot follow the new fashions except with great loss to their country."[85] Still others critiqued the inappropriateness of Western practices for the East, for example, taking off one's overcoat in Egypt where temperatures inside the house are as cold as, if not colder than, the outside.[86] Obviously, the writer is referring to Western architectural styles that retain the heat and the cold, rather than traditional styles that allow for greater ventilation. Finally, in 1923, Egyptians were at least partially vindicated when Westerners, influenced by the excavation of King Tut's tomb, began wearing pharaonic-style clothing.[87]

Nevertheless, the most vehement criticism of Western clothing came from those who feared a breakdown of the moral order as evidenced by women wearing immodest clothing.[88] Ihab Effendi Khulussy, one of the cartoonists for *al-laṭa'if al-muṣawwara*, frequently used this topic as a subject for satire. In a cartoon appearing in 1919, he represented the woman of yesterday and tomorrow (see figure 3.2). The picture depicts a woman cloaked in black from head to toe with an opaque *yashmak*, and within her, a younger woman clad in a Western, knee-length dress and stiletto heels, with a small

Figure 3.2 Yesterday and tomorrow
Source: *al-laṭa'if al-muṣawwara.*

veil and translucent *yashmak*. At first glance it might appear as though the author is trying to say that lurking within every traditional woman is a modern woman waiting to emerge. A more careful examination of both the cartoon and its caption reveal a different message. The traditional woman is larger and stronger than the frail wisp of a hunch-backed woman within her. The caption informs the reader that there is a great difference between the Egyptian woman of the past and her granddaughter, the woman of tomorrow, who exceeds the bounds of Europeanization and adornment.[89] In another cartoon, appearing in the same year, Khulussy points out the dangers of such dress. A gentleman clad in a suit and *tarbush* and his male companion in a speeding automobile, strain to catch a glimpse of an immodest beauty and run over an innocent man in the process. Khulussy points out that this type of dress creates two problems: undignified ogling and car accidents.[90] Not surprisingly, both of these cartoons appeared in the wake of the 1919 Revolution, a time when women took to the streets to protest British rule (see chapter 5).

Women were not alone in copying the fashion trends of the West, and critics like Muwaylihi satirized new styles of dress for men.While at the courthouse, the Pasha and Isa overhear a conversation between two fashion-conscious attorneys. One asks the other where he bought his tie, to which the second responds, "it came from my tailor in Paris with my other clothes, and it is the latest style."[91] A cartoon from 1922 entitled "The New Egyptian Fashion" highlights the bizarre mixing of Eastern and Western styles of clothing. In it we see a cigarette-smoking man clad in a collarless frock coat with sleeves that flare at the bottom and pants that are flared at the top.

Figure 3.3 The new Egyptian fashion
Source: *al-laṭa'if al-muṣawwara*.

The outfit is complemented by a *tarbush* with a sunbrim and pointed shoes with spats (see figure 3.3).[92]

Critics also attacked the influx of Western medicines and health/beauty products. Articles in the home economics section of *al-muqtaṭaf* encouraged women to steer clear of foreign products and to use what nature has given them. An article on powder warns women that toxic ingredients are mixed with powders and that grinding local cornstarch is better than using foreign substances. Another article, entitled "Water and Soap Is Not Rouge and Cremes", concludes by urging women to stop using dangerous compounds and to use the best cosmetics in the world: health, fitness, hygiene, and morals.[93]

Once again women were not alone in buying these new products. Turn-of-the-century advertisements for health/beauty products tended to target both men and women. Furthermore, as Elizabeth Frierson has argued in the Ottoman context, many were inclined to believe in the "efficacy of western science" and products thereof, at the expense of their budgets and traditional cures.[94] Such naïveté made users easy targets for caricatures. A 1922 cartoon from *al-laṭa'if al-muṣawwara* demonstrates these trends in a series of three pictures and captions. The first frame shows the front, profile, and back view of a man in a suit with carefully coifed hair. The caption informs the reader that people are surprised about the new medicines and creams for the hair that stylish young men use. The second frame depicts a variety of concoctions for the hair. Finally, in the third frame, the reader understands why these cosmetics are necessary: so that men can speed on their new motorbikes without messing up their hair.[95] Thus, the cartoon speaks to both the new cosmetics and the new mode of transportation.

Muwaylihi was also a critic of the new pharmacies and the new doctors. He does not necessarily eschew Western methods of medicine, but he has two major concerns. The first being the suitability of male doctors treating secluded women, and the second concern being the proliferation of quacks and elixirs.[96] Doctors traditionally had access to the *ḥarim*; however, they would not be left alone with the patient, nor would the patient remove her veil.[97] What concerned Muwaylihi more than an emergency visit under careful supervision, was the removal of previous restrictions and increasing numbers of visits.[98] Advertising in the mainstream and women's presses for medications, pharmacies, and doctors during this era sheds light upon Muwaylihi's concerns. As will be seen in chapter 4, patent medicines and pharmacies were among the most frequent advertisers in the late–nineteenth/early–twentieth centuries. With respect to doctors, as was the case in the Ottoman press, they rarely advertised prices; however, ironically, they often offered free service to the poor, who were rather unlikely to read the papers.[99]

Muwaylihi was critical of the diet and general lifestyle of Westerners and those Egyptians who imitated their practices. Speaking through the doctor, Muwaylihi condemns those who are overly fastidious in caring for their body: "Instead of drinking [ordinary] water, they drink mineral water; and they surrender appropriate health habits in order to take excessive care of the body, eating foods to which they are not accustomed." As a result, they suffer from imaginary illnesses, which are then treated by a multitude of unnecessary remedies.[100] These words of Muwaylihi still ring true a century later.[101]

Another target of criticism, to which Muwaylihi alluded, was the copying of foreign customs in food and drink. At one point in the story, the Pasha and Isa follow a country-bumpkin *ᶜUmda* [village chief] who is hoodwinked into spending large sums of money by a merchant and a profligate playboy. The *ᶜUmda* wanted to eat in a traditional kabab restaurant, but the playboy convinced him to go to a Western restaurant in Azbakiyya. The playboy ordered the same types of foods that appeared in the registers of the *Période Ismail*. The poor *ᶜUmda*, unaccustomed to such styles of food and drink, drank too much, bit into the butter, absconded with bread, ate off other people's plates, spilled food, wiped his hands on the tablecloth, broke a glass, drank from the finger bowl, cleaned his ear with a toothpick, and leered lasciviously at female patrons.[102] Although he had the financial wherewithal to partake of such luxuries, he obviously lacked the etiquette for doing so properly.

The press frequently critiqued Western patterns of consumption in tobacco, food, and drink. Use of tobacco in general, and Western-style cigarettes in particular, were sources of criticism in the women's, children's, and mainstream press. These articles highlight dangerous health issues, as well as beauty issues such as yellowing of the teeth and face.[103] In terms of food/beverages, critics warned against the expense of over indulgence, especially with regard to alcohol.[104] The press also expressed concern about the use of European wet nurses, who, through their use of wine, could spread disease (or even bad morals) to children.[105]

Abdullah Nadim was an early figure in Egypt's nationalist press, and he was best known for his role as the rhetorician of the Urabi revolt. In 1892, he wrote a scathing critique of the new patterns of food consumption in his journal *al-ustadh*. He begins by discussing the customs of the poor, the wealthy, and the *amirs* prior to the expansion of Westernization. Although the wealthy ate more quantitatively and qualitatively than the poor, the discrepancies were not that wide. Furthermore, people ate using simpler utensils and implements. After the intermingling of East and West, Nadim claims that the Westerners disfigured the Eastern economy with their luxury products, including specialized vessels for cooking and serving. Like Muwaylihi, he points out that neither the poor peasant nor the wealthy *amir* knows how to care for these new products, and that both end up squandering their money. The similarity between Nadim and Muwaylihi is not coincidental. Both men had families with vested interests in traditional patterns of consumption, Nadim having roots in an artisinal family. Nevertheless, he came from much humbler origins. Like Muwaylihi, Nadim was not against some intercultural borrowing; however, he warned against adopting Westernisms that were not congruous with Eastern morals and customs.[106]

Nadim also used fiction to depict this cultural struggle, in general, and the seepage of these Western patterns of consumption into the middle class, in particular. In his satirical journal, *Humor and Censure*, he includes a conversation between three women, a Muslim, a Christian, and a Jew. Each woman discusses how a man in her life has abandoned faith in the face of Western culture.[107] Using this fictional conversation, he depicts the costliness, in both morals and money, of following European trends. Furthermore, by writing this account in the vernacular, he was attempting to address issues of concern to the common man and reach an audience of readers and listeners beyond the upper middle class.

The new modes of transportation and the new pastimes were targets for criticism as well. A 1919 cartoon sent in by a reader of *al-laṭa'if al-muṣawwara* sets its aim at the new clubs established by the wealthy. The cartoon depicts a Notables' Club with entrance requirements including a car or two-horse carriage, a 15-centimeter mustache, a gruff voice, a scowling face when dealing with servants, sitting with one leg crossed over the other, and the ability to talk about important things, for example, the price of cars. The caption underneath suggests that the clubs and their members would not elicit such contempt from the masses if they followed the example of the Greeks in philanthropy and kindness to the poor.[108]

Poking fun at the habits and amusements of the wealthy, Muwaylihi creates a situation where the Pasha is nearly run over by a bike-riding judge in Ismailiyya. Isa explains to the Pasha, "this is a modern bicycle, which some people prefer to carriages ... [because] they do not eat or drink, nor do they grow tired and emaciated. This [bicycle] rider is a judge, who rides in order to exercise his limbs." The looming danger of speeding vehicles was a frequent rationale for attacking the new methods of transportation. The previously discussed cartoons regarding the well-coifed motorcycle riders and the ogling automobile driver fit into this category. Another obvious target of criticism was the extravagant cost of fancy carriages, imported automobiles, and expensive mass transit systems. In 1919 Talaat Harb, a key figure in Egypt's nascent industrial bourgeoisie, wrote a series of articles in *al-ahram* critiquing Egypt's foreign-financed and managed tramway company.[109]

Public transportation and new forms of amusement led to another form of disorder: the intermingling of the sexes. Khulussy of *al-laṭa'if al-muṣsawwara* frequently touched upon this volatile topic. In a 1917 cartoon we see four women compromised by new forms of transportation and amusement. The women all appear in clothing that is at least partially cloaked, and they all wear translucent *yashmaks*. One appears on the road, another at the cinema, the third on the tram, and the fourth in a store; all of them are surrounded by leering men. The caption describes the purpose of the cartoon as follows: "to demonstrate our moral, societal shortcomings that are not in keeping with our customs as an Arab, Eastern community . . . when we blindly follow the Westerners in that which is depraved . . . ."[110]

The same theme appears repeatedly in *ḥadith ᶜIsa ibn Ḥisham* as the Pasha visits the venues of corruption: hotels, bars, restaurants, gaming halls, dance halls, parks, clubs, and theaters. Over and over again, the Pasha is amazed by the sights, sounds, and smells of these places, and his companions must explain how things have changed. The dance hall is a den of iniquity where the stench of wine, sweat, smoke, and filthy bathrooms pervades the air. Furthermore, women were compromised in the company of men. To make matters even worse, many of these places also contained the intermingling of the classes.[111]

Aside from the moral and social concerns regarding these new amusements, there was also a concern that Egyptians were wasting their money and that the government was misallocating funds for that which was not directly benefiting Egyptians. Muwaylihi uses a visit to Azbakiyya to critique the government's allocation of funds for public use. The Pasha is amazed by the beauty of the Azbakiyya gardens. Its sights and sounds spur a discussion of land for public use. Muwaylihi, speaking through Isa, points out that while it is fine for foreigners to cultivate their spiritual side, Egyptians have more tangible, material issues to confront. A similar concern came through in the discussion of museums and libraries by the Pasha and one of Isa's friends. The friend could not see the utility in preserving old relics for the sake of foreigners, while ignoring the current needs of Egyptians.[112] In general, as the occupation became a permanent fixture in Egyptian life, the native population grew increasingly wary of foreigners, foreign companies, and that which the government performed on behalf of the foreign population.[113]

Another major target of criticism was conspicuous consumption in the home. An article in the home economics section of *al-muqtaṭaf* entitled "Gaiety is not Expensive Furnishings" clearly states this case. The author encourages the woman to use her own skill and creativity in furnishing her home instead of squandering her husband's money on expensive furniture and to devote her efforts to the care of her husband and children. Another article explains that most readers of the magazine are neither very rich, nor very poor. Thus, the mistress of the house should build her home gradually, buying quality items a little bit at a time. A third article from the same source criticizes the rich for using their homes and other means of conspicuous consumption as marks of distinction. Instead, the author encourages women to compete in other fields, for example, building *kuttabs*, schools, asylums, places of worship, and hospitals—or even in personal areas of consumption, by buying a book instead of a bonnet, and so on.[114]

Muwaylihi critiques both the new style of home and the conspicuous consumption therein. The Pasha's grandson's lifestyle exemplified the changes in architectural style and attitude. Rather than living in a traditional home with an inner courtyard and garden, he lived in a mansion, in the center of a garden—that is, when he was not staying at the hotel, another source of confusion for the Pasha.[115] Within the home, Muwaylihi critiqued the worst arena of conspicuous consumption: weddings. The Pasha is clueless as to the purpose of such an ostentatious event attended by people unknown to the family. A friend explains that inviting luminaries brings honor to the home, and people spend excessive sums for no real purpose.[116] While at the wedding banquet, the Pasha overhears a conversation between two men. An older fellow is critical of the groom, who blindly follows Western customs without understanding them. He states that nothing could be worse than copying these practices that have nothing in common with the groom's natural disposition.[117]

Nadim too was critical of the practices associated with weddings. In *Humor and Censure*, he includes a dialogue between two women on the visiting practices of women. One woman points out that women themselves are the worst factor corrupting other women and that weddings are particularly problematic. She gives the example of a woman who goes to a wedding content with her life, but returns home envious of the jewelry, fashion, and cosmetics of others. Once again, Nadim was concerned about the infiltration of these habits into the middle class, highlighting the desire of these women to emulate the aristocracy.[118]

The new stores and the products within them helped to create these new homes, and thus they too were the targets of criticism. Critics were amazed by the success of the new stores that seemed to prosper even when the economy did not.[119] Furthermore, these stores were owned by Westerners and/or sold only Western goods at the expense of local industry.[120] Finally, these stores lured women into the outside world, encouraging them to abandon the work of the home. This problem "threatened" to turn women into men.[121]

New stores contained products that threatened the old order. If women began to adopt all of the new Western gadgets, then they would lose their skills and waste their family's money. Ready-made clothes were not cheap, nor were the new sewing machines. One Lebanese reader of *al-muqtaṭaf* pointed out the dangers of relying on sewing machines, highlighting the superiority of hand-stitching and its importance for recycling clothing.[122] As we shall see in chapter 8, home economics textbooks from the same period echo similar sentiments.

Muwaylihi critiques both the omnipresence of stores and vendors, as well as the capitalist spirit. The Pasha is hardly able to recognize the site of his *waqf*, a fountain, which is now surrounded by a wineshop, pharmacy, and various other stores. Both the wineshop and the pharmacy were particularly emblematic of Western economic infiltration.[123] According to Muwaylihi, the foreigner compared to the Egyptian is industrious; however, it is at a cost. Hard work and the acquisition of material goods creates a vicious cycle, whereby the foreigner wants more and more, and he stops at nothing to continue this quest.[124]

While certain aspects of Western life were worth emulating, for example, the education of girls, all adaptations and borrowing were to take indigenous morals into account:

> If the Eastern young woman restricts herself in the customs of the foreigners [limiting herself] to seeking knowledge, strengthening the intellect, and gaining from the talent of providence and household administration, remaining modest and energetic; and [she] distances [herself] from carousing, opulence, playing, and dancing, then she will glean the advantages of the East and the West . . . [125]

Use of the term "Eastern" is interesting, reflecting the concerns of not only the Muslim community, but also Christians and Jews. Western-style education and/or governesses were an obvious source of criticism, which will be addressed in chapter 6. Nevertheless, critics were quick to point out that parents too had to shoulder the responsibility for the actions of their daughters. By allowing them to read Western novels, dress in Paris fashions, and engage in frivolous pastimes, parents sanctioned these new patterns of consumption.[126] Authors also critiqued Western feminism, which encouraged women to abandon their roles, resulting in lower marriage and birth rates.[127]

The depraved state of Western consumerist lifestyles was even depicted in fictional stories in the press, some of which were translated from European languages. In "The Good Year," which appeared in *al-sufur*, the main characters, Arthur and Laura, grapple with the greed of consumerist society. Arthur is unable to marry Laura because he does not meet her expectations. A small home, one servant, and a modest salary are not enough. He concocts a plan whereby he can have one good year with her. Arthur proposes that they marry, borrow a large sum of money, and then at the end of the year, he will drown himself, leaving Laura the insurance money. Reluctant at first, Laura finally agrees to the plan; and the two live in an "earthly paradise" up until the last few days before the year's end. After Arthur leaves to carry out the last phase of the plan, Laura is haunted by his spirit. She rushes to the shore and finds his body. He is revived, and she begs him not to carry out the plan. Laura tells Arthur that money is unimportant and that she will get a job. She can live in a small house with just one servant for his sake. The two realize that love is more important than material goods.[128]

Conclusion

Although Ismail failed in his efforts to make Egypt part of Europe and to attain greater independence, a number of legacies from his reign remained. First, his new patterns of consumption spread to the upper classes. They began to adopt Westernized styles of housing, dress, food, education, transportation, and leisure. Furthermore, as indicated by the indigenous critics of Western consumption, these new patterns also began to seep into the urban middle class, creating a cultural struggle for identity.

A second and related legacy left by Ismail was the network of roads, bridges, ports, railroad lines, and telegraph lines that helped to build the infrastructure necessary for consumption. By linking the sites of production and consumption, he attempted to reap the wealth of the countryside and provide the cities with modern goods and services. Chapter 4 examines the impact of these urban changes in creating modern shopping districts and the use of advertisements in educating the public to new products and services, while chapter 5 addresses the role of the press in buttressing the new role for the woman as *al-Sayyida al-Istihlakiyya* [Mrs. Consumer]. We first examine the evolution of these changes in Western Europe and the United States before moving to the Egyptian context.

Chapter 4

Advertising and Consumer Culture in Egypt: Creating *al-Sayyida al-Istihlakiyya*

The Rise of Consumer Culture and Advertising in the West

Consumerism, in the sense of conspicuous consumption, has existed for thousands of years as a means of distancing the upper class from the lower classes. Cultural artifacts, for example, *objets d'art*, magnificent tombs, sumptuary laws, and descriptions of feasts and festivals from all over the world, remain to demonstrate "goods . . . acquired not for themselves but for what they symbolize, for their associations, for their contribution to a particular image . . . ."[1] Nevertheless, modern consumerism and mass consumer culture are products of the nineteenth and twentieth centuries. Up until recently, the growing body of literature on consumption has focused on western Europe, specifically England, France, and to a lesser extent the United States and the Netherlands. Economic historians of the Middle East generally use the nineteenth century as a starting point, dealing with consumption only as it relates to Western products displacing indigenous ones.[2] This chapter offers a brief history of consumer culture and advertising in the West in order to highlight similarities and differences between their development in the two contexts. Traditional "coming of the West" accounts tend to overlook indigenous trends that predate the nineteenth century. Nevertheless, the incorporation of Egypt into the world economy, and consequently its greater contact with the West, had a profound influence on both patterns of consumption and the numbers of people consuming imported goods.

The birth of consumerism did not spring forth fully grown in nineteenth-century Europe, but rather, was the result of social and economic changes that had been taking place since the early modern period. The change lies in an increasing concern with material culture as more people had greater access to a wider variety of goods. Following the age of exploration and discovery, there was increasing demand for new goods to be used by more people for new social and cultural purposes. Furthermore, this desire for access was not necessarily limited to elites. At the same time that more goods were becoming available, households in western Europe were in the process of reallocating their productive resources, affecting the supply of goods, labor, and the demand for market products.[3]

Changing habits of consumption worked synergistically with the industrial revolution to create modern consumer culture. Over the course of the eighteenth and nineteenth centuries, consumption expanded quantitatively, qualitatively, vertically, and horizontally. In his landmark study, Neil McKendrick contends that much of this change is attributable to social competition that led to new characteristics of consumption: individualism, fashion, and decency. Building on the work of McKendrick, Grant McCracken points out that these developments meant that new conceptions of person were both driving and driven by new consumer patterns. Thus, by the nineteenth century, patterns that had been emerging since the sixteenth century were firmly established.[4]

Over the course of the nineteenth century, the continued development of the industrial and consumer revolutions were contingent upon the related revolutions in transportation, communication, and retailing. The expansion of the railroad network facilitated the more rapid movement of raw materials and consumer goods, as well as the movement of people toward urban centers. The growth of cities and the creation of better roads allowed for the use of horse-drawn omnibuses even before the arrival of the electric streetcar. From 1880 to 1914, the spread of the electric tramway helped to decrease the "size" of cities, while increasing their population, by making them more accessible. These improvements fostered the development of central shopping districts in large urban centers.[5]

Larger retail shops in this district could now thrive in comparison to smaller shops located in other sections of town due to their ability to draw customers from all quarters of the city, as well as from the suburbs. At mid-century, the most rapidly growing retail establishments were the dry-goods stores, or *magasins de nouveautés*. As the name implies, the stores carried a variety of goods, including fabrics, hosiery, lingerie, clothing, and other sundry items. These dry-goods stores developed into large department stores over the second half of the nineteenth century by introducing a number of innovations in retailing.[6]

First, these establishments offered set prices for cash only, emphasizing high turnover of goods. Credit and bargaining had been long-established links in the chain binding customer and small retailer. The new system seemed to offer advantages to the customer, who could comparison shop and take advantage of lower prices. Furthermore, with high turnover of stock, store owners could reap higher profits by investing in goods that would sell quickly, be replaced quickly, and sell again.[7]

The new department stores were also revolutionary in their diversification and departmentalization with respect to the location of goods, specialized personnel, and separate records. Store owners could now monitor the various departments and evaluate their goods, services, and employees. Diversification usually occurred through the introduction of new lines into an already successful department. Moreover, department stores worked to make shopping a more pleasurable experience. The use of iron and steel in the architecture caught the attention of potential customers, along with new forms of exhibition and promotion. Inside, the customer found dramatic interior architecture, elaborate lighting, and a magnificent array of goods. Furthermore, stores took advantage of new technologies, such as the telephone, the electric light, the cash register, and the escalator to increase the ease, efficiency, and safety of shopping, which became an activity rather than just a means to an end. New products and services—beauty salons, art exhibits, fashion shows, restaurants, concerts, and sales—offered new incentives. Department store owners became masters in self-promotion through the use of pamphlets, agendas, catalogues, trade cards, and advertising.[8]

Both the new department stores and advertising worked together to educate the public in how and what to buy. During the late nineteenth century, there were segments of the population that had growing purchasing power; yet they lacked the habit of spending, which advertising helped them to overcome. Advertising was not a nineteenth-century innovation. From handbills publicizing runaway slaves to the announcement of the arrival of new goods, advertising had served a variety of functions. The expansion of the press in the West at the turn of the eighteenth century brought an increased volume of advertisements, which resembled classified advertisements today. They were grouped in one section of the paper, close together, in a single font, and usually advertised new products and innovations. Ordinary household products did not necessitate advertisement.[9]

Over the course of the nineteenth century, rising literacy rates combined with the establishment of an inexpensive, advertisement-oriented press, allowed for further development. Nevertheless, as late as the 1860s, advertisements still resembled their earlier counterparts except that there were more of them. Generally, they included the name of the product, a brief description, and the address of the company. There were few sketches, borders, or varied fonts. Editors resisted breaking up their layouts with new formats. Furthermore, many potential advertisers were not yet convinced that advertising could encourage consumption, while others felt that more emphasis should be placed on product demonstration. Merchants would advertise for a few weeks at the beginning of each trading season and not advertise again until the following season, except to announce a special sale or event. These advertisements tended to be factual and informative, lacking great claims other than reasonable prices.[10]

By the 1880s and 1890s there were signs of change. Advertisers included book sellers, magazine agents, manufacturers of cheap miscellaneous goods, larger retail establishments, some ready-to-use food products, farm equipment, sewing machines, soap, cleaning compounds, and with increasing frequency, patent medicines. An analysis of major American advertisers in 1893 found that more than half of the firms that spent money on advertising were patent-medicine manufacturers. Not surprisingly, merchants were first able to see the power of advertising as customers began to request patent medicines by name, instead of asking for something for a headache.[11]

Patent medicine advertisers quickly earned a reputation for using distortions, hyperbole, superlatives, and outright untruths. With their claims to strengthen blood, cure rheumatism, and ward off whooping cough, these manufacturers paved the way for moving beyond simple, informative advertising. A natural outgrowth of the patent medicines was the early cosmetics industry. At first these products were marketed to remedy existing problems, rather than to enhance natural beauty. Furthermore, cosmetics were not marketed exclusively for women.[12]

While manufacturers of patent medicines were at the vanguard of American advertising, soap manufacturers in Britain were the pioneers. They were among the first to use pictorial advertising. According to Anne McClintock, "soap was a scarce and humdrum item and washing a cursory activity at best" in early nineteenth-century Britain. Most household laundering took place "once or twice a year in great communal binges." By the late nineteenth century a dramatic change took place as Victorians consumed massive quantities of soap and "advertising emerged as the central cultural form of commodity capitalism."[13] McClintock attributes the change in habits to the changes brought about by the colonial economy. Just as inexpensive cotton led to inexpensive textiles, so too did low-priced oils lead to low-priced soap.[14]

As advertising was becoming more sophisticated, a wide variety of new products arrived on the market during the 1880s. It is during this decade that new machinery was developed for making flour, cereal, canned foods, chemicals, matches, photographic film, and cigarettes. Factories could now process much larger quantities of raw materials. Consequently, many of these products necessitated new forms of marketing since they were entirely new products or were replacing homemade goods and unbranded merchandise. By 1910, these products began to replace patent medicines as big advertisers in the United States.[15]

Since women had been traditionally responsible for making and/or using several of the products turned out by continuous-process machinery, a significant proportion of early advertising was targeted specifically toward them. Ironically, as women were less needed in the productive realm, the number and complexity of household tasks multiplied and levels of consumption grew. As a result, their role as household managers expanded. To meet these new demands, advertisers informed women that new products could reduce labor and that smart consumers bought certain products.[16]

During the 1890s, advertising continued to evolve. Helen Damon-Moore asserts that "[a]dvertisements in the 1890s became bigger, better-illustrated, and slicker in tone. Catchy names abounded . . . [and] ad copy exhorted women to be modern . . . ." This trend meshed with late Victorian advertisements' plays on the prestige of science and appeal of modernity. At the same time, advertising blurred the lines between public and private. Advertising helped to turn previously public professions into activities that could be accomplished in the privacy of one's home, for example, shaving, photography, and shopping via catalogue.[17]

One reason for the development of advertising was the parallel development of the advertising agency. In the late nineteenth century, agencies functioned mainly as space brokers. By the turn of the century, agencies began to offer more services and advice to manufacturers; and they began hiring artists and copywriters to better serve their customers. Although outnumbered by men, women began to play a prominent role in advertising. Nevertheless, few women became generalists or executives; instead, they remained wedded to women's product accounts.[18]

During the first two decades of the twentieth century, the cosmetics industry blossomed with the creation of new lotions, cremes, dentrifices, and powders. While magazine advertising was limited before 1900, by 1920 cosmetics became a significant force in women's magazines. Rather than just attempting to remedy minor problems, these advertisements began to play on women's fear and anxieties. The shift of cosmetics from presenting information to creating demand by arousing fear, was symptomatic of a general trend in advertising in the West. Other products advertised themselves as serving society in general, and women in particular, by creating doubts about old products and values. While women were told that new forms of cleaning would make their lives easier and that certain products would ensure the health of their children, standards of household cleanliness and motherly attentiveness were rising. Building on the nineteenth-century idea that women were responsible for the love and happiness of the family, twentieth-century advertisers urged women to demonstrate this love by purchasing the appropriate products.[19]

By the 1910s and 1920s, the most innovative advertisers linked consumption of their products to more fulfilling marriages, better children, increased household efficiency, and greater political freedom. The use of endorsements by doctors, celebrities, and society matrons encouraged consumption for status where nineteenth-century advertisements had emphasized quality, durability, and practicality. Over the course of the 1920s and the 1930s, Western advertising moved further and further away from the old product-centered ads of the late nineteenth century, to a form that emphasized the consumer rather than the product. Raymond Williams has labeled this process the "magic" of advertising. According to Jennifer Scanlon, this shift in advertising not only created "artificial needs for new products but also artificial relationships among women and artificial definitions of womanhood."[20]

Both turn-of-the-century women's magazines and advertisements advanced these definitions of womanhood. Advertising trade journals also helped to shape a homogenous Mrs. Consumer, advising agencies of her importance. According to an 1895 brochure by the Lord and Thomas agency, "[s]he who 'rocks the cradle' and 'rules the world' is directly and indirectly head of the buying department of every home."[21] Similarly a 1916 advertising textbook suggested that certain products were by nature feminine, and therefore the advertiser should "know the foibles of the sex and base his campaign upon that knowledge."[22] In 1929 Christine Frederick, a contributor and household editor of the *Ladies' Home Journal*, saw an even more significant role for Mrs. Consumer, and she created a handbook for courting her patronage. In it she argued that women control at least 80 percent of household expenditures.[23]

Nevertheless, Mrs. Consumer was not a piece of clay in the hands of advertising executives and magazine editors. She had the ability to accept, reject, and/or refine the constructs of womanhood. Through letters to the editor, letters to manufacturers, responses to marketing surveys, and most importantly, her own purchasing power, Mrs. Consumer helped to fashion her own construct of womanhood. Before turning to her Egyptian counterpart, *al-Sayyida al-Istihlakiyya*, we must first look at the forces shaping consumer culture and advertising in Egypt.

The Creation of Consumer Culture in Egypt

It is erroneous to assume that notions of consumerism arose only with and in response to the West. For advertising to successfully promote consumerism, both a superstructure and infrastructure of consumption must be in place. Large corporations and retailers provide the superstructure of consumption, that is, the images that make a product or service seem "normal, appropriate, convenient, and popular." There must also be an infrastructure, what Damon-Moore has referred to as "a set of social conditions that predisposes an individual or group of individuals toward certain patterns of consuming."[24] For example, over the course of the eighteenth century, *dallalas* served the function of acquainting and persuading women to use certain luxury goods. Without this crucial indigenous link, shopping for European textiles, medicines, and furnishings in department stores and pharmacies would not have made sense for the upper class. Furthermore, the economic infrastructure of consumption, that is, roads, bridges, ports, railroads, and so on, had to exist in order for further development to take place.

The rise of modern consumer culture in Egypt was intricately linked to its incorporation into the capitalist world economy. Although most economic histories focus on the nineteenth century, when foreign investment intensified, it is clear that the roots of Egyptian capitalism lay in the eighteenth century. At that time, Egypt was an entrepôt of long-distance trading routes leading to Asia, Africa, and Europe. Cairo, like other large cities, served as a market for luxury goods, since it housed the individuals who could afford items such as imported weaponry, clothing, and furs. Meanwhile, in Europe, the industrial revolution led to economic demands for greater quantities of raw materials. France, compared to Britain, had "fewer options for procuring raw materials and marketing [its] manufactured products." In Egypt, France found much needed grain and a market for its luxury goods. Recent Syrian (Christian) immigrants served as a local client community purveying French goods to both the mamluk elite and the middle classes. French merchants went out of their way to understand the Egyptian market by surveying preferences, sending samples back to France, and having those samples copied.[25]

At that time shopping in Egypt took place in urban *suqs* [bazaars] where artisans and shops were concentrated. Stores were grouped together by common trade. As a general rule, they were fairly small, about six feet by four feet, enclosed by shutters or folding doors. The small, intimate setting of the store naturally made shopping a personalized business. A regular customer might expect to be offered coffee and tobacco during the process of a regular transaction, which could involve both bargaining and a conversation on matters unrelated to business. Such a transaction could take half an hour or more. In some markets, auctions conducted by brokers [*dallals*] were held once or twice a week. Additionally, *wakalas* housed merchants and served as a place to store and receive goods. According to Lane there were 200 such buildings in Cairo.[26] In the eighteenth century, Raymond estimates that about one-quarter of Cairo's population was involved in craft production and about one-tenth were merchants or retailers. By the turn of the nineteenth century, Cairo boasted some 74 craft corporations and 65 merchants' guilds.[27]

Prior to the rise of Muhammad Ali, Egypt in general, and Cairo in particular, had a thriving consumer culture. Nevertheless, most studies of commerce, banking, and industry begin with the changes that took place during his reign.[28] Muhammad Ali sought to develop industry in Egypt along the lines of the country's strengths and to avoid costly imports.[29] In addition to embarking upon his own efforts at industrialization, Muhammad Ali encouraged some foreign investment. By 1837, there were already more than 70 foreign mercantile firms operating in Alexandria. According to the Bowring "Report", Greece, France, England, Austria, Italy, and the Levant were the most heavily represented. Many of the foreign nationals who came to Egypt, particularly those from Southern Europe and the Levant, established permanent roots, the so-called *mutamaṣṣirun*.[30] By the 1840s and 1850s, the groundwork was laid for further foreign investment.

As discussed in chapter 2, Muhammad Ali's hand-picked and immediate successor, Ibrahim, preceded him to the grave, and the reins of government fell to Abbas Hilmi I (r. 1848–54), his grandson. Traditional accounts describe his reign as a period of reactionism and retrenchment. Toledano argues for a more sympathetic treatment of the misunderstood viceroy by demonstrating the many forces, indigenous and European, that would benefit from portraying him as a sexually deviant demon. Aside from the effusive praise of Nubar pasha, the more "balanced" views appear lukewarm at best. Toledano is successful, however, in providing context for Abbas's alleged hatred of Westerners, and hence the dismissal of a large number of his uncle and grandfather's advisors, as well as the dismissal (or relocation) of internal enemies linked to the same strategies. These moves surely earned him some degree of popularity within the country. Although he is often portrayed as reversing military policies, Toledano demonstrates that Abbas utilized the military for both "power and amusement"; however, financial need necessitated cuts. Similarly, he reduced spending on industry and education. Abbas preferred to place a higher premium on internal security, and thus he was responsible for two developments affecting the growth of consumer culture in Egypt. He improved the road between Cairo and Suez, shortening the route to India and the Far East; and he provided the British with a concession to build the first railroad line in Egypt, between Cairo and Alexandria, thus improving transit, trade, and communications.[31]

Said, Muhammad Ali's son, succeeded Abbas after his death in 1854. His francophile leanings gave him better contemporary European ratings than his predecessor; however, Egyptian nationalist historians distinguish his reign as the period in which Egypt flung open the doors of investment to the West and began a vicious cycle of loans and indebtedness. These criticisms not withstanding, Said is responsible for a number of developments associated with the growth of consumer culture in Egypt. He is most famous for granting the Suez Canal concession to Ferdinand de Lesseps. Additionally, he continued work on railroad lines in the delta and established telegraph lines between Alexandria, Cairo, and Suez.[32] Regardless of the fiscal and political implications of these policies, Said continued the development of the infrastructure necessary for modern consumer culture.

As previously discussed, Ismail expanded the transportation and communication networks in Egypt, extending them beyond the delta into the *ṣaᶜid*. Furthermore, he carried out municipal developments in the major cities of the delta, improving streets, sanitation, and public services. One of Ismail's more permanent legacies was the redevelopment of the Azbakiyya neighborhood, which came to include a number of European consulates and the Cairo Stock Exchange, as well as the most exclusive hotels, fashionable stores, and fine dining establishments. This neighborhood served as the nucleus for the modern shopping district in Cairo. By the end of this study, the district resembled a large triangle demarcated by Qasr al-Nil, Sulayman Pasha, and Fuad streets (Qasr al-Nil, Talaat Harb, and twenty-sixth of July streets today). The area around Sharif Street in Alexandria evolved into the same role. The new stores that arose in these districts were much like their counterparts in Europe and the

United States. Indeed, some of them, for example, Au Bon Marché and Printemps, were direct transplantations. Others, such as Sednaoui and Mauardi, were started by indigenous entrepreneurs and organized along Western lines.[33] Nevertheless, the old shopping districts did not cease to exist, and the new areas were inaccessible to all but the upper classes.

What became of the traditional shopping districts? There were some fields that continued to operate as they had in the past, such as the gold market and the tent-makers market, both of which continued time-honored traditions. The saddlery [*surugiyya*] continued to function on a somewhat more limited basis, since the tramway, and to a lesser extent the automobile, had begun to replace the horse-drawn omnibus, horses, donkeys, and carts/carriages. Other areas continued to be called by their traditional name, for example, the arms market [*suq al-silaḥ*], even as their function ceased to exist. New market areas emerged for those with limited means. The urban poor sought foodscraps, cigarette butts, and scrap metal at the *suq al-ᶜaṣr* on the edge of town; and the aspiring *effendi* might hope to find a used European-style suit at the *suq al-kantu*, near the entrance of Muski street.[34]

Between the British occupation in 1882 and World War I, the amount of foreign investment in Egypt grew tremendously, doubling between 1892 and 1897, and again between 1897 and 1902. After the financial crisis of 1907 and a change in Egypt's commercial law in 1908, many foreign companies went into liquidation. Nevertheless, commercial enterprises, while growing at a slower rate, did not decline. They could not have survived had there not been a demand for their new products and services. Nevertheless, consumer knowledge was limited; and advertising served to raise awareness among the upper classes.

Although there are some similarities, the course of advertising in Egypt does not follow the Western pattern in all respects. While both demonstrate an increasing concern for gender, a preoccupation with modernity, and a growing degree of refinement, Egyptian advertising never reaches the sophistication of American advertising in terms of both layout and psychological implications. Sketches and designs remain simple, and advertisements generally remain product oriented. Furthermore, with reference to women, Egyptian advertisements lack a concern for reducing labor and increasing efficiency; but they do emphasize the special needs of Egyptian women. Finally, Egyptian advertisements reflect the struggle of Egypt's incorporation into the world economy and its position as a colonized country.

In this study of advertising, one must recognize that the readership and target audience was mainly urban and clustered in the delta. This dichotomy relates to the distinction discussed in chapters 2 and 3 regarding the city as the site of consumption and the countryside as the site of production. Most of the stores, products, and services that advertised were available only in urban areas. Furthermore, the readership was disproportionately male, as well as disproportionately Christian and foreign (relative to their numbers in the population as a whole). Despite low literacy rates, women still had access to magazines and their advertisements. Girls in school read magazines purchased through block subscriptions. Furthermore, Egypt had a strong oral tradition, and reading aloud was not uncommon. According to Baron, "[r]eading aloud multiplied the size of a periodical's audience many times and provided an important source of information in the days before news was broadcast over the radio." Coffee shops were often the location where illiterate and semi-literate males listened to the paper and heard about the news of the day.[35] Successful nationalist journalists, for example, Abdullah Nadim, wrote in a manner such that key points would resonate with listeners. Similarly, as advertising became more sophisticated, ornate sketches, fancy borders, and varied fonts could catch the eye of onlookers.

Another major issue with the study of advertising is that of representation.[36] One must recognize that advertisements do not represent or even aim to represent the society to which they are directed. According to Roland Marchand, "advertisers quickly perceived [that] people did not usually want advertisements to reflect themselves . . . or their broader society exactly," but rather they wanted a "distorting mirror that could enhance certain images." Marchand points out that advertisements should not be overlooked as a viable source for history. While one could argue that it is not possible to gauge reader response, neither can we do so from more traditional sources, such as religious tracts or campaign speeches. Nevertheless, advertisements do tell us what products and services were sold in a given era, current fads, when products first attained mass distribution, and, in the case of testimonial advertisements, with whom advertisers thought consumers would identify and trust. They also specify the criteria by which consumers evaluate products.[37] Moreover, advertising is a two-way street, and consumer response, or lack thereof, shapes the advertising process. Foreign companies in Egypt had the added difficulty of attempting to understand the potential market. The symbols, images, and key phrases that sold products in the West might not have resonance in the Middle East.[38]

Finally, we must recognize that during this period advertising did not play as salient a role as it did in the West. The reading public in Egypt was still small, the number of publications limited, and many publishers used little or no advertising to finance their operations. Even into the early twentieth century, revenues for many journals came from subventions by the government or wealthy patrons and/or subscriptions.[39] A related problem exists in that advertisements frequently appeared as front or back material in a journal and were perhaps eliminated in the process of binding.

Early Press Advertising

The earliest advertisements that I examined came from 1865 and 1866 in *al-waqa*ᶜ*i al-miṣriyya*, the official government paper.[40] These format advertisements resemble the simple classified ads of the early-nineteenth century in the West, with no sketches, borders, or varying fonts; however, they differ from their Western counterparts in the language used. Like *al-waqa*ᶜ*i al-miṣriyya* itself, its advertisements are verbose and stilted in style. Nevertheless, they remain more or less informational and factual in nature. A large number of the ads, as one might expect from an official paper, deal with things that the government wants to sell, such as shares in its companies or surplus items.[41] There are also advertisements by individuals wanting to sell books, homes, and *waqf* property.[42] Most follow a formula whereby they provide information on what is being sold, whom prospective buyers must contact by a given date, and conclude by stating that goods will go to the highest bidder adhering to the specified terms. The target audience of these advertisements was upper- and upper-middle-class males who had an interest in keeping up with the administrative, economic, and judicial goings-on of the government. With respect to nongovernment publications, Shechter speculates that *Wadi al-Nil* was among the first to utilize advertising.[43]

Throughout the 1870s and 1880s advertising did not develop substantially. Where it existed, it was still limited to simple advertisements, many of which were for booksellers associated with the publisher of the newspaper or magazine.[44] By the 1890s, both the quantity and range of publications in Egypt had increased. The press had undergone a major transformation during the age of Ismail as writers engaged in a new discourse about the direction of Egypt's development. Ismail's deposition, the ascension of the European-leaning Tawfiq, the rise of a nationalist opposition movement, and the British occupation forged a new dialogue in the pages of the Egyptian press. Some suppression of journalists took place in the wake of the Urabi movement and the British occupation; however, by 1892 and the ascension of the Khedive Abbas Hilmi II, many of the imprisoned journalists had been released, the censorship laws loosened, and new publications firmly established. According to Abbas Kelidar, newspapers came to function as a substitute for political parties, each representing different solutions for Egypt's political woes. Editors and journalists ranged from Muslim to Christian to Jew, pan-Ottoman to pan-Arab to pan-Islamic to Egyptian nationalist, to pro/anti-British to pro/anti-French to pro/anti-Ottoman to pro/anti-monarchy. In the same year that Abbas Hilmi II took power in Egypt, the first journal for women, *al-fatat*, was published in Alexandria. It would be the first in a series of turn-of-the-century publications for women.[45]

These developments would have significant consequences for advertising in Egypt. With the rise of a more overtly political press, securing subventions from the government and from wealthy patrons could prove more difficult or restrict the purview of the publication. While political orientation might hinder support by patrons, so too might discourse that lacked the support of a specific platform. For this reason, many women's journals had to rely on other sources for funding. Advertising allowed the enterprising journalist to pursue a third course without recourse to wealthy patrons or the ability to sell large blocks of subscriptions.[46]

The editors of *al-hilal* were early proponents of advertising. In an 1897 article they discuss "The Benefits of Advertising," highlighting its importance as a means of gaining capital for prospective businesses, the great benefits that have accrued to Western companies by utilizing advertisements, and how they themselves have benefited from advertising. Early advertisements for advertising in *al-hilal* list prices and discuss the press's ability to produce both Arabic and Western characters. A later ad emphasizes the utility of advertising that reaches "thousands of readers fivefold." Some editors of the women's press were quick to see the advantages as well. Alexandra de Avierino was among the first to fully utilize advertising in her journal *anis al-jalis*. The publication was only 30–40 pages long, yet as many as 7–12 pages might be dedicated to advertising. In 1903 Alexandra de Avierino wrote an article entitled "The Benefits of the Overlooked," referring to advertising, in which she encouraged others to follow her lead. She asserted that advertisements would benefit the country by fostering not only the open exchange of goods, but also the open exchange of ideas as publications could proliferate.[47]

As more publishers saw the utility of using advertising, the amount, frequency, and sophistication of advertisements all increased.[48] Furthermore, editors of different orientations could seek different forms of advertising. At the same time, the numbers of industries, stores, products, and services that sought advertising multiplied. No longer were they limited to individual sellers seeking to find the highest bidders, rather there was now a varied group trying to attract large quantities of customers with their reasonable prices. Turn-of-the-century advertisements were peppered with phrases—"the utmost in moderate prices," "limited prices," "the utmost in reasonable prices," "the utmost in workmanship and moderate prices," "price and workmanship that cannot be surpassed," and the like. Aside from the claims of moderate prices, workmanship, variety, and quality, the wording of advertisements (outside the realm of patent medicines) remained informative and mostly factual.[49] Unlike the frequent calls to buy on credit that Frierson found in the late Ottoman press, I found no similar offerings in the Egyptian press.[50]

By the 1890s, a new era opened in Egyptian advertising that would last until about 1914. The number, range, and quality of advertisements would all increase. Like the West, the first big boom came from the realm of patent medicines and cosmetics; however, they differed from American ads because of their occasional association with a particular pharmacy. In both the mainstream press and in the women's press, and in Muslim, Christian, and Jewish publications, pharmaceutical agents and pharmacies represented the fastest growing segment of the advertising industry. Advertisements blurred the distinction between health, beauty, and even foods/beverages, informing potential consumers that they could add vitamins to their hair to restore its beauty and increase their vitality by drinking wine.[51]

Many of these advertisements appealed to women with sketches, testimonials, and claims to cure their ailments, for example, Bank's Pills and Hemagene Tailleur.[52] The sketches of women in Victorian clothing and the claims of the text are basically the same as advertisements found in the 1880s and 1890s in the West.[53] The lack of representation of indigenous women raises a number of questions. Was it simply that photographs were not yet widely used or that foreign companies utilized the same sketches used in their home campaigns? Or, was there concern about human representation in Islamic society—while photographs were fine for consumption in the home, trafficking in such images publicly was perhaps unacceptable. In her study of the Hamidian press, Frierson notes the lack of human representation, unless the individuals were clearly Western.[54] It was probably a combination of the aforementioned reasons. Publishers may have found the expense and technology of including photographic images prohibitive, and foreign companies usually had a variety of campaigns from which to choose. There was little need to risk alienating indigenous tastes regarding representation. Furthermore, there was little gender specificity in advertising, and most ads that claimed to help women, also claimed to help men, either in the same advertisement or in a different campaign.

A leader in this genre of double advertising was Doan's backache and kidney pills. The advertisements used three means for selling their product. First, some advertisements utilized both (Victorian) men and women to depict the anguish of back pain. Second, other advertisements used the testimonials of contented customers. Finally, some advertisements were plain text, explaining the benefits of the pills. Occasionally, the advertisements targeted at women state that most medicines are just for men, implying that the pills are specifically for women; yet the company continued to run advertisements with male pictures and testimonials, even in women's magazines.[55] With low female literacy rates, having advertisements with androgynous appeal was probably just smart marketing.

Similarly, Scott's Emulsion targeted a varied audience. The company's trademark picture of a fisherman remained the same, but the opening caption and text would change. One advertisement for women announced: "Relief for the pregnant." The text reads: "Women suffer from severe pain when they are pregnant. Although, if it were men in this agony, they would scream to heaven." The ad then points out that screaming does not really help the pain, but Scott's Emulsion is an effective cure. Other versions exhort its utility for those who have just suffered from illness, those currently suffering from a variety of illnesses, and for teething children.[56]

The names of foreign pharmaceutical agents and companies filled the advertising pages of Egypt's newspapers and journals. Nevertheless, there were also a small number of indigenous entrepreneurs marketing their elixirs, cremes, and dentrifices to the upper and growing middle class in Egypt. "Health Oil," an "Eastern" brand of fish oil, advertised its availability at the "Health Pharmacy." Mahmud Effendi Kamil promised to cure those afflicted by tooth problems with just one bottle of his remedy. Similarly, Faris Antun al-Shami developed a medicine for hair restoration that he licensed under the famous Eastern chemist Yusif Effendi Khury.[57]

As previously mentioned, the line between health and beauty products was blurred, and like the earliest cosmetics advertisements in the United States, most between 1890 and 1914 were not gender specific and were aimed at eliminating an unwanted problem rather than enhancing natural beauty. New products flooded the market, and everything from hair restoration cremes to hair removers targeted both men and women.[58] An 1897 advertisement for Rusma Ganibel hair remover contains a sketch of a woman in a sleeveless dress. The text advertises the price for a six-month supply for both men and women, with women paying 33 percent more.[59] Nevertheless, there was no distinction made about how either group would use the product.

Up until about 1915 there was not much gender-specific advertising, although women were clearly targeted in many ads. In comparing a mainstream newspaper, *al-mu'ayyad* and a woman's journal, *anis al-jalis*, I found far fewer differences than I had anticipated.[60] By current standards, a daily newspaper with a political agenda, edited by a Muslim male (Shaykh Ali Yusif) and issued from Cairo, clearly ought to be distinct in its advertising from a monthly woman's journal issued from Alexandria, edited by a female Syrian Christian (Alexandra de Avierino). Nevertheless, the two journals demonstrated roughly equal proportions of advertising dedicated to banking/insurance, as well as transportation and communcation. Both reflected the early-twentieth-century boom of advertising for pharmacies, medications, and cosmetics. The wording of the advertisements themselves did not differ greatly, nor did the strategies for selling health/beauty products.

The biggest difference was the lack of government notices in *anis al-jalis*, compared to *al-mu'ayyad*, which received support from the government of Abbas II.[61] *Anis al-jalis* filled this gap with more advertising in the realm of specialty shops, department stores, and elite service personnel.[62] With respect to the latter, *al-mu'ayyad* was more likely to run advertisments for doctors, lawyers, and dentists. While *anis al-jalis* contained a number of these advertisements, it was more likely to include other service personnel—tailors, governesses, music instructors, and photographers.[63] The localized nature of the readership and the more elite target audience meant that it was more financially rewarding for small entreprenuers to advertise, particularly if they were solicitous to the needs of secluded or semi-secluded women. *Anis al-jalis* advertisements were filled with explicit accommodations for these women, while in *al-mu'ayyad*, and in the mainstream press generally, such measures were either understood, unneccessary, or unavailable.

Another difference between the two publications was attributable to the religious inclinations of the respective editors. Although both *anis al-jalis* and *al-mu'ayyad* ran advertisements for elixirs that contained alcohol as a primary ingredient, I found no advertisements in *al-mu'ayyad* for alcoholic beverages, while they occasionally appeared in *anis al-jalis*.[64] Whether in Christian or in Muslim-edited publications, alcohol was more likely to appear in advertisements as a medication.[65] Interestingly enough, in the interwar period, the number of alcohol advertisements increases exponentially. According to Shechter, it "would lead one to believe that the consumption of whiskey was replacing that of water in Egypt."[66] In the pre-war era, advertising was not yet dominated by large multinational interests.

Anis al-jalis was somewhat unique among women's magazines for advertising and among those who advertised, for dedicating such a large proportion of the publication to ad copy. *Al-sa^{c}ada*, a women's magazine contemporary to *anis al-jalis* contained less advertising and less sophisticated advertising. For example, all of the advertisements for *anis al-jalis* were unique (although the same ad might run repeatedly), while many of the advertisements in *al-sa^{c}ada* were format advertisements, such that all pharmacies (or all tailors) had identical advertisements, except for the name and address of the businesses.[67] Even the few advertisements that contained borders or sketches shared them with others.[68]

Post–World War I Developments in Advertising

Between 1914/1915 and 1922 advertisements in Egypt developed further. They became more ornate, more highly decorated, with varying fonts, and illustrated with more frequent, improved sketches. Furthermore, there was greater gender specificity, and they reflected the expansion of foreign companies and the growing middle class. Nevertheless, traditional advertisements still predominated through the period under study. Even by the 1930s, advertisements remained product oriented, with uncomplicated text, few slogans, and simple illustrations.[69] The most sophisticated advertisements of the period between 1915–22 appeared in *al-laṭa'if al-muṣawwara*. This weekly journal was a pictorial compilation of current events, politics, famous people, social organizations, sporting events, fashion, and social criticism. The large pictures and simple text made the magazine more accessible than other publications of the day. A 1920 advertisement for *al-laṭa'if*'s advertisements promised immediate results due to the extent of its circulation: 40,000 readers.[70] Although this figure appears exaggerated, the magazine certainly had widespread appeal in Egypt and among Arabic readers as far away as Brazil.[71] The trends in *al-laṭa'if al-muṣawwara* demonstrate the overall trend toward greater gender-specificity in advertising.

Although some gender-specific advertising took place as early as the 1890s, its widespread use does not take place until after 1914. A series of advertisements for women's beauty products ran in *al-muqaṭṭam* in 1892; however, by 1896 the paper ran few of these advertisements. The removal of these ads perhaps occurred for two related reasons. First, some of the products, for example, a French weight-loss medication, may not have had resonance with the population. Many Egyptians, men and women, probably would have found the "before" picture more appealing than the "after." Second, advertisers may not have obtained sufficient response to advertisements.[72] As previously discussed, there were also a small number of elixirs for women, and there were some products for men only, for example, hernia belts.[73] Nevertheless, most advertisements were not gender specific until after 1914. Even products that previously made no gender distinction now included sketches/pictures of women (or men) or made reference to women (or men) in the text.[74] One Eastern entrepreneur, Wadia al-Hawawini, frequently advertised his products utilizing sketches of women; and in each ad, enjoined women to request his catalog for health and beauty products, including Purge Filles, Dr. Iskander's pills, lustrous hair restorer, and medications for headaches and dizziness.[75]

Although many advertisements after 1914 still called upon the reader to "request" or "use" their product utilizing the generic second person masculine singular command or the second person masculine plural command, increasing numbers of advertisers began to use feminine commands or specifically address women. The header of a 1915 ad for a department store is in bold letters and says "*ayyuha al-sayyidat*," or "[attention] ladies," to announce the arrival of the summer line. In a like manner, an advertisement for Nadko dye opens with "important news for ladies." Similarly, a 1917 De Ricoles mint elixir advertisement uses the feminine command form "request" [*uṭlubi*], although women's ailments are not actually discussed in the text.[76]

Men, as well, were courted with special cosmetics and an appeal for men's fashion. Not only did foreign companies and department stores target the stylish male consumer, but also indigenous companies. The Egyptian Clothing Company, in particular, ran a series of advertisements in 1922 aimed at creating the fashionable male. The ads are dominated by a large sketch of a man, clad in a European suit, wing-tip shoes, fancy tie, *tarbush*, and sometimes carrying a walking stick and/or cigarette. These advertisements emphasize style, reasonable prices, and quality (see figure 4.1).[77] The *tarbush* and cigarette are meant to target the rising class of new *effendiyya*, which included not just higher-level bureaucrats, but a growing middle class of clerks, civil servants, and teachers.[78]

Although advertising from 1890–1914 demonstrated a concern for modernity and modern products, this preoccupation increases in the period between 1915 and 1922, especially among indigenous companies. The picture used in Sednaoui advertising from 1915 to 1917 illustrates this concern. The spectacle of the store with its splendid cupolas, huge signs in Arabic and English, and its large windows dominates the central space of the advertisement. The store looms over a busy Midan Khazindar and is approached by people on foot, in automobiles, in carriages, and arriving by trolley. Although most of these people appear in Western clothing, a few figures appear veiled

Figure 4.1 Advertisement, Egyptian Clothing Company
Text: "The Egyptian Clothing Company. The best and strongest type of broadcloth. Prices cannot be beaten. Cut of the latest style, overcoats and suits for men, youths, and children of all ages. Come one and all to the stores of the Egyptian Clothing Company, near the Lyonnais Credit Bank of Cairo. Branches in Alexandria and Tanta."

Source: *al-laṭāʾif al-muṣuwwara*.

and cloaked. The modern wonder of Sednaoui was to have appeal for those with Western tastes, as well as those of a more conservative ilk.[79] The emergence of veiled women in advertising was a novelty, not only for Egypt, but for the late Ottoman press generally. Elizabeth Frierson discusses an anomalous advertisement for Haïm Mazza and Sons in 1897. This ad similarly depicts a variety of Western-dressed women, one man in frock coat and *tarbush*, as well as one veiled woman, examining the goods at the fabric counter. She reports that within one week this advertisement disappears and that she found no similar ad during the period under study.[80] Nevertheless, in Egypt this pattern was copied by other indigenous department stores and included similar images.[81]

The Egyptian Clothing Company's advertising between 1921 and 1922 attempted to create a positive image of modernity in the industrial process in hopes of selling more goods. These advertisements incorporated actual photographic images of the company's clean, white-washed exterior; its uniformly organized interior with rows of tables and machinery; and its neatly dressed workers (inside and outside the factory), clad in suits and *tarbushes*.[82] By depicting a kinder, gentler factory process and attempting to forge a relationship between the consumers and manufacturers, the Egyptian Clothing Company sought a more positive image of the industrial process and an association between their product and image. This effort meshed with the overall trend toward name-brand recognition, trademarks, and patents that had been introduced by Western companies.[83] Rather than associating a product with a small local storekeeper, the Egyptian would become accustomed to associating goods with large national and international companies. As well, these campaigns overlapped with "buy Egyptian" strategies (see the following), and once again the *tarbush* emerges as the embodiment of both modernity and cultural authenticity.

During the period between 1914 and 1922, advertisements became not only more gender specific and more preoccupied with modernity, but also more sophisticated in terms of marketing strategies. Advertisers begin to offer free samples, catalogs, and free services with the purchase of goods.[84] Others, selling products unfamiliar to the literate Egyptian public, needed to persuade potential customers to get more information without wasting undue space on advertising. Thus, catalogs came to be used as a means of stretching the marketing dollar.[85] Not only did catalogs help to educate the consumer in the large urban center, but they also helped to disseminate knowledge and products to more remote areas. Furthermore, they were part of the postal revolution described in chapter 2, which helped to provide secluded women with greater knowledge of the goods available on the market.

Other advertisers encouraged greater consumption by offering free gifts or services with the purchase of their products. Aziz Mansur offered free tailoring service for a suit or overcoat to those who purchased quality broadcloth from his store, promising the latest style made to suit the taste of the customer. Likewise, optometrists Lawrence and Mayo offered free eye examinations to their customers with a bold-faced header asking "Is your vision sound?" Yet another group of enterprising entrepreneurs offered free movie tickets to those who frequented their businesses, collected coupons, and purchased any daily paper. Thus, they were able to promote their products, reading, and a new pastime.[86]

Finally, one begins to see advertisements that do not look like advertisements. One for Morum department store appears to be a feature article of some sort. The bold-faced header commands the reader to read the following sentences:

1. Beauty has a standing that cannot be denied.
2. An indication of beauty is delicacy.
3. Delicacy is found in many things.
4. The most delicate article of men's clothing is the tie.
5. The tie gives the impression of beauty in the man.
6. The most delicate article of women's clothing is stockings.
7. Beautiful stockings increase the beauty of a woman.
8. Look for the most beautiful pieces of these two articles [of clothing].
9. Find them today at Morum.

Aside from the border, this example neither looks like nor reads like an advertisement until the last line. While appearing to be factual, it discusses "delicate," or rather intimate, subjects regarding the body of the man and the woman, without depicting either the articles in question or the human body.[87]

Even more innovatively, a Turkish patisserie owner ran an advertisement that resembled a human interest story. There is no border defining the advertisement, and two-thirds of the ad copy is a picture of the woman standing in the doorway of her establishment wearing a short-sleeved, ankle-length white dress and white scarf. The caption reads:

> This is a picture of the only Muslim lady who removed the veil from her face and plunged into the realm of work and diligence; she is a Turkish woman named Hala Hanum. She opened a small, charming, clean store that produces Eastern and Western confections and perfumes, selling them at the beginning of Sawaris Square Street in the capital. Her store, with respect to proficiency, cleanliness, quality, and service to the public, exceeds that which is displayed in European stores. So it is proper that these Egyptians and those who encourage her work go to her store, which is worthy of all help from Easterners. The name of her store is the White Rose.[88]

Were it not for the fact that the advertisement ran repeatedly, one might question whether or not it was an advertisement at all. Furthermore, it is interesting not only for its format, but for its strategy of encouraging Egyptians to patronize Eastern establishments and encouraging women outside the realm of the home. The use of the term Eastern is notable since it separates her from Westerners/foreigners and demonstrates a larger collective sense of identity, not surprising from the non-Egyptian editors of the magazine.[89] The Levantine-Christian editors judiciously highlighted the fact that Hala Hanum was Muslim, but chose to embrace her Eastern-ness instead.

Another change by the early 1920s is evidence of a growing middle class with greater purchasing power. One piece of evidence in this puzzle is the growth of advertising for affordable vacations and hotels. Previously hotel advertisements were mainly in the foreign press and guidebooks. These advertisements tended to be for the most exclusive hotels with numerous amenities and services (see chapter 3). Occasionally, advertisements for these first-class hotels would appear in Arabic journals as well.[90] By the early twenties, hotel advertisements begin to appeal to people of more modest means. Two 1922 advertisements in *al-laṭa'if al-muṣawwara* demonstrate this trend. A small hotel in Ras al-Bar merely advertised that it was a clean, family place with filtered water and reasonable prices. The other, somewhat flashier, advertisement encourages readers to leave the heat of Egypt for the beauty of Lebanon without exceeding the cost of an Egyptian vacation. Although the office of the company is located in stylish Midan Khazindar, it stresses affordability and accessibility over modern amenities and extensive customer services.[91] The previously discussed new *effendiyya* were targeted as the Egyptian economy stabilized in the postwar years.[92]

Although the periodization has some parallels with Western advertising, that is, greater gender specificity, concern for modernity, and increasing levels of sophistication, Egyptian advertising is distinct from Western advertising, especially where women are concerned. A major difference was the need for special services and accommodations for secluded and partially-secluded women. Ironically, department stores in the United States concerned themselves with men's need for separation, since shopping was viewed as the woman's domain. Therefore, stores often placed their men's department in a separate building or near an entrance so that men would not be sucked into the female vortex of shopping.[93] In contrast, advertisements in the women's press in Egypt, in particular, stressed the special needs of "national ladies" and those confined to the home.[94] As for the latter, they could call for ice cream delivery, be photographed by a female photographer in their home, be seen by a female doctor, tailored for by a female seamstress, or have goods from the Printemps department store sent to their home for a private showing.[95] Thus, many goods and services were available to women (often by or through women) in their homes.

As discussed in chapter 3, it was not only mixing of the sexes that bothered critics of Western consumption, but also interclass mingling. For those women who chose to leave their home, but wanted to avoid contact with unfamiliar males and unsuitable females, they could patronize stores with special branches, special salons, and/or partitions separating them from other customers. For example, Madame Massert's boutique advertised a special salon for "national ladies," and Maison Stein advertised a special branch for women's clothing.[96] The famous Egyptian feminist, Huda Shaarawi, writes in her memoirs of her early experiences in Alexandria's department stores. She would arrive on the scene cloaked and veiled, accompanied by a eunuch and a retinue of servants. She would then be led to the women's section and screened from view by partitions. Later she was able to reduce the chaos by convincing her mother to accompany her on shopping trips. She writes that her mother was "quick to see the advantages of shopping in person. Not only was there a wide range of goods to choose from but there was money to be saved through wise spending."[97]

Whether in their own homes or in protected environments, women could seek the services of other women. Although most female service personnel advertisements were placed by foreign women (either western European, Greek, Italian, or Syrian), a few were placed by Egyptian women. The women who advertised helped to blur the boundary between public and private by appearing as examples and by encouraging women to seek their services inside and outside the public sphere. As well, women working in establishments that catered to women served the same function. Contemporary observers remarked that most shop-girls were either foreign or Coptic.[98]

A second major difference between Egyptian and Western advertising targeted at women was the lack of emphasis on labor-saving devices and the lack of advertising for soap, cleaning agents, cleaning devices, and ready-made foods. These products played a major role in Western advertising, but scarcely appear in Egyptian advertising before 1922. Aside from a single one-line advertisement in 1904, the first soap advertisement I encountered was in 1922, and there were almost no others.[99] I found no advertisements for cleaning compounds, mops, or vacuum cleaners during the period under study, and there are almost no advertisements that actually show women doing housework. In an advertisement for Glaxo dry milk, a woman is depicted cooking, but this was an exception rather than the rule.[100] Moreover, processed foods were rarely advertised, aside from dry milk and children's formulas.[101]

The literate female public had little need for cleaning agents and ready-made foods. Even by 1917, the literacy rate in the governates of Cairo, Alexandria, and the canal district was only 17 percent among Egyptian women and other local subjects. Literacy rates tended to be lower among older and married women, and higher among unmarried, young women.[102] Among reading and even "onlooking" women, the vast majority did not need cleaning agents and labor-saving devices because they had at least one servant to do the most menial housework and/or certain tasks, for example baking or laundry, took place outside the home. As literacy seeped into the lower-middle class, many of those women were still too young to have their own household or a need for those products. With regard to soap, it fell into a category of products that had a long tradition in the region, and therefore needed no advertising. While soap may have been a nineteenth-century novelty in Britain, its regular use in the Middle East dates back to ancient times.[103] Indeed, soap was considered such a necessity that it frequently appeared in *nafaqa* [divorce maintenance] awards, along with items such as meat, bread, and oil.[104] As for depictions of women doing housework, even by the 1930s, these were rare.[105] Finally, the major exception to the processed-food rule can be easily explained by current advice in women's magazines and columns, which strongly advised women against the use of wet nurses (see chapter 3). For upper-class women who chose not to nurse, ready-made formula provided an easy solution. Egypt had extremely high infant mortality rates, and doctors in Egypt led campaigns for post-natal health, promoting breastfeeding or formula over unpasteurized milk. Dr. Shakhashiri went so far as to recommend the Glaxo brand, pointing out that "its only drawback is its price."[106] The enterprising staff at *al-laṭa'if al-muṣawwara* incorporated the endorsement in its 1922 Glaxo campaign.[107]

A third aspect of advertising in Egypt that is not a concern in the West, is the issue of imperialism and the clash of cultures. Over the course of the nineteenth century, Egypt was being incorporated into a world economy, not only financially, but also culturally, socially, and intellectually. The financial chaos brought about by Ismail meant a decline in foreign investment. However, after the British occupation and Egypt's return to solvency, foreign investment returned and advertising reflected the further infiltration of foreign companies. Much like the advertisements in the foreign language press in the United States that attempted to "Americanize" immigrants, foreign companies in Egypt sought to "Westernize" Egyptians by selling new products and a new style of living. Early on, these products included items to regulate life, for example, clocks and watches, as well as items for the proper home, such as electrical lights; Western-style bath fixtures; salon and bedroom furniture; pianos; sewing machines; and phonographs.[108] As previously discussed, advertisements for Western-style medicines, elixirs, and cosmetics, as well as for the modern pharmacies in which they were purchased, attempted to convince Egyptians of new means for coping with the challenges of modern life.[109] Other items, such as alcoholic beverages, false teeth, and surgical tools, also aided the "New Egyptian" in his/her assimilation to modern life.[110]

The availability of European and imported fabrics, as well as ready-to-wear clothing, meant that the latest European styles became accessible to the fashion-conscious Egyptian. During the nineteenth century, advances in dressmaking technology—patterns, the tape measure, and the sewing machine—made it easier for Egyptian women to keep up with the latest continental fashions.[111] Turn-of-the-century advertisers stressed the availability of imported broadcloth, fine satins, linens, and other fabrics, while tailors offered their services to create the latest styles. As ready-to-wear became more acceptable, more advertisements appeared for clothing.[112] Actual pictures/sketches of the garments, let alone women modeling the clothing, were rare.

Advertising in this era sought to make Egyptians take up new pastimes, for example, bicycling and photography. In particular, from 1921–22 Kodak waged a new campaign aimed at making photography seem easy, affordable, and accessible. These advertisements read much like the Kodak advertisements ten to thirty years earlier in the United States. For example, the header of one advertisement reads, "Use this camera and your success is guaranteed." The text explains the camera's compactness and affordability. Another advertisement shows a hand carrying five rolls of film, and the text reads, "Take this quantity of film, and you can make the most beautiful photographic pictures with Kodak." The text adds that one can learn how to use the camera in half an hour and that prices vary from 75 to 2,000 piastres.[113]

In order to be completely successful, Kodak had to incorporate the camera into the lifestyle of the bourgeois Egyptian, male and female, young and old. Much like the early-twentieth-century American advertisements, the Egyptian version associated the camera with the stylish traveler. A frequently run advertisement in 1921 portrays a chic Western-looking woman at the train station with a Kodak dangling by her side. The header reads, "Take Kodak with you," and the text encourages the reader to take the camera on all outings, once again stressing the ease of use. In 1922, Kodak began advertising its "Brownie" model, which would enable children to use Kodak products as well. Nevertheless, Kodak could not adopt Western methods and materials indiscriminately and achieve its objectives. In order to better approach the Egyptian woman, in late 1921, Kodak switched its model from a Western one to a Middle Eastern one, who appears in two separate advertisements. The new model is clad in a *tarḥa and yashmak*, but has her forearms exposed. She is grinning vacuously and holding a Kodak camera. The first advertisement has a catchy and familiar heading, "Don't let the good times pass, save them forever with Kodak," and once again the text stresses the ease of use—it now takes only five minutes to learn. The other header boasts, "If you want success in photography, use only American products," and the text goes on to discuss Kodak products (see figure 4.2).[114] Both of the advertisements mention the fashionable Midan Opera address of the company, located in the Shepheard's building.

Figure 4.2 Advertisement, Kodak
Source: al-laṭa' if al-muṣawwara.

The new Kodak model merits discussion on a number of levels. Aside from the previously discussed cloaked figures approaching department stores, she is among the first attempts at creating an indigenous representation of womanhood for an advertisement. Although it is a handrawn sketch, her features appear quite Western, and were it not for the *tarḥha* and *yashmak*, we might assume that she was Western. Furthermore, her arms exposed to the elbows undermine the authenticity of the representation. If she were home, she would not need the head-coverings, and if she were outside, she would be too scantily clad. Creating a model to appeal to the New Woman would not be easy, and it was only in its earliest phase as this study closes in 1922.

Another pastime promoted in Egyptian advertising was cigarette smoking, which was part and parcel of the new, reformed pace of *effendiyya* life in the late nineteenth century. As the twentieth century progressed and mechanization of cigarette production arrived in Egypt, the need to expand the market grew. Thus, beginning in the 1920s, there were efforts to attract female smokers.

Cigarettes make for an interesting contrast with the American context. Tobacco was a New World crop that reached Europeans and Middle Easterners by the seventeenth century. Unlike coffee or tea, whose consumption expanded as a result of imperial backing, tobacco consumption grew worldwide based upon consumer demand. In the American context, smoking was a gendered pastime associated with male consumption through pipes and cigars. When mechanization began in the 1870s, American tobacco advertising grew tremendously, as did the number of cigarette consumers. Nevertheless, there were taboos regarding women and tobacco. It was not until 1926 that the American Tobacco Company placed a woman in an advertisement, and it was another year after that before advertisements actually depicted women smoking. Similar to indigenous women not appearing in Egyptian advertisements, the use of Turkish/exotic women was common in American campaigns, although they did not appear smoking. Egyptian companies exporting to the United States and Europe used collector-series cards with pictures of women in sexually suggestive poses to entice male consumers.[115]

In contrast, by the nineteenth century, tobacco consumption in the Ottoman Empire in general, and in Egypt in particular, took place in all social classes, by both men and women.[116] What differed amongst these groups was the quality of the tobacco and the device used to consume it. Before mechanization, cigarettes were associated with the lifestyle of the *effendiyya* who lacked the time for elaborate smoking rituals. With mechanization underway, advertising among indigenous and foreign competitors blossomed.[117]

In 1922, four years before the American Tobacco Company broke the taboo, Dr. Bustany's Healthy Cigarette advertisements employed images of (Western-looking) women both to promote the glamour of smoking and to appeal to female smokers. In one of these advertisements we see a "flapper-type" woman in a sleeveless dress, with a burning cigarette dangling between her fingers, standing behind an advertisement bordered in cigarettes (see figure 4.3). The text reads, "Ask for Dr. Bustany's Healthy Cigarettes, free from harm, but not from flavor." Another advertisement depicts a woman's face emerging from the smoke of a cigarette burning in an ashtray. The text boasts, "the tobacco you will always smoke is (Dr. Bustany's) Healthy Tobacco," pointing out that these cigarettes are "sold everywhere, for men and for women."

Not only was Dr. Bustany "advanced" in his use of women, but also in the health claims made in his promotions. Yet another advertisement utilizing the image of a beautiful woman, calls attention to the reader with three bold-faced lines interspersed with explanatory text. The first reads, "a word on the side," followed by "your health, your health, your health," concluding with "void of lethal toxins." A fourth, text-only advertisement offers the most details on these health claims, by calling upon the reader to smoke this brand for the "sake of your interests and the interests of your children." Responding to people's frustrations with modernity, yet playing upon their modern concerns over health and family, Dr. Bustany claimed that his cigarettes were free from lethal toxins because they were hand-rolled. The ad points out that the reader knows nothing about the process by which machine-made cigarettes are produced, thus they should use Dr. Bustany's, which are "scientifically and medically guaranteed to be void of the dangerous elements found in other cigarettes."[118] Dr. Bustany was trying to make inroads with the female consumer at a time when supply was rapidly increasing due to the emergence of mechanization.

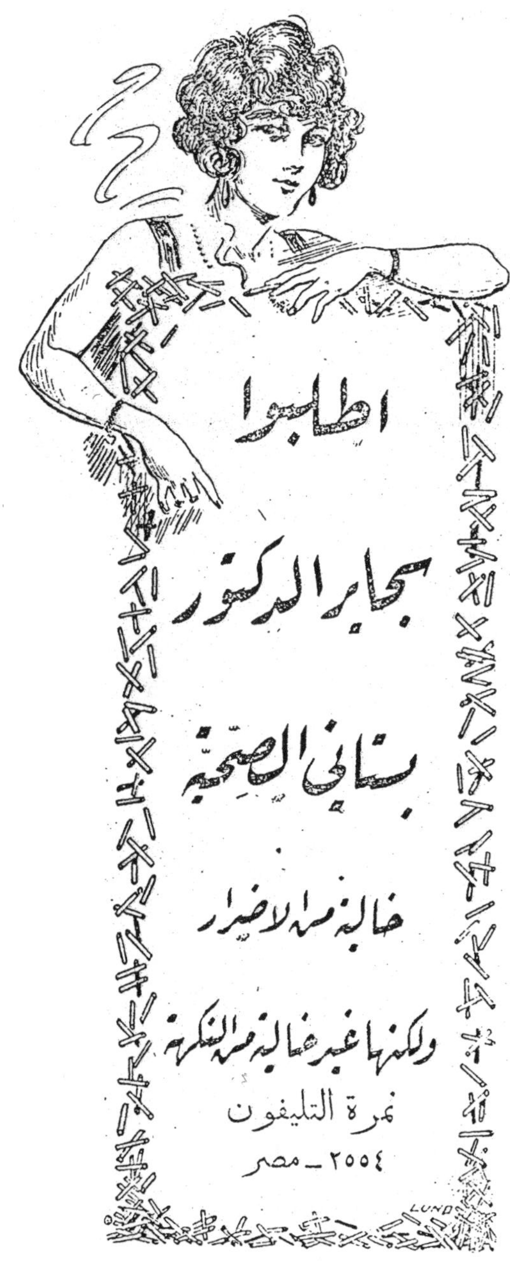

Figure 4.3 Advertisement, Dr. Bustany's Cigarettes
Source: *al-laṭa'if al-muṣawwara*.

Between 1890 and 1910, both Eastern and Western advertisers of the new specialty and department stores bragged about the quality of their goods, emphasizing their Western origins: "latest clothing from the best companies in Europe," "seller of English goods," "furniture made of Venetian wood," "announces the arrival of European goods," "Manchester wools," and the like.[119] However, by the teens and the twenties, as nationalist sentiment grew, few advertisers stated European origins outright.[120] Instead of announcing the arrival of the latest European clothes, housewares, or furniture, stores were more likely to simply announce the arrival of goods.

Similarly, early in the twentieth century, advertisers bragged at their association with the khedivial family. However, by the teens and the twenties few such advertisements exist. In 1901 the Widow Sagrestani announced that she was the oldest retailer of sewing machines, having served the khedivial family and other notable families, and in 1904 L. Kramer and Company highlighted its services as purveyors to the khedivial family.[121] These advertisements both occurred during the reign of Abbas II, who had considerable popularity and whose memoirs demonstrate a profound love of country.[122] As discussed in chapter 2, the British used the Ottoman entrance into the war as a pretext for deposing the vacationing Khedive, bringing in his uncle, who was viewed as a British tool. Whether it was the outbreak of war, the proclaiming of the protectorate, or the lack of a mobilizing ruler, associations with the royal family ceased. King Fuad (r. 1917–36) who ruled Egypt after his brother Husayn Kamil, had even fewer nationalist threads upon which he could cling. Having spent many of his formative years in exile, he never even mastered the language of the country over which he ruled. Thus, it is not surprising that I found no associations between products and the royal family in the last years of this study.

Not only were links to the royal family common in the early twentieth century, some advertisers appealed to protonationalist sentiments by advertising themselves as "national" [*waṭani*] or by demonstrating their concern for the needs of the country. As early as 1902, Hasan Bey Madkur advertised his store as the "biggest national commercial establishment in Egypt."[123] A foreign company, Walker & Meimarachi Limited, not only boasted about the variety and quality of its goods, but it also claimed to show concern for the needs of the government and the army.[124]

As the British occupation became more entrenched and the infrastructure of colonialism grew, response to the imperialism of goods and services became greater, particularly after the outbreak of World War I. In 1915, Ahmad Kamil advertised himself as a "national trader" with a "national store" carrying only "national products." He highlighted the quality of his merchandise and was careful to point out that his store was larger than foreign ones, offering all things necessary for men, women, and children. Similarly, Muhammad Amir advertised his store as an "Egyptian national sales showroom" [*ṣala al-biyu*^{c} *al-miṣriyya al-waṭaniyya*]. As previously discussed, the White Rose advertisement encouraged Easterners to patronize Eastern establishments, pointing out that the store's quality, cleanliness, and service surpassed that which was found in foreign patisseries. As well, the aforementioned Egyptian Clothing Company campaign stressed the quality, workmanship, and affordability of clothes produced by "the hands of Egyptian workers." Ilyas Addad's furniture store also featured "national craftsmanship" produced by "the hands of citizens" [*bil-warsha al-waṭaniyya wa bi ayadi ᶜummal waṭaniyyin*]. Finally, the previously mentioned movie offer was sponsored by a group of Egyptian national traders [*al-tujjar al-miṣriyyin*].[125]

In her study of the late Ottoman press, Frierson found consumer trends toward "anti-Western, buy-local" (later buy-Turk) sentiments that were similarly "adopted, internalized, and refined" by advertisers.[126] Nevertheless, she documents evidence of religious segregation, mandated by the state, although not necessarily observed by the consumers.[127] Some of the earliest and most successful commercial establishments in Egypt were run by Jews and Levantine Christians. These establishments were portrayed as "Egyptian" or "Eastern" in contrast to firms such as Printemps, Singer, or Kodak. The Egyptian press, with its significant Christian and Syrian elements, affirmed an Egyptian identity rooted in "Eastern-ness." The Egyptian flag chosen by nationalists during 1919 Revolution symbolized this identity. Aiming for Egyptian distinction, the color of the new flag was Nile green, unlike the Ottoman and khedivial red flags. It adopted the (Islamic) crescent and star of the nineteenth-century Ottoman flag, adding two additional stars; yet it was distinct from the khedivial standard that bore three crescents and three stars, which had symbolized Muhammad Ali's success on three continents (or his mastery over Egypt, Nubia, and the Sudan). Instead, the three stars would represent each of Egypt's religious communities: Muslims, Christians, and Jews.[128]

Political activism triggered by the 1919 demonstrations (see chapter 5) and continuing through Egypt's partial independence in 1922, encouraged more overtly political advertising. Ironically, it was foreign companies who took the lead. In much the same way that some products in the West tried to appeal to suffragettes by linking political freedom to consumption, a 1922 ad for a nursing supplement attempted to play on the nationalist sentiments of women who had participated in the 1919 Revolution (see figure 4.4). The central figures of the advertisement are two women carrying a banner. One of them is clearly upper class as revealed by her high-heeled shoes, mid-calf-length cloak, and light *yashmak*. The other woman is of more humble origins as seen by her slipper-type sandals, more modest cloak, and her *burquᶜ*. The banner reads, "Oh, nationalist mothers, among the most sacred of your duties is raising healthy children for the nation, use Lactagol." The text explains the benefits to both mothers and their children, as well as the availability of the product at all pharmacies. It also points out that Lactagol is available by mail from the foreigner Kingston Lorrie across from the Savoy hotel.[129] Foreign advertisers were well aware of the issues that would catch consumer attention, such as political activism and motherly concern for children's health.

A 1922 advertisement for Palmolive soap utilized pharaonic images to harken Egyptians back to their roots, while simultaneously appealing to their nationalist concerns in the post–1919 revolutionary period (see figure 4.5).[130] The advertisement depicts a fair-skinned, "Cleopatra-type" figure gazing contentedly as two dark slave men mix some sort of concoction in a large tureen. The text discusses how ancient Egyptians used olive and palm oils as natural resources for beauty, the same resources to which the modern Egyptian has access via Palmolive soap. Once again,

Figure 4.4 Advertisement, Lactagol
Source: *al-laṭa'if al-muṣawwara*.

by reading further one finds that the agents are foreign and that the product is manufactured in New York. This advertisement represented two common paths in American advertising, while adding an Egyptian dimension. First, it employed a character embodying traditional wisdom to market a modern product; and second, it depicted the parable of "civilization redeemed," that is, by looking to nature one could solve modern problems.[131]

It is not possible to gauge the reaction to the two forms of "nationalist" advertising, and thus we do not know for sure which was more effective, the flashier, yet overtly foreign, techniques or the "national" store approach. Furthermore, some of the "Egyptian" ventures were not as Egyptian as the image they tried to project, espousing a nationalist image to gain popular and governmental support, despite ties to foreign capital.[132] The only clue we have comes in advertising in the following period. Even this attempt is likely to only bring partial results, that is, we see what advertisers believe will work, and we assume that it is based upon past experience.

Figure 4.5 Advertisement, Palmolive Soap
Text: "In the days of the the ancient Egyptians, olive oil and palm olive oil were among the most important and greatest necessities and beauty aids. Palmolive soap is manufactured today from olive and palm oil, . . . "
Source: *al-laṭa'if al-muṣawwara.*

In the post-independence era *al-laṭa'if al-muṣawwara* continued to be a pioneer in advertising with its campaigns for the Egyptian Shoe Company employing pharaonic motifs and nationalist sentiments, as well as the veiled/non-veiled customer approach.[133] Its promotions for Shams Iskandarani and Sons encouraged the reader to "praise God" that we can buy from this "national" establishment and not resort to foreign ones. Yet another ad informed the reader that (s)he would raise the standing of Egypt and Egyptians by patronage of this store.[134] The advertising staff also began utilizing indigenous endorsements for products, that were not necessarily national, for example, Dr. Ross's Pills and the aforementioned Glaxo campaign.[135]

Other publications followed the lead and employed "national buying" as a major theme. The women's magazine *shajarat al-durr* utilized the terms "economic independence," "the Egyptian surpasses the foreigner," and the like in its post-independence advertising. An ad for the Eastern Sweets Factory cautions the reader that men have achieved political independence, but that it is incumbent upon "us," that is, women, to achieve economic independence, presumably through "our" purchasing power.[136] Nevertheless the magazine sold advertising space to foreigners as well. Throughout the 1920s, the association of consumption, local products/sellers, and national duty appeared repeatedly in advertisements. Consumers were even exhorted to buy Egyptian beer, since "this is the nation's duty, and the nation is above everything."[137] The common thread linking these campaigns was the staff of the publication itself, for where one such advertisement appeared there were usually more. With the passage of time, what constituted "national" had more explicitly porous boundaries. From the 1930s up through 1952, some "national" sellers advertised their imported goods.[138] Nevertheless, the push to "buy national," which began during World War I and increased steadily up through independence, must have had some resonance or its longevity would not have been so pronounced.

Reaction to imperialism represented more than just a struggle against political control, it was also a reaction to the spread of foreign ideas, customs, and beliefs. Nowhere was this threat greater than in the foreign and sectarian schools in Egypt. Muhammad Ali and Ismail's educational policies allowed a new bourgeoisie of technocrats, administrators, functionaries, and professionals to advance socially and economically over the course of the nineteenth century.[139] By the turn of the century, Egyptians had come to view education as a means of advancement in both the government and the growing private sector. As education gained significance, competition among schools and for positions in schools became fierce. The demand for primary education, in general, and female education, in particular, far outweighed the resources available from the government. Egypt's foreign and religious minorities had been creating their own schools for many years, some as early as the seventeenth century. As education became more of a commodity in the late nineteenth century and the foreign community grew, the number of these schools rose dramatically.[140]

Virtually all newspapers and journals covered educational issues ranging from tabloid-type coverage of school openings, celebrations, and visits by dignitaries to intellectual debates over curriculum and instruction.[141] The editor(s), orientation, and target audience of each publication steered the course of educational coverage. While women's education received widespread coverage in the mainstream press, it was the most frequently recurring topic in the women's press. Nationalist and Muslim publications laid more emphasis on announcements related to Muslim charitable organizations, while publications with Christian editors laid more emphasis on Christian charitable organizations and missionary efforts.[142]

Turn-of-the-century advertisements for schools reflect the struggles of Egyptian education and the range of options available. Newspapers and journals ran advertisements to suit the needs of their readership. Elite subscribers to publications such as *anis al-jalis* could find a European governess and/or a piano instructor for their daughters or find an appropriate school specializing in all of the "theoretical and practical sciences" necessary for girls.[143] *Al-muqaṭṭam* was one of the two most important papers of the late nineteenth century (the other being *al-ahram*). Its editors were products of the Syrian Protestant College and their paper was pro-British in orientation.[144] Not surprisingly, they ran advertisements for foreign schools in general and British schools in particular. Nevertheless, *al-muqaṭṭam* also ran advertisements for local schools, as well as individual *shaykhs*. Advertisements for foreign and local schools in *al-muqaṭṭam* emphasized instruction in both Arabic and a European language, as well as demonstrating the demand for girls' education.[145]

In the first decade of the twentieth century a number of new publications, avowedly nationalist in character, arose from the longstanding issue of the occupation, sparked by individual incidents, such as the Taba affair in 1906 and Dinshawai in 1907.[146] Mustafa Kamil, who tied Egypt's nationalism to a pro-Ottoman, pan-Islamic orientation, founded both the National party and its paper, *al-liwa'*. Educational advertisements in *al-liwa'* tended to be for "national" schools. The Kamal school simply advertised its willingness to take male and female students in preparation for the primary certificate, while the Husayniyya school gave more details about the qualifications of its instructors, including an English teacher. Like the advertisements in *al-muqaṭṭam*, many of these schools contained girls' divisions as well.[147] A nationalist-leaning paper, such as *al-liwa'*, was also more likely to carry advertisements for individual *shaykhs*, and I even found one for a *shaykha* in 1904.[148] In the face of competition from foreign schools and lack of indigenous schools, these go-getters saw the utility of using a new medium of communication to stress the need for traditional education. Furthermore, parents who insisted upon sending their children to foreign schools to gain the advantages of language instruction and greater career options could ameliorate the much-discussed shortcomings of the curriculum by hiring a *shaykh*.

Another interesting characteristic of the more nationalist papers was that they were likelier to carry classified advertisements for ordinary citizens, both men and women.[149] These papers offered widows the opportunity to sell their land and unneeded goods and other women a means of redressing grievances.[150] For example, one woman issued the following complaint:

> I am the wife Zaynab, daughter of the late Abd al-Rahman of Sayyida Zaynab. I announce that a man named Mansur Qasim married me and then left; and he has not returned, even until now. I have been unable to find the stamp imprinted with my name, so I have engraved another one. For that reason, I am not responsible to anyone for the previously mentioned [stamp], so if anything appears from this [stamp] it will be in error and will be null and void.[151]

Just as advertisements might empower women or allow them greater entrance into the public sphere, they could also be used to bring women back into line:

> On Thursday, December 24th, a girl named Fatima bint Khalifa, age 12, from my family, left my house on Suwali Street in Hasaniyya without reason and has not yet returned. So please, those who know her whereabouts, return her to us. Thank you.[152]

We can only speculate as to why Fatima left her home or her fate if she returned. The importance of this classified advertisement is the fact that the behavior of women was a public issue.

Conclusion

Advertising served to blur the boundaries between public and private in Egypt. In the public pages of the press, we see the call to women to take up concerns of the family and the nation through consumption. This linkage between family, home, and nation redefined the boundaries, and advertisers encouraged and stretched those limits.[153] They assumed that the woman would carry out the role of general purchasing agent as was the case in the West. The Egyptian woman would come to be seen as the arbiter of taste and consumption for the family, the unit upon which the reformed nation would be based. This woman could be reached through the pages of the press, whether she read the paper herself or merely looked on as her husband or children read to her. Nevertheless, *al-Sayyida al-Istihlakiyya* in Egypt was not the same as Mrs. Consumer in the West. While she lacked the Western concern for detergents and ready-made foods, she also demonstrated special needs related to her new public role and her burgeoning nationalist concerns. Chapter 5 demonstrates that *al-Sayyida al-Istihlakiyya* was but one face of the New Woman.

Chapter 5

al-Sayyida al-Istihlakiyya and the "New Woman"

The New Egyptian Woman and Her Western Sisters

As was the case in the West, *al-Sayyida al-Istihlakiyya* was created in the pages of the women's press, both in feature articles and in advertising. Nevertheless, there were significant differences. As discussed in chapter 4, advertising was not the principle source of revenue for many journals. Second, as was the case in Europe and the United States, the women's press was not devoid of men; however, in Egypt, as Marilyn Booth and Lisa Pollard have demonstrated, the woman's question was part of a much larger societal question that examined gender roles in the context of anti-imperialist nationalism.[1] Debates and discussion in the early "women's press" must be viewed in light of these issues, especially since many articles were unsigned. A third variation between contexts dealt with readership. The reading female public in Egypt was a much smaller and more elite group. Fourth, Western journals were more sophisticated in their exhortations to consumption, that is, there was more congruity between the text and the advertising. Thus, in the United States, a woman reading about the latest developments in kitchen technology, might view an advertisement for refrigerators on the opposing page or in the margins of the same page. In Egypt, even in the period up to 1952, such placement in mainstream or women's magazines was rare.[2]

Nevertheless, in some ways Egyptian publications for women surpassed Western ones, due to the difference in the readership. For example, the *Ladies' Home Journal* followed a strict advertising code that prohibited mail order ads of general merchandising, installment buying, alcohol, patent medicines, immodesty in text or illustration, financial advertisements, tobacco products, and playing cards. The target audience was middle-class white women with a grade school education, and circulation reached over one million households. In contrast, women's magazines in Egypt were targeted to a much wealthier, better-educated, smaller audience. Not only did advertisements appeal to Western-oriented modes of consumption, such as department stores and pharmacies, they were also geared toward a more wealthy woman with needs for specialty shops, tailors, governesses, and music instructors. Advertisements targeted the modern urban woman with sophisticated tastes and concerns, including many of the verboten ads from *Ladies' Home Journal*. Furthermore, the content of the journals was far more substantial intellectually, covering history, biography, literature, reform, and other topics of contemporary interest, in addition to topics anticipated in women's magazines.[3]

Other aspects of the "New Woman" differed from her Western sisters, and nowhere was this more evident than in Egyptian women's participation in international women's movements. While Egyptian, European, and American feminists could agree on suffrage, education, work, rights in marriage and parenting, and the "confinement" of separate spheres, Egyptian women took issue with polygamy and divorce (by unilateral repudiation). Meanwhile, Western women had more concern over property rights and legal personhood, issues that did not impact Egyptian women.[4] Thus, as we examine the construct of New Womanhood at the turn of the century, while acknowledging the similarity of the discourse, we must trace its evolution from different origins. Futhermore, these issues varied across social class and influenced the individual's view of politics in the period following independence.

Mrs. Consumer formed one facet of the "New Woman" who made her appearance in turn-of-the-century Egypt. After the publication of his *taḥrir al-mar'a* (1899) and *al-mar'a al-jadida* (1900), many considered Qasim Amin the "father" of the woman's movement in Egypt. Nevertheless, as Leila Ahmed has argued persuasively, his New Woman was neither new, revolutionary, nor particularly Egyptian. She points out that others, namely Tahtawi and Abdu, had already written on the subject, that his calls for education were no different than contemporary calls in the press, and that instead he opted for a class-based critique of Egyptian society.[5] The publication of Amin's two books created a flurry of criticism in the Egyptian press, and his work continued to be discussed in the pages of the press throughout the period under study. Nevertheless, he was merely one part of a larger discussion about the new Egyptian woman.

Many authors, mostly male and some female, penned new books (or translations) about this New Woman, ranging from her role in the home to her education and health. The following titles appeared in the years before and after the publication of Amin's books: *The Woman in the East, The Life of the Married Couple, The Egyptian Woman, Creation of the Woman, Education/Upbringing, Raising Girls, The Progress of Families in the Education of Daughters, Mothers' Advice, Organization of the Home, The Clear Study for Mothers of Today and Tomorrow, The Girl and the Home, Mistress of the House, Girls' Manners, The Girl's Upbringing, Women's Affairs, The Book of Women's Ailments, and Women's Lesson.*[6] Thus, Qasim Amin and his conservative critic Talaat Harb did not write in an intellectual vacuum. They were part of a much larger intellectual current, which included the press. Nevertheless, as Booth has convincingly argued, Amin was significant precisely because his work "generated a furious and more public debate" and because Egyptian feminists and those concerned with the "Woman Question" continued to revere him long after his death. The notion that a man in his position placed so much emphasis on Egyptian women and their role in defining Egypt's future, raised anxiety, inside and outside of his class.[7]

The New Woman, A Composite View

Despite differences in nuance and emphasis, the descriptions of the "New Egyptian Woman" in the press shared some common characteristics. Her most important roles were as wife to her husband, mother to her children, and administrator of her household. In the words of a contemporary male observer, "the Eastern woman is raised for married life, that is to be a wife, a mother, a household manager, and one who rears children."[8] With respect to her role as wife, most authors, male and female, viewed the woman as a partner to her husband. Guided by his/her distinct disposition, each partner would complement the other. The man, with his innate physical strength, was inclined to labor outside the home, thus providing the material basis of the couple's existence. The woman, with her gentle nature, served as a mental and emotional support to her husband, the pillar of her family, which in turn was the pillar of society. She depended on her husband, who was strengthened by her dependency. Nevertheless, she would be the strongest force in her husband's life, creating a "separate, but equal" partnership. Since one spent most of his/her life married, the entire happiness of the material world depended on the success of this partnership.[9] While this view sounds much like the Victorian, bourgeois view of companionate marriage, it emanates from a significantly different context.

Historically there existed little notion of separate spheres; however, the dictates of Islam as a system of belief and practice encouraged gender segregation as an ideal and marriage as an obligation. The Muslim woman could marry only a Muslim man, while the latter could choose to marry out of faith, as long as he married within the monotheistic tradition. He could take up to four wives, contingent upon his ability to provide equally for each wife; and he had access to unlimited concubines. Although Judith Tucker's recent work on law and family life does not deal with Egypt specifically, the findings of the courts in Ottoman Syria and Palestine do represent what we might term traditional Islamic notions of marriage and family life. She defines marriage as a "contractual relationship" uniting a man and woman. Whether written or oral, this contract traces the couple's lineage, specifies the *mahr*, and lists the witnesses. Furthermore, she holds that this institution was valued for all members of the community, emphasizing social suitability of mates and recognizing marriage's utility in channeling the male and female libido.[10]

The social suitability of mates usually meant marrying within one's class. For the upper class, political and economic issues were of far more significance than romantic notions of compatibility. Additionally, the wealthy were generally the only ones financially able to practice polygamy, purchase concubines, and have the leisure to seclude and veil their women, all of which shaped elite households. Despite the existance of these practices, elite women (free and enslaved) often wielded extraordinary political and economic influence.[11] Nevertheless, as Mary Ann Fay has argued, after "the demise of the household as a locus of power" over the course of the nineteenth century in favor of a centralizing state, elite women were left with the residue of polygamy, divorce, seclusion, and veiling, but none of the benefits of the old system. She views their strategies within women's organizations as an attempt to bargain for a better deal in the nascent Egyptian nation state.[12]

Changes in male and female education created new expectations for marriage at the same time that the elite household was being divested of its political function. Government schools for boys aimed at creating officers, doctors, teachers, and professionals implicitly and explicitly supported the notions of developmental idealism (see chapters 1 and 6) and changing patterns of family life. The expansion of the middle class created a new class of men that had not grown up in the traditional elite household, yet their material and social expectations were rising. These changes did not occur in a single generation or even two. We can examine some of these issues by comparing the marriages of Huda and Ali Shaarawi, Safiyya and Saad Zaghlul, and Ratiba and Ahmad Chafik.

Huda Shaarawi (b. 1879) was home-schooled in both traditional and modern subjects. When she was just 12 years old, she was betrothed to her married cousin and guardian Ali. Her mother Iqbal, a former slave, and her cousin/guardian Ali were worried about keeping Huda's significant inheritance within the family. Her late father, Sultan Pasha, had been one of the largest landholders in Egypt. Her mother had been influenced enough by changing patterns in society to stipulate monogamy as part of her daughter's marriage contract.[13] The marriage of the 13-year-old girl to the established man several decades her senior was not ideal for either partner. As per the marriage contract, Ali had divorced his first wife, although within a year she was impregnated and he had returned to her. Huda separated from her husband for seven years, and returned only when her brother insisted that he would not marry until she did so. After the reconciliation she bore her husband two children.[14] Shaarawi had married within in her class and stayed married due to family interests. While it was her mother's hope that she might have something resembling a new marriage, hers was quite traditional; and it undoubtedly impacted her activism for the rest of her life. Concerns for holding land and marrying within the family survived both independence in 1922 and the Revolution of 1952.[15]

Safiyya Zaghlul, the daughter of Mustafa Pasha Fahmy, was a woman of similar social standing and age (b. 1876). Her father, a member of the Ottoman-Egyptian elite, served as governor of Cairo and later served as prime minister for Abbas II. She was educated at home by a German governess, and she remained a devout Muslim. Given the family's standing, her father undoubtedly received numerous offers for his daughter's hand in marriage. Unlike Huda, who was betrothed at a relatively young age because of the family's economic concerns, Safiyya was not engaged until she was 20. The offer that Mustafa accepted was that of Saad Zaghlul, a man 20 years her senior with peasant origins, albeit wealthy peasant origins. His law-school training in France and his acceptance at the salon of Princess Nazli, made the social-climbing Zaghlul seem a good match for his daughter. Given his wife's position it would be difficult for Zaghlul to take a second wife. All accounts of the marriage describe it as harmonious, one that would later be an example to the nation.[16] Thus, Safiyya crossed class lines and created a bourgeois, companionate marriage. Nevertheless, the marriage was one that was presented to her by her father.

The situation of Ratiba, the mother of Egyptian feminist Doria Shafik, had some similarities with those of both these women. Like Safiyya and Huda, Ratiba came from a wealthy, notable family. Like Shaarawi, she was impacted by her father's death and manipulation by her guardian. Ratiba, her mother, and her two sisters moved into the home of her wealthy uncle and his Turco-Circassian wife. The latter arranged marriages for her own four daughters, as well as for Ratiba and her elder sister. While she married her own children to men of the family's standing, her husband's nieces were engaged to two brothers of distinctly middle-class origins. Ahmad Chafik was a struggling engineering student at the time that Ratiba was betrothed to him. Although he achieved success in his career, the couple's differing origins, lifestyles, and expectations were sources of conflict. Ratiba used her superior identity (perceived by both him and her) to dominate her husband. Doria's memoirs speak of her father as buying into the notion of companionate marriage. Her mother, while paying lip-service to the topic, always detested her inferior position vis à vis her cousins and other wealthy family relations.[17] Thus, Ratiba crossed class lines, but her unfulfilled (or partially fulfilled) material expectations affected her happiness.

All three of these examples demonstrate the types of transitions taking place in elite households, as well as the role that fathers, brothers, and guardians played in women's lives. The women who crossed class lines to marry carried expectations of their socially inferior husband, that is, their marriages would be "new" marriages. Women who married up or even horizontally lacked this power, which could also be impacted by the death of a father and one's relationship with her brother(s) or guardian. These changes that were just beginning to take place in the late nineteenth century, were well documented by the 1930s and 1940s. While memoirs usually reflect women's consent in these unions, there is often some kind of psychological duress involved. Furthermore, for women who did not socialize with men, what did consent mean?[18]

Conspicuously absent from all of these accounts, based upon women's memoirs, is the male perspective. Male memoirs are less likely to focus on these types of issues.[19] Certainly one's childhood experiences and education impacted such decision making. While we might never know how Ali Shaarawi felt about marrying his cousin or whether he was part of the plot by her brother to reconcile the couple once his child-bride had matured, we do know that as an elite male, he had a wide range of choice. Middle-class men had certain leeway as well; by marrying up, down, or horizontally they could arrange the type of household over which they presided. As the last vestiges of slavery waned, concubinage became less of an issue.

The early twentieth century was a time of flux in which old and new often stood side by side. Wealth gave men greater opportunity to seek the household of their choice, which could include marrying across cultural boundaries. As discussed in chapter 2, Abbas II married a Hungarian woman in one of the more noteworthy of such marriages. Another famous cross-cultural marriage was that of Eugénie Le Brun, a French woman and mentor to Huda Shaarawi, to Husayn Rushdi, a wealthy landowner and politician. Foreign brides were particularly objectionable from the perspective of elite women, who stood to lose the most through this practice. It also sheds light on elite women marrying middle-class men. Egyptian women of the middle and upper class vociferously condemned the practice in the women's press.[20] The problems emanating from it took on epic proportions in the sensational trial of Margaret Fahmy, a French woman accused of killing her Egyptian husband.[21] Nevertheless, some foreign wives were accepted into Egyptian society, particularly those that participated in the women's movement, for example, Louise Majorelly, the French wife of Wasif Bey Butros Ghali and Hilda Fanous, the American wife of Dr. Riad Fanous. Perhaps the practice was better accepted among Christians. Egyptian women frequently portrayed these liaisons as taking place with socially inferior European women, such as dancers, showgirls, and governesses.[22] Educator

Nabawiya Musa, who never even married, felt strongly enough about the issue to weigh in on the topic: "A man who marries a Westerner becomes with his children Westerners. As for an Egyptian woman, who marries a foreigner (e.g., a Muslim from Persia) she is capable of giving Egypt new Egyptians."[23]

A logical extension of the "New Woman's" role as wife would be as mother and primary care giver to her children. Obviously, the "old" Egyptian woman bore children and took care of them. Returning to Tucker and her study of the application of Islamic family law, she notes that while the judges were quite reticent with respect to the role of procreation in marriage, their discussions of mothering and fathering indicate that it was an anticipated outcome of marriage. With respect to parenting, the woman "was thought to be equipped [physically and emotionally] for the reproduction and care of small children," a task that fell to her relatives in the case of death. The man, on the other hand, was "more qualified to represent the interests of the child in the world outside the family and to provide material support," as well as to care for the child once (s)he reached a certain level of maturity.[24] Thus, the role of the mother was significant and bore some similarity to the new role; however, her previous incarnation had limited utility and was easily replaced once her children attained a certain age.

The New Egyptian Woman would take a more active, participatory role in this process due to the greater extent of her education. She, the mother, was viewed as a skilled gardener, who with her gentle nature, loving disposition, and wisdom, cultivated intelligent and moral children. The ignorant mother, who lacked these skills, or the mother who left the care of her children to servants, could prove detrimental to their well being. Her lack of skill would have consequences for the nation, the future of which depended on the proper upbringing of children. One author went so far as to describe the woman as having a greater impact upon society than any army, while another asserted that what an individual gleans from his mother remains imprinted upon his mind until death.[25] Thus, the future of Egypt lay in the hands of the "New Woman," for "the future of the child lay in the hand[s] of his mother, and the future of the nation [*al-umma*] lay in the hand[s] of its mothers."[26] Omnia Shakry demonstrates that this discourse was not merely a parroting of European models, but represented a specifically Egyptian, nonsecular notion of modernity. Even non-Muslim writers, for example, the editors of *al-muqtaṭaf* and *al-hilal*, wrote in a manner that supported and complemented the Islamic tradition.[27]

Finally, the "New Woman" was the general administrator and purchasing agent for her home. Whether wealthy or middle class, she was responsible for the careful and efficient running of her household. Although she was likely to have servants, the "New Woman" had to plan, monitor, and evaluate their work. Without this supervision, all comfort, happiness, and harmony would flee the home. This home was analogous to a small kingdom, whose future course lay in the wise governance of the woman. In order to provide guidance, the woman needed a proper education. To most effectively utilize the resources provided by her husband, the woman needed an understanding of the principles of economy, as well as a practical understanding of the work to be undertaken. Since the nation was nothing more than a collection of homes, once again the reform of the nation lay in the hands of the educated woman.[28]

Despite the fact that there were numerous articles on raising children and household administration, few articles gave concrete advice about how to undertake these activities. Most articles were, in fact, calls for the education of women under the rubric of another title. A series of four articles in *anis al-jalis* in 1899 exemplifies this trend, which was present in both the mainstream and women's press. In one of these articles, Alexandra de Avierino explains that *tadbir al-manzil* is not limited to care of the interior of the house and its furnishings, but rather is a more expansive field encompassing all aspects of family and social life and should be renamed *tadbir al-ḥayat* [life administration] or *tadbir al-dunya* [(material) world administration]. By expanding the definition of *tadbir al-manzil*, she opened the possibility for discussing the need for women's education, women's rights, and the proper roles of wives and husbands. All four of these articles acknowledge the importance of *tadbir al-manzil*; but they leave out any information on the practical, despite promises in the first article to address these issues.[29]

The elite readership and background of its editor made *anis al-jalis* more inclined to the theoretical aspects of *tadbir al-manzil.* Journals with a wider middle-class readership contained more practical information and items—household hints, sewing patterns, and the like. As we shall see in chapters 7 and 8, middle- and upper-class women viewed home economics differently. Many of the latter were making the transition from large, multigenerational households in which women were secluded, to nuclear households in which old gender boundaries were eroding.[30] These women had a full staff to complete the menial tasks of housework, and thus they needed little practical advice. They had much more concern for devoting their energies to renegotiating the patriarchal bargain through legal reform.[31] Meanwhile, many middle-class housewives were just entering the field of household management, and thus, they had a greater appreciation for journals that discussed its practical aspects. Efficiency was of more concern to this group, who had fewer (or no) servants. Neither they nor their mothers had experienced the effects of polygamy, concubinage, or strict seclusion.

The most informative and longest-running source on housekeeping and child-rearing comes from the "*bab tadbir al-manzil*" segment in *al-muqtaṭaf.*[32] Although this department contained numerous articles about the roles of women, women's rights, and women's education in the abstract, there were also many articles on how to actually carry out housekeeping and household organization.[33] Most issues contained a series of recipes and/or household hints ranging from how to make sponge cake to getting rid of ants, to removing stains from silk. The editors geared this department to the middle-class woman, whom they described as "neither very rich nor poor," with an income between £200–400 per year.[34] *Bab tadbir al-manzil* encouraged women to keep a watchful eye on her staff, likening the woman who leaves the administration of her home to servants to the man who leaves the administration of his work to servants.[35]

In keeping with the themes of self-improvement, efficiency, and thrift of the magazine, the male editors and their female relatives applied these principles to modern home economics. Women were to make the most effective use of their time, and they were encouraged to take advantage of scientific advances in housekeeping.[36] Furthermore, the department sanctioned and encouraged the role of the woman as the arbiter of taste and function for the household, with articles on interior decoration and finance. Such calls were not unique to *al-muqtaṭaf.* In her study of biography in the women's press, Booth found similar exhortations, as part of the modernist discourse on the New Woman.[37]

According to *bab tadbir al-manzil*, the woman had to strike a balance between the poles of frugality and tasteful consumption. She was expected to create the "proper" home without exceeding the finances provided by her husband. The husband and wife were to come to an agreement about household expenses based on a frank discussion of the husband's income. With this information, the wife was to budget appropriately, planning for all exigencies and emergencies. Quality, which was not measured by price, was to exceed quantity. Through thrift and proper management, a woman could have a "happy" home on a limited income, continuing to purchase the right items on a regular basis. She was responsible before her husband, children, and country for the care and appearance of her home, which was symbolic of both the family within it and the community surrounding it.[38] In Cairo, keeping up the new home required extreme vigilence, given the rampant influx of dust from the surrounding desert. Furnishings in the elite eighteenth-century home were somewhat easier to maintain in this environment. Only the pillows, trays, and mattresses that were being used were pulled out of storage closets, and all furnishings could easily be rid of daily dust and dirt. The new home with its new furnishings required more effort.

To carry out these duties effectively, the "New Woman" had to be a wise *Sayyida Istihlakiyya*. Articles in *bab tadbir al-manzil* explain both the theory and logistics of financial planning. Several articles discussed how to create a budget, likening the role of the woman of the house to that of the minister of finance and offering sample budgets. In order to effectively track her expenses, the woman had to keep a notebook specifically for household accounting. She was to scrupulously record all of her income and expenses daily. In doing so, she would avoid unnecessary expense and waste. The department also urged the woman to make her own purchases. Women who allowed their servants to shop had to carefully supervise them. They had to provide them with explicit instructions for buying, and they had to carefully examine all purchases. Furthermore, they were to keep up with current prices so as not to be cheated. Whether buying items herself or dispatching a servant, the woman was also supposed to adhere to the following rules: make a list; buy wholesale when possible; buy with cash rather than credit; buy when prices are down, but recognize that perishable necessities must be purchased daily regardless of price; buy non-perishable items in quantity; purchase quality rather than quantity; and patronize reputable merchants. Obviously, food purchases were among the most frequently recurring and needed the most careful planning. Articles in *bab tadbir al-manzil* offered concrete advice on selecting meat, fish, and produce. Buying the proper quantity was key so that both borrowing and waste could be avoided, and women were urged to recycle their leftovers in soups and stews.[39] Not only were women supposed to practice these habits themselves, but they were also to impart these values to their children.[40] Furthermore, they were to extend these principles of economy to their personal expenses for clothing and cosmetics, especially after the financial crisis of 1907 and during the war years.[41]

Although the role of the New Woman appeared to sanction and reinforce notions of public/private and male/female, these boundaries were actually in a process of erosion. Education and consumerism helped to blur these boundaries for both the middle and upper classes. The role of the new woman as general purchasing agent and household administrator meant that more women would leave their homes to enter both the traditional markets and the new stores, or at least to maintain a greater knowledge about them. Calls for women's education and its expansion necessitated leaving the private sphere to enter schools. To meet the demand for more teachers, more middle- and lower-middle-class-women entered the field of education.

At the same time, women of the upper and upper middle classes entered the public sphere in larger numbers through their charitable and women's organizations. They extended their role as caregivers to society at large by creating schools, hospitals, soup kitchens, and workshops. Upper-class women, like men, traditionally set up charitable endowments (*awqaf*) and gave alms to the poor. After the occupation, the British cut back on programs of social welfare and education; and elite women of all religions filled the vacuum with philanthropy. By the turn of the century, both Christian and Muslim women moved beyond the confines of religious institutions to create secular philanthropic societies. As Margot Badran points out, these new charitable associations brought elite women into direct contact with the people they assisted. Furthermore, as charity moved beyond the context of religious responsibility, it became a national duty.[42] Participation in these activities, as well as encouragement by the mainstream and women's press, helped to increase female activitism by the time of the 1919 Revolution. In the years after independence, it facilitated women's acceptance in the fields of medicine, education, and social work.

From Manly Rebellion to the Birth of a Nation: Gendered Aspects of Resistance in the Urabi Revolt and the 1919 Revolution

As Lisa Pollard has artfully demonstrated, the 1919 Revolution was "a family affair" attended by the New Woman, her husband, and their patriotic children. They were quite literally birthing and rearing the Egyptian nation, depicted as a woman. Indeed she refers to the nation as a "man's realm in feminine garb."[43] Elite nationalist males, who spearheaded the revolution, utilized the tropes of motherhood and maternalism, to articulate their readiness to take the control of the government. The pictures and newsreel footage, as well as the iconography of the period, demonstrate the important role played by women, the ideal of the "New Family" of citizens, and the expansion of visual culture. In contrast, the Urabi Revolt of 1881/82, which ultimately led to the British occupation, was a "manly" event, for the New Man emerged in society before the New Woman. Some visual imagery and political iconography exists from the period; however, the events of 1881/82 were far more aural in nature. By comparing the Urabi revolt and the 1919 Revolution we can see the clear emergence of the New Woman and the visual culture that helped to stimulate that emergence.

The Urabi revolt of 1881/82 was carried out by Egyptian army officers, who were dissatisfied with the differential treatment and promotion of native Egyptians versus the Turkish-speaking Ottoman elite. At the forefront of the movement was Colonel Ahmad Urabi, one of a handful of native Egyptians who had risen to that level in the army, supported by a coterie of (mostly) lower-ranking Egyptian officers. Marsot has characterized him as "a good-looking man" and "forceful speaker," who was able to attract audiences by weaving passages of the Quran into his speeches. The movement of army officers was supported by a group calling itself the Nationalist Party, and it included large landowners of both native Egyptian and Ottoman extraction. They sought a greater say in government and a reduced role for the khediviate, given the financial mismanagement of Ismail and the entrance of European creditors and consuls into the running of the country. Finally, the urban, intellectual bourgeoisie of Muslims and Christians promoted a government with some accountability to its people by means of indigenous morals and reformed legal institutions. Abdullah Nadim, the great orator of the Urabi movement, was a huge critic of blatant Westernization and he formulated speeches and articles that would resonate with the listening masses. Among all classes and walks of life there was a sense that foreign interests dominated in Egypt, whether from the Turkish-speaking elite or bond-holding Europeans. The oft-repeated slogan was "Egypt for the Egyptians."[44]

In opposition to this broadly based, yet loosely focused, group was the Khedive Tawfiq and the Europeans. Having participated in his father's unseating at the hands of European powers, Tawfiq was only too aware of how precarious his own position in the country was. He readily relied on the British, and to a lesser extent the French, for assistance. In Marsot's words, his immediate entourage of Ottoman-Egyptian elites "could offer nothing more than repeated attempts to assassinate Urabi and his friends; but since these attempts constantly miscarried, they only served to frighten Urabi into taking more drastic action."[45] The showdown between the two men boiled the conflict down to foreign versus indigenous concerns. The main events of the revolt were particularly masculine in nature, for example, the demonstration outside Abdin palace in which Tawfiq reportedly proclaimed that as Khedive he was free to do as he pleased, to which Urabi countered, "[W]e are not slaves and nevermore shall be possessed."[46] The British bombardment of Alexandria and their victory over the Egyptian army at Tal al-Kabir further attested to the male-dominated focus of the revolt. The British claimed to be temporarily restoring order, yet their forces would remain there more than 70 years. Where were the women? While presumably middle- and upper-class women would not have involved themselves in such affairs, the lower classes generally, and women, in particular, were conspicuously absent. The revolt was about the New Egyptian Man, and the resulting occupation brought about his emasculization. The Urabi revolt occurred less than ten years after the founding of the first government-sponsored primary school for girls. Aside from women of the palace, elite women were only in their first or second generation of new education. The New Woman was just coming into existance, and there was little visual imagery in the press to document her role, if any, in the events. The memories of the Urabi revolt are aural in nature: the slogan, the words that allegedly took place between Tawfiq and Urabi, the masterfully crafted speeches by the revolt's leaders, and the stories told by generation after generation of Egyptians, about where and how their families assisted the rebels.[47]

The 1919 Revolution was, in contrast, an event with greater female participation and feminine iconographic overtones. It was the sights, rather than the sounds of these events, that are remembered by Egyptians. In the years following the Urabi revolt, the rise of a women's press and women's columns in the mainstream press, the expansion of female education, the evolution of the Egyptian home and family as the locus for reform, and the continued struggle against the occupation, all served to bring women out of the confines of the home, both as subjects of a growing discourse on reform and as visible actors in demonstrations and organizations.

As World War I drew to a close, Egyptian nationalists eagerly awaited the implementation of Wilson's 14 points, with its promises of self-determination. When a delegation [*wafd*] composed of three nationalist leaders seeking to present Egypt's case at the Paris peace talks was rebuked by the British High Commissioner, the nationalist movement turned militant. Saad Zaghlul, the leader of the Wafd, became the chief spokesman. Soon afterward, the British attempted to quash the movement by exiling Zaghlul and two other leaders.

Rather than stemming the tide of militancy, the deportation served only to inflame nationalist sentiment from men and women of all classes. Newspapers and journals were filled with the iconography of the revolution: Egypt as pharaonic woman, a female warrior, or simply as a refined and indigenously dressed lady.[48] Egyptians showed their support by joining demonstrations, strikes, and walk-outs. Women of the lower classes participated in demonstrations alongside their husbands. Women of all classes watched from windows, balconies, and roof-tops, encouraging their husbands and sons. Upper-class women organized single-sex demonstrations, both on foot and in automobiles (see figure 5.1).[49] The Azbakiyya Garden Kiosk served as a waystation and meeting place for protestors of all sorts.[50] These are the images that remain etched in the minds of Egyptians, although few are alive that actually witnessed these events firsthand. At least 800 Egyptians were killed and many more wounded in the demonstrations and conflicts during this period. "The Ladies of Egypt" sent a note to the Americans complaining of the "persistance of the British in employing brute force even toward women," highlighting the active participation of women.[51]

Upper-class women provided a network of organization throughout Egypt for the nationalist movement. In early 1920 a group of Muslim and Coptic women headed by Huda Shaarawi formed the Wafdist Women's Central Committee (WWCC). These women played a crucial role for two reasons. The arrest and deportation of male nationalist leaders left a vacuum in the planning and execution of critical events. By involving their wives and daughters, these leaders insured the continuation of the movement. Furthermore, the women were crucial links in disseminating information. The WWCC worked through female associational networks, linking them with middle- and upper-class women throughout the country.[52]

One of the most effective actions taken by the WWCC was to sponsor a boycott of British goods and services in January of 1922. These actions did not emerge from a void. Booth argues that the genre of biographies written by, about, and for women "helped to prepare the discusive ground for nationalist economic activism." They did so by choosing exemplary women and focusing on those characteristics that would benefit the current situation. Booth suggests that the biography of Zenobia of Palmyra, who wore only Eastern cloth and encouraged indigenous industry, could have sparked activism.[53] Surely the examples of women in colonial New England or the more recent Swadeshi movement in India could have served a similar function.

Figure 5.1 Women's participation in the 1919 Revolution
Source: *A Woman Tenderfoot in Egypt.*

The boycott organizers recognized the important role played by women as general purchasing agents for their homes. It was part of a larger protest against the British occupation in general, and the arrest and exile of their leaders, in particular. The women circulated a petition calling for the end of martial law and the protectorate, as well as the return of Saad Zaghlul. Afterwards, they agreed to an economic embargo of British goods and services, including merchandise, merchants, banks, artisans, functionaries, doctors, pharmacists, and dentists. According to Badran, "the women sealed their resolve with a 'religious' oath":

> We swear by God . . . to boycott the British agressor, to deny to ourselves and to the people close to us everything that those usurpers have manufactured . . . their shops are forbidden to us . . . their factories are forbidden to us . . . [and] all that is connected to them is forbidden to us. God is our witness, and we steadfastly swear by him. . . . We implore you, God, to bring back to us our honest Sa^{c}d, safely and in good health, for his sake and the sake of his devoted compatriots, and to bring victory to Egypt and defeat to her deceitful enemies.[54]

The work of the boycott began as a handful of women making telephone calls, and within a few hours it evolved into about two dozen women seeking the cooperation of merchants. Ultimately, the WWCC boycott reached thousands of women through women's committees in the provinces.[55]

Apparently, the boycott was not taken seriously at first. In fact, the British did not acknowledge its significance until after the Wafd announced its support on January 23, two days after the British had received the WWCC's telegram. While the women suffered no ill consequences other than some snickering, the male signatories of the Wafd manifesto were ordered arrested and the newspapers publishing the manifesto were suspended. Nevertheless, the women took their work quite seriously. Madame Zaghlul herself served only native cakes and tea to an American visitor, explaining "everything is made at home because of the boycott," while Hidiya Afifi (Barakat), wife of a prominent Wafdist official, carried her complaints to the streets, monitoring foreign stores and shaming potential customers.[56]

Due to its timing, the boycott lacked serious long-term consequences for British merchants. The protectorate ended about a month after the start of the boycott, and public support waned. Furthermore, many British merchants relied on the large foreign community for support, rather than the middle and upper Egyptian classes. Nevertheless, according to a contemporary American observer, Grace Thompson Seton, the boycott did have some serious short-term consequences: "Some firms closed, some suspended business and others had liquidation sales."[57] Furthermore, the women did receive the support and admiration of Wafdist men. Wasif Ghali praised the women's efforts as "the most powerful and effective of our peaceful weapons in our legitimate struggle," and Saad Zaghlul indicated his appreciation after his return from exile.[58] In addition to the boycott, the WWCC carried out other economic activities with greater long-term significance for the nationalist movement. The women of the Wafd realized the importance of founding a national bank. They organized committees to sell shares for the fledgling Bank Misr, and they even bought the first shares.[59] Furthermore the women of the WWCC created new associations, for example, the New Woman Society, and interacted with others spawned in emulation, such as the Society of the Egyptian Women's Renaissance and the Society of Mothers of the Future.[60]

The WWCC boycott of British goods is symbolic of the new role of women for two reasons. First, its organizers were part and parcel of the growing nationalist movement, and they received the tacit support of Wafdist men for this new and public role. Second, by organizing a boycott and working through women's associational networks, they were acknowledging the growing role of middle- and upper-class women in the public sphere and empowering them to take part in the nationalist movement. It made the women feel as though they were doing something at a time when both men and women felt impotent. Ellen Fleischmann's use of oral history as a source for the Palestinian Great Revolt of 1936–39 underscores the positive feelings generated by the economic boycott there. More than five decades after the events in question, she records the recollections of two women, who as teenagers, participated in an economic boycott, even carrying it years beyond its official cessation. They discussed their feelings of great pride, as they refused themselves the joy of the Jewish-owned cinema, despite their great desire to see *Gone with the Wind*.[61] Cast in this light, the "national" advertisements of the 1920s, discussed in chapter 4, are more clearly understood.

Nevertheless, the weakness of the boycott highlighted the uneven nature of consumer development in Egypt. The targeted stores and items had an elite and limited audience. Unlike the United States where the new shopping districts and new stores tended to drive old-fashioned establishments out of business, in Egypt, the new stores developed in a system parallel to the old shopping network. Thus, the foreign patisseries, which Madame Zaghlul scrupulously avoided, did not displace the traditional *makhabiz*, nor did the new department stores with their modern housewares divisions replace the old copperwares market. While the pattern of Western consumer development could be replicated in the capital and other large cities of the delta, it never overtook or even overshadowed the consumer society that existed before it.

The people who shopped at the stores affected by the boycott were the same people with access to the advertisements in the press. The audience of those advertisements had grown both vertically and horizontally between the 1860s and the 1920s. No longer were ads merely aiming at upper-class men, who were able to read the stilted prose of *al-waqa*^{c}*i al-miṣriyya*. As we have seen, the audience grew to include both men and women, and by the 1920s it reached into the middle class with promises of affordable vacations, new hobbies, and fashionable clothing. The growth of publications, such as *al-laṭa'if al-muṣawwara*, encouraged these trends. One no longer needed a higher education to read, or even listen, to the new magazines.

Feminism, Political Activism, and the New Woman

The role women could take in buying for their home, participating in charitable activities or even participating in the 1919 demonstrations did not necessarily mean that all women were politically activated or would remain inclined to activism. The story of two women, Dorrya Fahmy and Doria Shafik, both of whom studied at the Sorbonne, is telling of these circumstances. Dorrya Fahmy (b. 1902) had a privileged upbringing.[62] Her Turkish grandfather was a legal advisor and judge for the government and her father, a lawyer. Her mother, orphaned at a young age, received an education at a Franciscan School run by the Italian community, where she remained until she was married at the age of 16. Doryya received no early schooling outside her home, where she had a French governess. Not surprisingly, in terms of reading and writing, Fahmy always felt more conversant in French than in her native tongue. As she approached the age at which her family felt that she ought to be married and made preparations in that direction, Fahmy penned a series of anonymous articles in *La Reforme* and *La Bourse* disparaging arranged marriages. She confided in only one family friend that she had written these articles, and this individual passed the information along to Ali Maher, who at that time was the Minister of Education. He suggested that Fahmy could solve her dilemma by studying in France. At first Dorrya was somewhat concerned since she had never attended any formal type of school nor did she have any diploma whatsoever. Whereas most educational missions had focused on sending women to England, Doryya had the opportunity to go to France and attend the École Normale Supéreure of Sèvres. Her sister was completely shocked and humiliated that Doryya's goal in life was to become a teacher. In 1925, when she was in her early twenties, she boarded the ship for France, discarded her *yashmak*, said goodbye to her life in Egypt, and felt a tremendous sense of liberation.

Fahmy continued her studies in France for more than ten years. After receiving her teaching certificate she went on to the Sorbonne, where she studied French literature, civilization, and history, in addition to musicology. She met her husband, an Egyptian, who also had come to Paris to study. Her first child, a daughter, was born in France; and she brought the child back to Egypt, returning to complete her *doctorate d'état* in

French literature in 1935. Not only was this a rare event for an Egyptian girl, but for French women as well. Fahmy's recollection was that it was just weeks before her when the first French woman received *doctorate d'état*. When she returned to Egypt, there was literally no place for her in the university system, which not only lacked women, but in the case of the French department, also lacked Egyptians. Her husband, in archeology, faced similar discrimination.[63]

She believes that if it had not been for the efforts of Ahmad Lutfi al-Sayyid, then rector of the Egyptian University (later Fuad I/Cairo University), she may not have ever worked. Lutfi al-Sayyid, the liberal intellectual and nationalist, felt it was important for Fahmy to join the faculty and facilitated her entrance. She remained there until the opening of Alexandria University (then Faruq I University) in 1945, and she continued working until the mid-1980s.[64]

I asked Fahmy if she were involved with the women's movement in Egypt. She rolled her eyes and stiffened her posture, informing me in no uncertain terms that she was not a "feminist." Clearly this came as somewhat of a shock at first—a woman who rebelled against an age-old institution and sought an acceptable solution; cast off her veil aboard ship, à la Huda Shaarawi; completed a degree that was rare not only for Egyptian women or men, but even for French women; published her first research on author George Sand, and faced horrendous discrimination by French nationals in the university and continued working until she was more than 80-years-old—yet, she rejected the feminist label. After she explained her reasoning, the situation became clear. Her feeling was that by the 1930s the feminist movement had become too intwined with politics, for which she had no interest. Learning the history of another New Woman, Doria Shafik, sheds further light on this issue.

Doria Shafik's (b. 1908) story bears uncanny resemblance to Fahmy's, yet it departs from it in significant ways. Although not part of the Ottoman-Egyptian elite herself, through her mother's family she was connected to the world of privilege. Unlike her cousin who had a European governess, she had one from the Levant. Initially, she could only afford "the miserable Italian nuns' school in Mansura." Eventually she moved up the pecking order of schools enrolling in a more presitigious French mission school, Notre Dame des Apôtres, the same school her mother had attended. Like Fahmy, French was her preferred mode of written expression.[65]

Although the status of the school improved, conditions there were not ideal. Harsh discipline and the constant comparison with her wealthier relations often depressed Doria, not to mention the separation from her mother. When she was not yet 13, Doria's ailing mother betrothed her to the wealthy nephew of one of her least favorite relatives. After her mother's death, Doria must have confided her feelings to her father, who together with her, broke the news to her grandmother that she did not wish to marry this fellow. She then moved to Alexandria with her father and studied at a French mission school there. Doria contemplated various careers, including secretarial work. Her elder sister Soraya, like Fahmy's sister, was concerned about the choices her sister was making; however, she couched her complaints in terms of concern for her sister rather than the family name. Soraya was able to dissuade Doria from secretarial work, arguing that it might wreak havoc upon her marriage prospects.[66]

After watching her brothers get sent to Europe for their studies, Doria wrote a letter to Huda Shaarawi seeking assistance so that she too could go abroad to study.

Shortly thereafter, Doria won an essay contest, writing on the subject of Qasim Amin (d. 1908) on the twentieth anniversary of his death, and she was invited to appear at the Azbakiyya Theater with Madame Shaarawi. The next day, Doria received word from the Ministry of Education that a scholarship had been arranged for her to attend the Sorbonne. Refusing to conform to the ministry's notion of what a woman ought to study, she insisted upon philosophy.[67]

Like Fahmy, Shafik found an Egyptian husband in Paris, yet hers came after two false starts, namely, two broken engagements. Ironically, she ended up falling in love with the son of her mother's cousin. The couple returned to Cairo in 1939, although Doria had to go back to Paris the following year to defend her two theses, one on Egyptology and one on women's rights in Islam.[68] For awhile she worked as an inspector (of French) for the Ministry of Education; however, she craved something different. Shortly thereafter, she accepted an offer sure to anger her mentor and benefactress Huda Shaarawi. Princess Chivekiar[69] invited Doria to edit a new journal, the French-language paper for her New Woman Society [*La Femme Nouvelle*].[70]

The offer, the circumstances surrounding it, and Doria's reasons for acceptance were all probably part of the reason that Fahmy so eschewed the notion of feminism and the women's movement. Within a year of Egypt's partial independence in 1922, Huda Shaarawi broke away from the New Woman Society and created the Egyptian Feminist Union (EFU) in 1923, with a decidedly political platform, while the former maintained the profile of a benevolent association with Princess Chivekiar as its patroness. These two women remained competing poles of elite feminism and philanthropy on the one hand, and party politics and the monarchy on the other.[71] Chivekiar, with her numerous ex-husbands and sychophants, was at the center of a number of palace controversies, once again creating an intersection between the politics of the royal family and women's roles within the nation. Accepting Chivekiar's offer would be tantamount to a slap across the face for Shaarawi and her partisans. Furthermore, it would mean tacit support for the monarchy, which was quickly losing face amongst the Egyptian people. Nevertheless, Shafik believed that working through existing power structures and utilizing available funds were the most expedient means of helping other women and advancing women's causes. She later founded her own magazine, *bint al-nil* in 1945, and her own leading women's association after Shaarawi's and Chivekiar's deaths in 1947.[72]

Conclusion

Although the New Woman was part and parcel of the debate regarding the future of Egypt and the activism of the 1919 demonstrations, allegiance to politics would not necessarily define her. The efforts of the first generation of feminists were rewarded in the 1920s with some modest gains; however, their aggressive agenda was not achieved. While they could claim victory in the realm of compulsory primary education for girls and boys, the government lacked the human and material resources to make the dream a reality. Discrepancies between male and female education at the higher levels remained huge, but were improving. Similarly, in the arena of family law, the EFU demanded an end to polygamy and *bayt al-ṭa*ᶜ*a* (a legal precept that could force a wife to return to the home of her husband), as well as some restrictions on divorce. While these goals were not achieved, they were successful in raising the age of marriage and extending the period of maternal child custody.[73] Leadership and patronage of groups such as the EFU, tended to fall within the upper class, individuals who either experienced polygamy, concubinage, and early marriage in their own household or within their parents' household. Divorce by their husband's unilaterial repudiation was something that Egyptian women of all classes feared. The discourse in the women's press tended to focus more on the creation of the proper household to circumvent such a circumstance, rather than trying to prevent men from this course of action altogether. Great emphasis was placed on creating a happy and harmonious home, the entire responsibility of which fell upon the shoulders of the New Woman.[74]

In the years after independence, particularly after the creation of the *bint al-nil* union, more middle-class women began to enter feminist associations, yet they remained marked with the vestiges of competing personalities and elite politics. Ultimately, the New Woman's role within the home, thus creating the nation as a family of homes, was more important. The New Woman could achieve this goal by raising the new generation of Egyptians or teaching them. Part two of this work focuses on schools, educational discourse, and textbooks. In particular, chapter 6 provides an overview of women's education in Egypt. As we shall see, the new forms of education that arose in the nineteenth and twentieth centuries, like the new commercial districts, did not immediately displace traditional structures. Furthermore, the existence of parallel systems of education fit neatly with the British notion of a bifurcated system of education based upon class, as well as elite Egyptian class interests.

Part II

Teaching the New Woman

"The Mother is a School"
Hafiz Ibrahim
Translated by Mona L. Russell and Laila S. Russell

. . .

The mother is a school; if you prepare her, you prepare a nation well from its roots. The mother is a garden; if you water it, it will flourish.

. . .

I am not calling for women to move about freely among men, unveiled in the bazaars; roaming about as they please, unconcerned about being watched or protected. In their homes their concerns are numerous, as are the concerns of the lord of the sword and the spear.
Nor am I calling upon you to be excessive in seclusion, restriction, and oppression. Your women are not ornaments or jewels that you place in a safe, fearing for their loss. Your women are not pieces of furniture that you acquire [for your] homes, as is common among the swindlers.

. . .

Be moderate between these two extremes, for evil comes from [both] restriction and liberty.

. . .

"The Mother is a School," al-hilal 18, 10 (1910): 582–583

Chapter 6

Education: Creating Mothers, Wives, Workers, Believers, and Citizens

Introduction

The extract from Hafiz Ibrahim's poem represents the tensions, ambiguities, and characteristics of the "New Woman" in Egypt at the turn of the century. Her role in the home and in raising the children was supreme and unquestioned, and it was necessary for the cause of the nation. Nevertheless, as she entered the new stores, schools, and professions, the extent of her liberties remained a source of debate and contention.

The role of the state in women's education in Egypt, as in education in general, has contracted and expanded according to its developmental needs, as well as its need to assert hegemonic leadership. The increasing role of the state in women's lives over the course of the nineteenth and twentieth centuries increased educational opportunities for women, but at the same time it has also changed the nature of women's education. Up until the nineteenth century, women's education in Egypt was related to religion and pursued for its own sake by the upper classes.[1] In the nineteenth and early twentieth centuries, education spread vertically and horizontally in order to serve the needs of the state and the growing needs of the population as women became educated in order to enter the medical and teaching professions, as well as to become better wives and mothers. Nevertheless, the state was slow to spread this education. Private enterprise, both foreign and domestic, filled the gap. The British occupation added another confusing dimension to this process. Foreigners played a critical role, and the occupation heightened awareness of female education and the role of curriculum therein. With the emergence of the New Man, middle- and upper-class Egyptians sought education for their daughters that would prepare them to become not only capable wives and mothers, but also responsible citizens.

Pre-Nineteenth-Century Female Education in Egypt

In addition to elite women, discussed in chapter 2, women of humbler origins received education by attending *kuttabs*, which were theoretically open to women, studying with male and female teachers in their homes or informal mosque classes, attending more formal classes on an informal basis, or by studying with their learned male and female relatives. The curriculum in the *kuttabs* usually included Quran and *ḥadith*, and in some cases poetry, mathematics, and Arabic. The quality and quantity of the curriculum varied from school to school and teacher to teacher. From what evidence exists, girls who attended these schools, albeit few in number, received the same education as boys. Nevertheless, we also find evidence from the writings of *ᶜulama'* that suggest that women were taught to read but not to write, and that poetry was a dangerous subject area for women. To what extent women were excluded from these subjects depended upon both the school and the teacher. According to Edward Lane, even few boys learned how to write, except those who were destined for occupations in which writing was a necessity. Women who were taught in the home might have more limitations placed on their curriculum; however, they also might be allowed more leeway. In addition to the subjects taught to boys, girls learned needlework and embroidery from their female relatives or a special teacher [*muᶜallima*]. Wealthy merchants also housed small schools in their homes for their children and dependents. With respect to Coptic girls, they too could attend the Coptic equivalent of the *kuttab*; however, they needed their mother's permission. In Cairo, girls generally did not attend, whereas in upper Egypt attendance was somewhat more common, at least up till the age eight or nine. Home education was also an alternative for Coptic girls.[2]

Government Entrance into Female Education

The nineteenth century marks a distinct break with the past in the social, political, economic, and cultural dimensions of Egyptian life. With respect to women and education, this break meant a change in the state's need, opportunity, and ability to integrate women into the workforce in untraditional ways. In terms of the country as a whole, the expansion and development of the world economy necessitated changes both within Egypt and in Egypt's relations with other countries. Muhammad Ali, who rose to power in 1805, was able to formulate a development program that enhanced the changes underway.[3]

The army and expansion were at the core of Muhammad Ali's program for development. In order to facilitate this plan, he had to modify the educational system. Rather than building upon the existing system, Muhammad Ali built a parallel system. He started at the top with specialized schools for military science, engineering, and medicine. He then worked his way down to the primary level. Initial recruitment for the advanced schools would come from the traditional schools, but later his new primary and preparatory schools would prove more fertile training ground. Muhammad Ali supplemented his program with the use of foreign advisors, translators, and educational missions to Europe. A paternalistic state sponsored the entire system, covering tuition fees, books, other educational expenses, and even personal expenses. Whether in primary, preparatory, or specialized schools, as well as on missions abroad, the state strictly governed Egyptian students with careful supervision, continuous observation, and numerous regulations. Punishment for wayward pupils included public reprimand, confinement, a bread and water diet, corporal punishment, and expulsion. The state was attempting to foster both the student's character and intellect to better serve its needs.[4]

Two integral components of Muhammad Ali's development scheme were a thriving army and a healthy population.[5] French doctor Antoine B. Clot, medical advisor to Muhammad Ali, suggested the training of female doctors; and he took great personal interest in the project. Having been trained in France, Clot had experience with the French model for training midwives.[6] In Egypt, his concern was twofold. First, he wanted to spread the latest innovations in medicine to women, who avoided contact with unfamiliar males; and second, he wanted to thwart an outbreak of venereal disease in the army. Although training women in medicine seemed a simple solution, putting the plan into action required surmounting the same obstacles as the initial problem itself. In other words, the whole idea of training women doctors was to avoid putting women in contact with unfamiliar males; but how was the government to train an initial group of women without contact with male instructors, or worse yet, male European instructors? The same forceful methods that Muhammad Ali employed to find recruits for the army, industry, and public works projects could not be used with women. Nevertheless, the idea was not completely novel to Egyptians since *dayas* had long been practicing the trade of midwifery.[7]

Clot's initial solution to the problem was to procure slaves, who would first be taught basic literacy and then receive the same instruction as male medical students. Clot himself chose the first students, ten slaves of Sudanese and Abyssinian origin. In keeping with cultural mores and consistent with the practice of surveillance and regulation in other schools, Clot appointed two eunuchs to keep an eye on the students (and teachers) and later to serve as instructors. He also employed a third eunuch to monitor the behavior of the other two.[8]

The School of Midwifery opened in 1832, but the problem of finding and maintaining students remained. The first students progressed well intellectually, but they did not thrive physically in their new surroundings. Three of the slaves died of consumption and one from dysentery. The remaining six continued their studies and other slaves were procured, but Clot preferred to find a means of recruiting indigenous girls. The first opportunity presented itself when a group of indigent girls remained unclaimed in the teaching hospital. Clot secretly enlisted these orphan girls in the School of Midwifery, and after teaching them the basics, officially enrolled them in the school. The heavy-handed conscription and *corvée* policies of Muhammad Ali left many girls fatherless, and the School of Midwifery provided institutional support. Like other government schools, its students received free housing, clothing, food, tuition fees, and pocket money. The school even had its own bath attendant, although her salary was deducted from the students' allowances. As word of such perks spread, the School of Midwifery was able to attract some students. In fact, Clot encouraged students to visit their relatives in the provinces in order to recruit their sisters and cousins. The school perpetuated itself by utilizing the older students and graduates as tutors and teachers to the younger pupils. Abugideiri insightfully points out that this tutoring built upon established precepts in Islamic learning, while simultaneously "bringing Egyptian midwives in line with French maternity training."[9]

Despite incentives for attracting pupils, recruitment remained a perennial problem, and by 1840 there were only 11 students, despite Clot's grandiose plans for expansion. According to Abugideiri, recruits were generally unmarried teenagers with indigent backgrounds; however, she maintains that they would eventually represent a wider geographic and social spectrum. Nevertheless, they "were ultimately a minority corps of trained medical officers whose numbers were consistently disproportionate to the growing Egyptian population."[10] The bottom line was that most Egyptian women were not interested in becoming medical officers for the state. Medicine was not yet a prestigious career, even for men. Furthermore, the School of Midwifery was plagued with illness among both students and faculty. Only women with few options in life came to the school.

The curriculum of the School of Midwifery encompassed more than simple obstetrics and gynecology. The women also learned Arabic, vaccination, neo-natal pediatrics, pharmacology, surgery, and hygiene. Graduates received the same rank as men from the School of Medicine. The government attempted to extend its authority over the graduates of both schools by arranging marriages between them. In this way, couples could be dispatched to the provinces to work as a team. The arrangement was not incumbent upon the women, but there were a number of material benefits: promotion in rank and salary, a small furnished home, a monetary award, and manumission (for slaves).[11] Fahmy contends that the women were "not permitted to leave the school until they found a suitable husband from among the Egyptian doctors," thus emphasizing the foreboding, paternalistic nature of the state, a view shared by Mervat Hatem. As discussed in chapter 5, marriage was considered a community obligation. Furthermore, the indigent origins of many of the midwives, as well as their education, might have impacted their ability to find a mate—suitable or otherwise. Even as the practice of arranging these marriages waned in the late nineteenth century, the notion of companionate marriage was still in its infancy. The state increased the chances of women continuing to practice after marriage by marrying them to doctors; and furthermore, women must have found some incentive to do so, or the practice would not have continued up through the early 1880s.[12]

The state continued to support medical education for women and believed that educated women could contribute in other ways. In 1836 Muhammad Ali created the Committee of Public Instruction to oversee the organization and implementation of the new schools. Committee members agreed that the progress of society depended upon the contribution of all of its members. Although they believed in the importance of female education, their collective plate was already full in the creation and implementation of a new system of education for boys.[13]

While the government did little to sponsor female education, the viceroy, by example, promoted education in the royal *ḥarim*. Education amongst upper-class women was not uncommon, and prior to the nineteenth century, the curriculum focused on (reading) Arabic, Turkish, and Persian; poetry; Quran; and *ḥadith*. Muhammad Ali and his son Ibrahim began the process of employing European governesses for their children. Nevertheless, the wide-scale use of European governesses did not take hold until the age of Ismail. Another way in which the royal family generally, and its women specifically, participated in the education process was through charitable support. The viceroy's daughter Zaynab served as an example to other women by employing one-fifth of her estate in *awqaf*, some of which supported schools, and by maintaining her own literary salon.[14]

The royal *ḥarim* set the trend for upper-class women later in the nineteenth century. The memoirs of Huda Shaarawi (1879–1947) indicate that she followed an educational path similar to the one described in chapter 2. She and her brothers, as well as two companions, received home instruction together under the supervision of a eunuch. While she excelled in the new curriculum, Huda felt that she had not mastered the Arabic language. Her eunuch impeded her quest for this subject as he did not feel it was appropriate for young ladies, and her parents either did not know or did not care.[15] The major difference between Shaarawi and the women of the royal *ḥarim* seems to be the degree of support and interest from her family. Concern for female education amongst the upper class clearly ran the gamut from those who fastidiously monitored their daughters' education, to those who merely sponsored it, to those who ignored it entirely.[16]

The Government Tries Again

Female education must be seen in light of overall educational and development policies. As the fortunes of Muhammad Ali waned after 1840, there was less need for the new educational system with expansion and industrialization halted. His successors were neither able nor willing to continue sponsoring education to the same degree. Egyptian nationalist historians use the most scathing words to describe the rulers and their role in education. According to al-Rafii, "Abbas hated knowledge and learning," and Said continued his predecessor's policy of apathy toward education.[17] The latter is oft quoted as saying to his tutor, "why open the eyes of the people, they will only be more difficult to rule."[18] In reality the situation was more complicated. The economy simply could not sustain these extensive educational programs. Nevertheless, Abbas and Said were not blameless. Said completely disbanded the Ministry of Public Instruction [*diwan al-madaris*]. By the end of his rule, only the military and medical schools remained, despite significant economic improvement.[19]

Ismail reformed and revitalized the educational system established by his grandfather. In addition to some foreign advisors, he was surrounded by a cadre of officials who had been brought up through the Muhammad Ali system of education—Tahtawi, Ali Mubarak, and Ibrahim Adham, and others. Early on in his reign, Ismail reestablished the *diwan al-madaris*, combining it with the Ministry of Public Works and the *waqf* administration, with an eye toward greater government control and seizing upon the relationship between municipal reorganization, education, and finance. In addition to reopening the specialized schools, Ismail began to work on the base, spreading primary schools throughout the provinces. He attempted to place the *kuttab* system under government administration and seized some of the *awqaf* that administered these schools. He also took measures to regularize testing, curriculum, and instruction.[20] Ismail began the controversial policy of introducing fees in the schools; but this policy applied only to those who were able to pay, and the proportion of paying students remained under 30 percent up till the arrival of the British. At the same time, however, Ismail raised the standard of quality for those still receiving government assistance.[21] He greatly increased the budget for education and set a personal example for the wealthy by providing funds to support free schools.[22] Ismail's Western admirers tout his accomplishments in education, and even his critics begrudge him some success.[23] Ismail's plans also included education for women. He established a commission in 1867 to study the possibility of founding a primary school for girls. Always concerned about appearances, his hope was that he could have the school open by the time of the Suez Canal festivities. Nevertheless, the two-year time frame proved insufficient.[24]

The first government primary school for girls did not materialize until 1873. Ismail's third wife, Jashm Afit Hanum [Cheshm Afet, Shams Iffat] sponsored the Siyufia School. Nevertheless, there seems to be a dispute as to whether the princess actually financed the school or not. According to Ellen Chennells, the school "was founded by the Khedive," and kept up "entirely at his expense," but it was called the School of the Third Princess because he liked to "associate his family with his undertakings." Zaynab Farid speculates that the school was publicized in such a fashion so that it would gain greater acceptance by the population.[25] Yet another interpretation might be that Ismail paid or encouraged this wife to pay for the school to buttress his family image. Its opening occurred the same year that he arranged the grand-slam wedding event for four of his children (see chapter 2).

On the other hand, it is plausible that Jashm Afit Hanum sponsored the school herself and continued to serve as its patroness. First, princesses in the royal family were active patrons of education. Furthermore, from what little is known about this woman, she seems inclined toward education and its importance. Having no children of her own, she adopted a slave child whose education she enthusiastically sponsored. According to Yacub Artin, she did encourage Ismail to open the school and was actively involved in its planning. Artin's words regarding her influence over Ismail are supported by circumstantial evidence. Namely, he chose to make her his official wife (third), yet she bore him no children, while he was compelled by the Sultan to marry the mother of his heir apparent. Nevertheless, his affection for her might also be a reason for him to put the school in her name. Abbas II's memoirs are equally vague. He credits his grandfather with being a revolutionary with respect to secular, national education generally, and girls' education specifically; however, he too credits the princess with founding the school. Regardless of sponsorship, Jashm Afit continued to publicly support the school by making visits with the royal family at examination time.[26]

The actual development of the school, its clientele, and its curriculum are far more interesting than the debates over who financed the school. The third princess donated an old palace in the neighborhood of al-Siyufia and saw to its renovation. In keeping with the royal family's tastes, the school was sumptuous, with a large open courtyard and accommodations to serve 200 internal and 100 external students.[27] According to contemporary observers, the school called upon parents of all classes to send their daughters to be educated, housed, clothed, and fed at government expense. The announcement in the official government paper, as well, indicated the school's willingness to accept orphans, poor girls, and daughters of the wealthy, under the auspices of the government. Two years after the school's opening, an article in *Le Courrier de Port-Said* supported these claims, informing readers that al-Siyufia accepted girls "without distinction of belief, class, or origin . . . ."

The issue of who actually attended the school is a bit more difficult. Apparently it was several months before any students applied for matriculation. According to McCoan, the appeal of free room and board, clothing, and education appealed to the lower class; but once the initial prejudice against the school was broken, al-Siyufia had a wider appeal and applications exceeded the number of positions available by 1878. Ellen Chennells writes in her memoirs that she found "children of all classes" treated equally at the school. According to Yacub Artin, the first students at the school were white slaves from the royal family and other prominent families. As for girls from the lower class, Artin reports that few parents of this class sent their daughters to school, despite the material advantages, because they needed their daughters' labor and educated girls were thought to be difficult to control.[28]

The school's curriculum contained elements that would appeal to both groups of students. The commission charged with studying the issue of female education in 1867 envisaged a program similar to European schools of the time with an Ottoman-Egyptian flavor. The curriculum would include reading, writing, religion, Arabic, Turkish, arithmetic, drawing, geometry, childcare and hygiene, cooking, home economics, and needlework.[29] From Dor Bey, the Inspector-General of the public schools, we find that the five-year curriculum came to include these subjects, as well as French, the history and geography of Egypt, weights and measures, natural history and physics, Arabic and European calligraphy, and music for those who so desired.[30] Turkish, French, music, and art all had upper-class appeal. These are courses that would make the white slave contingent refined wives, mothers, and companions. The history and geography of Egypt indicate burgeoning nationalist interests.[31] Finally, the needlework and home economics classes would appeal to the lower and lower middle classes since they would provide income-producing skills. Traditionally, girls of this strata learned how to use the spindle, while middle- and upper-class girls learned sewing and embroidery. Most likely these girls were in the internal division and received extra training in home economics since they were responsible for the school's upkeep, laundry, and cooking. Supervisors oversaw the division of chores, and the girls rotated positions on a weekly basis. The school held periodic sales of the goods produced (beyond the needs of the students), and the proceeds went toward a dowry fund for the poorest girls. Once graduated, these girls could seek employment in factories that produced clothing for government schools, continue their education in the School of Midwifery, or seek employment in the private sector.[32]

The staff included men and women, as well as Europeans and Egyptians. Hassan Effendi Salih was the director of the school, serving as liaison to both the Ministry of Public Instruction and parents. The actual running of the school was in the hands of a Syrian headmistress, Mlle. Rose Najjar. Three *shaykhs* taught religion, an *effendi* taught Turkish, and another, drawing. Eight women rounded out the remainder of the teaching staff, four for needlework, one for piano, one for laundry, and two supervisors.[33]

The Siyufia School ran quite efficiently and grew in popularity. When Ellen Chennells visited the school in the mid–1870s, she "found everything in excellent working order" and "in perfect cleanliness," after having "inspected every part of the building." At the time of her visit, there were two hundred boarders and one hundred external students.[34] Owing to the success of the first school, Ismail quickly decided to open another, al-Qarabia, along the same lines. The curriculum and staff were similar to al-Siyufia, although al-Qarabia was designed along somewhat more modest lines and had a greater emphasis on domestic service. By 1875 al-Siyufia had attracted almost 300 pupils and al-Qarabia, 152. Artin reports that the two schools operated on a grand scale and required large sums of money for support. In the year prior to his deposition, Ismail began plans on a third school for Cairo, as well as plans to spread female education in the provinces. The third school was to be smaller and more exclusive, specializing in the education of noble girls. Although a mansion was constructed to house the school, it never opened. By this point the royal family and the government were suffering severe financial setbacks, and both Jashm Afit Hanum and the *waqf* administration had to cut back on expenses at the two schools. After Ismail's abdication, Jashm Afit withdrew her support. The two schools were merged and placed under the *waqf* administration.[35]

The trials and tribulations of the Siyufia School indicate the confusion over the mission of female education in Egypt. The extensive curriculum indicates an effort to please too many people. The school would have continuous difficulties, particularly in trying to attract girls of different classes. The School of Midwifery had already provided a case study for girls' education in Egypt. Its emphasis on vocational education meant that it never attracted large numbers of students, and those who came were girls with limited options.[36] The curriculum at the School of Midwifery was not suitable for middle- and upper-class girls, and parents were concerned about their daughters mixing with girls of other classes and with the teaching staff at both schools. While lower- and lower-middle-class families might be attracted by the material support provided by both government schools and the promise of their daughters attaining income-producing skills, they were concerned that education would make their daughters "uppity" and perhaps unmarriageable. The small but growing middle class, composed of urban professionals who had advanced through the modern educational system, saw the advantages of female education; however, they were skeptical about the curriculum and the use of male instructors in public and private schools for girls. The highest strata of society was unconcerned about these issues since home education was easily attainable. Nevertheless, the quality of home education was only as good as the governess supplying it.[37] The creation of the Qarabia school and the plan for the School for Noble Girls would have provided some relief and clarity to the system.

Another factor that further clouded the issue of female education was the suppression of the slave trade in 1877. This measure effectively reduced the population of potential students at al-Siyufia, that is, the white slave contingent. Furthermore, it affected the availability of domestic slaves. The American Consul-General in Egypt spoke to Ismail about the issue of female education and the slave trade. According to

Edwin de Leon, Ismail hoped to substitute educated Egyptian peasant girls as servants in place of slaves.[38] With the change in clientele, al-Siyufia limited its mission to preparing girls of modest means for entering domestic service; and this development essentially turned the school into an orphanage.[39] Furthermore, the reduced financial base affected both the quality of instruction and the material support provided by the school. The competent headmistress was dismissed without notice or provocation, and she never received appropriate reparations. By the time that the school returned to the Ministry of Public Instruction in 1889, the ministry saw the need to dismiss the headmistress, chief agent, and officer of the school. As for the students, by this time, they barely had clothes on their backs.[40] Despite these problems, al-Siyufia remained the only school for girls and applications exceeded the number of positions available.[41]

In 1892 Yacub Artin, who studied the issue of female education for the Ministry of Public Instruction, advanced the following criticisms of al-Siyufia [al-Sania]:

> Its curriculum, its programs, its very premises, show the effect of this absolute lack of a fixed and determined goal. Everything about this establishment is vague and complicated; pompous in theory and on paper, its program produces nothing or almost nothing in practice upon which one could base the hope for a normal [course of] development for female education in Egypt . . .[42]

The fate of al-Siyufia and Artin's suggestions for improvement is discussed in the section on education under the British occupation.

Alternatives to Home and Government Education: The Foreign and Mission Schools

Although the foreign/minority schools and the mission schools in Egypt had distinct origins, the two worked to increase both the quantity and quality of education in Egypt. While the goal of mission schools was to spread Christianity and Western education, the goal of the foreign/minority schools was to preserve language, culture, and heritage. Both types of schools affected and were affected by government trends in education. As education became a sought-after commodity in the late nineteenth century, more Muslim Egyptians entered both types of schools. The government was particularly slow in meeting the growing demand for female education, and Egyptian girls entered these schools in larger numbers than boys.

Missionary education spread most rapidly under the reigns of Said and Ismail; however, it was Muhammad Ali who laid the groundwork for the movement's flourishing. He had invited some foreign business interests into Egypt, and the missionaries followed the path of the entrepreneurs. The viceroy must have realized that he could not bear the burden of education alone. Thus, he granted missionary societies free land and buildings. Additionally, he allowed their workers free travel by train, and their personal effects/equipment entered Egypt duty free. Nevertheless, providing the means was not enough to have made the schools succeed. There must have been some demand for education in order for the movement to have blossomed. The focus of many of the missions was Copts, although some concentrated on the Jews. French, English, Scottish, and American missionaries spread schools throughout Egypt in addition to those built by the Greek, Italian, German, Armenian, Jewish, and Coptic communities.[43]

The British were the first to send missionaries in large numbers, with the Methodists operating between 1823 and 1835; the Church Missionary Society (CMS) between 1826 and 1873; the Christian Mission to the Jews (CMJ) between 1847 and 1863; and the Church of Scotland between 1859 and 1864. Britain's missionary interests began to wane at mid-century under the francophile governments of Said and Ismail; however, they picked up again after the occupation in 1882. The economic interest of these missionary groups was quite apparent. For example, one-third of the CMS's commissioners in 1801 were either bankers, brokers, or merchants. Nevertheless, a distinction should be drawn between those planning missions, and the earnest missionaries who relocated and faced numerous adversities in their effort to spread the word of God. Egypt was a target since it was more tolerant toward Europeans than elsewhere in the Ottoman Empire.[44]

The CMS was one of the earliest missionary efforts in Egypt. It opened a press in Malta in 1815 for printing the New Testament in Arabic; and it sent its first agents to Egypt in 1815 and 1825. Apparently discouraged by the prospect of converting Muslims, the CMS directed its activities toward the Copts. Among the early CMS goals was a school for girls. Plans were scuttled and resuscitated a couple of times due to illness among the missionaries and concerns that Copts would not send their daughters to the school. Mrs. Dunsap, a former (black) slave and wife of a French doctor, encouraged the plan and advised the missionaries to include sewing and knitting in the curriculum. The CMS did include sewing and embroidery in the school's curriculum, along with Arabic reading and writing. Most of the original ten students, eight Copts and two Muslims, were quite poor; and the commercial value of their education did not escape their parents' attention.[45] Even some Muslims allowed their daughters to attend, despite the fact that Arabic was taught by means of the Bible. The sewing skills provided the necessary incentive, as documented by Bowring's visit in 1840.[46] Finished articles produced by the girls in school were picked up by a *dallala* and then sold in the market. Given the fact that all mission schools for girls faced high rates of attrition, the program of study was intensive, lasting from eight in the morning until five in the afternoon. The school grew in popularity, and by the time of Bowring's visit, it had 100 students, most of whom were Copts. The CMS girls' school was, in fact, more successful than the one for boys, since it did not have to contend with loss of students by conscription or *corvée* labor, only early marriages. Ultimately the school achieved some degree of status by attracting students from some prominent Coptic families and by sending female missionaries to tutor the women in the royal *ḥarim*.[47]

French Catholics had long-established ties in Egypt. The arrival of Syrian Christians in Egypt in the eighteenth century strengthened the existing Franciscan community, encouraging further growth. The resurgence of trade with Europe, in general, and France, in particular, helped to foster an environment of intellectual growth for both the Christian and Muslim upper classes in Egypt during the eighteenth century.

The second wave of Syrian immigration in the nineteenth century, along with the increased interest in education, led to the growth of French schools. Unlike the early British schools, French schools sought more actively to spread French language and culture.[48] By the mid-nineteenth century, they became interested in the education of girls. The first Catholic school for girls, *Maison du Bon Pasteur*, opened in 1846 as a result of the efforts of the French consul and a church official. The school's benefactor was European, it was located in the European quarter (Muski), and its main clientele was also European. It is difficult to ascertain if any Egyptian, or even Syrian, girls attended the school during its early years. Regardless, the school provided free primary education. In the same year, Franciscan missionaries opened another girls' school, *Soeurs de la Providence*, in Alexandria, owing to the large Catholic (foreign) community in the port city. Unable to meet the demand for education by Catholic communities, the Franciscans were followed by the Lazarists. Both orders established schools, hospitals, and orphanages in Cairo, Alexandria, and other major port cities, with Muhammad Ali donating both land and buildings for many of these establishments.[49] Under Abbas, one French girls' school opened, *Filles de la Charité* of Alexandria. In particular, this school later concerned itself with orphaned refugees from Lebanon. In general, the early work of the French missions was not aimed at the indigenous population. Instead, it was directed primarily toward European Catholics and secondarily toward Syrian Catholics.[50]

Under Said, the Scottish Mission and the CMJ worked to convert and educate the Jewish community of Alexandria. The Scottish Mission opened a boy's and a girls' school there. Although these schools catered mainly to Jews, they accepted children of all races and creeds. The curriculum included Arabic, English, French, Italian, writing, arithmetic, and history, in addition to needlework for the girls. Girls were of particular interest to the missionaries, who had established a ladies' association in Paisley to promote the Christian education of girls in Alexandria.[51] Similarly, the CMJ opened a school for girls and a school for boys in the mid–1850s, both of which laid a heavy emphasis on foreign languages.[52] Given the prominent role played by Jews in commerce and banking, such an emphasis is not surprising.

During the reigns of Said and Ismail, Catholic efforts gained speed, and the government became more involved in donating land and buildings for projects that were increasingly beneficial to the indigenous population. Between the years of 1863 and 1879 alone, 129 private schools opened in Egypt, the majority of which were Presbyterian or Catholic. A group of Franciscan nuns opened *Maison des Soeurs Franciscans* in 1859. Located in Cairo, this school was directed toward abolitionist activities. It purchased black slaves, trained them in domestic service, and then released them as free women. The school took in about 50 women at a time, and it continued to function as such until the patron who purchased the slaves died in 1882. By this point, the slave trade was officially abolished; and it was functioning more as a hospice/training center.[53] Upon accession to power, Ismail had granted the Franciscan Sisters a gift of 50,000 francs and an annual subvention in wheat, allowing the mission to expand, adding a school and an orphanage. According to Dor Bey, the school admitted all nationalities; however, Italians were in the majority. Ismail encouraged the work of the Franciscan Sisters and other French missionaries, who opened schools in Shubra in 1861, Bulaq in 1868, Mansura in 1872, Kafr al-Zayyat in 1873, and Ismailia in 1874.

These schools continued to spread in the capital and in port cities with large foreign contingents. The French did not concern themselves with the indigenous population until later in the century, when competition grew with the spread of American and English Protestant groups.[54]

The CMS, Mary Whately, and the American Mission differ from the early French efforts due to their attempt to reach the indigenous population in general, and females in particular. Mary Whately, daughter of the Archbishop of Ireland, started her own school in a popular quarter of Cairo in order to spread the gospel to the lower classes. Contemporary observers describe her as energetic, devoted, and one of the "chief educational forces in Egypt." She spent the better part of 30 years and her personal fortune in establishing schools.[55] Nevertheless, Whately came to Egypt loaded with class and cultural biases. She felt that Egypt's underclass could be uplifted through religious education, and that at least there was "no drunkenness to contend with . . . ."[56] Whately believed that her work was more urgently needed in the cities where greater numbers of women could be reached and where transmission to the countryside was still possible. Despite warnings from the European community and educated Egyptians that her chance for success among Muslim girls was all but nonexistent, she proceeded with her plans.[57] When questioned about her mission, she repeatedly stated that she could not convert her students.[58] She held the key to a sought-after commodity (education), and students had to accept the proselytizing in order to obtain that commodity at the bargain price for which it was offered. She charged no fees.

Whately took a grass-roots approach in creating her school. She rented a room in a popular neighborhood, enlisted the aid of a Syrian Christian girl in her building, and set out into the streets to "drum up business." Within three days the tenacious Whately had secured herself 14 female students.[59] Over the years, she was able to enlist over 100 girls in her school (at a time); however, she had numerous problems with attendance, attrition, and early marriage. Whately never lost sight of her goals, and periodically would take to the streets to "beat up for recruits" and visit the mothers of her pupils to recapture lost students.[60] Whately viewed herself as something of an animal trainer, who took in wild, dirty, uncivilized beasts and turned them into respectable individuals "under Christian influence."[61] For Whately, her mission was to clean, civilize, and educate these students. The one prerequisite for attendance was to "do so cleanly."

In addition to her girls' school, she also started one for boys that included both Copts and Muslims. Interestingly enough, she found that students who had attended convent schools were not much ahead of her raw recruits because their learning was based solely on rote memorization.[62] Although Whately repeatedly emphasizes that her school catered to Muslims of the poorest classes, McCoan indicates that her clientele also included a minority from the middle class and higher. Furthermore, the religion and class of her clientele may also have changed over time, particularly as more options became available to Muslim parents. According to a letter from the Minister of Public Instruction in 1880, her school was devoted to "the Coptic and Levantine population."[63]

Whately could not operate alone. Initially, she had little knowledge of Arabic, and thus, it was necessary to secure the aid of the Syrian Christian neighbor and her mother.

In fact, one has to wonder about how much (or how little) her early pupils learned. Whately described herself and an early teacher as "Sanford and Merton," one lame and one blind, since she lacked linguistic skills and her assistant lacked experience. As time passed she had other such instructors of varying degrees of quality, but ultimately her best assistants were her own students. She attempted to install the girls as quickly as possible in positions of responsibility, owing to the problem of early marriage. She viewed using her pupils as preferable to recruiting English teachers who lacked the language skills and necessitated transplantation far from their homes. Egyptian girls, on the other hand, were "not first-rate instructors," but "with careful supervision," could surpass English teachers because of their knowledge of the people, language, and customs.[64]

The most important aspect of Whately's curriculum at both her girls' and boys' schools, was "the word of God," viewing foreign languages, geography, history, and accounts as unnecessary frills.[65] The main inducement for girls (and their mothers) to attend school, was needlework. Apparently, her operation roused anger amongst indigenous teachers, who periodically raided her school to regain clients. Just as the *mu^{c}allima* could raid the Bible class, so too could missionaries raid indigenous sewing schools. A pamphlet from the American Mission discusses the visit of a female missionary to "a little Moslem sewing school" where students eagerly listened to the story of Mary.[66]

Whately competed with indigenous teachers for both students and government funding. Since the time of Muhammad Ali, the government had a growing interest in dealing with the poor. Of particular concern were the "deserving poor," among whom were orphans and poor children, who, if properly educated, would become productive citizens rather than beggars.[67] Whately had received government support in the form of land, housing, and subventions since the time of Ismail; however, she had to petition for these funds, invest her own money, and solicit contributions from English travelers.[68] Even smaller, indigenous operations could also hope to claim government attention. A woman, Sitt Zahra, requested funds from the government for her Eastern School [*al-madrasa al-sharqiyya*], in which she taught Egyptian girls [*lil-binat al-muwaṭaniyyat*] reading, writing, and needlework. Her students included orphans, whom she instructed without compensation.[69] Sitt Zahra expanded her curriculum beyond the scope of the traditional sewing teacher, who merely taught the trade. With the spread of the sewing machine and ready-made clothing, many women fiercely guarded these skills, and they actively sought to attract and maintain students for their livelihood. Earlier in the century, women involved in dressmaking and embroidery were not affected by the growth of European imports, and these professions remained lucrative.[70] However, by the 1890s and the spread of new stores, such skills were beginning to be threatened. Learning handiwork alone would no longer suffice.

In the last quarter of the nineteenth century, a number of women, Egyptian and foreign, started small schools for girls. Syrian and Coptic women were active in the Faggala neighborhood of Cairo, as well as in other cities, such as Tanta, Mansura, Fayum, and Minya. The schools differed in curriculum; however, the staple was basic Arabic literacy and handiwork, with many also offering French and music.[71]

Whately was just one woman with a single school for girls and one for boys. In contrast, the American Mission brought numerous missionaries and established many long-lasting institutions of learning. By 1850 Protestant groups in the United States in general, and Presbyterians in particular, came to see the importance of women both as missionaries and as targets of mission. In the words of a female missionary: "The whole world was going to learn that a nation can be lifted no higher than its women will permit. . . . the citadel of heathendom was in the heathen home, and that citadel could be taken only by the assault of women," achieved by the education of girls.[72] While there was little success on the conversion front, there was more in the areas of education and welfare.[73] The Americans firmly believed in the use of women to institute social change.[74] Women trained in mission schools were expected to carry out positions of education and leadership in their homes and communities.[75] In the words of Patricia Hill, the movement was a form of "cultural imperialism that aimed at transforming the non-Western world and its symbolic relationship with changing cultural paradigms of ideal womanhood in America." The mission allowed women not only to spread Western standards, but also to stretch and confront those standards.[76]

Women like Helen Montgomery justified their role by drawing distinctions between themselves and the women of the Orient, who suffered wrongs "buttressed behind sanctions of religion." While overlooking verses that demonstrate the equality of believers, Montgomery uses Sura IV:34, to demonstrate the inherent inequality of Islam. She then initiates a tirade against polygamy and divorce, quoting from both Qasim Amin and Lord Cromer, as was common among Women's Board publications.[77] Ironically, as Western divorce rates increased and Egyptian ones decreased, divorce as a marker of flawed family life has been removed from Western discourse, while polemics about the veil continue to this day.[78]

Women's missionary work was dual pronged. First, there was "harem work," which involved seeking out women in their homes to spread the gospel; and second, there was the creation of a network of girls' schools. Life for female missionaries in Egypt was not easy. They had neither the means nor the inclination to live the ritzy hotel life described in chapter 3. Accounts of the early missions indicate that many missionary women died or left the country ill. Nevertheless, even the blind could be engaged in harem work, reading from the scriptures, conversing, and praying with the "inmates of the home." Female missionaries enjoyed these visits despite the large cultural difference that existed between them and their hosts.[79]

Female missionaries provided a link between the harem work, the mission of the schools, and the condition of Egyptian homes. They hoped that the skills their students learned in school would be applied in their homes and in the lives of their families, and teachers took great pride in their achievements. The creation of the proper home would be the first step in their students' (and subsequently their families') advancement toward "proper" Christianity. As photography became more accessible to the amateur, the missionaries used pictures to record these successes.[80]

Female missionaries carried an extra burden. Virtually all women, nurses and doctors excepted, were teachers, whereas male missionaries had a variety of functions. Furthermore, the girls' schools attracted more students and received more attention. Boys had greater options, in terms of both government schools, which provided passports to government employment, and more schools established under the auspices of the Coptic church. The curriculum in the girls' schools necessitated greater contact between teachers and their students outside the classroom due to its emphasis on moral training and home economics. In contrast, male teachers viewed these activities as beyond the scope of their duties. This linkage made female teachers more active in the lives of their students and contributed greatly to the success of the schools. Finally, as previously discussed, the missionaries believed that by reaching women, they were reaching families and future generations. Dor Bey's visit to the schools seems to substantiate a significant difference in quality between the girls' and boys' schools. He found the latter unacceptable in terms of both staff and curriculum. The girls' schools, on the other hand, were in general both better organized and better suited to the needs of the population with regard to curriculum.[81]

The work of the Americans began during the reign of Said. He granted them property and a building in Muski in 1854. Within two years of their arrival, they opened a training school for girls, two girls' primary schools, and a primary school for boys in the capital. Within another year they opened schools in Alexandria and Fayum. In 1861, they benefited from the departure of the CMS, taking over its boarding school for girls in Azbakiyya. Similarly, in Alexandria, they took advantage of the departing Scottish Mission, taking over its girls' school.[82]

The American Mission continued to thrive under Ismail. During his reign, the Americans opened 36 schools, about one-third of which were girls' schools or coeducational facilities. They spread their base of operations in the delta and moved into upper Egypt. In Cairo, they were forced to give up their Muski location in order to make way for Ismail's municipal developments. Not lacking in generosity, however, the Khedive offered a new spot in Azbakiyya, along with a donation of £7,000, to build a new facility.[83]

These early American Mission schools ranged in quality and in the number and religion of the students. The premier school was the new Azbakiyya location, which could house over 150 students, in addition to the Cairo missionary staff and their families. At the other end of the spectrum, the girls' school in Mansura was no more than a room in a missionary's home overseen by his wife and an assistant. Some of the schools were almost entirely Coptic, while others had significant Muslim minorities. Some of the schools were merely day schools or training centers, while others were more intensive programs with boarders. The missionaries felt that they could make significant inroads at indoctrination by keeping the children at school, and they often complained about intrusive parents whose "frequent visits and untidy habits retarded the good work of training their children."[84] Another incentive for boarding schools, particularly in upper Egypt, was the opportunity to reach girls who lived in remote areas. McCoan reports that nearly all of these schools were free; however, records of the missionaries indicate that they collected over $500 per year in tuition between 1870–75, and by 1880, the figure catapulted to $3,225. It appears that over time the missionaries may have instituted a sliding pay scale at their schools.[85] Over the course of the period under study, the American Mission continued to flourish in both the delta and upper Egypt. By the turn of the century, there were 119 schools serving some 8,000 students, and within another two decades there were 2,000 students in Cairo alone, with schools established in 175 villages. Although Copts formed the majority of the student population, there was always a significant minority of Muslims.[86]

The curriculum varied from school to school and developed over time. The earliest girls' school limited its curriculum to reading, writing, arithmetic, and needlework. Similarly, the first girls' school in any given location was likely to follow this basic formula. Missionaries themselves frequently started small schools that taught only basic literacy, and Egyptians associated with the church also initiated such schools. By the turn of the century, more formal instruction was given in mission schools offering three, five, seven, nine, and eleven year courses of study, in addition to the Cairo Girls' College that offered three years of higher education. Home economics became a core part of the curriculum, encouraged and supported by the community. For example, the director of girls' school in Faggala sought to equip a room to "meet the need for home training"; and with the help of an Egyptian pastor, the congregation provided the furnishings. Practicality was an important factor given that the overwhelming majority of girls never completed more than three years of study. By the early twentieth century, the curriculum included Arabic reading and writing; English reading, writing, and conversation; object lessons; arithmetic; hygiene; and Bible Studies. Students who advanced beyond the "beginner's level" also studied geography, home economics, drawing, teacher training, and ethics. The most advanced schools in Cairo, Alexandria, and Assiut offered music, French, and art.[87] Writing in 1910, one female missionary even went so far as to claim that the curriculum in mission schools was more progressive than that which was available in the United States.[88]

For parents seeking to give their daughters a Western education, music, painting, languages, and home economics were particularly important, even at schools where music lessons boosted the tuition price by thirty percent. For missionaries, teacher-training was an important aspect of the curriculum. As we have seen, at both government and private schools, the shortage of trained female teachers made the use of older students a necessity; and this necessity had to be utilized before the student married. Furthermore, the missionary women were often in charge of more students than they could adequately supervise, and thus they used older pupils to supervise younger ones. What started as an *ad hoc* program of "pupil teacher" training ultimately turned into more formal teacher training programs and kindergartens. At the same time journals, such as *al-muqtaṭaf* and *al-hilal*, were running stories about the importance of the kindergarten movement in developing children's minds and bodies.[89]

The rapid spread of the American Mission created a huge response in terms of other missions, the foreign and minority communities, and the Muslim majority. In effect, it served to improve education in Egypt both quantitatively and qualitatively. The Catholic orders that had been content servicing the Catholic community and providing some small-scale indigenous programs now worked harder to reach Egyptian Copts, particularly after the arrival of the Jesuits in 1879. They also moved beyond the major cities of the delta and into upper Egypt.[90]

The Coptic community, which formed the backbone of the student and native-teacher population, had an ambivalent relationship with the American Mission. On the one hand, thousands of Copts benefited from the mission schools; and on the other, certain elements of the church hierarchy found it difficult to watch another group encroach upon their territory. The Copts developed a number of schools with the help of the American Mission. Some of them received financial and managerial assistance, while others depended on the mission only for teachers and curriculum materials. These activities began as early as the 1860s, and by 1896 the number of schools directly or indirectly associated with the American Mission numbered 168, of which 35 were for girls and 133, for boys. At the same time, some Coptic priests grew suspicious of the Mission's work in Cairo. According to Andrew Watson, an early missionary, as female attendance at schools and meetings grew in 1863–64, priests threatened not to carry out their traditional role of helping to arrange marriages. In 1867 the Coptic Patriarch issued a patriarchal bull in reference to the new school for girls in Assiut, warning parents to "deliver them not into the hands of those ravenous ones who cause them to drink cups of wickedness instead of morality."[91] By 1868, the Coptic community of Assiut endowed its own school for girls. Meanwhile, in response to the girls' schools in Cairo, the Coptic community opened schools in Harat al-Saqqain and in Azbakiyya, raiding the American Mission for teachers. Due to the large-scale inability of missionary teachers to teach Arabic, the schools relied heavily on the Coptic community for teachers. The curriculum at the Coptic schools for girls contained the usual staples: Arabic, mathematics, and needlework. Dor Bey was extremely impressed by the work done by the Copts with respect to female education.[92]

Just as the activities of the American Mission spurred the Coptic community into action, the work of the Scottish Mission and the CMJ served to stimulate the efforts of the Jewish community. Among the Jews of Egypt there was a long-standing tradition of education, the premier career track being medicine. Schools and informal circles of learning had long been associated with synagogues. As well, Jews were involved in urban professions—banking, commerce, and metal work—all of which necessitated some type of education or apprenticeship.[93] Sources on the education of girls are lacking, but it would appear that their education was similar to the Muslim and Coptic communities, that is, it was more informal and limited to the upper classes.

By the mid-nineteenth century, as education became more significant among urban professionals, the Jewish community and European Jewish sponsors actively sought to advance education among both boys and girls. Adolphe Crémieux, a Jewish political activist who visited Egypt in the 1840s, helped to sponsor schools with a new curriculum for Jewish children: Judaic Studies, Hebrew, Arabic, French, and mathematics. Girls would study the same subjects as boys, although they would also learn needlework in exchange for a little bit less of everything else. Nevertheless, these schools suffered from financial problems, cholera, and a general opposition to the innovations that they provided. The two schools closed in 1842.

It was nearly 20 years before another school for Jewish girls opened. In 1860, sponsors in France created the *Alliance Israélite* to sponsor the education of Jewish boys and girls in Egypt. As in the other Jewish schools, language played a prominent role in the curriculum including French, English, Hebrew, and Arabic, as well as Egyptian history and geography. Girls received additional instruction in handiwork. The founding of the Jewish school for girls was motivated by concerns that their daughters were being Christianized in the school formerly run by the Scottish Mission and taken over by the Americans. By 1876, there was only a handful of Jewish schools in Cairo and Alexandria. There were not nearly enough to service the education-oriented Jewish community.[94] Like the Coptic community, it sought to sponsor more primary and elementary schools from the 1860s onward, in response to the missionaries and the growing numbers of foreign schools.

The Greeks formed another significant minority group in Egypt. Prior to the nineteenth century, the community was small, sponsoring a few schools associated with churches and monasteries in Cairo and Alexandria. As discussed in chapter 3, large numbers of Greeks came to Egypt during the reign of Said to take advantage of the Capitulations. As the community grew, so too did the number of schools as the Greeks sought to retain their heritage through a classical curriculum. The Greek community followed contemporary trends and developed their schools in a fashion similar to the Coptic community. The Greeks resided mainly in Cairo and Alexandria, the latter community being wealthier and hence more active in establishing schools, churches, and hospitals. By the reign of Said, the Greek communities of both Cairo and Alexandria had taken up the torch of girls' education, although the Cairo community lacked Alexandria's financial wherewithal. Under Ismail the schools continued to thrive, and Dor Bey gave favorable reports to both the boys' and girls' schools in Cairo and Alexandria. These schools offered Greek, French, Arabic, arithmetic, geography, and history, in addition to needlework and music for girls. Although the schools were founded with the goal of preserving Greek culture, they were open to the non-Greek community.[95]

Egypt's other minority communities included the Italians, Germans, and Armenians. Italian and German Catholics took advantage of the Franciscan and other Catholic schools. By the turn of the century there were some Italian, German, and Armenian schools for boys in Cairo and Alexandria, and the Germans and Armenians had opened schools for girls. Since these communities were much smaller, it was more difficult to establish community schools for girls.[96]

The spread of the American Mission, as well as growing competition from government schools, profoundly influenced all of the foreign and minority communities in Egypt. In turn, the government watched the growth of foreign schools with a cautious eye.[97] Government schools for boys always had the advantage serving as a stepping stone to public service. The growing number of positions in foreign and indigenous mercantile establishments meant jobs for men with the linguistic skills provided by the Europeanized government schools and the prestigious foreign schools.[98] Missionary schools fared much better among middle- and upper-class girls because the incentive was based more purely on the curriculum and standards in the schools. While early missionary efforts aimed at reaching Egyptians of the lower classes through a curriculum that included needlework, by the turn of the century, many of these schools attracted girls of the upper classes with a curriculum aimed at creating refined mother-educators. Meanwhile the government could meet neither the growing demand for girls' education nor the specific needs of the population in terms of curriculum. With the arrival of the British and the rise of the nationalist and women's presses, the debate over which women should be educated and what the curriculum should encompass gained both energy and depth.

The British Occupation and Female Education

The British revamped the educational system by limiting access to education, increasing fees and the number of people paying them, changing the composition of the student body, and changing the curriculum within the schools.[99] The imprint of the British was most clearly laid by its first High Commissioner (1883), Lord Cromer (Sir Evelyn Baring), who had first come to Egypt as Commissioner of the *Caisse de la Dette Publique* (1877–79) and later as Controller (1879) during the reign of Ismail. Cromer's previous experience in colonial administration was in assisting his cousin Lord Northbrook, who was appointed viceroy of India in 1872. It was in India that he developed his opinions regarding subject races, "White Man's Burden," and the like.[100]

Cromer's feelings with respect to Egyptian education were shaped by the fact that his family owned a significant portion of the Egyptian debt and what he viewed as "mistakes" made by the British in India. Returning Egypt's finances to order was always his foremost concern in all facets of administration. With respect to education, he was afraid of creating a westernized elite that would be critical of the British occupation.[101] Nevertheless, he could not ignore the educational views of Lord Macaulay, the architect of India's educational system:

> . . . To trade with civilized men is infinitely more profitable than to govern savages that would, indeed, be a doting wisdom which in order that India might remain a dependency would make it a useless and costly dependency which would keep a hundred million men from being our customers in order that they might continue to be our slaves.[102]

Thus, his approach was a two-tiered system aimed at promoting literacy among the masses and providing for a small corps of individuals "suitable for the requirements of government service."[103]

As for the latter goal, the British placed their own officials and other suitable foreigners in the highest ranking positions; however, they sought an increasingly educated class of Egyptians to fill the lower ranks, as well as the liberal professions. The easiest way to carry out this aspect of the program was to raise fees in primary schools, limiting access to the higher track of education, and simultaneously working toward the necessity of a secondary certificate for public service. The class-conscious British, in alliance with the Egyptian ruling elite, believed in limiting the higher track to children of the upper classes. In their view, raising fees at the primary schools served to "raise the moral standard" by not admitting "children of the class which sends its children to elementary schools" who would "harm their peers." Second, they hoped to raise the standards in the upper division of the higher primary schools such that candidates who did not seek secondary education would be better prepared for government service and more students would seek the secondary certificate.[104] Ultimately, the British phased out the primary certificate examination as a passport to public service, replacing it in 1907 with a civil service examination and later eliminating it entirely.[105] There was even support amongst some sectors of the population for such restrictions, with arguments centering upon the fact that the diffusion of education would make the masses lose their desire for manual labor and would water down the level of the government schools.[106]

The British justified raising fees in the primary schools by insisting that the increased revenues would go toward the funding of elementary schools, which provided basic vernacular education.[107] Furthermore, Cromer believed that fees were "one of the surest tests of the popularity of education." In his *Annual Report*, he boasted that the number of paying students climbed from 5 percent in 1879 to 86 percent in 1898.[108] He maintained that such a system was not "reactionary," but rather, an improvement that would help the masses gain an education "of a more truly national and popular character." Moreover, he stated that free spots had been monopolized by "the rich and powerful," while many needy pupils had been forced to pay fees, bringing down the level of the government schools. Despite the increase in fees, the numbers of students continued to rise.[109]

Cromer's efforts allowed him to direct his energy toward bringing Egypt's finances back to solvency and expanding agricultural output, while still allowing a modest expansion of education without an increase in its budgetary allotment. After Saad Zaghlul took office as Minister of Public Instruction in late 1906, there were some steps taken to insure that students of exceptional ability and insufficient means could find positions in the better schools. There were also some adjustments made in the poorer regions of upper Egypt given the students' relative inability to pay. The government then channeled these funds to support the lower tier of the educational system: the elementary schools, vocational schools, and *kuttabs*. Cromer did not want to train more government employees, but rather he sought to "equip the pupil with sufficient knowledge to take care of his own station of life." Nevertheless, he expressed concern that the *kuttabs* would serve as asylums for young men seeking to avoid work or military service. Therefore, he established age limits for male students.[110]

The easiest method for building the lower tier of the educational system was for the government to gain control over the network of *kuttabs* and native elementary schools already in existence, in addition to offering greater opportunities for vocational and technical education. In 1888 the government removed native boys' and girls' elementary schools from the jurisdiction of the *waqf* administration and placed them under the Ministry of Public Instruction, in order to inexpensively expand basic education while also regularizing curriculum, instruction, and sanitary conditions within these schools. In 1898, the British began a program of providing such schools, which adhered to government standards, with subventions for support. In order to receive these funds, schools had to offer (Arabic) reading, writing, and arithmetic, in addition to religious instruction. Schools that offered a foreign language were not considered for support, and thus a number of Coptic *kuttabs* were ineligible for assistance. Many of the native elementary schools did not meet these standards. In 1904, of 124,000 students in such schools, 81,000 lacked instruction in writing, 70,000 in arithmetic, and 54,000 in reading. Nevertheless, by the following year, more than half of the 4,859 *kuttabs* under government inspection received grants.[111]

The British maintained that if Egyptians were truly concerned about education, then elites and communities would work together to sponsor more schools. The royal family had been taking an active lead in establishing free schools for the poor since the mid-nineteenth century.[112] A large number of indigenous societies, Muslim and non-Muslim, had also arisen in the last quarter of the nineteenth century.[113] In Cromer's *Annual Report* of 1905, he wrote that such societies existed in 11 different provinces and had created nearly 800 new *kuttabs* and repaired numerous others. In the same year, the government began a formalized program of land grants to societies and individuals for building schools. Within two years, the government had received some 555 applications, of which 457 had been granted, 86 refused, and 12 remained under consideration. A note to the Council of Ministers in 1909 listing the location and sponsors of a number of schools indicates that the Coptic community, as well as other foreign and minority groups, benefited from this and other such programs. Muslim societies and individuals were able to profit from the program as well, building schools for both boys and girls. Some provinces were extremely active in establishing schools. In Daqahliyya, the Society for the Amelioration of *Kuttabs* established *waqf* funds to maintain and construct some 268 schools, about half of which could accommodate 80–100 students. By 1908, some 1,692 *kuttabs* had been constructed or rebuilt under the auspices of this program. While the British firmly supported the efforts of private benevolent societies, there was always an underlying concern that the education be of a "suitable" nature, that is, in Arabic and limited to basic skills.[114]

Congruous with British desires to support private and local initiative, and given the more responsive attitude of Cromer's successor, Sir Eldon Gorst, the government sought to meet Egyptian demands for education with further programs. Influenced by the nationalist leadership of Saad Zaghlul in the Ministry of Public Instruction, Egyptians demanded a greater voice in education, increased government expenditure, and an education of a more national character. To meet the first of these demands, the British agreed to create provincial councils that would supervise all forms of vernacular education (*kuttabs*, agricultural schools, and technical schools). Seventy percent of the revenue provided to the provincial councils was to go toward building, maintaining, and improving the standards in *kuttabs* and elementary schools. The remainder of the money was to go toward agricultural and technical education, building new facilities, taking over existing ones, and/or subsidizing private schools.[115]

With respect to female education, traditional interpretations of British involvement (or lack thereof) seem to indicate that the British were attempting to avoid a cultural clash with the Egyptians.[116] Ironically, the British occupiers, like the missionaries, rationalized their role based on the lowly position of women in Egypt. Cromer wrote that veiling and seclusion "cramp[ed] the intellect and wither[ed] the mental development" of women in Muslim countries, while polygamy ravaged the moral-social fabric of society. He linked the advancement of women to the advancement of civilization. The "obvious remedy" for Cromer was the education of women, which he wrote ought to be undertaken with "vigour."[117] Nevertheless, the standard that Cromer hoped to apply in Egypt, the Victorian ideal of domesticity embodied in the mother-educator, was one that gave women a "serious—and quasi-political—purpose in life," while simultaneously blocking access to political life.[118] Indeed, in Britain, Cromer was an active opponent of women's suffrage. Thus, he endorsed a platform that would rationalize Britain's position as an occupier, while serving as an obstacle to the rising tide of feminism in Britain.[119]

Despite the lip service paid to the significance of female education, applications continued to exceed the number of positions available in the government schools for girls, even after the introduction of fees. The British preferred to depend on missionary efforts and private charitable enterprise to meet the rising demand for female education. While Cromer believed in the necessity of female education, he also felt that the process "ought to be slow."[120]

Although the British position was seemingly contradictory, their program for female education fit neatly within their two-tiered scheme. Despite the growing demand for primary and higher education, the British developed such schools only to the extent that they were needed to provide for positions in nursing, midwifery, and teaching. As for the masses, the British felt that girls in the provinces could attend *kuttabs* alongside boys. In order to encourage female attendance, they provided subventions on a per capita basis, with each girl being counted as two boys. Due to such efforts, girls entered *kuttabs* at a proportionally higher rate than boys. Additionally, the government supervised a number of *kuttabs* for girls. These schools, along with other government schools, were to serve as models for those established through private enterprise.[121]

Not surprisingly, the British paid little attention to the upper tier of the girls' educational system. First, they failed to acknowledge the important role played by the graduates of the School of Midwifery. Attendance at this school had always been free and sponsored by the state. In 1892, the British limited the number of free positions to six and began assessing fees. Previously, women had received a more stringent course of study and attained the same rank as male graduates of the medical school. Now women received only three years of training, half that of their male counterparts. Furthermore, their hours of study were less rigorous, and they lacked practical training. The program became more oriented toward producing nurses and conventional midwives. A small number of qualified candidates could continue their studies to become doctors. Abugideiri has referred to this process as the "colonization" of Egyptian medicine, which ultimately led to the creation of "an elite corps of urbanized, upper-class Egyptian males, fluent in English."[122]

The Siyufia school, the other branch of the upper tier, remained problematic for the government. Writing his annual report to the Khedive, Minister of Public Instruction Ali Mubarak wrote that reorganization of the school was "an absolute necessity." In 1889 the government removed the school from the jurisdiction of the *waqf* administration and placed it under the Ministry of Public Instruction. At that time its main purpose was as a school for domestic service. Since it was the only government primary school for girls, Mubarak felt that it was necessary to raise its standards. In order to demonstrate the extent of the changes in goal and curriculum, the ministry changed the name of the school from al-Siyufia to al-Sania. Furthermore, it introduced a system of fees into the school, such that external students would pay fees, and internal positions would remain free for the orphaned and indigent. Fathers (or guardians) of the students received letters explaining that the school was no longer being used to train domestic servants and that major changes would be made in personnel. These changes did not come quickly or easily. Mubarak's report indicates that the school continued to stress practical instruction for orphan and indigent girls. Girls from the upper class would receive this same practical, domestic training;

however, they would also receive a more "fully developed classical instruction," suitable for teacher-training. Additionally, the school contained a section for the blind and one for the deaf. Finally, there was a division to prepare girls for the School of Midwifery.[123]

Changing the name, governing authority, and personnel of the school did not clarify its mission any further; however, the school did run more smoothly and efficiently. Mrs. Yacub Sarruf, wife of the editor of *al-muqtaṭaf* and *al-muqaṭṭam*, visited the school in 1890 and was pleasantly surprised by what she encountered. She expected to find a small, wretched building with 20–30 students learning basic literacy and needlework. Instead, she found an immaculate building offering quality instruction to about 100 girls. She saw deaf girls learning craft skills, blind girls reciting the Quran, and other students studying mathematics. She was particularly impressed with the order and cleanliness of the school, as well as the fact that the girls produced their own clothing. Nevertheless, in the conclusion of her article, Mrs. Sarruf expressed her concern that daughters of the wealthy were learning certain domestic skills at the expense of more refined skills, which properly complete the education of young girls. Parents of the students shared such concerns, and they began to demand another school to address these problems. The government continued to study the problem, but took its time in finding a solution.[124]

The government put Yacub Artin in charge of studying the issue, and writing in 1892, he felt that the school still lacked a definitive goal. In his conclusion, Artin highlighted proposals for improving the education of young girls in Egypt. He felt that the Sania school ought to be closed and replaced with a smaller school, with only internal, non-paying students, who would later enter the School of Midwifery or the Normal School section of the new school. There would also be a small primary school attached to this school for external, paying students, who would be taught by students from the Normal School. Finally, he suggested the creation of another such primary school for girls attached to the Nasriah School.[125] In other words, he sought a more rigid demarcation between the departments of the school and expansion through teacher education programs. Nevertheless, Artin's report was slow to circulate through the proper channels. Seven years after the report was submitted to the Khedive, the Council of Ministers charged the Higher Council of Public Instruction to study the report in preparation for presentation to the Council of Ministers.[126]

Female education was not a high priority, and the government moved slowly to address its weaknesses. A second school for girls, the Abbas school, finally opened in 1895; and it helped somewhat in addressing the class concerns of parents. The new school would deal more exclusively with girls of the lower classes, while the Sania school could focus on middle- and upper-class girls. The curriculum at the two schools remained similar; however, the Sania school attracted better teachers. In fact, some teachers at the Abbas school lacked even a primary certificate.[127] Ten years after the opening of the Abbas school, a note from the Ministry of Public Instruction to the *majlis al-nuẓẓar*, indicated the distinction between the schools:

> Day by day, the Sania school for girls takes the form of a school intended for girls of the highest class among the people. Recently, it has moved to a magnificent building. Applications for admission exceed the number of positions currently available. Consequently, it appears necessary to choose the best students for this school. The [most] effective method [for doing so], without a doubt, would be to increase fees.... As for

> the people who cannot pay the aforementioned fees, they can send their daughters to the girls' division of the Abbas school, which follows the same program as the Sania School, but the fees remain the same.[128]

By the following year, all of the pupils at the Sania school, internal and external, were paying fees, while almost two-thirds of the female students at the Abbas school paid no fees. In his *Annual Report* for 1907, Cromer proudly indicated that the Sania school was representative of the changes in education, boasting that the number of students reached 265, and "every girl . . . is a paying pupil." Nevertheless, parents continued to demonstrate a concern for the education their daughters were receiving. They continued to request a more general education, without undue emphasis on teacher-training.[129]

Despite the continuous demand for expansion, extension, and improvement, the government was slow to respond. Even in the capitals of the provinces, primary schools for girls did not open until 1909. By 1922, a number of new government schools opened that offered parents a greater diversity of curriculum and expanded programs of study. In 1910, the government created a School of Practical Housewifery, in order to complete girls' education in domestic science. Girls coming to this school, and others following its model, were expected to be proficient in Arabic and mathematics. In other words, it was to serve as a "finishing school" for *kuttab* and elementary graduates. In 1916, the government created yet another class of schools for girls between the *kuttabs* and the primary schools called higher elementary schools. The higher elementary schools, like the *kuttabs*, stressed basic vernacular education but added an emphasis on domestic education, including needlework, cookery, laundry, ironing, and household administration. In 1920, the first secondary school for girls opened in Cairo. In the same year, a *lycée* for girls of the upper classes opened, and it radically changed the character of the Sania school. Now the school could be more effectively utilized as a training ground for the Sania Normal School, while most of the wealthier girls flocked to the new school.[130]

At the time that the Sania Normal School opened in 1900, no Egyptian woman had any formal training in teacher education. This new division of the Sania School served as the training ground for primary school teachers and administrators. Since only a few hundred girls attended primary schools, while thousands attended elementary schools, the need for elementary teachers was much greater. In 1903, the Bulaq Normal School opened to meet this ever-increasing demand. Strong prejudice still existed amongst middle- and upper-class Egyptians regarding their daughters entering the field of teaching. Nevertheless, after the opening of the two teacher-training colleges in Cairo, girls of the lower middle class began to enter the ranks of teaching in larger numbers. Under the leadership of Saad Zaghlul, the Ministry of Public Instruction encouraged greater Egyptian participation and expanded programs of female teacher training in the provinces. By 1919, 10 of the 14 provincial councils had established teachers' colleges for women. Nevertheless, the annual output of female teachers remained under 200 per year, while the need was estimated at 900. In 1907 the government also began a program of sending a small number of girls to England to complete their training in teacher education.[131]

The lack of indigenous, female teachers remained a perennial problem for the expansion of education. The profession of teaching, for males and females, never attained status in Egypt during the period under study. In fact, teachers did not even receive government pension benefits until 1880. In his study of educational and career choices of Egyptian students under the British occupation, Donald Reid notes that (male) students viewed the Teacher Training College as "a dead-end street." He points out that the low status of the job was accompanied by an equally low pay, which was actually cut during the inflationary years of World War I. The government made periodic efforts to improve conditions for teachers; however, when belt-tightening measures were needed, the educational system, in general, and teachers, in particular suffered. Educated males preferred to enter more financially and socially remunerative positions in other sectors of government service or in private enterprise. The *Annual Report* of the British Consul-General gave yearly witness to the shortage of teaching personnel, and as dire the need for male teachers, the need for female teachers was even greater. Despite the introduction of fees in all other areas of the upper track of the educational system, the government continued to offer free instruction to males and females pursuing a career in education. As an extra incentive, female students received free room and board, in addition to free tuition. Students at the Sania school with excellent attendance and superior conduct received an additional monthly allowance.[132]

The problem of finding qualified female teachers had been an issue since the establishment of the School of Midwifery. All institutions of learning grappled with the problem of finding qualified, female personnel. At both public and private schools for girls, conditions necessitated the employment of foreign females (Western and Levantine), as well as male teachers, particularly for some subjects, such as Arabic and religion. The existence of male teachers, and to a lesser degree foreign females, provided parents with a justification for prohibiting or limiting their daughters' education.[133]

Women of the upper class had the greatest flexibility regarding their education. They had the means to employ their own tutors, conduct literary salons in their homes, or to seek knowledge at the best private facilities available. When the Egyptian University was established in 1908, 31 women, of whom 3 were Egyptian, attended lectures with men at the new school. Nevertheless, the university did not open its doors to all women. The memoirs of Nabawiyya Musa poignantly demonstrate the difficulties facing women seeking higher education. She was told that there was no "special space prepared for women," and she was moved to write a letter to the director indicting Egyptian men for their failure in educating women despite their promises regarding its necessity. Perhaps the university made no accommodation for Muslim females. Regardless of its ambiguous entrance policies for women, the university solicited one journal edited by, contributed to, and written for women.[134]

Early in 1909, Huda Shaarawi helped to plan a special lecture series at the university for women, inviting French feminist Margarite Clement to speak. The initial lecture was so successful that the women turned it into a series held on Friday afternoons, when the university was not in session. Malak Hifni Nasif, an Egyptian writer, teacher, and feminist, contributed to this series. Among the issues that she addressed were the importance of education (religious, moral, and practical) for girls, women's rights, and the importance of not following the customs of the foreigners. European men also lectured in this series, which included discussions on education, health, and hygiene.[135]

By the fall of 1909, the university established a more formal program of study for women under the direction of Mlle. A. Couvreur from the *Lycée Racine* in Paris. According to Reid, the audience for Mlle. Couvreur's lecture series "could not have been more upper crust," including eight princesses, the wives of beys and pashas, Christian notables, and the wives and daughters of future prime ministers. Couvreur's lectures were in French, the language of the highest tier of society. Her course covered psychology, philosophy, education, and feminism. She requested authors for the library including Herbert Spencer, Gustav Le Bon, and Friedrich Nietzche. The university published two of her works: *La Femme aux Différentes Epoques de l'Histoire* and *Psychologie et Morale Féminines*. Couvreur's message of greater educational opportunity for women and the importance of women to the home, family, and nation rang true to her audience. Writing in the spring of 1911, Mlle. Couvreur informed the university secretary that the women were progressing well and were ready for studies of a more critical and analytical nature. During that academic year, Couvreur received some assistance from Labiba Hashim, a Syrian Christian writer with her own women's journal, *fatat al-sharq*. Hashim lectured in Arabic on the subject of education/upbringing [*al-tarbiya*]. A number of her speeches were reprinted in *al-muqtaṭaf*, as well as in her own journal. She opened her first lecture by explaining that "the life of a nation is its men and its women, and there are no men and women without sound bodies and high morals, both of which stem from a strong education." She went on to discuss the important role of both parents in providing the proper material and moral upbringing for their children.[136]

By 1911 greater facilities were made available to the women, and the program of study expanded to include lectures given in Arabic on history and home economics. Mlle. Couvreur continued to lecture on education and morals in French. The history course covered both ancient and modern history, including the significant changes in government, the most famous queens of Egypt, Egypt and the Islamic state, the influence of Islam on the customs of Egypt, the mamluk state, and the French invasion. The university hired Nabawiyya Musa to deliver these lectures. Ironically, history was one of Musa's worst subjects. She was the first Egyptian girl to sit for the secondary certificate examination, and she received only 11 points out of a possible 25 in history. Finally, the women's section included a course on home economics, discussing the history of the subject, finance, hygiene, home selection, married life/family happiness, and household manners/morals. This segment was to be taught by a prominent Syrian Christian, Mrs. Rahma Sarruf. The women also had the option of attending lectures in Semitic languages and in ancient history given by members of the university's regular teaching staff.[137]

Although there was support for the lecture series by the rector, Prince Fuad, as well as from the university's administrative council, the series was discontinued because of public opposition. The women's section lectures were held during morning hours and on Fridays to avoid conflict and overlap with male students. These scheduling efforts did not stop demonstrators, who forcefully prevented the women from entering the buildings. Furthermore, the university secretary, Abd al-Aziz Fahmy, received threatening mail. Although many secondary sources cite the fact that disturbances occurred, there is no information given on the make-up of the opposition. Baron indicates that male students were the source of the opposition, and that they materially benefited from the cancellation of the women's section for the 1912–13 academic year—three additional male students were sent on educational missions abroad. Meanwhile, it was not until 1928 that Egyptian women were formally admitted into the university.[138]

Conclusion

The strong public reaction to the women's section of the university was part and parcel of a strong public interest in education, in general, and women's education in particular. Over the course of the nineteenth century, the choices for girls' education dramatically expanded, and by 1900 they included a range of public and private facilities offering education from kindergarten to post-secondary. In 1800, aside from home-schooling, the best opportunity a girl might have was to study in a *kuttab*, up until she started showing the signs of physical maturity. With the growth of the centralizing state and boys' educational programs, girls' horizons slowly broadened as well. As we shall see in chapter 7, in many ways the discourse on female education in Egypt mirrored that of boys' education with concern for expansion, the evils of foreign education, and the importance of a "national" curriculum. As education became a desired commodity, the demand for schools increased, particularly the demand for higher-track schools. Nevertheless, debates regarding curriculum for girls divided along lines of gender and class.

Chapter 7

The Discourse on Female Education

Modern discussions of the necessity of female education in Egypt can be traced to the noteworthy efforts of Rifaat Rafia al-Tahtawi, who had traveled to France with an early educational mission during the time of Muhammad Ali. Rather than viewing him as a precocious anomoly, Peter Gran argues that he was a product of the religio-cultural-trading center of Tahta in upper Egypt, where Tahtawi studied subjects beyond those usually found in the *madrasa*. His ability to tutor while just a young student at Azhar lends credence to his bountiful early education. At al-Azhar, Tahtawi studied under Shaykh Hassan al-Attar, and once again his curriculum expanded beyond the norm encompassing history, literature, and geography. Rather than viewing his tenure in France between 1826 and 1831 as a complete departure from his past, we should view it as an expansion and continuation.[1]

His writings on the education of girls represent both his upbringing and early education, as well as his experience in France. In *murshid al-amin lil-binat wal-banin* [1872], Tahtawi begins with traditional argumentation that the education of girls does not violate religious convention. He demonstrates this point by discussing early exemplars of female learning and the encouragement of learning in the Quran and *ḥadith*. Thus, his first concern was to demonstrate the congruity of girls' education with Islam and to silence any traditionalist opposition. He then tries to counter those who might argue on scientific grounds that women should not be educated, contending that women are as capable of learning as men, despite some biological differences. Furthermore, he argues that the benefits derived from female education outweigh any disadvantages, by pointing out the evils of laziness and the importance of education for a harmonious marriage. Consequently, an improved family life would stem from a more harmonious marriage. Based upon this rationale, Tahtawi believes that boys and girls should receive an equal (primary) education. He does point out that most women are not suited for the study of government administration; however, he also cites historical examples of great female rulers in the East and the West. Finally, he concludes that an improvement in the lives of men, women, and families would necessarily lead to reform of the nation [*al-waṭan*]. In other words, as Qasim Amin would be a quarter century later, Tahtawi was a proponent of developmental idealism. At the same time that Tahtawi was writing about these subjects, Ottoman thinkers as well underscored the important role played by women in the home and the need to inculcate children with sound morals and patriotism.[2]

Advocates of female education writing in the years after Tahtawi advanced few new arguments, rather, they recast his arguments with varying degrees of emphasis and offering new details on different aspects.[3] The most novel arguments dealt with the appropriate curriculum for girls' schools. Among the first to write were the Syrian Christians in *al-muqtaṭaf* and *al-hilal*, beginning in the 1880s. A series of female-penned articles appearing in the *bab tadbir al-manzil* section of *al-muqtaṭaf* in 1884 demonstrate the concern of this community for the education of their daughters. The first author in the series, Mrs. Salma Tanus, argued

> The woman is . . . the one who binds society together, and were she not mannered, moral, and of delicate character, then society would waste away . . . . They [women] are the mistresses of families and homes, undertaking their administration and organization . . . Thus, women are the foundation of civilization . . . . They must be educated in the sciences . . . but their education regarding housework and the needs of the family must not be overlooked.

She goes on to liken the woman without education to the professional man without vocational education. One noteworthy aspect of Mrs. Tanus's arguments is that girls' education must include a balance of scholarly education and practical education in home economics, in addition to knowledge of a craft or skill.[4]

Mrs. Maryam Jurji Ilyan read Mrs. Tanus's article, and she felt compelled to continue writing upon the subject. She discusses similarities and differences between men and women to demonstrate the need for female education; and she points to the example of great female rulers in the West. The thrust of her argument, as is the case in most of this discourse, is that women are responsible for their children and their homes, and "without good homes civilization does not exist." Mrs. Ilyan concludes that the woman must receive an education equal to that of the man, because she "is the foundation and pillar of the country's success."[5] Yet another woman, Mrs. Shams Shahadi read Mrs. Ilyan's article, and she too participated in the discourse. Mrs. Shahadi did not differ radically from either of the previous writers, again emphasizing the mother-educator role of the woman. The distinguishing feature of her article was that she addressed herself to other women, in particular, and emphasized their role in improving their own condition. She called upon her sisters to discuss women's issues rather than the trivial topics of food, clothing, and new stores.[6]

These articles are interesting because they are representative of the genre that would follow for the next 40 years. There are numerous discussions of the differences between men and women; women's complementary equality with men and their ability to learn; the importance of the woman's role as wife, mother, and household administrator; historic and religious exemplars of female learning; the hinging of societal reform upon reform of the woman, the home, and the family; and what specifically female education should entail. Although the women contributing to *al-muqtaṭaf* in 1884 were discussing the situation in Syria and the Syrian community in Egypt, more writers began to address the conditions in Egypt specifically by the following decade. The arrival of the British in 1882 encouraged further debate. While the British rationalized the occupation of Egypt based upon the lowly position of its women, they also cut back on government spending.[7] As the British anglicized the curriculum and the language of instruction in all schools, the notion of a "national" curriculum emerged, with respect to religion, language, and history.[8] We must first look at this larger current in the discourse on education before examining that which specifically deals with girls.

Many Egyptians preferred to send their sons to government schools to avoid the influence of foreigners; however, the more significant factors were their high standards, instruction in a foreign language, and thus greater opportunities for employment. Students in these schools often learned European languages outside the language classroom. Certain subjects, such as math and drawing, were frequently taught by foreigners, given the shortage of native teachers. Egyptians began to demand more instruction in their native tongue. Prior to the occupation, most Egyptian boys in primary school studied French as a foreign language.[9] Although the British repeatedly claimed that Egyptians were free to select a foreign language, more and more students studied English due to the possibility for government service and the reality of administrative control by the British. Nevertheless, they were not successful in overtaking was the law school, which remained a nerve center for anti-British propaganda.[10]

The Egyptian push for Arabic instruction came shortly after the turn of the century, around the time that Saad Zaghlul became Minister of Public Instruction in late 1906. This effort was part of a larger effort to nationalize the curriculum, with greater emphasis on Arabic, religion, and national history. The battle to nationalize the curricula manifested itself in a struggle against Douglas Dunlop, the much-hated and frequently lampooned British advisor to the Ministry of Public Instruction. The only person who appears to have a kind word for Dunlop is Cromer, who chose his hard-working and irascible tennis partner to implement his educational policies. Cromer gave him the title advisor for public education; and Dunlop, who had first come to Egypt as a missionary/teacher, held this post for nearly 20 years. Despite some 30 years of service in Egypt, Dunlop allegedly never learned a word of Arabic. Furthermore, he mistrusted colleagues who did learn the language, favoring those who did not.[11]

A 1908 article in *al-tarbiya*, a children's magazine edited by the staff of *al-liwa'*, nicely summarized Egyptian objections to Dunlop. First, it contended that Dunlop shunned the study of French, because he believed that it would encourage nationalism among the Egyptians. Instead, he endorsed English language instruction in hopes that it would reinforce the occupation. The article then asserted that Dunlop viewed Arabic as an even greater "messenger of nationalism," thus he "suffocated" its use in the public schools. Similarly, the article accused him of curtailing religious education, as well as pharaonic and Islamic history, in an effort to weaken the students' love of their homeland.[12]

As discussed in chapter 6, Eldon Gorst began working with Saad Zaghlul to address some of these concerns in 1907. Gorst was a younger, more open-minded individual than Cromer, who was prone to moodiness and tantrums. From the memoirs of Abbas Hilmi II, we learn that Gorst's father had been Minister of Public Education in England and that he frequently traveled with his family to Egypt for the season. In addition to vacation time spent in Egypt, Gorst also served in the Ministry of Finance and the Ministry of the Interior before replacing Cromer. Thus, he was in Egypt during the

Dinshawai incident and felt that amends ought to be made. For all of these reasons, Gorst was more amenable than Cromer to the demands of Saad Zaghlul.[13]

The first order of business was to teach more subjects in Arabic. In primary schools, all subjects, except English, would be taught in Arabic. In secondary schools, most subjects would be taught in Arabic; however, some instruction would remain in English given the shortage of native teachers.[14] Second, students would be able to respond to the secondary school examination questions in Arabic, as long as the subject had been taught in Arabic. Finally, for primary students, classroom hours in religion increased by 30 percent. This new allotment not only provided more time for religious and moral instruction, it also served to reinforce the study of the Arabic language and Islamic history. Christians and Jews would be separated from their Muslim classmates for such lessons. To better accommodate the new arrangement, religion class would be held at the end of the day so that non-Muslim students could leave if no provision was made for their instruction.[15] Thus, there was some effort to meet Egyptian demands for boys' education. Nevertheless, the changes were slow in implementation. Three years later, at the Egyptian National Congress in Brussels, the delegate speaking on education complained that Egyptian children were "ignorant of their own language" and that the curriculum in the primary schools "disregard[ed] the study of national history."[16]

The demands for a greater voice in education, reduced fees, increased expenditure for education, and a "national" curriculum continued through the 1919 revolutionary period. After independence in 1922, politicians could no longer blame the British for these problems, and they became the new targets. A cartoon from *al-laṭa'if al-muṣawwara* from August of 1922 demonstrates continuing Egyptian concerns (figure 7.1). On one side of the picture lies the "shore of light and knowledge,"

Figure 7.1 From the shore of ignorance to the shore of knowledge
Source: *al-laṭa'if al-muṣawwara.*

and on the other, that of "ignorance and darkness." A member of the elite, labeled "administrators of Egyptian schools," is about to launch a boat from the shore of ignorance, across the river, to the shore of knowledge. The boat, labeled "Egyptian schools," is filled with "the [male] children of the wealthy" and sacks of money. The "children of the poor," including one girl, remain on the shore of ignorance, while an *effendi* begs the boatswain to carry these children across for a reasonable fare. The man responds, "A reasonable fare, [that] was ages ago, as for now, so long (peace be upon you)."[17] According to Salmoni, the curriculum between 1923 and 1952 "did not evince . . . an early conscious commitment to social and political change."[18] Even Saad Zaghlul, known for his advanced views on education had this to say in response to a 1926 proposal to increase the number of free positions in government schools: "All rich and poor are Egyptians equal in rights, and the rich may be stronger and more able to make use of education."[19]

The discourse on female education reflected a concern for these same issues, which affected women to a greater extent, given foreign domination over female education. Alexandra de Avierino, a Syrian in Egypt, used her magazine, *anis al-jalis*, as an early forum for this discussion, and as mentioned in chapter 5 sometimes used household organization as an entrance into the subject. In addition to calling for the education of women and chronicling its development, she took time to praise those men who advanced this cause, pointing out their importance in helping women achieve their role as "a partner in service to the nation." She published her own articles, as well as those from other male and female authors. Most of the contributors were in agreement that "the woman is the first and best school" for the child, that women need education for the sake of the family, and that this education had important implications for the future of the nation.[20] Other contributors to the women's press followed the strong lead of Avierino and the aforementioned women contributing to *al-muqtaṭaf*.[21]

Since girls were less likely to attend government schools and there were such shortages of female Egyptian teachers, the fear of "foreign-ness" predominated the discourse in the press. While boys too might be at risk, some men went so far as to argue that women were at even greater risk since they were more "susceptible" to succumbing to the moral standards of foreigners.[22] Their predominance in foreign and mission schools made them even weaker in Arabic than their male counterparts. Men, in particular, seemed to fear that their daughters would become completely Europeanized because of their foreign language instruction.[23] One man, writing in 1901, vehemently insisted that "[t]he Arabic language must be taught to the girl before any foreign languages, for it is the language of her mother, her father, her ancestors, her husband, and her country."[24] Women too expressed concerns over the evils of foreign education. One mother indicted all Egyptian schools, complaining that foreign schools "lure the women of this country" into abandoning their language, clothing, and customs, and that the government and native schools blindly follow the programs of the foreign schools.[25]

Even after the reforms of 1907, public schools for girls were slow to Arabize the curriculum due to the shortage of Egyptian teachers for all subjects.[26] The press targeted Dunlop as the source of the problem. An article, supposedly written by a female student, critiqued Dunlop's view of Arabic. During a visit to the author's school, Dunlop asks the girl what language she prefers, to which she responds, "Arabic, because it is the language of the noble Quran and the beloved national language."[27] Similarly, the public discourse displayed concern for girls studying "national" religion and history, rather than that of the foreigners. Both Muslims and Christians generated an especially great concern over their daughters' instruction in religion and morals.[28]

Although the content did not differ radically, the first two decades of the twentieth century witnessed a quantitative increase in the number of people writing about women's education. There were greater discussions about the curricula in girls' schools and which girls should be educated, as well as more nationalist calls for education. Up until World War I, Syrian Christians, who dominated the Egyptian press, were more likely to speak in terms of the Arab nation, the Ottoman State, the East, or the community.[29] Egyptians took great pride in being part of the East, even in the period following independence.[30] As increasing numbers of Egyptians contributed to this discourse, writers began to speak more about the importance of female education for "the" nation [*al-waṭan*], as opposed to *al-bilad, al-umma*, or *al-awṭan*. By the first decade of the twentieth century several Egyptian newspapers appeared: *al-mu'ayyad* (1889), *al-liwa'* (1900), and *al-jarida* (1907). These and other Egyptian publications began to contribute to the growing discourse on girls' education. The magazine *al-tarbiya* specifically encouraged girls' education. The cover prominantly displayed sketches of a young girl studying, alongside those of schoolboys playing and reading. Furthermore, it contained a special section just for girls, which was later renamed the girls' and women's section. Articles in this department lamented the pitiful condition of female education, highlighted its importance, and linked it to the progress of the nation:

> The education of girls is among the most important necessities because they will sit at the throne of a kingdom, which despite its small size, has an extremely important position . . .
>
> . . . There is no way for nations to advance or uplift themselves, except with the education of girls and the cultivation of their minds.[31]

The discourse on female education frequently made references to and comparisons with the West. The writers of *al-tarbiya* were quick to point out that "the Egyptian girl is capable of being educated and civilized like the Western woman, when she is provided with the means."[32]

The nationalist press tried to find new ways to advance the cause of universal education, in general, and female education, in particular. Another article in *al-tarbiya* masqueraded as a complaint against forcing girls at the Sania school to "lick their plates clean." The author begins by discussing the reprehensible policy of forced eating, which he claims leads to health problems and compels the student to take measures such as hiding her food inside bread. Punishments for such infractions were severe, with offenders being locked inside dark bathrooms. The author concludes by calling upon the Chief Medical Officer to look into the complaint, the principal to end the policy, and the Minister of Education to call for "compulsory education instead of compulsory food," thus revealing the true agenda of the article.[33]

Similarly, an article in *al-mu'ayyad* asks who is more worthy of education, fathers and mothers or sons and daughters, in order to highlight the dismal state of education amongst all sectors of the population. The author ponders whether parents need it first because they raise children, or whether children need it first because of their future role. Not surprisingly, the author concludes that neither generation (nor gender) can be ignored.[34] An even more inventive article proclaims that "he who educates the girl closes the prison." The author asks, "what can the poor husband do with an ignorant wife, who does not answer any question he asks, except with words [that hit] like stones or with greater force?" He points out that the husband has no choice but to remove her from the home, leaving him with no one to do his housework. The author asserts that this turn of events will lead the wife to court, where she will seek maintenance [*al-nafaqa*] from her hapless husband, who will then be "strangled at the neck" by the ruling. He will be forced into poverty; and when he is unable to make payments, his ignorant wife will cause him to lose his freedom in prison. Finally, the author traces the source of the problem to the lack of female education.[35] Although the argument is creatively cast, the story is familiar. Uneducated women create inharmonious marriages, which in turn have greater implications for society.

All the participants in the discourse seem to be in agreement that there was a need for some form of female education, upon which society as a whole depended. In no article could I find anyone rejecting the notion of female education outright. Men and women, Muslims, Christians, and Jews all supported education for their daughters. This is not to say that there were no Egyptians who objected; but rather, those who did object did not or were not able to participate in the discourse taking place in the press.[36]

According to Rashid Rida, there were conservative *azhari* *ᶜulama'* who cited questionable *ḥadith* that prohibited teaching women to read and write,[37] but such opinions did not emanate from the press. Additionally there were men and women who objected to female education for precisely the same reason that led others to support it: they believed that an educated wife could be the cause of an inharmonious marriage, if the husband were uneducated or educated to a lesser degree. Thus, support for female education could have a class dimension.

Those contributing to the discourse in the press were from the middle and upper classes, many of whom had benefited from the modern educational system established by Muhammad Ali and his successors. Nevertheless, some felt that female education should be confined by class:

> We are striving toward the happiness of the family, wanting to advance the nation [*al-umma*], so this point of departure is the education of the girl today and the wife of tomorrow and the mother of the future. It is necessary to limit the education to the daughter of the educated class and the middle class . . .[38]

The more typical opinion was that of Mrs. Sarruf in her discussion of the Sania school. She felt that education should not be limited to a certain class, but that the intermingling of different classes should not take place in the schools.[39] Many supported the founding of schools for the masses [*al-ṭabaqa al-ᶜamma*] and commented upon the utility of education for this group.[40] An article in *bab tadbir al-manzil* had the following to say on the subject with respect to girls:

> It is known that if *fallahin* girls are educated, then it is difficult for them to return to the houses of their fathers and marry men from among their people. Thus, their education does not benefit them, it harms them. The [female] children of the *fallahin* do not profit

> because they are not prepared for it. [Nevertheless], the *fallahin* are the backbone of the country, and the reform of their affairs is the most important reform needed. We have heard about a boarding school in Assiut that teaches girls what is necessary to run the home, along with reading, writing, and the principles of science . . . It [the school] aims to reform the homes of the *fallahin* and make them like the peasant homes in Europe . . .

The author then concludes that this school is proper for its station and that the country is in need of other such schools.[41] Similarly, Alexandra de Avierino suggested that it was far better to send poor girls to school, rather than having them run wild through the streets.[42]

Another area where contributors to the discourse disagreed was the extent, purpose, and content of education. Without dismissing female education entirely, some contributors believed that certain limitations were necessary. One particularly negative article appeared in 1885 in *al-muqtaṭaf.* After a rather misogynous discussion of biology, genetics, anatomy, and physiology, the author concludes a number of things about the education of girls. First, (s?)he points out that schools should be built with proper ventilation, lighting, and accommodation for physical activity. Second, he urges parents and teachers to encourage girls to participate in physical education. Third, he feels that girls should not study more than four hours per day, with an additional two hours for preparation. Fourth, he asserts that girls should not spend too much time on the sciences, since "knowledge of what is not beneficial is like ignorance of that which is beneficial." His final two suggestions deal with mental and physical health. In summary, he felt that the woman should be challenged both physically and mentally, but not overtaxed by the burdens of education during the critical years of her adolescent development.[43]

An interesting aspect of the previous argument was the author's concern for the introduction of physical education into the girls schools. He felt that girls needed special encouragement to participate in such activities because of their "natural inclination" toward "calmness and modesty." Furthermore he argued that good physical health was necessary to perpetuate healthy future generations.[44] A number of articles in *al-muqtaṭaf,* in particular, encouraged greater physical activity for girls/women and propounded the benefits of female health.[45] In her discussion of curriculum, Mrs. Tanus also argued that good physical health is necessary for girls' education and that its neglect by mothers and teachers leads to "fatigue, misery, distress, and anxiety for both girls and their families."[46]

Discussions of physical education received little press time compared to the far more common push for domestic education. A small minority felt that girls should receive an education similar in content to boys; however, the overwhelming majority called for a more practical curriculum, emphasizing those skills that the woman would need for her home. These suggestions had class implications, since privileged women had servants. Most believed that girls of the upper classes needed at least some theoretical instruction in home economics. What divided contributors to the discourse was how much of the more practical aspects was necessary. The following dialogue, printed in *bab tadbir al-manzil* exemplifies these concerns:

> We recently heard a [female] principal, who is famous for girl's education and moral upbringing, complain about the entrance of cooking into [the curriculum] at one of

the higher girls' schools, [which was] founded to graduate girls in the art of education. After some days, we heard the following conversation between a man and a woman:

Man: I heard that your sister finished her studies and got her degree. Did she learn the science of cooking?

Woman: My sister does not want to cook, not even in a palace or a hotel, nor does she desire to be a teacher of cooking.

Man: That is not what I mean, but [after all] there is a kitchen in every home, and if she marries, then she will be expected to concern herself with her husband's kitchen and what is cooked in it.

Woman: I did not learn the science of cooking, and in less than a month, I knew how to cook more food than what one learns in a higher school. Her parents paid for her education so that she could associate with a man able to hire a servant to cook. If the husband cannot hire a cook, then he must make do with what the woman can cook, even if she did not learn the science of cooking. Furthermore, there are more ready-made foods available, which are made by specialists. The woman used to gather the wheat, crush it, sift it, wash it, grind it, mix it, knead it, and bake bread; [she would] spin cotton and wool, thread them, weave them, embroider clothes and sew [with] them; [she would] squeeze olives and make soap. She would make just about everything. Now she scarcely makes any of these things because they are made in special factories more inexpensively. She buys ground flour or bread and fabric or sewn clothing. She buys oil and soap without toiling to make them, and she buys cheese, sardines, pickles and many other foods for less than she could make them with her own hands . . . all without learning how to do these things. Cooking is a vocation for which great chefs or cooking instructors require education, and sewing is a vocation for which seamstresses or sewing teachers necessitate education. So why don't all of your sons learn shoe-cobbling, carpentry, masonry, and dying . . .

Man: Take it easy, I do not aim to educate your sister in the vocation of cooking so that she [will] become a chef at the Ritz hotel or at the Cecil hotel, rather that she learn enough so that she . . . knows what is required of her in her home . . .

Woman: Oh, how remarkable! Did you not understand what I just said. I did not learn the science of cooking nor that of embroidery and sewing, but nonetheless I am able to run my home as you [can] see.

Man: However, if you learned the basics of practical cooking, then it would be easy for you to learn the causes of many errors that the cook sometimes makes . . . If you learned the principles of embroidery and sewing, then you could save your husband a lot of money. . . . I liken the affluent woman's education in the science of cooking to her husband's education in the principles of agriculture, were he a large landowner. He does not strive, through his education, to become a peasant plowing the land with his [own] hands . . . Cooking is a chemical science, whose knowledge gratifies the senses [in] everyone no less than the gratification of learning math, history, and geography. So why don't our daughters learn it like they learn those sciences . . . The same applies to the science of embroidery and sewing, both of which are based on the principles of engineering . . . How nice it would be if our daughters, all of them, learned the science of preserving health, caring for the ill, . . . for the woman is the true nurse of her children . . .

The man had not yet finished his discussion when I saw the family of this virtuous woman gleam, and she said to him, I do not grant you a thing from what you have said . . . Visitors entered and the subject was changed.[47]

From this discussion two things that characterized the discourse on female education are evident. First, an overwhelmingly large number of men contributing to the discourse felt that girls' education needed a more practical aspect. Likewise, in 1904, Yusif Effendi Ghanimat al-Baghdadi complained that girls spend too much time studying geography, science, history, and chemistry without taking an interest in learning how to raise children or in home economics. He and other professional men felt that it was not necessary for women to exert much effort in such subjects because they were not going to enter the workforce. Instead, they suggested that girls spend more time preparing themselves for marriage, motherhood, and household administration.[48] Although Lord Cromer wrote in his *Annual Report* for 1905, that "the younger generation [of men] are beginning to demand that their wives . . . possess some qualities other than those which can be secured in the harem," clearly many felt a certain amount of intimidation regarding their wives and daughters obtaining the wrong type of education, or worse yet, pursuing a career that could displace them. Juan Cole has argued that these concerns took on a class dimension, stating that given their simpler homes and modest incomes, "petite bourgeois intellectuals tended to advocate a much more modest sort of education for their women." Furthermore, the new agrarian capitalists of the upper-middle class sought an education for their wives and daughters that would emphasize the values of thrift and efficiency, eschewing the old Turco-Circassian habit of conspicuous consumption.[49] Thus, while they may have shared a sympathetic view with the woman in the dialogue with respect to providing their daughters with a non-vocational education, they valued practical instruction in home economics as a means of achieving greater household efficiency and consequently freeing up funds for investment.

Regina Awwad, the Syrian editor of *al-sa^{c}ada*, shared this view and painted a less rosy picture than Cromer. She could not understand why young men seemed to prefer uneducated women. Like many men, she consistently pressed for the importance of a domestic and practical education for girls:

> The woman enters her husband's home in order to work, to toil sleeplessly through the night, to labor in the kitchen, to raise the children. These are the occupations of the normal woman. If the intention of marriage is raising a family . . . then why do our schools not teach our girls anything about cooking, household organization, and rearing children?[50]

Similarly, Rahma Sarruf, who lectured at the women's section of Cairo University, complained that while there has been "renaissance" in girls' education in Egypt, it has fallen short of its mission because of the lack of home economics in the schools. She called upon mothers and fathers to press for its inclusion in girls' schools.[51] A young Egyptian (female) contributor to *al-sufur* magazine held similar views, and pressed for a domestic practical curriculum based upon her early experience supervising servants.[52]

Despite the support for the domestic curriculum by some women, the response of the woman in the dialogue represents a second interesting point. Many women of the upper-middle and upper class viewed domestic labor as below their station, and thus viewed instruction in cooking, laundry, ironing, and cleaning as both demeaning and unnecessary. Like the woman in the dialogue, Mrs. Sarruf expressed class-based concerns in her discussion of the Sania school:

> . . . if women from the [class of] *amirs*, pashas, and leading merchants entered the school, and they saw the girls helping with the laundry, kindling the fire, and separating the rice, they would not want that for their daughters. There is no doubt that they would demand that they be instructed in music, drawing, and other such things that complete [their education], which are not needed by the remainder of girls.[53]

Despite such concerns, the British and the Egyptian ruling elite believed in the necessity of a more "practical" curriculum. In 1897, Miss Forbes, the English headmistress of the girls' division at the Abbas school, wrote in her annual report that needlework was a subject that Egyptian girls are eager to learn and "must learn completely." Furthermore, she pointed out that more room was necessary for instruction in this important subject. Miss Forbes also mentioned that students would benefit from cooking lessons. She was particularly concerned that the girls receive "practical" instruction in preparing "the foods used in this country." In other words, she did not wish for them to learn *haute cuisine*, but that which would be useful, in the short term, for preparing lunches for both divisions of the school, and in the long term, for their own homes.[54]

The administration was responsive to the demands in the press and those of school administrators like Miss Forbes. The Sania school underwent special renovations in 1910 to meet the "demand for more practical education," with the installation of a new room for lessons in domestic economy and cooking.[55] The following statement by Lord Kitchener in 1913 demonstrates continuing British efforts to this end:

> The demand for girls' schools shows no tendency to decrease . . . In the elementary schools specially set apart for girls, the education authorities are endeavoring to develop instruction on practical lines and to give early training in household management. Mistresses have been specially appointed with this object, their duties including the supervision of cleanliness and the physical condition of the children. In order to provide a course of training in these domestic subjects, a new section has been added to the elementary training college for women at Boulac. Similarly, in the girls' primary schools, kitchens and laundries have been attached to the building and personnel staff strengthened by the appointment of trained domestic science teachers. Following on the same lines, the special necessities of girls' education are being kept in view in the preparation of new girls schools to be erected in Cairo and Alexandria.[56]

Provincial councils aided the government in providing technical and vocational education for girls, once again pressing for more practical skills. A girls' *kuttab* in Beni Suef included a special workshop for basket and wicker work, and a vocational school at Bulaq instructed girls in needlework, cookery, laundry, and gardening, in addition to "the usual book subjects."[57] The School of Practical Housewifery in Cairo was instituted in order to prepare girls "to be better wives and mothers" by providing them with both theoretical and practical instruction. The facilities at the model school included special rooms for cooking, laundry, and needlework. To completely press the practical aspect of instruction, students would be expected to carry out the housework of the school, and they would be given practical examinations in cooking, needlework, laundry/ironing, and household management. Their only written examination was in mathematics/household finance, and the only subject that did not have a direct link to home economics was religion.[58]

Administrators beefed up the domestic curriculum in all the girls' schools and apportioned examinations to reflect the more practical outlook. In 1914, the distribution of points and subjects in the written primary certificate examination was adjusted to address the new focus, with 60 of 145 total points dealing with various aspects of home economics. Furthermore, the girls had to complete practical examinations in cookery, laundry (washing and ironing), and needlework.[59] The new program instituted for girls' elementary schools in 1916 included the following improvements: kindergarten; needlework; physical education; and practical instruction in cooking, laundry, and ironing.[60] That same year, the government created higher elementary schools. Adly Yeghen, the Minister of Public Instruction, described these schools as "organized on the same basis as higher elementary schools for boys, but specially adapted to the practical exigencies of female education."[61] The strong domestic emphasis manifested itself in the curriculum, with 12 sessions per week in domestic science/needlework classes, 6 in mathematics/household finance, and 2 in health/hygiene compared to 3 in religion, 8 in Arabic, 2 in calligraphy, 2 in drawing, and 1 in history.[62]

In addition to renovations at the Sania school, its teachers' division underwent a restructuring in 1915. Students could now choose to specialize in either general education or in home economics for the final two years of study. According to Gafar Waly, the Minister of Public Instruction, "the goal of this division was to prepare a group of students to specialize in home economics, which has great significance for girls' education [*tarbiyat al-banat*]."[63] Students in the home economics division would receive the same amount of instruction in religion, hygiene, and education, but they would reduce the number of lessons in English, translation, mathematics/household finance, geography, history, and drawing, in order to receive more intensive training in the theoretical and practical aspects of home economics. The bulk of the difference would be made up for in needlework, cookery, laundry, and housewifery.[64]

Conclusion

The British reorganized the Egyptian educational system to fit the needs of the occupation. The domestic and practical bent in female education was part of their effort to tame, sanitize, and control the Egyptians. The emphasis on the Victorian ideal of domesticity served to both justify the occupation and to quell the rising tide of feminism in Britain. These views, which held Britain as the pinnacle of civilization and domesticity as the key to advancement, were held by both high- and low-level administrators, as well as by males and females.[65] While the Egyptian ruling elite viewed such reforms as necessary for the lower tier of the educational system and supported a domestic curriculum for their daughters, the measures were somewhat less popular among women of the upper classes and proved difficult to carry out. Interestingly enough, Salmoni found that this continued to be mantra of male public opinion that was repeatedly criticized by women after independence.[66]

Juan Cole attributes the distinction in views between elite men and women to the quality and nature of their respective educations. Among the ruling elite were the new agrarian capitalists, who placed a high value on rational economizing and received superior educations, while their wives and daughters "continued to be superficially educated" and "remained outside" their culture and values.[67] While certain characteristics can be drawn regarding the education of upper-class boys graduating from the Europeanized government schools and the more prestigious private schools, one cannot categorize women's education at the turn of the century as "superficial." Can one place a woman who studied at home with a German governess and native *shaykhs* in the same category as one who studied with Mary Whately, or equate the education of the girl who studied for a few years at a French convent school with that of one who graduated from the American (Mission) College? As seen from the discussion of the women's press in chapter 5, at least a significant minority of educated women had something more than a superficial education. Many of the women who owned, edited, and contributed to the women's press had a substantial knowledge of history, literature, and geography. Furthermore, many of them valued the qualities of economy and efficiency. Although a number of the pioneers in this field, for example, Alexandra de Avierino, were educated in Syria, many contributors were Egyptian and educated in Egypt.

The common thread in women of the upper classes' objection to the domestic and practical bent of education was not necessarily their experience (or lack thereof) in the classroom, rather it was their view of what family life should entail. Like the woman in the dialogue, they felt that they should not have to settle for less than that to which they were accustomed. For women of the lower and middle classes, education was an assurance of marriage to a partner of equal or better status. In other words, they felt that they should aspire to do less work than their mothers, not more.

Due to the unpopular response and logistical difficulties, many of the reforms in education were short lived. The new primary certificate examination, which aimed to reflect the goals of female education, proved difficult to grade and it had a high rate of failure. The Minister of Public Instruction called for its repeal the following year.[68] The domestic science division of the Sania Teachers' College was such an utter failure that by 1921 it existed "in name only" because students overwhelmingly chose the general education division. Thus, even women from the middle and lower middle classes did not value these skills. Given this state of affairs, the Minister of Public Instruction, Gafar Waly, proposed reducing the time allotted to some aspects of home economics and putting more effort into those subjects that would prepare them for teaching: handiwork, science, and nature study. He also suggested that the entrance examination exclude hygiene and include history. Furthermore, graduates of government schools, as well as those under government inspection, would not have to take practical entrance examinations in home economics since it would be assumed that they possess such skills. Eliminating these students from the practical examinations would prove to be easier logistically as well, given the shortage of appliances and the difficulty of assessing these exams. Finally, Waly proposed that the teachers' license examination exclude needlework, cooking, washing, ironing, and household administration, since these skills were not necessary for teaching.[69]

Despite these problems, the British viewed the results of female education quite positively. They measured success of the system by the willingness of parents to pay fees and the number of applications exceeding the number of positions available. Nevertheless, these were less signs of support than indications of a lack of schools and a greater desire for girls' education. The two-tiered educational system instituted by the British did not work as well for female education. For males it meant reserving positions in government service and the liberal professions for children of the upper classes. Additionally, it allowed for a lower level of education that the ruling elite, including Egyptians, believed would keep the peasant or small shopkeeper content with his station in life.[70] Arguments in the press might center upon which educational track was more important or more in need of development, but the division itself was not questioned.[71]

The vocational and practical bent of the upper educational tier did not mesh with the goals of the upper class and those who aspired to the upper class. They did not want their daughters becoming teachers, nurses, or doctors nor did they want them associating with the class of women who desired to enter those professions. Some administrators shared these concerns. Amin Sami felt that rather than attaching the Normal School to al-Sania, it should have been attached to the Abbas school, since many of its students were non-paying and seeking a career in teaching. Instead, he felt that the Sania school ought to have a post-primary division for upper class, paying students.[72] Many parents with such concerns over class and curriculum chose to educate their daughters at home. Others sent their daughters to the numerous foreign and minority schools, where the curriculum was better suited to their daughters' lives. In addition to the basics, at the most exclusive of these schools, girls learned some handiwork and perhaps a small dose of theoretical home economics. More importantly, they received instruction in refined subjects, such as music, art, and languages.

By providing competition with the government schools, the foreign schools helped spur the government to create more schools and to rethink the curriculum. While many educated Egyptians felt that there was much to admire in foreign (Western) education, most felt that certain limitations and adjustments were necessary. In particular, foreign schools were weak with respect to a national curriculum, and this concern grew in the two decades preceding the 1919 Revolution. The presence of these foreign schools fostered the growth of community and national schools: Muslim, Coptic, and Jewish.[73] The British occupation and the strong presence of foreign schools stimulated the debate in the press over what was to be admired from the West and what was to be avoided. Qasim Amin and his conservative critic Talaat Harb were merely two variations on this theme, with Amin representing the extreme pro-Western viewpoint and Harb representing the extreme pro-Islamic element. The well-studied issue of the veil is merely a metaphor for their positions, and thus is not dealt with here.[74] Interestingly enough, in her study of women's biographies in the Egyptian press, Marilyn Booth found the issue (of veiling/unveiling) largely absent.[75] What was far more important was women's education and comportment. As we see in the following chapter, textbooks provided a blueprint for women in these arenas, whether they chose to restructure society from within their home or whether they were to educate the next generation in schools.

Chapter 8

Textbooks: Defining Roles and Boundaries

Introduction

Since the 1960s, there have been numerous studies of contemporary American textbooks by specialists in curriculum and instruction, sociology, and psychology. These studies highlight the significance of textbooks for understanding cultural norms and values. Textbooks have the advantage of being more accessible than what is taught in the home or learned from other sources. Nevertheless, many of these studies fail to examine the historical and political context from which these textbooks emerge. According to Apple and Christian-Smith, textbooks are more than "delivery systems of 'facts'," they reflect much more "profound political, economic, and cultural relations and histories."[1]

As these studies have advanced, scholars have begun to utilize textbooks as a means of examining power relations in society, including biases against women, minorities, and the working class. More recently, studies have turned to older textbooks as a means of studying such relations historically.[2] Most studies of Arabic and Egyptian textbooks, however, focus on the contemporary period. Many of these authors are modernization theorists with an Orientalist bent, that is, they seek to show the "backwardness" of Egyptian society, its lack of modernity, its selective cultural borrowing, and its essentialist Islamic element, particularly with respect to issues of women and gender.[3] Furthermore, they share many of the same structural weaknesses as traditional American studies of textbooks, and they utilize the same techniques of analysis.[4] Recently a number of more innovative studies have been carried out by historians, anthropologists, and political scientists.[5]

Much like the advertisements discussed in chapter four, textbooks do not mirror society exactly, but rather they present distorted or idealized images of reality as conceived by the ruling elite and textbook authors. Curriculum serves as a powerful means of social control by legitimating existing power relations and projecting this socially constructed image as natural.[6] Indeed, "[h]egemonic leadership involves developing intellectual, moral and philosophical consent from all major groups in a nation."[7]

Turn-of-the-century Egypt was a site of struggle between the British occupiers, the Egyptian ruling elite, and the intellectuals, over what constituted an Egyptian identity. The Egyptian elite shared the British desire to limit the higher track of education and to attain fiscal solvency. Nevertheless, like many journalists and urban professionals, they desired a curriculum with greater emphasis on religion, morals, and Arabic, as discussed in chapter 7.

The "official" textbook itself is but one link in a chain that connects the government, the educational bureaucracy, the teacher, and the student. The historical context helps to explain the ideal as conceived by the government and textbook authors, but it does not necessarily address other factors in the equation—who is reading the textbooks, where those textbooks are being used, what is understood from the textbooks, and how teachers are conveying (or not conveying) this information to their students.[8]

By examining the textbooks used in girls' schools by the second decade of the twentieth century,[9] we can study the differing agenda of the two educational tracks, witness the governmental attempt to meet the public demand for a domestic curriculum in girls' schools, and examine new modes of consumption. At the same time, the textbooks display an attempt to forge a national identity, which valued traditional morality, yet called for a new form of identification as citizens. Textbooks targeted both the individual and the home as sites of reform, the springboards from which the new nation would emerge.

Two Textbooks for Two Educational Tracks

As discussed in chapter 6, by the turn of the century, there were two lingering problems in government schools for girls: ambiguity over mission and lack of female teachers. The two-tiered educational system did not clarify matters, it only clouded them further. The lack of teachers necessitated the recruitment of women from the lower middle class into the upper track of the school system (primary, secondary, and higher schools of education). Nevertheless, at the same time, the government sought to provide an education suitable for upper-middle-class and upper-class girls, which would prepare them to become good wives, skilled mothers, and loyal citizens.

The lower tier of the educational system (the *kuttabs*, elementary schools, and vocational/technical schools) also had a specific agenda. It was to provide the student (male or female) with basic literacy and mathematics skills, which would equip him/her "with sufficient knowledge to take care of his [or her] station in life." Many of the schools in the lower educational track were traditional *kuttabs*, and thus a religious emphasis is not surprising. Even in the newer elementary schools religion played a major role. Although Cromer questioned the validity of increasing the number of lessons in religion from two to three, he accepted the change for the stated purpose of attracting more charitable endowments to fund the lower educational track. Furthermore, religion classes helped to serve as a form of control, even in the upper track of the educational system, in order to defend "against evil passions," "strengthen the ties which unite individuals," and set the individual on "the path to righteousness in this world." These ideas regarding education's utility for this purpose were new neither to Egypt nor to Islam. Furthermore, Copts as well as Muslims shared these opinions. Wahib Dus Bey was noted as saying "religion is the spirit and consciousness of the elite and . . . the bridle of the commoners."[10] For the lower educational track, social control was reinforced through lessons in hygiene, as evidenced by a comparison of the different syllabi used for the two educational tracks.

In elementary schools, hygiene classes for girls often filled the function of the more varied curriculum found in hygiene, morals, and home economics classes at the better schools. Elementary boys and girls required an extra year, and the curriculum was far more detailed, particularly regarding personal hygiene. Furthermore, they covered topics not mentioned at all in the primary school syllabus, for example, perspiration, vermin, the evils of alcohol, and the cleanly use of latrines. Girls in both primary and elementary schools covered additional topics relating to the care of children and the convalescent.[11]

A comparison of two textbooks bears out the differences in the two types of schools. Dr. Sarubyaq's primer on health, *Hygiene for Elementary Schools*, consisted of two versions, one for boys and one for girls, the latter being nearly fifty pages longer. Both the male and female versions begin with three detailed chapters on personal hygiene. The text then moves on to the basic principles of anatomy and physiology as related to nutrition and digestion, including a discussion of the dangers of alcohol. The remaining chapters deal with clothing, sleep, housing, childcare, first-aid, and home nursing, with greater detail in the girls' version. Sarubyaq employs sketches to reinforce his message of cleanliness and morality. To demonstrate the evils of alcohol, he juxtaposes two sketches of the same man, one before and one after an alcoholic binge. Before descending into the throws of an alcoholic stupor, the man is well groomed, clad in a tie, suit, and *tarbush*. Afterward, he is dirty, unkempt, has lost his *tarbush*, and his clothing is disheveled. These pictures are followed by one of a man in a straitjacket.[12]

This text's discussion of hygiene and temperance demonstrates the concerns of the ruling class for control of the masses. As discussed in chapters 2 and 3, the ruling elite tried to sanitize, organize, and tame the mess of the cities with public works projects, public services, and new forms of order. The government hoped to extend its sphere of influence into the home by teaching the principles of hygiene, morals, and home economics. The ruling elite shared the British occupiers' fetishism with cleanliness, which embodied the bourgeois values of monogamy, industrial capital, and class control.[13] Ironically, Islamic culture is predicated on rituals of cleanliness and ablution. Furthermore, there was an indigenous tradition of instructive literature [*wa*ᶜ*ẓ*], directed at men to instruct women on hygiene, as well as caring for the home and the family.[14] Thus, the British were imposing their own more recently adopted models of cleanliness on a culture that had a longstanding tradition of hygiene.

With respect to alcohol, the mainstream, women's, and children's press frequently ran articles warning about its dangers, from both a health and a morals standpoint.[15] Nevertheless, the literate population received mixed messages from the press, which also secured revenue from alcohol advertisers. Alcohol consumption among certain segments of the upper class was well established from the ruling family down. According to Timothy Mitchell, the concern for such habits spreading among the lower classes was of far more interest to reformers and social critics, who feared the spread of alcoholism, promiscuity, disease, and insanity amongst the lower classes.[16] Nevertheless, alcoholism remained an upper-class phenomenon. Unlike Europe, which had a ready supply of inexpensive alcohol for the working classes, Egypt had mainly expensive imports. Even the more inexpensive locally produced wines and beers were inaccessible to the masses. While alcohol was the drug of choice for the upper classes, locally grown hashish remained the vice of the lower classes. The lower classes lacked the leisure and money to recklessly pursue promiscuity, and they tended to care for the mentally ill in their own homes rather than institutionalizing them.

In contrast to the social control manifested in *Hygiene for Elementary Schools*, Muhammad Rushdy's *General Management of Health and Illness* was designed to create savvy nurse-mothers/consumers among upper-middle-class and upper-class girls in private and primary schools. While it covers many of the basics discussed in the elementary text, it lacks detail on cleanliness and hygiene. The book covers anatomy and physiology in a more comprehensive manner. The sketches are simple and scientific, covering topics such as the nervous and digestive systems. Like the Sarubyaq text, it contains a section on the dangers of alcoholic beverages, although it seems to send a mixed message to potential consumers. It warns that alcohol can be dangerous to one's health and can lead to disease; however, this warning is followed by information on the percentage of alcohol in various drinks and an endorsement of alcohol for medicinal purposes. While there is some coverage of personal hygiene, it lacks the detail of the elementary text.

The entire textbook has a magazine-like quality, with advertisements for various products, such as Evian mineral water, Delmar Insecticide Powder, the Burroughs-Wellcome syringe, and Nestle's baby formula. Thus, in order to be a good mother, one not only needed to know how to raise healthy children and care for sick ones, but she also needed the proper products to do so. Rushdy includes a listing of "necessary medical supplies" at the end of the book, reiterating the names of all of these products.[17]

Home Economics: Cleanliness, Consumption, and Virtue

The theme of cleanliness and the importance of the home for the nation came through for the primary and higher elementary schools by means of textbooks on morals and home economics. The lines between hygiene, morals, home economics, and even civics were blurred since the creation of a strong, healthy nation necessitated strong, healthy individuals who created strong, healthy homes.[18] Chapters on cleanliness of body were juxtaposed with those on behavior, which were then followed by chapters on maintaining the home physically, spiritually, and emotionally. The introductions and conclusions frequently linked these matters to the health of the nation. These textbooks sought to create mother-educators/consumers who would carry out the task of improving the nation through their own exemplary behavior, by carefully raising their children, and by sustaining a proper home. As discussed in chapter 5, these books were part of a larger genre of books on the proper roles of and morals for girls and women.

The majority of these books were written by men, many of whom were Syrian Christians, but there were also female, Egyptian, and Muslim authors. Some of these works were direct translations from foreign books. For example, *Elementary Education and Morals* was a French text adopted by Education Minister Ahmed Hechmat when he found nothing to his satisfaction amongst Egyptian textbooks.[19] By the second decade of the twentieth century, however, there were more titles by indigenous authors, who sought to provide books specifically for Eastern girls in an Eastern context. Speaking in terms of "Easterners" was not uncommon in textbooks, particularly given the prominent role of Syrian intellectuals in education and government administration. There were also texts with a more strictly Egyptian nationalist/Islamic agenda. In writing *adab al-fatat*, Ali Effendi Fikry received inspiration from Talaat Harb's *tarbiyat al-mar'a*, and his message does not stray far from that of Tahtawi, namely that female education would foster an improved home life and Islam affirms such an education.[20]

By examining two home economics textbooks, we can examine the important linkage between individual, home, and nation, as well as the themes of cleanliness, consumption, and virtue. The differences between the two textbooks reflect variations of opinion on the proper education of girls, as well as slightly different target audiences. Furthermore, the texts reflect the tension between what is to be admired and adopted from the West and which traditional values should be maintained.

Francis Mikhail, author of three widely circulated textbooks on home economics and architect of Egypt's plan for home economics schools, read numerous foreign books before undertaking the composition of his own book for "girls of the nation" [*li-banat al-waṭan*].[21] Similarly, Antun al-Gamayyil, author of *The Girl and the Home*, points out that "there are many books on female upbringing from all nations," but that they are not suitable for "our Eastern life and our national customs [*ḥiyatna al-sharqiyya wa ʿadatna al-qawmiyya*]."[22] While Mikhail does not admit to seeking advice from any female informants, merely other textbooks, Gamayyil was assisted by a "virtuous woman" and educator, G.S. Dubuk.

Both of these authors link the education of girls, the state of the home, and the condition of the nation early in their texts. In Gamayyil's first chapter, he explains that home economics is a "special science" that enables the woman to bring "order, organization, cleanliness, and ease of mind and body" to her "small kingdom." This knowledge of home economics encompasses both moral and practical dimensions and is necessary because "the happiness of the family depends on the excellence of the organization of the mistress of the house." He closes with the following assertion:

> For the happiness of the family and the future of the community [*al-umma*], and in the noble name of marriage and the majesty of motherhood, the young woman's education must be among the most important and exalted matters.[23]

Likewise, according to Mikhail, "the happiness of civilized nations . . . depends upon familial happiness . . . the foundation of which is the upbringing of girls and their education," because they raise the "citizens" and "mothers" of the future.[24] In the introduction of another text he writes that home economics has great significance for family life, and that it aims to help girls understand their duties in the home. Such knowledge "increases familial happiness" and "dresses the country [*al-bilad*] in new clothing, clothing of freedom and movement," pulling it "out of darkness."[25]

The Mikhail and Gamayyil texts offered girls of the middle and upper classes detail on consumption for the home, while still stressing the themes of cleanliness and order. These mothers of the future were to bring the order of the major cities into their home by maintaining proper hygiene for themselves and their children, maintaining a clean domicile, and furnishing it in the proper manner. Instructions for personal hygiene lack the nuts and bolts detail of the elementary schools. Mikhail points out that it is possible for people of all classes to own a tub; and that in a warm country such as Egypt, regular bathing is important. Rather than dwelling on how to use a sponge or loofah, he discusses what the bathroom should look like, how it should be furnished, when to bathe, what toiletries should be placed there, and how to avoid catching cold.[26] In *Household Organization* Mikhail even offers details about the cost of necessary furnishings and implements for the bathroom. The picture that follows the text displays a modern bathroom, with a four-legged tub, chairs, and fine cabinets.[27] He recommends that women change their clothing every four days in the summer and every week in the winter; however, for women who do their own housework, he suggests changing the clothes every other day or so. The convalescent and the nursing mother were held to an even higher standard, requiring a daily change.[28]

Like Mikhail, Gamayyil also discusses the arrangement of the bathroom, the universality of the bathroom in the home (whether modern or traditional), when to bathe, and danger of catching cold. He adds information on the dangers of heating the bathroom by coal.[29] His only instructions for bathing are to use a loofah with soap, and he offers no advice on the frequency of changing one's clothes.

Gamayyil's text is targeted to the wealthy girl with servants, while Mikhail's remarks reflect a more diverse audience, from those with a complete staff to those with few or no servants. Gamayyil devotes an entire chapter to a discussion of servants, while the subject receives little attention in the three Mikhail texts.[30] Since these girls had a full staff to complete the menial tasks of housework and their mothers were long experienced in the chores of household management, Gamayyil's advice was of a more general nature. Meanwhile, the middle-class readership of Mikhail's textbooks was just entering the field of household management, and thus these girls needed greater details for carrying out its practical aspects. Efficiency was of greater interest to this group, who had few or no servants. Finally, given the sharp increase in the cost of house rents, as well as a signicant increase in domestic servants wages, many Egyptians were making due with fewer servants.[31]

In addition to keeping themselves clean, women were also responsible for maintaining clean children. According to Gamayyil, "uncleanliness causes various types of illness in the child, so it is necessary to wash him completely every day with warm water."[32] Once again, he does not specify how often to change the child's clothes;

however, he does stress the necessity of having enough clean clothing for all seasons. Mikhail, on the other hand, has less stringent requirements for the frequency of bathing, at least once per week, although he does advocate using two sponges, one for the head and one for the body, in order to maintain proper sanitation. To protect her clothing and her own cleanliness, Mikhail suggests that the mother wear a leather or rubber apron.[33] Such a suggestion was unnecessary for Gamayyil's readers, who would probably not do this chore themselves.

The home too had to be maintained in the most sanitary of conditions, the first step of which was choosing the proper home. According to Mikhail, it is "the most important thing in an individual's life on this earth."[34] Gamayyil points out that while economy and taste are important considerations, hygiene is the most important.[35] Both authors stress the significance of ventilation, sunshine, and wide streets, and the avoidance of locations near hospitals, factories, and cemeteries. Nevertheless, the two differ upon whether or not one should be located in the midst of town. Mikhail asserts that "the home should be located close to the market, so that the individual does not have far to go to buy things necessary for the home," and that this location should also be close to the husband's work and the children's schools. Gamayyil, on the other hand, is clearly dealing with a more elite group. He views markets as in the same category as other crowded and unsanitary places to avoid, preferring an isolated location above the city. His target audience is unconcerned about the distance from the market and the cost of transportation, both of which Mikhail finds important.[36]

Gamayyil describes choosing a home as "among the most difficult matters which merit the attention of the mistress of the house." Mikhail, on the other hand, delegates the responsibility to the man; however, he also goes over contractual terms for buying, selling, and renting, indicating that the woman should have an informed role in the process. Furthermore, he recommends that a new dwelling meet the woman's standards before any contract is signed.[37]

In the same way that the ruling elite, since the time of Ismail, concerned itself with structuring the cities, textbook authors believed that this same method of organization could be brought to the home. In his *Household Organization*, Mikhail not only defines the divisions of the house, but explains the differences between the small, medium, and large homes.[38] In *Modern Household Management*, he discusses only the large home, carefully outlining its structure and layout. The ground floor was to contain the kitchen, pantry, lavatory, bathroom, dining room, foyer, *salamlik*, and perhaps a room for the reception of female visitors. The first floor was reserved for the bedrooms and dressing rooms, and the higher floors were to be used for servants' quarters and the washroom. These divisions were important for sanitation, ventilation, and organization. Finally, Mikhail suggests an iron fence enclosing the house and garden, reminiscent of Cairo and Alexandria's public parks.[39] As discussed in chapter 3, these "divisions" of the home were innovations.

Both Gamayyil and Mikhail take the reader on a room-by-room tour of the house in chapters entitled "Divisions of the House," describing the materials, furnishings, and care of each room. Both authors assume at least a middle-class standing; however, Gamayyil targeted the wealthier girl. He makes it clear that servants cannot be relied upon to maintain the home because they are ignorant, "most of them coming from the countryside . . . [bringing] with them their habits of filthiness and squalor." The mistress of the house is ultimately responsible for the upkeep of her home, regardless of the fact that she does not necessarily undertake this work herself. He points out that experience and training are important, and that parents should encourage their daughters in this role by making them responsible for the upkeep and decoration of their rooms.[40] After each room description, he explains how often that particular room needs cleaning, and at the end of the chapter on divisions of the home he adds a schedule for housecleaning.[41] Gamayyil establishes a correlation between the condition of the individual, the home, and society: men with dirty, noisy homes find it necessary to escape, seeking refuge in taverns and gambling establishments, where they lose both their health and their wealth.[42]

In all of his textbooks, Mikhail goes into much greater detail than Gamayyil, and he offers illustrations or pictures to reinforce his points. He has a greater fascination with modern gadgets, objects, furniture, and services. His description of the foyer is an excellent example. He meticulously narrates every facet, from floor to ceiling, regarding lights, color, materials, paint, and furnishings. He recommends decoration with oriental crafts, antiques, and even the skins or horns of predatory animals. Mikhail also makes practical suggestions, including a place for visitors to leave their walking stick and a tray for visitors' cards. He closes with a warning: "No screen, or anything like that, which is usually placed at the door of the *ḥarim*, should be placed there; [because] it is against the conditions of health, and it is an out-moded form of decoration."[43] Although allowing for some traditional items, he clearly encourages Western forms of consumption and behavior. Photographic pictures, which were not all that common in textbooks of the time, reinforce his suggestions. Following his discussion of salons, he shows pictures of small salons, knick-knacks, large salons, and even one depicting how to arrange the corner of the salon. These pictures displayed Louis XIV-style furniture, Western-style lighting fixtures, English tea services, statuettes, and even a bearskin rug. The following section discussed further details on interior decoration, with pictures detailing the artistic decoration of a piano, the organization of the fireplace and its implements, and the arrangement of plants and flowers.[44]

The decorating hints in the Mikhail text display a Westernized outlook. He explains that the salon is used to receive visitors of all sorts, many of whom are not well acquainted with the family. Consequently, he suggests placing photographs of the family in this room, in addition to a portrait of the lord or lady of the house, taken by a reputable photographer or drawn by a well-known artist. Traditionally, displaying images of people was not common, let alone images of one's wife and children in a location under quasi-public scrutiny. Similarly, as was customary in Europe, Mikhail encourages decorating with pictures of the royal family, famous ministers, and/or other great personages.[45] Such a display would be symbolic of the home's modern outlook, as well as its political orientation.

Mikhail's discussion of the library similarly illustrates his encouragement of Western-style tastes, consumption, and behavior. Historically, personal libraries were not uncommon amongst the elite, but what Mikhail proposes is a Western-style den. In both *Modern Household Management* and *Household Organization*, he goes into great detail over the requisite furnishings for this important room. He describes the every aspect of the proper desk and suggests having a small safe for documents and valuables. Furthermore, he recommends a number of decorations that function as instruments of precision and measurement: the clock, the thermometer, and the calendar. The den was to function both as a "work room" for the man of the house and as a family library. Mikhail firmly believed in the value of reading, and he encouraged the family to budget money for reading materials citing moral, intellectual, and nationalistic reasons:

> The individual cannot dispense with books and journals. The best homes are those that are adorned with a bookcase or bookcases . . . Books are a good form of entertainment and the best type of solace . . . they fill [one's] spare time with a useful activity.
>
> . . . the individual cannot dispense with newspapers from which [s]he reads the news of his [or her] nation [*waṭanihi*] and the events, happenings, and politics that take place outside his [or her] country [*biladihi*].[46]

Mikhail even explains how the books should be organized, discussing their placement on shelves by subject in alphabetical order. The maintenance of the family library was the woman's responsibility; and to do so properly, she had to make an index of family holdings, as well as a card catalog. She was also responsible for keeping the family records, including a notebook chronicling its significant events. While women traditionally maintained such information through an oral tradition, keeping a "golden family book" for the sake of one's children and their progeny was an importation. With respect to general record-keeping, once again Mikhail offers practical information on filing, and on storage containers. The pictures following the section on the library/den suggest that the room was to be used for more than just reading. Since his model budget also allowed for hobbies and recreation, it is not surprising that two pictures display "work rooms" with billiard tables.[47]

Mikhail was extremely concerned not only about having the proper furnishings, gadgets, and implements in one's home, but how to use those items correctly. He is much more elaborate than Gamayyil in describing the processes of the home—setting the proper table for a formal family breakfast in the dining room, the less formal breakfast table, the lunch (dinner) table, serving sit-down and buffet-style meals, and the five o'clock tea table. Finally, he lists necessary utensils and serving vessels, including cost.[48]

Gamayyil's style is much simpler, leaning toward the theoretical basis of housekeeping. The following is his description of the salon and reception rooms:

> These are the rooms used for sitting during the day and for receiving visitors and guests. It is necessary that they be furnished according to the wealth and the social standing of the owner of the house.
>
> It is difficult to designate the furnishings that should be used in the reception room because it depends upon what can be paid to that end. It is not proper . . . [to] spend beyond our means . . . cleanliness, proper arrangement, and good taste are still the primary conditions, especially in the reception room, which is the mirror of the house . . . It is necessary . . . that all the seats, tables, pictures, and furnishings appear in good taste and order.[49]

Gamayyil's advice is much vaguer, offering no details on furnishings. He merely advocates cleanliness, order, and thrift.

By examining these home economics textbooks, we can see the significant role of the woman in a new Egypt and how these changes reflect Egypt's incorporation into a financial, social, and cultural world economy. These developments envisaged a perceived break with the past. According to Gamayyil,

> in our age, the role of the mistress of the house is not limited to what it was in the past: she must organize the needs of her home, administer its accounts . . . indeed, she must know how to use her mind and her time, whatever her position in society, in order to make the best use of . . . whatever life brings her.[50]

For women of the middle and upper classes these changes meant becoming the general purchasing agent for and financial manager of the home. Women of means in Egypt had long been responsible for household administration, but the new method would be modern, scientific, and democratic.

According to Mikhail, not only was the husband responsible for providing the wife with a mutually agreed-upon allotment for household expenses, he was to provide an additional allowance for the wife's "personal necessities" that she was free to spend in any way that she wished. This allowance was above and beyond what she received annually to "encourage the woman in her work."[51] Gamayyil gives even greater female control of income by simply stating and restating that "the man earns and the woman organizes this earning." Furthermore, he implies that the woman's job is harder since "spending *dirhams* requires greater reason than earning them." Finally, he again advocates early training for this role by making girls responsible for their own clothing budget.[52] Both authors make suggestions for sample budgets, allotting money for housing, food, clothing, furniture, and savings. Mikhail goes into greater detail about other modern expenses, such as education, insurance, and recreation, while Gamayyil refers only to other "miscellaneous" expenses.[53] Perhaps Mikhail was attempting to acquaint his middle-class readers with information already familiar to elite girls. One has to question what type of education boys were receiving regarding their role in the home, since even in the period after independence this seemingly important subject was neglected.[54]

Gamayyil and Mikhail both recommend that women spend a small amount of time each day attending to the fiscal needs of the household. They go into great detail about the different notebooks necessary for tracking income and expenses on a daily, weekly, monthly, and yearly basis. These records were part of the professionalization of housewifery. In addition to basic book-keeping, the authors recommend using a date book, making "to do" lists, and keeping records of addresses, prices, and reputable merchants. Mikhail reminds the reader that special notebooks can be purchased in stationery shops for these purposes.[55]

Lessons in household accounting were reinforced in the mathematics classroom. In fact, in girls' schools, mathematics classes were usually entitled arithmetic and household finance. All students in Egypt, primary and secondary, male and female, devoted a portion of each academic year to an understanding of the weights, measures, and currencies used in Egypt.[56] Textbooks often employed practical questions facing the Egyptian consumer, such as "what measure does the grocer use for vinegar" or "convert 96 English pounds to *milims*."[57] This unit in textbooks reflected the economic and political standing of the country. For example, an 1891 textbook includes conversion of Turkish, Egyptian, French, and English currencies, but in an 1898 text, the Turkish is eliminated; and in a 1926 text, the French is eliminated.[58] Currencies and finance also made their way into the higher levels of education, including the teachers' colleges and the short-lived women's section at the Egyptian University.[59] I was unable to locate mathematics textbooks specifically for girls for the period under study; however, judging from the illustrations in primary and elementary textbooks, it appears that boys and girls used at least some of the same textbooks. An undated textbook, that appears to be from the early twenties, demonstrates a concern for understanding currency and an appeal to both male and female students. The book employs pictures to demonstrate word problems, for example, a picture of a pair of earrings for £3 and two bracelets for £10, and the figures include both boys and girls.[60] Nevertheless, in the text of most books, even beyond the period under study, examples use words such as "man," "artisan," "peasant" or just third person masculine singular in word problems relating to purchases and conversions.[61] Thus, these textbooks lagged behind in representing the role of the woman as the general purchasing agent for her home.

Home economics required more than just a knowledge of finance, but also an understanding of how to reduce costs and how to spend time and money wisely. For Gamayyil, this meant that the wife had to know what to buy, when to buy it, and what price to pay for it, regardless of whether she bought the goods herself or dispatched a servant to do her buying. He lays out a schedule for how often to purchase certain goods, suggests appointing special times and days for shopping, and recommends that the mistress of the house consult regularly with the cook. Furthermore, he describes the lady of the house as "more knowledgeable than her husband of the true needs of her house and the quantities of necessary provisions for consumption."[62]

Mikhail felt that a "spirit of order" was the basis for economy, and he offered more practical advice, for example, choosing meat, poultry, and produce, as well as tips for the preservation of food. Additionally, he offers information on the latest gadgets, such as a new device for making butter.[63] In order to demonstrate economy of time, he offered a model schedule for the housewife, which included sewing and (useful) reading during spare time, overseeing children's studies, and management of family accounts, in addition to the cooking and housework.[64]

Gamayyil agreed as well that economy came in knowledge of handiwork and sewing, explaining that "the needle is the woman's best friend," and that ready-made clothes lack the care of hand-sewn garments. Furthermore, for the poor woman, such knowledge offers a means of subsistence; and for all women, handiwork provides a "moral benefit," allowing them to fill their free time with a useful activity. While Gamayyil asserts that practice is more important than theory, he gives absolutely no practical advice.[65] Mikhail, on the other hand, gives much greater detail, while still emphasizing the moral and economic benefits. Beyond the savings of making one's own clothes, Mikhail advocates the recycling of old clothing, turning them into children's clothes, pajamas, or work clothes.[66] Yet another way to stretch one's clothing budget was to periodically dye clothes, giving old items a new appearance.

Gamayyil makes no such suggestions to his elite readers. Instead, he recommends donating old clothing to the poor. Another practical kernel of wisdom offered by Mikhail is the purchase of a sewing machine. He vows that it is "certainly worth its price" and recommends the Singer brand, explaining that its machines are famous for their "durability, speed, and proficiency" and the company offers free lessons to consumers. Finally, Mikhail follows his chapter on handiwork with one on sizing and how to take measurements.[67]

The two authors introduce girls of the middle and upper classes to new standards of consumption and order, but the differences between them reflect the varying audiences. Mikhail plays to a more diverse audience, and like the gentleman in the dialogue discussed in chapter 7, he felt that even elite girls needed instruction in the practical aspects of housekeeping, such as the necessity of cooking: "Nothing prevents the princess or the lady, or even the queen, from knowing this art, whether it is done with her own hands or under her supervision."[68] He follows this introduction with sections on preparing traditional foods.[69] In contrast, the Gamayyil text does not have a single chapter or subsection on cooking, but he does devote a small section to the fine arts, which he views as useful for girls as long as they do not neglect their other duties.[70]

Both authors did see, however, a more active role for women in the countryside. According to Gamayyil, agriculture "is the pillar of the community's wealth, the foundation for its richness, and the origin of its happiness." Thus, the woman of the countryside had special and important duties to fulfill "both inside and outside" the home. She had to have knowledge about raising fowl, caring for livestock, and gardening, in addition to knowing the more complex accounts of her household. Gamayyil recognized that she would not carry out the manual labor herself, but that she had to supervise the servants and the field hands.[71] Once again, he offers only an outline of the necessity of such work, without describing what was actually involved. In part one of *Modern Household Organization* Mikhail offers similarly vague information on the duties of the rural wife, explaining that she must know the principles of agriculture and how to care for fowl and livestock. Nevertheless, in part two, he gives more practical information on caring for birds, raising poultry, milking cows, and making cheese.[72] Even elite women benefited from these skills since life on the rural estate often involved the running of dairy product factories and an extensive knowledge of agronomy.[73]

Regardless of the differences between the two texts, the books shared some common characteristics. They seemed to offer a dual message to girls of the middle and upper classes. While girls were exhorted to consume and consume along modern (Western) lines, they were continually reminded of the importance of thrift and economy. This ambiguity was apparent in Gamayyil's description of reception rooms. While he pointed out that they are an important reflection of one's social standing, he also noted that order and hygiene were more significant. Throughout the text Gamayyil utilized homilies to remind the reader of the importance of thrift,—"he who purchases what he does not need is forced one day to sell that which he does need."[74]

Mikhail's textbooks display an even greater amount of hypocrisy with his lavish descriptions and illustrations interspersed with information on the importance of economy. In *Modern Household Management* he includes a chapter entitled "Economy of Expenditures," in which he describes the precarious balance between wants, needs, and resources, and a chapter simply entitled "Economy," in which he discusses the importance of saving; how to cut corners on expenses for clothing, food, and housing; the concern parents should have for training their children to spend money wisely; and the use of banks.[75]

A balance between justified consumption and thrift was required for a "happy" home, which was symbolic of both the family within it and the community surrounding it. The creation of this home depended upon the partnership of the man and the woman, who, according to Gamayyil, had specific roles:

> The man undertakes outside work, exerting himself and taking his work seriously in order to provide sustenance for his children; the woman is concerned with internal matters, and she judiciously uses the money provided for her, which is returned to the family with ease, harmony, and comfort.[76]

The wife was also to be the moral exemplar for the family, exhibiting "modesty, compassion, and tolerance" and serving as a "school" in which her children learned community values.[77] Nevertheless, Gamayyil never tells us what she should do or how she should do it.

Mikhail, refers to the husband and wife as "partners in this life, neither of whom has a need for another and for each of whom are rights and distinctions that undoubtedly . . . preserve . . . the family and society."[78] Like Gamayyil, he placed a complementary value on the work of the two partners: "just as the husband works outside [the home] earning a living, she [the wife] works as well, arranging the household subsistence and the economy of expenditures . . .".[79] He too felt that it was the wife's job to impart proper values to her children, which, incidentally, he mentions right after his discussion of the necessity of bathing them, once again equating physical and moral cleanliness. Furthermore, he gives explicit advice from proper visiting behavior and hand-shaking etiquette to appropriate comportment in speech, movement, and bodily function. He offers both traditional and Western pieces of advice. In his discussion of visiting, he explains traditional reasons for when and why visits should take place. Mikhail breaks with tradition by implying that men and women socialize. He does so by indicating that women should shake hands only with other women. Nevertheless, he recommends that they avoid the distasteful Eastern habit of excessive hugging and kissing, except with relatives.[80]

Despite the fact that the two authors delineate marriage as a complementary partnership, it was not an equal relationship. Gamayyil writes that "the man wants to be the lord who is unchallenged in everything . . .". However, he also points out that the woman is usually able to win the man over to her opinion.[81] According to Mikhail, "the wife must submit to her husband and give him legally sanctioned obedience," although he too put restraint upon the powers of the senior partner:

> The husband must work earnestly and actively in order to earn his potential and make a living. He [must also] bring his wife the sources of his wealth and income; and he cannot spend anything from them without her notification . . . He cannot spend his time in taverns, cafes, or places of pleasure and amusement, nor should he eat outside his home or far from his children. Rather, they [should] be together, hand in hand, so that their morals can become infused with his . . .[82]

Indeed, both authors intermingled the subjects of morals and home economics, for the two were inextricably linked. The home was a microcosm of the community and the proper roles of husbands and wives were necessary to create familial and communal happiness:

> . . . when the married couple conducts themselves in the manner that we have presented, then they will have a happy life and a content existence that cannot be spoiled or disrupted, and this is what is intended from marriage and this is what is called familial happiness.

Furthermore, for Mikhail, working toward these goals was a service not only to the nation, but also to mankind.[83]

While both authors set up the bourgeois nuclear family as the building block of the reformed nation, there is no discussion of how to choose a marriage partner in either textbook. Presumably, this was a matter to be undertaken by the parents of the girl and those with a vested interest in her future. Even into the 1940s, in upper-class households, there was little personal choice with respect to marriage mates. According to Magda Baraka, of much more significance was marrying into a "good family," while the notion of love "was considered a maverick kind of concept."[84]

Before departing from the subject of home economics textbooks, we should pause a moment to consider the undertaking of such textbooks for girls. Why would Francis Mikhail and Antun al-Gamayyil embark upon writing these textbooks? Aside from the fact that Mikhail published a number of books on home economics, helped to plan the government's schools for housewifery, and had a Christian name, little else is known about this figure. According to Beth Baron, he owned the Tawfiq press, which published *al-^{c}a'ila*, edited by Syrian Jew Esther Moyal, and *al-jins al-laṭif*, edited by Egyptian Copt Malaka Saad. The latter wrote her own competing textbook, *rabbat al-dar*, also published on Tawfiq press.[85] It is not clear whether the women sought out Mikhail because of his familiarity with the topic matter, whether he came to the topic as a result of his association with female magazine editors, or whether he was merely an available, reasonably priced publisher. His own textbooks were published by the government.

A bit more is known about Antun al-Gamayyil (d.1948). Prior to assuming a number of different government posts, during which time he authored the textbook in question, he founded the literary magazine *al-zuhur*, which ran from 1910–14. After Egyptian independence, Gamayyil served in the *majlis al-shuyukh* and later as editor of *al-ahram*.[86] It is noteworthy that someone who would rise through the ranks of literature, politics, and publishing would author a home economics textbook. Furthermore, that he would include (within the text) endorsements of his book by noted judge and bureaucrat, Ismail Pasha Sabri and noted author, Mustafa Lutfi al-Manfaluti, is again telling of the significance with which home economics was invested in turn-of-the-century Egypt.[87] Unlike Mikhail, who admitted no female assistance, Gamayyil candidly stated that he sought out the advice of a female expert. Nevertheless, within the text, the reader has no idea to what extent the ideas and information are his and to what extent they belong to his female informant.

Who is the New Woman?

As discussed in chapter 6, education became more "Egyptianized" with the creation of the Sania Training College in 1900, the opening of the Bulaq Normal School in 1903, and the expansion of educational missions abroad after 1907. By the closing years of the first decade of the twentieth century, a growing number of Egyptian women, mostly of middle- and lower-middle-class origin, entered the field of education and became responsible for conveying the ideals seen in the textbooks to their students.[88] This raises the question of whether or not these women, who in their own lives rejected the hegemonic conception of womanhood, accepted the new construct in their lives as teachers?[89] In other words, how did they react to the concepts employed in the textbooks?

The "New Woman" depicted in the textbooks was roughly the same New Woman who appeared in the pages of the women's press. The upper-middle-class and upper-class women contributing to these journals, who helped to fashion this construct of professional housewife, went out of their way to point out that they were not neglecting their true vocation by writing.[90] Nevertheless, as Cathlyn Mariscotti has pointed out, this attempt at the professionalization of the role of wife and mother did not necessarily work for female teachers and other women with ties to the lower middle class. According to Mariscotti, many of these women adopted an oppositional construct of womanhood, which they espoused in their own writing and in their own lives.[91]

How did this vision translate into their training and teaching? Did they accept the role of the woman as mother-educator, general purchasing agent, and household administrator? The largest single piece of evidence that these women did not necessarily accept the ideology of domesticity in its entirety is the large-scale refusal of future teachers to enter the domestic science track of the Sania Teachers' College. Obviously, these women felt that spending their time in the general education courses was more worthwhile for their personal and professional lives than spending half of their time in home economics classes.

Whether by choice or by economic necessity, female teachers did not fit the construct of professional housewife. How did these women respond to the message of the textbooks, and how did they convey this message to their students? Aside from a few guidelines, teachers had a great deal of pedagogical freedom. Their only requirements were to use the books selected by the school director, cover a certain number of lessons per week in each subject, and retain a copy of class notes in ink.[92] These requirements neither necessitated going through the textbook verbatim, nor did they prohibit alternative readings of the text. In simple terms, a teacher who never used napkins in her own home could choose to skip the pages in Mikhail's text covering the proper way to fold napkins. At a more sophisticated level, the teacher could seek to teach her students alternative constructions of womanhood within the texts at hand. As a general rule, teachers adhered to the age-old technique of reading and explicating texts.[93] As we have seen, textbooks did not necessarily offer a clear and unambiguous message, as seen by Mikhail's lavish descriptions interspersed with his admonitions against profligacy. Similarly, by examining a morals textbook we can find two alternative constructions of womanhood and speculate as to how this book was used at the different levels of the school system. *A Book of Morals for Girls*, by Muhammad Ahmad Rakha and Muhammad Hamdi, was used in primary schools, elementary schools, and in institutes for teachers.[94] Thus, the book was used in the different educational tracks and amongst different age levels. The first four sections of the textbook endorse the construct of womanhood seen in the press and in home economics textbooks, and they offer similar social commentary. However, the final section of the book offers an alternative vision.

The first section of *A Book of Morals for Girls* is dedicated to manners. The authors employ short stories about girls who fit the proper pattern of behavior. They begin in the home and work their way outward into society. The first chapter is about a girl named Labiba, who obeys her parents, does not shout, stays clean, and passes her time only with useful amusements. The authors then move into the classroom to describe Faiqa, an exemplary student who lives up to her name (excellence). The third chapter of this section is on proper comportment in the street. This chapter abandons the story format by simply conveying the information. The reader learns that polite young ladies stick to the path, taking only necessary trips, and that they dress plainly in loose-fitting clothing, avoiding extremes in adornment. The pictures accompanying this chapter depict women in traditional black garments and light facial veils; but elsewhere in this section, photographs reveal women in the home wearing open-necked European dresses. The other photographs accompanying the text depict fathers and children in Western clothing, as well as European furniture, art, and gadgets. Although the text seems to endorse Western modes of consumption in the home, the authors quote from Sura 24:31 to endorse traditional standards of modesty and propriety outside the home. The next chapter returns to the story format, conveying a dialogue between a mother and daughter. The daughter wants to leave all the housework to the servant and go visiting. Her mother will not allow her to engage in frivolities at the expense of her housework, warning her against the evils of laziness. Finally, this section closes with a chapter on "please" and "thank you."[95]

Once established in what to do, the second section of the book continues to discuss other laudable behavior, and it discourages many traditional practices that the authors deem as unworthy. Moderation, thrift, and consumption all appear in this section. Another chapter reinforces lessons learned in the home-economics class. It opens with one woman asking another where she purchased the material for her dress and who made it for her. The second woman responds by explaining that her husband bought the material, and that she made the dress. The first woman is surprised, not understanding where her friend finds the time for sewing or why she does sew, since she can afford to pay a seamstress. The second women answers these queries by explaining that she sews in her free time to guard against laziness, and she enjoys setting the proper example for her children. Moreover, she points out that her husband will wear clothing sewn only by her hands. Thus, if a girl missed the message in her home economics class, she might still learn the importance of sewing in her morals class. Finally this section contains several chapters warning against traditional pastimes/occupations of women: folk medicine, superstition, tomb-visiting, saint worship, and the *zar*.[96]

Section three is entitled "Stories," and it consists of parables that both reinforce the previously covered material and introduce new material, including kindness to animals, the danger of haste, and the notion that money cannot buy health and happiness. One of the stories gives a dual-pronged lesson. It outlines the requirements of a proper urban home, while reinforcing the idea that this lifestyle is not for everyone. In this vignette, two city girls visit a farm and meet a young peasant girl. After learning about her life, one of the two city girls asks if the peasant girl has been to Cairo and if she would like to live with them, enticing her with food, furnishings, clothing, servants, and a carriage. The peasant, having visited Cairo once, explains that she prefers her simple life to the cramped life of the city. When the two astonished girls tell their father, he explains to them that the peasants are "active and content," and that those in the city have them to thank for their wealth, for they are "the source of happiness."[97] In other words, there was one standard of consumption and behavior for the upper-middle-class urban girls and another for the peasant. In her study of the Egyptian upper classes between 1919 and 1952, Magda Baraka points out that the word "*fallaḥ*" was undergoing a "semantic transition" from its usage as a derogatory slur to a source of pride in Egyptian nationalist terms.[98] Textbook depictions of the peasantry connote such ambiguity. On the one hand, as previously discussed, servants bring literal and metaphorical dirt from the countryside, while on the other they represent authenticity and true "Egyptian-ness."

Section four of the Rakha and Hamdi text is a series of anthems for sleep, work, and motherhood.[99] Finally, section five is a review of famous women.[100] The first four sections of the text seem to reinforce the hegemonic construct of womanhood. Women appear mainly in traditional roles: mothers, daughters, sisters, wives, aunts, and peasants. In only two cases do women appear in the urban work force, one of them taking place in Europe and the other regarding a teacher and student. Section five departs from this format and includes the biography of non-traditional, yet exemplary, women.[101]

The series begins with Bilqis, the Queen of Sheba, and her encounter with Soloman.[102] It is not particularly surprising that the review should begin in the pre-Islamic era, since the story has Quranic credentials. The Rakha and Hamdi version differs slightly from the Quranic version (27:23–44). It is told from Bilqis's perspective rather than that of Soloman. Like the Quran, this version depicts her as an able ruler; however, there is much less emphasis on her seeking advice from her chiefs. The reader sees that Bilqis ultimately follows the path of light and truth, which is also in keeping with the Quranic version, given that Sura 27 deals with lessons of true and false worship and the triumph of faith.

The second woman in the review also has Quranic credentials: Asiya, wife of pharaoh.[103] Asiya's treatment combines two Quranic descriptions. Although not mentioned by name, wife of pharaoh first appears in Sura 28:9, in which she saves the life of Moses, and she is mentioned again in Sura 66:11. This sura deals with harmony between the sexes, and the wife of pharaoh is upheld as an exemplar to other women along with Maryam (Mary), the mother of Jesus. Interestingly enough, despite the fact that Maryam appears much more frequently and is mentioned by name in the Quran, she is not chosen for Rakha and Hamdi's review of famous women. Perhaps these Muslim authors, writing in a sea of Christian authors and for schools that were in competition with numerous private and mission schools, chose to overlook Maryam and move on to key Islamic figures.

The review then skips ahead in history to the Islamic conquest, but then the following chapter brings the reader to a more predictable choice: Khadija, the first wife of the Prophet Muhammad.[104] In traditional Islamic sources, Khadija appears, along with Asiya, Maryam, and Fatima, as one of four perfect women.[105] The Rakha and Hamdi vignette discusses the meeting and marriage of Khadija and Muhammad, and it is told in light of Khadija's skill as a businesswoman. According to the two authors, unlike other women of her time, Khadija understood the value of money. She saw that it had a purpose other than its use in buying fine clothing and jewelry. They stress this aspect of Khadija's personality, as opposed to her role as the first convert to Islam; the mother of Fatima, who continued the Prophet's line; or even as the "woman behind the man." They bring up the issue of buying fine clothing and jewelry for a specific and modern reason. While seventh-century Mecca was a flourishing center of trade, it lacked modern standards of fashion and individualism. The lesson of Khadija had a great deal more resonance in early-twentieth-century Cairo and Alexandria, in the midst of numerous department stores, boutiques, and jewelry stores.

The authors next choice is not surprising either: Aisha, the beloved wife of the Prophet Muhammad.[106] Aisha is a somewhat controversial figure in Islamic history. On the one hand, she is revered for her wisdom and closeness to the Prophet, while on the other, her reputation is sullied by her role in the Battle of the Camel. Rakha and Hamdi's text highlights the most positive aspects of her personality. Initially, she is described as both beautiful and renowned for her wisdom. The authors also discuss Aisha's role in the Battle of the Camel, however they omit certain details. They depict her as concerned about avenging the death of Uthman, without mentioning her role in the events prior to his assassination. Furthermore, they do not elaborate upon the gory details of the First Civil War, leaving the story incomplete. Aisha's description concludes with a discussion of her role as an advisor to and source of wisdom for the Islamic community.

The authors continue with other notable members of the Prophet's line. The next is Fatima, the Prophet's great granddaughter.[107] Rakha and Hamdi describe her as a beautiful woman, whose moral fortitude and religiosity resembled that of her grandmother and namesake. The main part of the narrative focuses on her role in the Battle of Karbala, where her father was killed. The review then skips back chronologically to Zaynab, the daughter of Ali.[108] She shares the same basic characteristics as Fatima, except no mention is made of beauty; and once again the story focuses on her role at the battle of Karbala. The authors then move on to discuss Sakina, the daughter of Husayn, who is clever, beautiful, and virtuous.[109]

The chronology moves on to Nafisa, the daughter of Hasan.[110] Unlike the five previous vignettes, which focused on how the women were pivotal in the lives of their men, this one focuses primarily on Nafisa's religiosity and life. From the text, the reader learns that she made the pilgrimage 30 times, fasting by day and praying by night, and that she memorized the Quran with remarkable *tajwid*. The text then discusses her move to Egypt, where the Imam Shafii sought her audience and received *ḥadith* from her. Her story concludes by stating that she prayed for the Imam Shafii upon his death and that she died four years later while fasting and reading from the Quran.

The review of famous women continues in the eleventh century with a surprising choice, a heterodox Fatimid: Sitt Malak, daughter of al-Aziz bil-lah al-Fatimi.[111] Once again, the authors depict her as a woman who combines outstanding beauty with intelligence. They describe her as a wise administrator who helped her brother al-Hakim run affairs of the state. They also explain that she served as regent for al-Hakim's son after his disappearance. Nevertheless, the authors neither discuss the extent of her brother's eccentricities, nor do they mention the theory that perhaps it was Sitt Malak who was responsible for her brother's disappearance.

The subsequent vignette takes us to the thirteenth century, and it is another selective interpretation of history: the story of Shajarat al-Durr, the wife of al-Malik al-Salih al-Ayyubi.[112] Like the description of Sitt Malak, that of Shajarat al-Durr focuses on her ability to counsel her husband on matters of the state, including military campaigns. The text relates the familiar story of her concealing her husband's death in order to avoid demoralizing the troops during an important campaign against the Crusaders. According to Rakha and Hamdi, her concern was in saving the throne for the son of her husband. The authors briefly mention that this stepson was assassinated by the mamluks, but they offer no details. Instead, they move on to discuss Shajarat al-Durr's nomination to Queenship by the mamluks, who pledge her their obedience. She is described as a capable ruler who cared about her subjects and distributed money to the poor. The authors then explain that when pilgrims passing through Egypt found a woman on the throne, she was compelled to marry the mamluk general, Aybak. The text ends by stating that her rule lasted another 80 days, without discussing either Aybak's assassination or her own. From this account, the reader sees only her intelligence, generosity, and ability to rule. The issues of rage, greed, and jealousy that characterize most versions of the story do not appear.

The review of famous women then jumps ahead several hundred years and across the Mediterranean Sea to Queen Elizabeth I of England.[113] The reader learns nothing about Elizabeth's controversial mother, her being proclaimed illegitimate, or any other controversies surrounding the House of Tudor. Rakha and Hamdi merely describe her as "among the greatest rulers." They discuss her knowledge of language, history, and science, highlighting the fact that men sought her advice in political affairs. The text also discusses the prominent position of England vis à vis Spain during her reign. The authors take time to mention the Spanish king's hatred of Elizabeth, while conveniently leaving out the fact that she had rebuked his marriage proposal. The narrative continues with the confrontation between Elizabeth's navy and the Spanish armada, emphasizing the significance of this event for English history. In particular, the authors attribute this success to the strength of Britain's navy, without mentioning the weather or other factors. Obviously, this story had resonance for an Egypt under British occupation for nearly 40 years.

The review of women takes another great leap forward chronologically with two stories from nineteenth-century England. First, the authors discuss Victoria, Queen of England and Empress of India.[114] The text emphasizes the people's pleasure with her rule, how they attained greatness in knowledge under her reign, and how she instilled morals in the army. In other words, she combined wise leadership, virtue, and morality. The second nineteenth-century English heroine is of much more humble origins. She is Grace Darling, the daughter of a lighthouse keeper, who with her father braved a rough storm to save the survivors of a shipwreck.[115] Grace exemplified the virtues of industry, obedience, modesty, and piety; and thus she seems a likely candidate for the review. Nonetheless, one has to question how this young woman, who attained semi-legendary status in her own country, but was virtually unknown outside England, made her way into the pages of an Egyptian morals text for girls. The real Grace Darling died of consumption in 1842, four years after her great deed; but she lived on in the annals of English newspapers, books, poems, songs, and commemorative pottery, the peak of her fame coming in the late nineteenth century with the spread of girls' magazines.[116] Thus, it seems likely that Rakha and Hamdi perused contemporary British literature in the process of writing their book, selecting this woman on the basis of her virtues. Since women's biography was becoming a staple of the women's press, they may have found the example there.

The authors then select another Western woman of humble origins: Laura Secourd of Canada, Heroine of the War of 1812.[117] Upon hearing about American plans for invasion, Secourd crossed enemy lines to warn the British-Canadian forces about the impending attack, saving her country from foreign occupation. Like Grace Darling, Laura Secourd became much more famous posthumously, but remained virtually unknown outside her country. Obviously, she contained the right combination of intelligence, bravery, and nationalism to be chosen for a 1918 textbook. In a like vein, the text then covers another ordinary woman, Lina of Italy, doing the extraordinary for her country.[118]

Rakha and Hamdi's review ends with Florence Nightingale, who was the subject of numerous biographies in the mainstream and women's press.[119] The authors describe her as a "symbol of humanity," discussing her role in the Crimean War and the founding of the Red Cross. Nightingale exemplified a number of important characteristics for the modern girl: virtue, industry, compassion, and service to country.

In examining the review of famous women as a whole, it is interesting for both who is included and excluded, as well as the information provided on those who are included. Why, for example, are Bilqis and Asiya included, while Maryam is excluded? Why do the authors emphasize Khadija's role as a businesswoman over that of early convert and mother? Why is Fatima, the daughter of the Prophet excluded, but her daughter and granddaughters included? The juxtaposition of Aisha, Fatima, Zaynab, and Sakina is also worthy of note. They are not arranged chronologically by generation, but rather they are placed thematically in a selective discussion of the first two civil wars in Islam. Why are the stories of Sitt Malak and Shajarat al-Durr juxtaposed? Both of these women are portrayed as able leaders and administrators, without discussing the more controversial aspects of their personality and historical roles. The review then jumps into a discussion of notable European women. Elizabeth, Victoria, and Florence Nightingale are not surprising choices. They frequently appeared as exemplars in the women's press, along with figures such as Catherine the Great and Madame Curie. Nevertheless, the authors then choose a series of women who were national heroines, but virtually unknown outside their country of origin: Grace Darling of Britain, Laura Secourd of Canada, and Lina of Italy. From where do the authors select these women and why do they choose them over others? Why are there no women from the region after the thirteenth century?[120] Like the biographies that appeared before and after them in the women's press, they were meant to be "instructive as well as entertaining, even if it was not always clear which facets of a life were to provide instruction."[121] It would be up to the teacher to guide her students.

In looking at all of the women, it is clear that there are some shared values. The common denominator was intelligence and virtue; however, no other characteristics can be applied to all. Other important traits included wise governance, oratorical ability, poetic ability, generosity, religiosity, compassion, nationalism, and beauty. Although the text explicitly states that these women were the most remarkable of their times, the implication is clear that their distinction also transcended time and place. Their virtues could be applied to contemporary Egyptian girls, who were embarking upon new roles, but were in need of traditional wisdom and guidance.

The women chosen for the review, nonetheless, seem to defy the roles for women outlined in the previous four sections of the book. None of these women are discussed in the context of their role as mothers; and in fact, a number of them were childless and/or virgins. This seems a bit odd, given that one of the authors' main purposes was to prepare women for their role as mothers. Nor are the women described as great wives or household administrators.[122] Even those of humbler origins are not discussed in the context of these roles.

On the other hand, the women chosen help to create a distinct relationship between home, family, and nation, reinforcing the notion that a civilization can be measured by the condition of its women. The series goes beyond the "behind every great man is woman" concept.[123] Instead, the text emphasizes the fact that even women in non-traditional roles have something to offer the nation. By presenting these women as "exceptional," the authors do not upset the patriarchal system. They clearly avoided the example of contemporary suffragettes and feminists who would offer such a challenge.

In teaching the lessons of this textbook, it was up to the teacher to direct the nature of the discussion. There were no prepared questions or guidelines in the text. Whereas the young elementary or primary student might enjoy memorizing the songs and looking at the pictures, older students could spend more time discussing the significance of the parables and the selection of the great women. Perhaps, the teacher might ask the students who is more worthy of praise or which women were the best role models for their times? In the case of girls studying at teachers' institutes, they could be motivated and encouraged by role models—Sitt Malak, Shajarat al-Durr, Queen Elizabeth, Queen Victoria, and Florence Nightingale, and so on. These were all women who moved freely in the public sphere without compromising their character. In presenting this material, teachers did not necessarily stress their exceptionality, but could instead use them as oppositional constructs of womanhood. Nevertheless, this is merely a matter of speculation, as is how the message was received by students. What is clear is that in the decades following the publication and use of these textbooks, women began to enter the urban workforce in larger numbers. Twenty years after the publication of Rakha and Hamdi's text, the number of women in the labor force had increased more than 600 percent.[124] Nevertheless, the curriculum in the girls' schools continued to stress home economics. Career paths for women reinforced the role of mother-educator, as more women became teachers, nurses, pediatricians, obstetricians/gynecologists, and social workers.[125]

Conclusion

The study of early-twentieth-century textbooks highlights the distinctions between the two educational levels and demonstrates the ambiguities over the mission of female education. Both tiers of the educational system sought to impose the ideals of order, hygiene, organization, and moderation. The expanded curriculum in the upper track of the educational system allowed many venues for these lessons by means of classes in home economics, hygiene, morals, and religion. Meanwhile, girls attending *kuttabs*, elementary schools, and vocational schools combined these lessons in hygiene and religion classes. Class-based assumptions buttressed the curriculum. Thus, girls in the lower track learned how to wash their hands after meals, while girls in the upper educational track learned how to set the proper table.[126]

Nevertheless, the class divide between the two educational tracks was not as clear as in the boys' schools. The vocational emphasis of the upper track discouraged many upper-middle and upper-class girls from attending government schools. Instead, they could choose a private school that reflected the needs of their families. Girls from the wealthiest strata, with a full complement of servants to carry out their housework, might prefer schools that adhered to the Gamayyil principles of home economics and offered refined subjects, such as art, music, and languages. Middle class girls of more modest origins might also seek private schools, which would keep them from having to mingle with girls seeking an occupation in teaching or medicine, while also offering them the practical instruction shown in the Mikhail texts. Thus, there were many girls from the middle and lower-middle-classes in the upper track of the educational system. These girls were given a view of the home and consumption which, for many, was far beyond their means. Textbook authors addressed this issue with calls for economy, thrift, and moderation.

These textbook authors were graduates of the new schools in the Middle East. Some were Syrian Christians who had been educated in mission schools, while others were Egyptians who graduated from the schools established my Muhammad Ali and Ismail. While the authors were sensitive to issues of traditional morality and burgeoning nationalist issues, their educational experience in Western-style schools profoundly influenced their worldview. The architects of the new school system were men like Tahtawi and Mubarak, who had participated in early educational missions to Europe. While they maintained the need for certain cultural differences, they were fascinated by European life and customs. Both men wrote books on life in Europe. Mubarak's account was a fictional work entitled *ᶜalam al-din* in which visitors from Egypt travel to France, where they are amazed by the order and organization of the port, capital, mercantile establishments, public gardens, and people. After witnessing the disparities between Egypt and France, the protagonist highlights the source of the difference: "it stemmed from elementary rules of discipline and methods of educating the young, to which everything else goes back."[127] Mubarak made the ideals of organization and discipline the foundation of the new educational system.

Tahtawi was also profoundly influenced by his experience in Europe, and when he returned, he translated and supervised the translation of numerous books on history, medicine, geography, philosophy, and military science. As well, he wrote an account of his stay in Paris, entitled *takhlis al-ibriz ila talkhiṣ Bariz* in which he details the physical composition of Parisian homes, including the layout, furnishings, and decorations. In this discussion he comments upon the importance of the den, decorated with portraits, and reading. Furthermore, he provides information on table manners, customs, and even utensils.[128] Tahtawi does not uncritically accept all aspects of the Parisian lifestyle. For example, he finds that women's clothing lends itself to licentiousness.[129]

One cannot help but be struck by the similarity between the Mikhail texts and Tahtawi. It is as though he read *takhlis al-ibriz* and elaborated upon it, providing sketches and photographs. Nevertheless, the wholescale adoption of European architecture and furnishings did not necessarily make sense in Egypt. As discussed in chapter 3, the traditional home provided much greater circulation of air, and hence greater comfort in the summer and the winter. While a fireplace might provide many months worth of use in northwestern Europe, it had far less utility in Egypt. Furthermore, the exigencies of living on the fringe of the desert, as in Cairo, meant dealing with an abundance of dust in the home. Fireplace mantels, fancy armoires, Louis XIV-style furniture, *bric-a-brac*, and pictures were all places where dust could settle. The simplicity and/or portability of traditional furnishings made them far easier to maintain. Ironically, while authors were attempting to integrate the lessons of order, discipline, and efficiency that they had learned into textbooks for girls, they were advocating models that actually created more housework for Egyptian wives and servants.

Chapter 9

Conclusion

The discussion of textbooks brings this study full circle from an investigation of new patterns of consumption amongst the elitist of the elite to new ideals to which middle-class Egyptians aspired. The ideal home depicted in textbooks was a small-scale version of the "house that Ismail built." Its structure and organization were Western, with its all-important divisions, layout, and surrounding gates, just as the country itself had been dissected by roads, railway lines, and telegraph cables. Inside the home, the individual was to decorate with European-style furnishings, *bric-a-brac*, and portraits, just as the cities had been adorned with modern buildings, houses, parks, and gardens. The responsibility of maintaining this home belonged to the "New Woman," defined by her ability to serve her husband, raise moral children, keep her house clean, and maintain her family's accounts. The home was a small kingdom in and of itself, and it was a building block for the Egyptian nation. The new nation as well needed someone at its helm, and the British, the monarchy, and the politicians all vied for this role.

Ismail sought to create an image of the royal family as both a symbol of dynastic grandeur and as an example of modernity in his realm. The familial link to his Ottoman suzerein facilitated the change in succession to primogeniture, and he imposed "new" marriages upon his children. Arranging a marriage between his heir-apparent Tawfiq and Amina, with her dual royal lineage, would suit his purposes well. Nevertheless, the circumstances that brought Tawfiq to the throne and his continued manipulation by European powers, meant that he would not be the great dynast about which his father dreamed. Despite Tawfiq's unpopularity, Amina was beloved for her philanthropic work, and helping to guide her son, Abbas II, in the early years of his reign. While Abbas's relationship with the nationalist movement was at times strained, he did fulfill the role that his grandfather had desired. For that very reason, the British deposed him at the outset of World War I. The reign of Husayn Kamil (r. 1914–17) was short-lived and highly regulated by the British. He and his unassuming (non-royal) second wife would garner little public respect or interest. The British then placed Fuad on the throne, who at the time was divorced from his first (royal) bride, Chivekiar. In 1919 the non-Arabic-speaking Fuad married Nazli Sabry, daughter of the Minister of Agriculture and descendent of the legendary French mercenary, Suleiman Pasha.[1] The 19-year-old, distinguished (but non-royal) beauty could well have served the role of the premier New Woman of the country, balancing Fuad's deficiencies. However, her

51-year-old husband preferred to keep his bride a "royal captive . . . [in] a gilded cage."[2]

In both the public and private schools of Egypt the "New Woman" received training in the duties that would prepare her for her role as the guardian of her own kingdom. Nevertheless, middle- and upper-class Egyptians were not united in their belief over what this education should entail. While there was a general consensus among the classes and the sexes that a woman's education should prepare her for her future role, there was a wide range of opinion regarding what a suitable curriculum should encompass.

The upper-class girl was moving from a world of strict gender seclusion and large multigenerational households with full serving staffs and retainers, to a world in which she would have greater access to the public sphere through education, shopping, and philanthropy. Her household was also in the process of change. Formerly, the elite home was both a symbol of conspicuous consumption and a seat of power. As the dynasty of Muhammad Ali gained strength over the course of the nineteenth century, such households became things of the past. While they still employed a full retinue of servants, no longer did they require retainers to defend the master's interests. The nuclear family, while not displacing the extended household, did become an ideal. Nevertheless, the elite woman while finding herself in a world of new educational and consumer possibilities, still faced the challenges of polygamy, unilateral divorce, and the last vestiges of concubinage.

The dimunition of the political role of the elite household corresponded to the rise of the New Man and the New Woman. While the New Man challenged the monarchy for a greater voice in government, the elite woman demanded new rights in marriage and divorce. The British occupation complicated matters by reducing the role of the monarchy, thwarting the aims of the New Man, and creating tensions in the life of the elite woman. On the one hand, she could agree with the British that the position of Egyptian women ought to be improved, an argument frequently used by the British to justify the occupation. On the other hand, she could pressure her husband and men of his class to raise the status of women in readiness for self-government. As we have seen, the condition of the woman and the family was inextricably linked to notions of development and modernity.

The upper-class girl's education needed to reflect these changes in her home and in her country. Furthermore, as upper-class men sought education in Europe and in the Europeanized schools of Egypt, many sought wives with a comparable and compatible background. Thus, upper-class men and women believed that a woman's education should include theoretical home economics, foreign languages, and the fine arts. The education of choice was a home education, where the curriculum could be tailored to meet individual needs. In some families this might also include more traditional instruction in Quran, *ḥadith*, poetry, and Turkish; while others might merely employ a European governess to focus on French, music, and art. The new education encouraged these women to utilize their organizational and managerial skills outside the home. Both philanthropy and the nationalist movement brought these women further into the public sphere, and elite men supported these roles for their wives and daughters. Nevertheless, if the woman were to receive a salary for doing such work, it would be considered a disgrace.

The middle class was less unified in its interests and its beliefs regarding girls' education. Lower-middle-class men, namely, *ᶜulama'*, small merchants, artisans, and low-level bureaucrats, were members of professions that had lost a certain degree of wealth and status with the rise of capitalism and the Egyptian state. Their economically tenuous position made them a bit apprehensive regarding girls' education, as they feared women pursuing careers that could potentially displace them. Furthermore, their household accounts were not particularly complex nor could their income support servants. Thus, they believed in a modest education for girls; however, they insisted upon one with a practical emphasis.[3] In their opinion, girls did not need frills, such as languages, history, and geography, nor did they even need to spend an extensive amount of time in mathematics class. Instead, they felt that girls should spend their time learning the practical skills involved in running their homes: cooking, cleaning, laundry, and childcare. They tended to send their daughters to schools where these skills were emphasized, such as the School of Practical Housewifery, the new higher elementary schools, and the government-run *kuttabs* for girls. Those who were poor enough to desire an income for their daughters could send them to one of the teachers' training colleges or the School of Midwifery. Nevertheless, these men tended to be more conservative regarding the role of their wives and daughters in the public sphere, adhering to old Turco-Circassian values, rather than Western ones.[4] Understanding the mindset and experience of lower middle class women is more difficult. The one small piece of evidence that we have is the large-scale refusal of future teachers, most of whom were lower middle class in origin, to enter the domestic science track of the Sania Teachers' College. Women overwhelmingly chose the general education division, which emphasized language, mathematics, geography, history, and drawing over needlework, cookery, laundry, and housewifery.

The men of the middle and upper middle classes tended to come from families whose condition improved over the course of the nineteenth century. These were people whose fathers and grandfathers had advanced socially and economically due to their education, moving into positions in the upper levels of the bureaucracy and the liberal professions. These were also men who received land grants from the government and who invested their own money in land. Women in these upwardly mobile families were just being introduced to the concept of household management, and their household accounts were becoming increasingly complex. Thus, there was a greater need for the science of home management. Nevertheless, men more than women believed in the necessity of some practical education for girls. Few in this class could afford home education for their daughters. For most, government schools were not a viable alternative either due to the vocational bent of the curriculum. The private, community, and mission schools offered a variety of alternatives at a wide range of cost.

Middle- to upper-middle-class women contributing to the discourse on education did not speak with a unified voice. Some, for example, Regina Awwad, pressed for a more practical curriculum for girls. Nevertheless, others were proud of their newly attained position in society and wished to emulate the model of the elite. In other words, they felt that cooking was the vocation of a cook and that a girl's time in school was better spent engaged in other subjects. Regardless of their view on practical home economics, the women of this class had less experience with issues related to polygamy and concubinage, and they placed more emphasis on creating the proper home, rather than dismantling the improper one.

Education reinforced divisions in society, particularly in the government schools for boys, where the bifurcated system tended to cut along class lines. Nevertheless, the multiplicity of choices for girls also tended to divide along class lines. The type of education a girl received reflected both her family background and the type of man she might marry. The rise of companionate marriage without the concommittant rise of personal choice in partners meant that education, along with family reputation, was a leading criterion for decision making.[5] The textbooks adopted for individual schools reflected the class outlook of the particular school. Schools that catered to a more prestigious clientele might opt for the Gamayyil home economics text, while a somewhat more modest school might adopt only part one of Mikhail's *Modern Home Management*, while a school catering to the middle to lower middle class might utilize both parts one and two of the Mikhail text.

Furthermore, the textbooks delineate the distinction between the countryside and the city, reinforcing the respective roles of production and consumption. Authors point out the importance of the peasant for the economy; but at the same time, they depict peasants as simple, ignorant, and dirty. Even though city dwellers owe the peasant gratitude for their well being, the culture of the countryside was rejected in favor of the Westernized culture of Cairo and Alexandria.

Education was part of a larger struggle for cultural identity. Textbooks in particular, represent a hegemonic struggle between the interests of the ruling elite and the British occupiers on the one hand, and indigenous customs and values on the other. An intellectual bargain was reached between the occupiers, the elite, and the nationalist intelligentsia whereby curriculum would espouse a vision of Western civilization tempered with traditional Eastern values. Thus, home economics textbooks exhorted girls to consume along Western lines, create Western-style homes, and to live up to the Victorian mother-educator ideal. History, geography, and mathematics classes also buttressed a Eurocentric world view with their emphases on empire and the culture of the West. At the same time, however, classes in religion, Arabic, morals, and civics encouraged students to follow traditional standards of modesty and propriety, while also encouraging a new form of identification as citizens. Students learned their roles as members of individual families and as part of the collective national family.

Education in household management and consumption continued beyond the walls of the classroom as women read and listened to the growing literature of the home in the women's and mainstream presses. Articles offered advice that ran the gamut from the abstract, theoretical rights and duties of women to nitty gritty advice on how to get rid of insects and remove stains. Furthermore, advertising informed women of the new products and services available in large cities. Indeed, there was a great deal of overlap between what girls learned in school and what they found in advertisements. In school they read about visitors' cards, new types of furnishings, modern medicine, and services such as banking and insurance. These were the same types of products and services that advertised in both presses.

The repeated images and words in advertising, as well as in prescriptive literature, fed Egyptian women a near-constant diet of ways to improve her home through consumption.[6] In the years after 1915, one the strongest messages sent, despite consumption of foreign and Western-styled (indigenously made) goods, was to purchase "Egyptian." While we do not know how readers perceived these advertisments, the staying power of this method of marketing, meant that advertisers believed in its utility. According to Marshall McLuhan, "[e]ffective advertising gains its ends partly by distracting the attention of the reader from its presuppositions and by its quiet fusion with other levels of experience . . . it is the supreme form of demogogic flattery."[7] Consumption of national goods, or even goods that improved the quality of the home, helped women to contribute to the larger effort of the country. Their identity was vested in the home and the marriage that they created. By the same token, the economic boycott, or non-consumption of British goods, was an active demonstration of their self-identification as Egyptian citizens.

Abbreviations

AHA: American Historical Association

Annual Report: Parliamentary Papers, *Report by Her/His Majesty's Agent and Consul General on the Finances, Administration, and Condition of Egypt and the Soudan, 1898–1914*. London: Harrison & Sons.

AUC: American University in Cairo

DW: *Dar al-Watha'iq*, Egyptian National Archives

AT: *muḥafiẓ ᶜAbdin, taᶜlim* series

MW: *majlis al-wuzara'*

NM: *niẓarat al-maᶜarif*

NSH: *niẓarat al-ashghal*

SJ: *shirkat wa jamaᶜiyat*

PI: *Période Ismail*

IFAO: L'Institut Français D'Archéologie Orientale

IJMES: *International Journal of Middle East Studies*

MESA: Middle East Studies Association

PA: Presbyterian Archives, Philadelphia, PA

SUNY: State University of New York

Notes

1 Introduction

1. Qasim Amin, *The Liberation of Women and The New Woman*, translated by Samiha Sidhom Peterson (Cairo: AUC Press, 2000), 115–16.
2. Arland Thornton, "The Developmental Paradigm, Reading History Sideways, and Family Change," *Demography* 38, 4 (2001): 451. Amin mentions by name a number Thornton's purveyors of the developmental paradigm: Rousseau, Marx, and Spencer.
3. Lavern Kuhnke did the pioneering research on *ḥakimas* first published in the mid-1970s and updated in her *Lives at Risk* (Berkeley: University of California Press, 1990). Since that time Khaled Fahmy, Mervat Hatem, and Hibba Abugideiri have argued that there existed a "less rosy picture" emanating from the training of *ḥakimas*. See Fahmy's "Women, Medicine, and Power in Nineteenth-Century Egypt," in Lila Abu Lughod, ed., *Remaking Women: Feminism and Modernity in the Middle East* (Princeton: Princeton University Press, 1998): 35–72; Hatem, "The Professionalization of Health and the Control of Women's Bodies as Modern Governmentalities in Nineteenth-Century Egypt," in Madeline Zilfi, ed., *Women in the Ottoman Empire* (New York: Brill, 1997); and Abugideiri, "Egyptian Women and the Science Question: Gender in the Making of Colonized Medicine, 1893–1929" (Ph.D. diss., Georgetown University, 2001). Mario Ruiz is in the process of writing "Illicit Lives, Intimate Danger: Gender, Law, and Violence in Colonial Egypt, 1848–1922" (Ph.D. diss., University of Michigan, 2004) and discussed this topic in a recent MESA presentation: "Virginity on Trial: Sex and Violence in Khedive Ismail's Egypt (1863–79)," November 2002.
4. See entry I.1.i for woman, www.oed.com (2003).
5. See e.g., Ann Heilmann, ed., *The Late-Victorian Marriage Question: A Collection of Key New Woman Texts* (London: Routledge/Thoemmes Press, 1998); Judith McArthur, *Creating the New Woman: The Rise of Southern Women's Progressive Culture in Texas, 1893–1918* (Urbana: University of Illinois Press, 1998); Hu Ying, *Tales of Translation: Composing the New Woman in China, 1899–1918* (Stanford: Stanford University Press, 2000); Lynne Attwood, *Creating the New Soviet Woman: Women's Magazines as Engineers of Female Identity, 1922–1953* (Basingstoke: Macmillan, 1999); James McMillan, *France and Women, 1789–1914: Gender, Society, and Politics* (New York: Routledge, 2000); Helen Hopper, *A New Woman of Japan: A Political Biography of Kato Shidzue* (Boulder: Westview Press, 1996); Sharad Srivastava, *The New Woman in Indian English Fiction* (New Delhi: Creative Books, 1996); Frances Elizabeth Willard, *The Ideal of "the New Woman" According to the Woman's Christian Temperance Union*, edited and introduced by Carolyn De Swarte Gifford (New York: Garland, 1987); Patricia Marks, *Bicycles, Bangs, and Bloomers: The New Woman in the Popular Press* (Lexington: University of Kentucky, 1990); Maggie Andrews and Mary M. Talbot, eds., *All the World and Her Husband: Women in Twentieth Century Consumer Culture* (London: Cassell, 2000). Barbara Sato, *The New Japanese Woman* (Durham: Duke University Press, 2003).

6. See e.g., Elizabeth Frierson, "Unimagined Communities: State, Press, and Gender in the Hamidian Era," (Ph.D. diss., Princeton University, 1996); Camron Michael Amin, *The Making of the Modern Iranian Woman: Gender, State Policy, and Popular Culture, 1865–1946* (Gainesville: University Press of Florida, 2002), Akram Fouad Khater, *Inventing Home: Emigration, Gender, and the Middle Class in Lebanon, 1870–1920* (Berkeley: University of California Press, 2001); Afsaneh Najmabadi, *The Story of the Daughters of Quchan: Gender and National Memory in Iranian History* (Syracuse: Syracuse University Press, 1998); a number of the essays in Lila Abu-Lughod, ed., *Remaking Women*; Monica Ringer, "Rethinking Religion: Progress and Morality in the Early 20th century Iranian Women's Press," paper presented at the AHA, January 2003; Ellen Fleischmann, *The Nation and its "New" Women: The Palestinian Women's Movement, 1920–1948* (Berkeley: University of California Press, 2003).
7. Mary Ann Fay, "The Ties That Bound: Women and Households in Eighteenth-Century Egypt," in Amira Sonbol, ed., *Women, the Family, and Divorce Laws in Islamic History* (Syracuse: Syracuse University Press, 1996), 155–72; Afaf Marsot, *Women and Men in Late Eighteenth-Century Egypt* (Austin: University of Texas Press, 1995), esp. chapters 3 and 4; Jane Hathaway, *The Politics of Households in Ottoman Egypt* (Cambridge: Cambridge University Press, 1997), esp. chapters 2, 6, and 7.
8. Judith Tucker, *Women in Nineteenth-Century Egypt* (Cambridge: Cambridge University Press, 1985). With respect to Cairo, see Mine Ener, *Managing Egypt's Poor and the Politics of Benevolence, 1800–1952* (Princeton: Princeton University Press, 2003).
9. Although she could reside portions of the year outside these cities, she still had regular and repeated contact with the urban, delta world.
10. Fleischmann, *New Women*, 65–66.
11. The original quotation was regarding the Iranian context, see Ringer, "Rethinking."
12. Mary Lyndon Shanley, *Feminism, Marriage, and the Law in Victorian England* (Princeton: Princeton University Press, 1989), 6–7.
13. Fatma Müge Göçek, *Rise of the Bourgeoisie, Demise of Empire* (New York: Oxford University Press, 1996), 5. See also Göçek, *East Encounters West* (New York: Oxford University Press, 1987), 24.
14. Göçek, *Bourgeoisie*, 28.
15. Fay, "Households," 155–56; Hathaway, *Politics*, 17–18, 24–25.
16. Eve M. Trout Powell, *A Different Shade of Colonialism* (Berkeley: University of California Press, 2003), 5–7. See also, Frederick Cooper and Ann Laura Stoler, eds., *Tensions of Empire: Colonial Cultures in a Bourgeois World* (Berkeley: University of California Press, 1997).
17. Abbas Hilmi II, *The Last Khedive of Egypt: Memoirs of Abbas Hilmi II*, translated and edited by Amira Sonbol (Reading: Ithaca, 1998), 39, 53, 125. Sonbol argues that documents, letters, and other materials support the gist of these claims. The recent memoirs by Prince Hassan Hassan reflect the spread of this view through the various branches of the royal family. See *In the House of Muhammad Ali* (Cairo: AUC Press, 2000).
18. This work depends heavily upon the pioneering work in Egyptian education done by Aḥmad ^{c}Izzat ^{c}Abd al-Karim and John Heyworth-Dunne. Regarding the former, see *tarikh ta^{c}lim fi Miṣr fi ^{c}aṣr Muḥammad ^{c}Ali* (Cairo: Maṭba^{c}at al-Naṣr, 1938) and *tarikh al-ta^{c}lim fi Miṣr min nihayat ḥukm Muḥammad ^{c}Ali ila awa'il ḥukm Tawfiq* (Cairo: Maṭba^{c}at al-Naṣr, 1945). Regarding the latter, see his *An Introduction to the History of Education in Modern Egypt* (London: Cass, 1968). For women's education in particular, see Leila Ahmed, *Women and Gender in Islam* (New Haven: Yale University Press, 1992), 127–88.
19. See e.g., Badran, *Feminists, Islam, and Nation* (Princeton: Princeton University Press, 1995); Beth Baron, *The Women's Awakening in Egypt* (New Haven: Yale University Press, 1994).

20. Badran, *Feminists*, 12–13. For two other opinions regarding the appropriation of the feminist movement by the nationalist movement, see Mervat Hatem, "The Enduring Alliance of Nationalism and Patriarchy in Muslim Personal Status Laws: The Case of Egypt," *Feminist Issues* (Spring, 1986): 19–43; Juan Ricardo Cole, "Feminism, Class, and Islam in Turn-of-the-Century," *IJMES* 13 (1981): 387–407.
21. Baron, *Women's Awakening*, 3–4, 191–93.
22. Lisa Pollard, *Nurturing the Nation: The Family Politics of Modernizing, Colonizing, and Liberating Egypt, 1805–1923* (Berkeley: University of California Press, 2005).
23. See e.g., Baron, *Women's Awakening*; Abbas Kelidar, "The Political Press in Egypt, 1882–1914," in *Contemporary Egypt Through Egyptian Eyes: Essays in the Honor of P.J. Vatikiotis* (London: Routledge, 1993); Juan R. Cole, *Colonialism and Revolution in the Middle East* (Princeton: Princeton University Press, 1993), esp. chapter 4; Ami Ayalon, *The Press In the Arab Middle East, A History* (New York: Oxford University Press, 1995); Frierson, "Unimagined Communities"; Palmira Brummett, *Image and Imperialism in the Ottoman Revolutionary Press, 1908–1911* (Albany: SUNY Press, 2000); Shaun Lopez, "The Culture/Gender Wars: Margaret Fahmy and the Shaping of Sexuality in 1920s Egypt," paper presented at MESA, November 2002 and his 2004 dissertation from University of Michigan. See also Frierson, "Cheap and Easy: The Creation of Consumer Culture in Late Ottoman Society," in Donald Quataert, ed., *Consumption Studies and the History of the Ottoman Empire, 1550–1922 An Introduction* (Albany: SUNY Press, 2000), 243–60.
24. Heather Sharkey, *Living with Colonialism* (Berkeley: University of California Press, 2003), 3.
25. Grant McCracken, *Culture and Consumption* (Bloomington: Indiana University Press, 1990), 117.
26. Göçek, *Bourgeoisie*, 37.
27. See Quataert, *Consumption*; Relli Shechter, ed., *Transitions in Domestic Consumption and Family Life in the Modern Middle East: Houses in Motion* (New York: Palgrave, 2003).
28. For the classic view on this subject see Christine Frederick, *Selling Mrs. Consumer* (New York: The Business Bourse, 1929), 12.
29. John K. Galbraith, *Economics and Public Purpose* (Boston: Houghton Mifflin, 1973), 29–37, 233–40.
30. Vivian Gornick, "Consumerism and Women: A Redstocking Sister," in Gornick and Barbara Moran, eds., *Women and Sexist Society* (New York: Basic Books, 1971), 480–84. See also, Stuart Ewen, *Captains of Consciousness* (New York: McGrawhill, 1976), 175–78.
31. See his "Transformations in a Culture of Consumption: Women and Department Stores, 1890–1925," *Journal of American History* 71 (1984), 342. See also Leach, *Land of Desire* (New York: Vintage Books, 1994). Rachel Bowby presents a more nuanced view of gender and consumption in "Soft Sell: Marketing Rhetoric in Feminist Criticism," in Victoria de Grazia and Ellen Furlough, eds., *The Sex of Things: Gender and Consumption in Historical Perspective* (Berkeley: University of California Press, 1996), 381–87.
32. Neil McKendrick, John Brewer, and J.H. Plumb, *The Birth of Consumer Society* (Bloomington: Indiana University Press, 1982), 1–11; McCracken,*Culture and Consumption*, 22.
33. Traditional accounts of capitalist development have focused on European economic penetration over the course of the nineteenth century and have characterized the change as both abrupt and transformative. See e.g., Charles Issawi, "Egypt since 1800: A Study in Lopsided Development," in his *The Economic History of the Middle East, 1800–1914* (Chicago: University of Chicago Press, 1966); Issawi, "Middle East Economic Development, 1815–1914: The General and the Specific," in M.A. Cook, ed., *Studies in the*

Economic History of the Middle East (Oxford: Oxford University Press, 1970). Although adhering to traditional periodization, Roger Owen documents such changes as both slower and uneven in nature. See *The Middle East in the World Economy, 1800–1914* (London: Methuen, 1993). Peter Gran challenges these studies with respect to both the origins and the periodization of the rise of capitalism. See *Islamic Roots of Capitalism, 1769–1840* (Austin: University of Texas Press, 1979).

34. On Ottoman citizenship and identity, see Brummett, *Image and Imperialism*, 11–12. See also Bernard Lewis, *The Multiple Identities of the Middle East* (New York: Schocken, 1998).
35. See F. Robert Hunter's *Egypt Under the Khedives, 1805–1879* (Pittsburgh: University of Pittsburgh Press, 1984) and Timothy Mitchell's *Colonising Egypt* (Cambridge: Cambridge University Press, 1988).
36. This quotation comes from Powell, *Different Shades*, 51. See also, 26–63.
37. Rifa^{c}at Rafi^{c} al-Ṭahṭawi, *manahij al-albab al-miṣriyya fi mabahij al-adab al-^{c}aṣriyya*, 2nd edition (Cairo: Maṭba^{c}at Shirkat al-Ragha'ib, 1912), 350–51.
38. Ministry of Public Instruction, *al-madaris al-ibtida'iyya al-darja al-ula* (Bulaq: Maṭba^{c}at al-Ahliyya, 1885); Ministry of Public Instruction, *lycee: madrasat al-normal, qism al-mubtadiyan, brugramat* (1887); Ministry of Public Instruction, *Syllabus 1892*; Ministry of Public Instruction, *Syllabus 1901* (Bulaq, 1901); Ministry of Public Instruction *Syllabus of Secondary Courses of Study* (Cairo: National Printing Department, 1905); DW, MW, NM, box A23, Report on Curriculum in Primary Schools, June 7, 1897; DW, MW, NM, box A23, Changes in Secondary Curriculum, October 28, 1902; DW, PI, box 12, George Robb, *Educational Progress in Egypt During the Period of 1882–1922*.
39. See e.g., Muḥammad Ḥamid, *mu^{c}ayyan al-ṭulab ^{c}ala al-ḥisab* (Maṭba^{c}at al-Amiriyya, 1891); *al-nafahat al-^{c}abbasiyya fil-mabadi' al-ḥisabiyya* (Cairo: Maṭba^{c}a al-Kubry al-Amiriyya, 1898).
40. Egyptian, Islamic, and Ottoman history were still taught; however, the perspective and focus changed with the arrival of the British and their empire-based methods of teaching. For the British opinion regarding the teaching of history and geography, see DW, AT, box 230, "The Teaching of Geography," and "The Teaching of History," *The Indian Practical Teacher* 1, 8 and 1, 9 (Dec. 1909 and Jan. 1910), resp., 2.
41. DW, MW, NM, box A23, Projet d'extension de l'enseignement religeiux dans les écoles primaires, April 2, 1907.
42. See e.g., Israel Gershoni and James Jankowski, *Egypt and the Arabs: The Search for Egyptian Nationhood, 1900–1930* (New York: Oxford University Press, 1986); Erez Manela, "The Wilsonian Moment and the Rise of Anticolonial Nationalism: The Case of Egypt," *Diplomacy and Statecraft* 12, 4 (December 2001): 99–122.
43. Nancy Reynolds translated a portion of Fathi Radwan's memoirs that graphically depict these parallel structures with respect to commerce in the 1920s. See her "*Sharikat al-Bayt al-Miṣri*: Domesticating Commerce in Egypt 1931–1956," *Arab Studies Journal* (Fall 1999/Spring 2000): 80.

2 The House, City, and Nation that Ismail Built

1. Afaf Marsot, *Egypt in the Reign of Muhammad Ali* (Cambridge: Cambridge University Press, 1984), 1, 21. Although Marsot credits him with founding modern Egypt, recent studies, e.g. Khaled Fahmy's *All the Pasha's Men* provide a more nuanced view of his ethnicity and worldview. (Cambridge: Cambridge University Press, 1997).
2. Afaf Marsot, *A Short History of Modern Egypt* (Cambridge: Cambridge University Press, 1985), 54. This function, a ceremony of investiture for his son Ahmad Tusun as

commander of the expedition force against the Wahhabis, marks the beginning of his program of expansion.

3. Although Muhammad Ali is frequently credited with bringing the *Rumi* style to Egypt, the more accurate description might be that he popularized it, since the home of al-Alfi Bey, completed in 1797, was already built in this style. The *Rumi* style shares characteristics with Greek, Albanian, Bulgarian, and Ottoman architecture of the same era. Nihal Tamraz, *Nineteenth-Century Cairene Houses and Palaces* (Cairo: AUC Press, 1998), 5, 17–24, plates 2.1–2.13.
4. ^{c}Abd al-Raḥman al-Rafa^{c}i, *^{c}aṣr Isma^{c}il* vol. 1 (Cairo: Dar al-Ma^{c}arif, 1987 [1932]), chapters one and two, esp. 15, 18, 20, 21, 33–34, 48; Ehud Toledano, *State and Society in Mid-Nineteenth Century Egypt* (Cambridge: Cambridge University Press, 1990), 52–55; Tamraz, *Cairene Houses*, 28.
5. Toledano, *State and Society*, 62.
6. Ismail's succession was tainted by the fact that his elder half-brother Ahmad Rifat was killed in a train accident. Since Ismail had chosen not to attend this function, some members of Ahmad's family have pointed a finger of suspicion at him. Marsot argues that there is no evidence to support this claim. See her *Short History*, 67.
7. See comments in early 1863 by W.S. Thayer, General Princeteau, and Le Moyne in Georges Guindi Bey and Jacques Tagher, eds., *Ismail D'Après Les Documents Officiels avec Avant-Propos et Introduction Historique* (Cairo: IFAO, 1946), 14–15.
8. Afaf Marsot, "The Porte and Ismail Pasha's Quest for Autonomy," *Journal of the American Research Center in Egypt* XII (1975), 92; Marsot, *Short History*, 68. According to Prince Hassan Hassan, Ismail wanted to be known by the title *al-Aziz al-Masri*. See his *In the House of Muhammad Ali* (Cairo: AUC Press, 2000), 78.
9. John A. Todd, *The Banks of the Nile* (London: A. and C. Black, 1913), 94; ^{c}Ali Mubarak, *al-khiṭaṭ al-tawfiqiyya al-jadida li Miṣr wal-Qahira wa mudunha wa biladha al-qadima wal-shahira*, vol. 1 (Cairo: Dar al-Kutub, 1979), 210, 213; Mahmoud El-Gawhary, *Ex-Royal Palaces in Egypt* (Cairo: Dar al-Ma^{c}arif, 1954), 15–16, 38; Janet Abu-Lughod, *Cairo: 1001 Years of the City Victorious* (Princeton: Princeton University Press, 1971), 113; Tamraz, *Cairene Houses*, 32–33.
10. Abu-Lughod, *Cairo*, 108; Nina Nelson, *Shepheard's Hotel* (London: Barrie and Rockliff, 1960), 29; Tamraz, *Cairene Houses*, 28–30; Mubarak, *khiṭaṭ*, vol. 1, 212; DW, PI, doss. 62/5, Letter from the Chief Engineer to Barrot Bey Regarding Work on the Gezira Gardens, Cairo, March 14, 1874. See DW, PI, doss. 62/4 for information regarding the zoological gardens at Gezira; Mrs. William Grey, *Journal of a Visit to Egypt, Constantinople, the Crimea, Greece, &c. in the Suite of the Prince and Princess of Wales* (New York: Harper & Brothers Publishers, 1870), 125–26. Part of the original palace has been incorporated into a Marriott hotel, and the original grounds extended to where the Cairo Tower stands and also included what is now the Zamalek Fish Grotto. See Hassan, *In the House of Muhammad Ali*, 81–82.
11. Jean-Pierre Barillet-Deschamps, former chief gardener to the city of Paris, had been appointed by Ismail several years earlier to work on the Azbakiyya park and gardens. He continued to work for Ismail on several other projects, including the Orman gardens, which remained incomplete at the time of his death in 1874. Mubarak, *khiṭaṭ*, vol. 1, 212–13; DW, PI, doss. 62/5, Letter from the Chief Engineer to Barrot Bey Regarding the Garden of the Salamlik at Giza, Cairo, March 30, 1874; Abu-Lughod, *Cairo*, 105, 112, 142; Tamraz, *Cairene Houses*, 30–31, plate 2.45.
12. Mubarak, *khiṭaṭ*, vol. 1, 213; El-Gawhary, *Palaces*, 85; Mary Broderick et al., eds., *A Handbook for Travellers in Lower and Upper Egypt* (London: John Murray, 1896), 403; al-Rafa^{c}i, *Ismail*, vol. 2, 32; DW, PI, doss. 15/7 contains the affairs of the *Mahrussa*;

Alfred Butler, *Court Life in Egypt* (London: Chapman & Hall; New York: Scribner & Welford, 1887), 131; Hassan, *In the House of Muhammad Ali*, 78.

13. Fatma Müge Göçek, *East Encounters West: France and the Ottoman Empire in the Eighteenth Century* (New York: Oxford University Press, 1987), 5.
14. Blanchard Jerrold, *Egypt Under Ismail Pacha* (London: Samuel Tinsley & Co., 1879), 16–17.
15. Pierre Bourdieu, *Distinction: A Social Critique of the Judgement of Taste*, trans. Richard Nice (Cambridge: Harvard University Press, 1984), 77, 185, 190–92, 196.
16. DW, PI, doss. 10/12, Letter from Gianchi to Abdel Magid Bey, Milan, May 22, 1875. See also, Mubarak, *khiṭaṭ*, vol. 1, 213; See e.g., Grey, *Journal*, 26; Butler, *Court Life*, 51–52. For actual costs see DW, PI, doss. 10/12, Correspondence from A. Defoer and L. Eude, L. Chanee & Cie. Regarding Shipments 22 and 23, Paris, March 1875. DW, PI, doss. 10/13, Letter from A. Defoer, Paris, January 1876.
17. Tugay, *Three Centuries: Family Chronicles of Turkey and Egypt* (London: Oxford University Press, 1963), 305. See Tulay Artan, "Aspects of the Ottoman Elite's Food Consumption: Looking for 'Staples,' 'Luxuries,' and 'Delicacies' in a Changing Century" for a discussion of types of meat and palace/capital consumption, in Donald Quataert, ed., *Consumption Studies and the History of the Ottoman Empire, 1550–1922: An Introduction* (Albany: SUNY Press, 2000), 133–37.
18. See e.g., DW, PI, doss. 10/3, 10/4, 10/5, 10/6, 10/11, 10/13, and 10/17. Göçek points out that although consumption of wine was forbidden in Islam, Ottomans consumed it anyway. Göçek, *East-West*, 42–43. With respect to Ottoman Egypt, Muslims occasionally consumed alcohol, but left its production to Christians and Jews. Stanford Shaw, *Ottoman Egypt in the Age of the French Revolution* (Cambridge: Harvard University Press, 1964), 132. By the turn of the twentieth century, Lord Cecil reports that elite Egyptians bragged about their drinking. See his *The Leisure of an Egyptian Official* (London: Hodder & Stoughton, 1921), 270–71.
19. DW, PI, doss. 10/10, Correspondence from A. Defoer Regarding Shipment of Kitchen Utensils, January 1873; DW, PI, doss. 10/5, bill from Orfevrerie Christofle, Paris, March 21, 1868; DW, PI, doss. 10/15, Correspondence from Orfevrerie Veyrat to Barrot Bey Regarding Purchase of Silver, Paris, February 10, 1878. According to Ḥanafi al-Maḥalawi, the Khedive used silver implements for ordinary occasions and gold ones for special occasions, al-Maḥalawi, *ḥarim muluk Miṣr min Muḥammad ᶜAli 'ila Faruq* (Cairo: Dar al-Ameen, 1993), 87. See also Douglas Sladen, *Queer Things About Egypt* (London: Hurst & Blackett, Ltd., 1910), 83. According to Lane, even Egyptians of the upper classes did not use forks and knives. Spoons were used for rice, soup, and other items not easily eaten by hand. See his *An Account of the Manners and Customs of the Modern Egyptians* (London: M.A. Nattali, 1846), vol. 1, 198. Nevertheless, in a supplement on late innovations he states that some of the wealthy have adopted the fork and knife. See fifth edition (New York: Dover, 1973), 558. Göçek points out that in the eighteenth century, Ottomans did not use tablecloths, napkins, knives, forks, plates, or salt. Göçek, *East-West*, 38.
20. Grey, *Journal*, 126–27, 32–34; Lane, *Manners.*, vol. 1, 198.
21. See e.g., DW, PI, doss. 10/10, Letter from A. Defoer to Abdelgalil Bey, January 18, 1873. Doss. 10/8, 10/10, 10/11, and 10/16 contain numerous cigar orders. Tobacco was a New World crop, which first spread in the Ottoman Empire during the early seventeenth century, first for medicinal and later for recreational purposes in pipes or waterpipes. Cigars and cigarettes were nineteenth-century innovations. Göçek, *East-West*, 104; Relli Shechter, "The Egyptian Cigarette: A Study of the Interaction Between the

Consumption, Production, and Marketing in Egypt, 1850–1956," (Ph.D. diss., Harvard University, 1999), 10.

22. De Kusel, *An Englishman's Recollections of Egypt, 1863–1887* (New York & London: John Lane Co., 1915), 126.
23. Shechter, "Cigarette," 41, 44.
24. See DW, PI, doss. 10/4. According to Mrs. Grey, women of the *ḥarim* sometimes wore the Khedive's picture set in stones as a piece of jewelry.
25. Graham-Brown, *Images of Women* (London: Quartert Books, 1988), 38. See also Nancy Mickelwright, "Personal, Public, and Political (Re)Constructionists," in Donald Quataert, ed., *Consumption Studies*, 282.
26. Nancy Mickelwright, "(Re)Constructionists," 263. See also her contribution to Relli Shechter, ed., *Transitions in Domestic Consumption and Family Life in the Modern Middle East: Houses in Motion* (New York: Palgrave, 2003).
27. DW, PI, doss. 10/14, Bill from Paschal & Cie. for clothing, cologne, etc., March 31, 1877.
28. See e.g., DW, PI, doss. 10/3, 10/4, and 10/14. Items ordered by the princesses are indicated as such, however, it is not clear for whom Ismail intended other purchases.
29. DW, PI, doss. 10/13, Correspondence from Savory & Moore to Barrot Bey Regarding Medication and Other Products, London, June 23, 1876.
30. Lisa Pollard, "Nurturing the Nation: The Family Politics of the 1919 Revolution" (Ph.D. diss., Berkeley, 1997), 31.
31. Emmeline Lott, *The English Governess in Egypt: Harem Life in Egypt and Constantinople* (Philadelphia: T.B. Peterson & Brothers, 186–?), 58.
32. DW, PI, doss. 10/12, Correspondence from A. Defoer Regarding Shipment of Clothing for the First and Second Princesses and Prince Ibrahim, Paris, April 6, 1875 and May 24, 1875.
33. The most reasonable assessment, between 150 and 200, including slaves and eunuchs, comes from Emmeline Lott who actually resided in the *ḥarim*. Lott, *Harem Life*, 121. See also Grey, *Journal*, 39; William McEntire Dye, *Moslem Egypt and Christian Abyssinia* (New York: Atkin & Prout, 1880), 30; al-Maḥalawi, *ḥarim*, 86 and 88.
34. Grey, *Journal*, 39.
35. Clara Boyle, *Boyle of Cairo: A Diplomat's Adventures in the Middle East* (Kendal: Titus Wilson & Son, 1965), 36. For the cost of a tailor, see e.g., DW, PI, doss. 4/12, Letter from the Secretary of the Khedive [unsigned] regarding Zeinab's account with *couturiére* Mlle. Marie Gilbert, February 26, 1874.
36. Ellen Chennells, *Recollections of an Egyptian Princess by her English Governess* (Edinburgh: William Blackwood & Sons, 1893), vol. 1, 252–53; vol. 2, 121.
37. Mrs. Cromwell Rhodes to Douglas Sladen, in Sladen, *Egypt*, 89. Grey, *Journal*, 141–42.
38. Sladen, *Egypt*, 83–84.
39. See e.g., DW, PI, doss. 10/4, Instructions from L. Rouvenat, Fabrique de Joallerie, Bijouterie, Objets d'Art, Paris, undated [1867].
40. DW, PI, doss. 10/9, Letter and Bill from A. Defoer to Barrot Bey, Paris, May 28, 1872; doss. 10/13, Accounting Sheet from Pharmacie de S.A. Le Khedive, June 1876.
41. Margot Badran, "Huda Shaarawi and the Liberation of Egyptian Women," (Ph.D. diss., St. Antony's College, Oxford, 1977), 36 as cited in Graham-Brown, *Images*, 81. For examples, see the pictures in Charles Chaille-Long, "Princes of Egypt," *The Cosmopolitan Magazine* 26, 3 (1899): 253–62; al-Maḥalawi, *ḥarim*, 101–13; and in Dar al-Hilal, *sijill al-hilal al-muṣawwar, 1892–1992* (Cairo: Dar al-Hilal, 1992), 1: 691, 2: 1002–03.

42. Lott, *Harem Life*, 164.
43. al-Mahalawi, *harim*, 84.
44. Grey, *Journal*, 38. There was no need for European-style washing materials since palaces contained Turkish baths. Tugay, *Family Chronicles*, 307.
45. al-Mahalawi, *harim*, 90; Hassan, *In the House of Muhammad Ali*, 66.
46. See account by Ahmed Shafiq Pasha of his mother-in-law in his *mudhakkirati fi nusf qarn* as cited in al-Mahalawi, *harim*, 87–88. See also Tugay, *Family Chronicles*, 307.
47. Dye, *Moslem Egypt*, 8–9. His estimate of cost appears exaggerated. See also, Hassan, *In the House of Muhammad Ali*, 69–70.
48. Chennells, *Recollections*, vol. 1, 252–53.
49. Grey, *Journal*, 42–44. It is interesting to note that this wedding took place over the course of three days, while the later ones took place over the course of a week.
50. Ken Cuno, "Ambiguous Modernization: The Transition to Monogamy in the Khedivial House of Egypt," paper presented at MESA, November 2001. On companionate marriage, see Beth Baron, "The Making and Breaking of Marital Bonds in Modern Egypt," in Beth Baron and Nikki Keddie, eds., *Women in Middle Eastern History* (New Haven: Yale University Press, 1991), 275–91.
51. Cuno speculates that perhaps even Said had tried to cultivate the image of monogamy with his wife Injy, who was quite popular among Western female visitors. Nevertheless, it was Malak Barr Hanum, who bore his children. See Cuno, "Ambiguous Modernization" and al-Mahalawi, *harim*, 66.
52. al-Mahalawi, *harim*, 79–83. The choice of marriage mates is interesting since three of the children were married to descendents of Ismail's late half-brother Ahmad Rifat and two to daughters of Ilhami Pasha, perhaps to quash unhappiness from those branches of the family with regard to the change in the law of succession.
53. Foreign women could attend the "male" functions, while Ottoman-Egyptian females went to festivities over which the Queen Mother presided. Chennells, *Recollections*, vol. 1, 241.
54. DW, PI, doss. 4/12, article from *Le Journal* dated September 9, 1875.
55. Lord Cromer, *Modern Egypt* (New York: Macmillan, 1908), vol. 1, 18. Marsot, *Muhammad Ali*, 85; al-Rafa^c^i, *Ismail*, vol. 1, 74; P.J. Vatikiotis, "Ismail Pasha," in *The Encyclopedia of Islam*, vol. 4, 192–93; Abbas Hilmi II, *The Last Khedive of Egypt: Memoirs of Abbas Hilmi II*, translated and edited by Amira Sonbol (Reading: Ithaca, 1998), 37, 53; Hassan, *In the House of Muhammad Ali*, 110.
56. Box 258, Abdin, Letter from Ibrahim Pasha to Sami Bey, October 31, 1839 as cited in Guindi and Tagher, *Documents*, 5.
57. See comments made by Prince Metternich as reported by Bonfort to Artin Bey, Vienna, December 20, 1844, Box 1, Abdin, as cited in Guindi and Tagher, *Documents*, 6–7; al-Rafa^c^i, *Ismail*, vol. 1, 74. On French in the empire, see Göçek, *East-West*, 80.
58. DW, PI, doss. 44/1, Abonnement a divers journoure par l'agence Havas Bullier pour Son Altesse le Vice Roi, Cairo, April 15, 1866; Order to withdraw 2,500 francs for *la Turquie*, Constantinople, May 13, 1866; Note de journeuxe arasequels est abonne S.A. le Khedive d'Egypte, undated [1871]; DW, PI, doss. 44/1, Letter from Mrs. Fariman of the *Levant Times* to S.A. La Princesse Mere, London, April 2, 1874.
59. Yacub Artin, *L'Instruction Publique en Egypte* (Paris, 1890), 134.
60. See e.g., Ellen Chennells, *Recollections*, vol. 1, 2; vol. 2, 140–43; and Tugay, *Family Chronicles*, 198.
61. See e.g., DW, PI, doss. 2/9, Correspondence between Riaz Pasha and Maclean Regarding Governess for Princess Zeinab, November 1867; Letter from John Larking to Barrot

Bey Regarding the Hiring of Ellen Chennells for Princess Zeinab; Letter from Dor Bey to Barrot Bey Regarding Mlle. Stettler, July 30, 1874; Letter from Moustapha Pasha Regarding Djemilah Hanim's Governess, July 21, 1875.

62. Letter from Ismail to Hassan [in French], Constantinople, August 23, 1867, doss. 2/3, Abdin as cited in Guindi and Tagher, *Documents*, 10.
63. DW, PI, doss. 4/12, Letter from Zeinab to Ismail, Ras el-Tin, June 12, 1871; Letter from Ismail to Zeinab, unsigned and undated.
64. Chennells, *Recollections*, vol. 2, 24–25; vol. 1, 214; Tugay, *Family Chronicles*, 193.
65. For specific *ḥadith* relating to education, see Zaynab Farid, *ta^{c}lim al-mara' al-^{c}arabiyya fi turath wa fil-mujtama^{c}at al-mu^{c}aṣira* (Cairo: Maktabat al-Anglo al-Miṣriyya, 1980), 6 and Sophie Babazogli, "L'Education de la jeune fille musalmane en Egypte," (Thesis, L'Ecole des Hautes-Etudes Sociales, 1927) (Cairo: Paul Barbey, 1928), 42.
66. Jonathan Berkey, "Women and Islamic Education in the Mamluk Period," in Keddie and Baron, eds., *Women in Middle Eastern History*, 143–57.
67. Farid, *ta^{c}lim*, 43.
68. Tugay, *Family Chronicles*, 178–79. Nevertheless, Göçek reports that the curriculum in the imperial Ottoman *ḥarim* included writing. Fatme Müge Göçek, *Rise of Bourgeoisie, Demise of Empire* (New York: Oxford University Press, 1996), 24.
69. Lott, *Harem Life*, 60.
70. DW, PI, doss. 4/8, 4/9, and 4/12.
71. Chennells, *Recollections*, vol. 1, 14, 203; vol. 2, 55, 94, 116–17.
72. Lucie Duff Gordon, *Letters from Egypt*, reedited with additional letters by Gordon Waterfield (New York: Praeger, 1969), 332–33; Demetra Vaka, *Haremlik* (Boston: Houghton-Mifflin, 1909), 119–25.
73. Chennells, *Recollections*, vol. 2, 111; Tugay, *Family Chronicles*, 308; Farid, *ta^{c}lim*, 20–25; Lane, *Manners*, vol. 1, 255.
74. Chennells, *Recollections*, vol. 1, 14 and 163; Tugay, *Family Chronicles*, 192–93; Lott, *Harem Life*, 187.
75. Tugay, *Family Chronicles*, 308.
76. Tugay, *Family Chronicles*, 308; Farid, *ta^{c}lim*, 30–31. See also, Mary Ann Fay, "Women and Households: Gender, Power, and Culture in Eighteenth-Century Egypt," (Ph.D. diss., Georgetown University, 1993), 76, 81.
77. A.B. DeGuerville, *New Egypt* (London: William Heinemann, 1906), 138–39.
78. The mother of Prince Ibrahim Hilmi bought a Circassian slave for her son and sent her to a convent school in Italy for training prior to their marriage. Tugay, *Family Chronicles*, 202. Prince Hussein, married in one of the 1873 ceremonies, remarked that he was glad that his father "bestowed upon him an educated wife instead of a mere doll . . . " Chennells, *Recollections*, vol. 2, 146–47. According to F. Robert Hunter, Nubar Pasha's wife was well-educated, serving as an advisor to her husband and a "tactful and charming hostess" to his guests. F. Robert Hunter, *Egypt Under the Khedives* (Pittsburgh: University of Pittsburgh Press, 1984), 168.
79. See Leslie Peirce, *The Imperial Harem: Women & Sovereignty in the Ottoman Empire* (New York: Oxford University Press, 1993); Fanny Davis, *The Ottoman Lady* (Westport: Greenwood Press, 1986).
80. See e.g., DW, PI, doss. 83/8, "Chronique Locale," *Moniteur Egyptien* 4, 269 (November 24, 1877); untitled feature in *al-waqa^{c}i al-misriyya* (November 11, 1877).
81. al-Rafa^{c}i, *Ismail*, vol. 1, 99; Marsot, *Short History*, 66.
82. See e.g. Jean-Marie Carie, *Voyageurs et Ecrivains Français en Egypte*, vol. 2 (Cairo: IFAO, 1956), 359–67.

83. Edward Dicey, *The Story of the Khedivate* (London: Rivingtons, 1902), 75.
84. al-Rafa^c^i, *Ismail*, vol. 1, 99.
85. Dicey, *Story*, 78.
86. Dicey, *Story*, 76–77.
87. Timothy Mitchell, *Colonising Egypt* (Cambridge: Cambridge University Press, 1988), 63; Hunter, *Khedives*, 124–31; al-Rafa^c^i, *Ismail*, vol. 1, 258; Ordre Supérieur à Nubar Pacha, Ministre des Travaux Publics, December 7, 1864, Register 539, "Ordes Supérieurs," as cited in Guindi and Tagher, *Documents*, 143; ^c^Ali Mubarak, *al-khiṭaṭ al-jadida li-Miṣr al-Qahira wa mudunha wa biladha al-qadima wa al-ahira* (Bulaq, 1887/88), vol. 9, 49–50; DW, Diwan Majlis al-Khuṣuṣi, Daftar al-Qararat wal-Lawa'iḥ al-Ṣadira, Daftar 10/8/11, for the period 1283–84 as cited by Nihal Tamraz, "Nineteenth Century Domestic Architecture: Abbasia as a Case Study" (M.A. thesis, AUC, 1993), vol. 1, 21.
88. Todd, *Nile*, 94; Marcel Clerget, *Le Caire: Etude de Géographie Urbaine et d'Histoire Economique* (Cairo: E & R Schindler, 1934), vol. 1, 194; Mubarak, *khiṭaṭ*, vol. 1210–211; al-Rafa^c^i, *Ismail*, vol. 2, 29–30; Abu-Lughod, Cairo, 106; Edwin De Leon, *The Khedive's Egypt* (London: Sampson Lew, Marston, Seale, & Rivington, 1882 [1877]), 32; Karl Baedecker, *Egypt & the Sudan, Handbook for Travellers* (New York: Charles Scribner's Sons, 1914), 52.
89. The French headquarters were in Azbakiyya, and according to Doris Behrens-Abouseif, they created new streets and established taverns, cafes, restaurants, theatres, and dance halls. Once in power, Muhammad Ali continued these trends. Behrens-Abouseif, *Azbakiyya & its Environs from Azbak to Ismail, 1476–1879* (Cairo: IFAO, 1985), 74–88; Mubarak, *khiṭaṭ*, vol. 1, 214–16.
90. Abu-Lughod, *Cairo*, 107; Behrens-Abouseif, *Azbakiyya*, 90–99; Mubarak, *khiṭaṭ*, vol. 1, 210–11; al-Rafa^c^i, *Ismail*, vol. 2, 30; Butler, *Court Life*, 61; James C. McCoan, *Egypt* (New York: Peter Fenelon, 1898), 49; Broderick, *Handbook*, 327.
91. Despina Draneht, *Twilight Memories* (Lausanne, n/d), 86 as cited in Trevor Mostyn, *Egypt's Belle Epoque 1869–1952* (New York: Quartet Books, 1989), 75.
92. Abu-Lughod, *Cairo*; Afaf Marsot, *Short History*, 68; De Kusel, *Recollections*, 89. Operas, ballets, and concerts, performed in a specially constructed building for a specific audience was unknown to the Ottomans before the eighteenth century. Göçek, *East-West*, 46. See also Yaḥya Ḥaqqi, *safaḥat min tarikh Miṣr* (Cairo: al-Hay' al-^c^Amma al-Miṣriyya lil-Kitab, 1989), 67; Hassan, *In the House of Muhammad Ali*, 107.
93. Since the time of the French invasion, ancient Egyptian art and relics had been smuggled out of the country despite legislation forbidding this practice.
94. "The Egyptian Museum and its Founder Mariette Pasha," *al-hilal* 11, 4 (1902): 114–18.
95. Mubarak, *khiṭaṭ*, vol. 1, 210–11; al-Rafa^c^i, *Ismail*, vol. 2, 9–15, 29–30; Abu-Lughod, *Cairo,* 110–111; Lettre de la Maia a la Zaptieh du Caire, June 26, 1863, Register 531 "Turc," as cited in Guindi and Tagher, *Documents*, 101; Preambule du texte de la concession pour l'eclairage au gaz de la ville du Caire, March 31, 1870, doss. 31/1, "Abdin," as cited in Guindi and Tagher, *Documents*, 151.
96. See letters to the English Consul, E. Stanton, October 7, 1869 and February 8, 1875, in Guindi and Tagher, *Documents*, 103 and 100, respectively; Ordre Superieur, September 12, 1863, Register 1910, "Ordres Arabes" and letter to E. Stanton, Alexandria, September 9, 1865, both cited in Guindi and Tagher, *Documents*, 103–04. See also Mitchell, *Colonising*, 96–98.
97. DW, PI, doss. 62/3, Direction Générale de Promenades et Plantations de l'Egypte, *Jardin de l'Esbekieh Cahier Des Charges Clauses et Conditions Générales Relatives Aux*

Diverses Concessions du Jardin de l'Esbekieh au Caire (Cairo: Typographie Française Delbos-Demouret, 1871); Letters from Barillet to Riaz Pasha Regarding Azbakiyya Park, May 20, 1879 and March 28, 1871; Délibération, Administration de Promenades et Plantations, July 26, 1871; Behrens-Abouseif, *Azbakiyya*, 93–95; Broderick, *Handbook*, 326–27.

98. Nelson, *Shepheard's*, 8, 16, and 25; Behrens-Abouseif, *Azbakiyya*, 91, 93, and 96; Broderick, *Handbook*, 327.
99. Mubarak, *khiṭaṭ*, vol. 1, 214; Behrens-Abouseif, *Azbakiyya*, 92; Abu-Lughod, *Cairo*, 107.
100. In 1897, Alexandria's foreign population comprised about 15 percent of its total population of about 140,000. Egypt, niẓarat al-maliyya, *ta^{c}dad sukan al-quṭr al-miṣri, 1897* (Cairo: al-Maṭba^{c}a al-Kubra al-Amiriyya bi Bulaq, 1898), 95.
101. al-Rafa^{c}i, *Ismail*, vol. 2, 31; Mitchell, *Colonising*, 67.
102. See e.g., comments by R. Beardsley, U.S. Consul, November 9, 1872 and September 15, 1872 as cited by Guindi and Tagher, *Documents*, 146–48.
103. Mubarak, *khiṭaṭ*, vol. 7, 87 as cited in al-Rafa^{c}i, *Ismail*, vol. 2, 19. al-Rafa^{c}i also cites the Cave Report, which indicates that Ismail laid down 1,200 miles of railroad track. See also, Bayard Taylor, *Egypt and Iceland in the Year 1874* (New York: C.P. Putnam's Sons, 1874), 133.
104. McCoan, *Egypt*, 250–52; al-Rafa^{c}i, *Ismail*, vol. 2, 22–24.
105. Heather Sharkey, *Living with Colonialism* (Berkeley: University of California Press, 2003), 63.
106. al-Rafa^{c}i, *Ismail*, vol. 2, 298.
107. The new architectural form did lead to the development of larger ensembles. Costume changes also accompanied the new context. Nevertheless, it is not until the 1920s, '30s, and '40s that Western music makes large-scale inroads into popular forms of music. Interview with ethno-musicologist Dwight Reynolds, August 26, 1997.
108. De Kusel, *Recollections*, 89; Nelson, *Shepheard's*, 37.
109. De Kusel, *Recollections*, 89.
110. Butler, *Court Life*, 61. The financing of *Aida* required huge sums of money. Madame Delphine Baron of Paris designed the costumes. Among the props were gold and gem-encrusted jewelry and solid silver weaponry. Soprano Teresa Stolz refused an offer of 100,000 francs for the lead role. Mostyn, *Belle Epoque*, 78–80. According to al-Rafa^{c}i, Ismail spent £160,000 on the opera house. al-Rafa^{c}i, *Ismail*, vol. 1, 289.
111. Sir I. Gardner Wilkinson, *A Handbook for Travellers to Egypt* (London: John Murray, 1867), 95; al-Rafa^{c}i, *Ismail*, vol. 1, 289–90.
112. al-Rafa^{c}i, *Ismail*, vol. 2, 26; vol. 1, 236–37; "Organisation de la Bilbliothèque Nationale," *Journal Officiel* 352 (April 10, 1870) as cited by Guindi and Tagher, *Documents*, 117.
113. DW, PI, doss. 70/2, *Statuts de la Societe Khediviale de Géographie* (Alexandria: Imprimerie Francaise A. Moier, 1875); al-Rafa^{c}i, *Ismail*, vol. 1, 109–53, 200. Quotation from Eve Troutt Powell, *A Different Shade of Colonialism* (Berkeley: University of California Press, 2003), 106–07.
114. DW, PI, doss. 70/1, Letter to Barrot Bey from the President of *L'Institut d'Egypte*, Alexandria, July 3, 1875.
115. Abbas Kelidar, "The Political Press in Egypt, 1882–1914," in Charles Trip ed., *Contemporary Egypt: Through Egyptian Eyes: Essays in Honor of P.J. Vatikiotis* (London: Routledge, 1993), 3.
116. al-Rafa^{c}i, *Ismail*, vol. 2, 250–51; Kelidar, "Political Press," 3–4; Juan Cole, *Colonialism & Revolution in the Middle East* (Princeton: Princeton University Press, 1993), 126–32.
117. Juan Cole, *Colonialism*, 124–25. For circulation figures, see Ami Ayalon, *The Press in the Arab Middle East: A History* (New York: Oxford University Press, 1995), 148.

Irene Gendzier's *The Practical Visions of Ya'cub Sanu'a* remains an outstanding study of one of the earliest and key figures of the opposition press. (Cambridge: Harvard Middle Eastern Monographs, Center for Middle Eastern Studies, 1966).

118. For a brief summary of these issues, see the extract from the Cave Report entitled "Progress and Indebtedness under Ismail, 1863–75," in Charles Issawi, ed., *The Economic History of the Middle East* (Chicago: University of Chicago Press, 1966), 430–38.
119. Marsot, "Ismail," 95–96.
120. Standard Egypt textbooks, e.g., Marsot's *Short History* or Arthur Goldschmidt Jr.'s *Modern Egypt* (Boulder: Westview Press, 1988); as well as monographs, e.g., Marsot's *Egypt Under Cromer* (New York: Praeger, 1968) and Pollard's, "Nurturing the Nation" all support this depiction.
121. Clara Boyle, *Boyle of Cairo*, 38. al-Maḥalawi, *ḥarim*, 80, 92. See also Pollard, "Nurturing the Nation," 33–34, 140.
122. Tamraz, *Cairene Houses*, 15; al-Maḥalawi, *ḥarim*, 91–96. Sultan Abdul Hamid II conferred the title of *Valde Pasha* upon her, placing her in rank with senior Ottoman princesses. See Abbas Hilmi II, *Memoirs*, photograph 3.
123. Yunan Labib Rizq, "al-Ahram: A Diwan of Contemporary Life," *al-Ahram Weekly*, September 22, 1994. Pollard, "Nurturing the Nation," 127–28.
124. Abbas Hilmi II, *Memoirs*, 23.
125. Abbas Hilmi II, *Memoirs*, 50.
126. For Djavidan's views see her *Harem Life* (London: Noel Douglas, 1931). On the two wives, see al-Maḥalawi, *ḥarim*, 96–100; Cuno, "Ambiguous Modernization," and Mervat Hatem, "Through Each Other's Eyes: The Impact on the Colonial Encounter of the Images of Egyptian, Levantine-Egyptian, and European Women, 1862–1920," in Nupur Chaudhuri and Margaret Strobel, eds., *Western Women and Imperialism* (Bloomington: Indiana University Press, 1992), 35–57.
127. Hatem, "Colonial Encounter," 53; see also Samir Raafat, "From Mag-Arabs to al-Magary," *Egyptian Mail*, April 13, 1996; Samir Raafat "Queen for a Day," *al-Ahram Weekly*, October 6, 1994.
128. Abbas's memoirs demonstrate that he was on an ordinary vacation in Istanbul before the war broke out. Abbas Hilmi II, *Memoirs*, 18, 307. According to Prince Hassan, Husayn Kamil twice rejected the offer; however the British indicated they were ready to overturn the dynasty with a new candidate waiting at the Shepheard's hotel. See *In the House of Muhammad Ali*, 80.
129. In 1873 he married Princess Ayn al-Hayat Ahmad. She bore him four children between 1874 and 1879, and she lived with him until 1885. al-Sultana Malak (Malak Jashm Afit) bore him three children, beginning in 1888. There is scant information available on this wife. al-Maḥalawi, *ḥarim*, 124–31.

3 Patterns of Urban Consumption and Development, 1879–1922

1. Fatma Müge Göçek, *East Encounters West* (New York: Oxford Press, 1987), 117–19.
2. P. J. Vatikiotis, *History of Egypt* (Baltimore: Johns Hopkins Press, 1980), 434; ᶜAbd al-Raḥman al-Rafaᶜi, *ᶜaṣr Ismaᶜil* , vol. 1, 53
3. Egypt, Ministry of Finance, *The Census of Egypt Taken in 1907* (Cairo, 1909).
4. Sir I. Gardner Wilkinson, *A Handbook for Travellers to Egypt* (London: John Murray, 1867), 69, 109–10; François Levernay, *Guide Général d'Egypte* (Alexandria: Imprimerie

Nouvelle, 1868), advertisements; Mary Broderick et. al., eds., *A Handbook for Travellers in Lower and Upper Egypt* (London: John Murray, 1896), 327 and advertisements; *Egypt & How to See It* (New York: Doubleday, Page, & Co., 1909); Karl Baedecker, *Egypt & the Sudan, Handbook for Travelers* (New York: Charles Scribner's Sons, 1914), 35; Nina Nelson, *Shepheard's Hotel* (London: Barrie and Rockliff, 1960); DW, PI, doss. 68/3, Pamphlet from La Maison de Santé du Docteur Grant, July 1876; Advertisement for al-Ḥayat Hotels of Helouan in *al-muqtaṭaf* 46, 3 (1915); Lucie Duff Gordan, *Letters from Egypt*, reedited with additional letters by Gordon Waterfield (New York: Praeger, 1969), introduction; Helen Miles, "The Rise and Fall of Cairo's Great Hotels," *al-Ahram Weekly*, 17–23, August 1995, 16.

5. C.E. Coles, *Recollections and Reflections* (London: The Saint Catherine Press, n/d), 30, 150–52; Lord Edward Cecil, *The Leisure of an Egyptian Official* (London: Hodder & Stoughton, 1921), 145–47. See also Douglas Sladen, *Queer Things About Egypt* (London: Hurst & Blackett, Ltd., 1910), 133 and *Egypt and How to See It*, 27.
6. Baedecker, *Egypt*, 35; *Egypt and How to See It*, 11–12.
7. Nancy Mickelwright, "London, Paris, Istanbul, and Cairo: Fashion and International Trade in the 19th Century," *New Perspectives on Turkey* 7 (Spring 1992), 134.
8. Charlotte Jirousek, "The Transition to Mass Fashion System Dress," in Donald Quataert, ed., *Consumption Studies and the History of the Ottoman Empire, 1550–1922* (Albany: SUNY Press, 2000), 209, 223.
9. Bayard Taylor, *Egypt and Iceland in the Year 1874* (New York: C.P. Putnam's Sons, 1874), 26, 33, and 144; Sladen, *Egypt*, 83.
10. See e.g., *anis al-jalis* 1, 3 (1898), 1, 5 (1898), 4, 8 (1901): 775–79, 4, 9 (1901): 814–15, 5, 2 (1902): 968–69; *al-laṭa'if al-muṣawwara* (February 21, 1916): 7 (December 31, 1917): 3, "Wedding Dresses and the Trousseau," (April 7, 1919): 3; "Today's Fashion for Ladies," (June 30, 1919): 6; "The Latest Fashion from Paris," (July 7, 1919): 6; "Our Ladies Page," (July 21, 1919): 6.
11. See e.g. *sijill al-hilal al-muṣawwar 1892–1992* (Cairo: Dar al-Hilal), vol. 1, 94–95; vol. 2, 1014, 1015, 1023, 1026.
12. Mary Ann Fay, "Women and Households: Gender, Power, and Culture in Eighteenth-Century Egypt" (Ph.D. diss., Georgetown University, 1993), 140–44; See also Edward Lane *An Account of the Manners and Customs of the Modern Egyptians* (London: M.A. Nattali 1846), vol. 1, 58–77; Afaf Marsot, *Women and Men in Late Eighteenth-Century Egypt* (Austin: University of Texas Press, 1995), 114–17.
13. Alfred Butler, *Court Life in Egypt* (London: Chapman & Hall; New York: Scribner & Welford, 1887), 6–7; Hunter, *Egypt Under the Khedives, 1807–1879* (Pittsburgh: University of Pittsburgh, 1984), 102; See also Edward Lane, *Manners*, vol. 1, 40–50; Fatma Müge Göçek, *Rise of Bourgeoisie, Demise of Empire* (New York: Oxford University Press, 1996), 83.
14. Cecil, *Leisure*, 269.
15. Relli Shechter, "The Egyptian Cigarette: A Study of the Interaction Between Consumption, Production, and Marketing in Egypt, 1850–1956" (Ph.D. diss., Harvard University, 1999), 41–42.
16. Pierre Bourdieu, *Distinction: A Social Critique of the Judgement of Taste*, trans. Richard Nice (Cambridge: Harvard University Press, 1984), 162–63; Wilkinson, *Handbook*; Broderick, *Handbook*, 982–92; *Egypt and How to See It*, 25–26 and 180; Baedecker, *Egypt*, 9 and 42; DW, MW, SJ, box B4, series 359, Note to the Council of Ministers from the Law Firm of Briscoe & Aicord Regarding the Union Club, June 17, 1904; DW, PI, doss. 18/4, Correspondence Relating to the Founding of the Khedivial Club, September

1874; Abbas Hilmi II, *The Last Khedive of Egypt: Memoirs of Abbas Hilmi II*, edited and translated by Amira Sonbol (Reading: Ithaca, 1998), 155–56; Hassan Hassan, *In the House of Muhammad Ali* (Cairo: AUC Press, 2000), 29.

17. Cecil, *Leisure*, 8, 85, 89, 118–19; Butler, *Court Life*, 99; Coles, *Recollections*, 150, see also 39, 155–63.
18. DW, MW, SJ, box B4, series, 359, Basic Law for the Tawfiq Literary Club, undated.
19. *al-hilal* 2, 17 (May 1, 1894): 538.
20. "Women's Societies," *al-muqtaṭaf* 13, 9 (1889): 624; "A Troop of Egyptian Girl Scouts," *al-hilal* 29, 3 (1920): 270–72; and *sijill al-hilal*, vol. 1, 427. Elizabeth Cooper, *Women of Egypt* (New York: Frederick Stokes, 1914), 239.
21. DW, MW, NSH, box 2/1, Correspondence from the Ministry of Public Works Regarding the Lighting of the Opera Theatre, October 10, 1887–June 7, 1890; *Annual Report* (1911), 33.
22. DW, MW, NSH, box 2/1 Correspondence between the Committee of Theater Ministry of Public Works, and the Council of Ministers, December 23, 1881–January 4, 1882; Letter from A. Rouchdy (Minister of Public Works) to the Council of Ministers Regarding Support for the Theatre, April 15, 1885; The Opinion of the Finance Committee in Agreement with the Request of the Theatre Committee for £4000 for the Khedivial Opera Theatre, April 24–26, 1890; The Opinion of the Finance Committee in Agreement with the Request from Public Works for £500 for the Khedivial Opera Theatre, November 30, 1890. Announcement regarding the salary increase of the Opera House director, *al-muqaṭṭam* (June 21, 1892): 3.
23. Broderick, *Handbook*, 991; Cecil, *Leisure*, 146; *Egypt and How to See It*, 27–28.
24. See e.g., announcement, *al-muqaṭṭam* (April 27, 1900), 2; Wilkinson, *Handbook*, 95.
25. Butler, *Court Life*, 137.
26. "Azbakiyya Garden Theatre," *al-muqaṭṭam* 9, 2379 (1897): 4.
27. See e.g., advertisement, *al-muqaṭṭam* (October 2, 1896): 4; al-Rafaᶜi, *Ismail*, vol. 1, 289.
28. Magda Baraka, *The Egyptian Upper Class Between Revolutions, 1919–1952* (Reading: Ithaca, 1998), 122–23.
29. Mitchell, *Colonising Egypt* (Cambridge: Cambridge University Press, 1988), 117.
30. See e.g., Douglas Sladen, *Oriental Cairo, the City of "Arabian Nights"* (London, 1911), 22, 61, and 118; Sir Thomas Russell, *Egyptian Service, 1902–1946* (London: John Murray, 1949), 178–79; A.B. DeGuerville, *New Egypt* (London: William Heinemann, 1906), 79.
31. Bruce Dunne, "Sexuality and the 'Civilizing Process' in Modern Egypt" (Ph.D. diss., Georgetown University, 1996).
32. Trevor Mostyn, *Egypt's Belle Epoque 1869–1952* (New York: Quartet Books, 1989), 146.
33. Ehud Toledano, *State and Society*, 237–39. See also Jarrod Hayes, *Queer Nations* (Chicago: University of Chicago Press, 2000), 23–49.
34. "The Egyptian Museum," *al-hilal* 2, 18 (May 15, 1894): 571; "The Egyptian Museum in Giza," *al-hilal* 4, 17 (1896): 674; "The New Egyptian Museum," *al-hilal* 5, 16 (1897): 633; "The Egyptian Museum and its Founder Mariette Pasha," *al-hilal* 11, 4 (1902): 114–18; Aḥmad Muḥammad ᶜAguby even reified the museum in a poem, "The Egyptian Museum," *al-hilal* 28, 5 (1920): 439. The Egyptian Museum remains at its Qasr al-Nil location. See also Donald M. Reid, *Whose Pharaohs?* (Berkeley: University of California Press, 2002).
35. *Annual Report 1903*, 69; *Annual Report 1904*, 88–89; *Annual Report 1905*, 94; *Annual Report 1906*, 97; *Annual Report 1907*, 41–42; *Annual Report 1909*, 49; Ministry of Public Instruction, *Regulations Concerning the Reading Rooms & Loan Department of the Khedivial Library* enacted by Ministerial Order No. 966, July 11, 1903 in *Regulations 1914* (Cairo: Government Press, 1914); Cecil, *Leisure*, 43–44.

36. DW, MW, SJ, box B4, series 224, Correspondence Relating to the Creation of a Public Garden in Alexandria, August 19, 1883–September 20, 1883; Correspondence Relating to the Establishment of a Public Park in Alexandria, September 1886–December 1889; Series 630, Note to the Council of Ministers from M. Fakhry Regarding Land around the Old Ismailieh Canal, November 20, 1920.
37. Announcement, *al-muqaṭṭam* (June 8, 1892): 3.
38. The "events" section of *al-hilal* and page three of *al-muqaṭṭam* frequently listed these events.
39. *Annual Report 1901*, 46; *Annual Report 1906*, 99; *Egypt and How to See It*, 26; "Children and Zoological Gardens," *al-muqtaṭaf* 33, 6 (1908): 515–16.
40. John A. Todd, *The Banks of the Nile* (London: A. anc C. Black, 1913), 95; DW, PI, doss. 62/4, Letter to S.A. Ismail Pacha from Georges Andrea Regarding an Orangutan, Cairo November 16, 1873; DW, PI, doss. 62/4, List of the Animals at the Gezira Garden, October 4, 1878; *Annual Report 1909*, 24.
41. "Preferability of Electrical Light," *al-muqtaṭaf* 5, 1 (1880): 25; "The Gilded Electrical Bathtub Heater," *al-muqtaṭaf* 6, 3 (1881): 159–60; "Electrictity," *al-muqtaṭaf* 8, 1 (1883): 56–57; "Electricity for Cooking," *al-hilal* 14, 5 (1906): 312; "Cooking with Electricity," *al-muqtaṭaf* 43, 4 (1913): 387; "Household Organization and Electricity," *al-hilal* 24, 1 (1915): 82; "Mechanical Devices Instead of Servants," *al-hilal* 24, 8 (1916): 681–82; "Electric Cooking," *al-hilal* 25, 1 (1916): 65; Aḥmad Muḥammad ᶜAguby, "Electricity," *al-hilal* 28, 7 (1920): 655; "Electricity," *al-hilal* 29, 2 (1920): 217; "The Wondrous House," *al-hilal* 29, 10 (1921): 982–85; "Is the Servant Disappearing," *al-hilal* 31, 1 (1922): 84; "Electric Furniture," *al-hilal* 30, 10 (1922): 950–52.
42. "The Story of Egyptian Cinema," in *sijill al-hilal*, vol. 1, 530–33; Advertisement for Cinematograph Metropole, *al-laṭa'if al-muṣawwara* (April 17, 1922), 14. See also Walter Armbrust, *Mass Culture and Modernism in Egypt* (New York: Cambridge University Press, 1996).
43. See e.g. "Secrets of the Cinematograph," *al-hilal* 29, 4 (1921): 345–52 and "Cinema of the Future," *al-hilal* 30, 1 (1921): 54–55. On the phonograph, see "Teaching Language by Phonograph," *al-hilal* 22, 2 (1913): 157; and "Teaching Languages by Phonograph," *al-hilal* 22, 3 (1913): 235.
44. Baraka, *The Egyptian Upper Class*, 124–25.
45. "Popular Arts," *sijill al-hilal*, vol. 1, 457–58.
46. "Physical Exercise—Part One," *al-muqtaṭaf* 4, 10 (1879): 270–72; "Physical Exercise—Part Two," *al-muqtaṭaf* 4, 11 (1879): 292–95; "The Bicycle and the Tricycle," *al-muqtaṭaf* 7, 4 (1882): 251; "Advice to the Wife," *al-muqtaṭaf* 15, 3 (1890): 201–03; "Exercise for the Wife," *al-muqtaṭaf* 15, 5 (1891): 235–36; "Questions and Suggestions," *al-hilal* 9, 14 (1901): 417; "What Preceded Us While We Were Sedentary," *al-hilal* 10, 3 (1901): 77–82; "Physical Exercise Among the Ancient Egyptians," *al-hilal* 10, 13 (1902): 403–06; "Types of Exercise," *al-muqtaṭaf* 33, 3 (1908): 253–54; "The Best Types of Exercise for Women," *al-muqtaṭaf* 56, 6 (1920): 529; "Exercise for Girls," *al-muqtaṭaf* 59, 2 (1921): 172–74; *Annual Report 1903*, 61.
47. DW, PI, box 1/6; "Lighting Homes of the Capital with Gas," *al-hilal* 1, 4 (1892): 180 and Untitled announcement in *al-muqaṭṭam* (June 2, 1892): 3; Coles, *Recollections*, 62, 75–81, 95–105, 113–27; Russell, *Egyptian Service*; DW, MW, NSH, box 1/6, Demande de Concession au Gouverment de S.A. Le Khédive de l'Enterprise générale de numerotage des maisons des villes du Caire et d'Alexandrie, May 29, 1883.
48. Janet Abu-Lughod, *Cairo: 1001 Years of the City Victorious* (Princeton: Princeton University Press, 1971), 132–34.

49. "The Alexandrian Tramway," *al-hilal* 6, 2 (1897): 69.
50. Abu-Lughod, *Cairo*, 135.
51. Mubarak, *al-khiṭaṭ al-tawfiqiyya al-jadida li Miṣr wal-Qahira wa mudunha wa biladha al-qadima wal-shahira* (Cairo: Dar al-Kutub, 1979), vol. 1, 211; Nihal Tamraz, *Nineteenth-Century Cairene Houses and Palaces* (Cairo: AUC Press, 1998), 57.
52. Wilkinson, *Handbook*, 151.
53. Tamraz, *Cairene Houses*, 47, 58–59, 72–73.
54. Tamraz, *Cairene Houses*, 56–57.
55. Abu-Lughod, *Cairo*, 138–39.
56. *Egypt and How to See It*, 47–48; Baedecker, *Egypt*, 119.
57. Robert Ilbert, *Heliopolis* (Paris: Centre Nationale de la Recherche Scientifique, 1981), 116; Baraka, *The Egyptian Upper Class*, 108–09.
58. *al-muqaṭṭam* (October 2, 1896), 3. Several issues of *al-laṭa'if al-muṣawwara* lampooned the tramway. See e.g., untitled cartoon and critique, *al-laṭa'if al-muṣawwara* (November 21, 1921): 4 and "The Difficulty of Transportation in Egypt," *al-laṭa'if al-muṣawwara* (April 14, 1919): 2–3. See also *sijill al-hilal*, vol. 1, 20. An 1896 guidebook indicates that "no white people can use a tram except to Heliopolis or the Pyramids." Broderick, *Handbook*, 43.
59. "Garden Cities," *al-hilal* 30, 10 (1922): 907–10; Abu-Lughod, *Cairo*, 142. Another site for British residency was the southern suburb of Maadi. See Samir Raafat, *Maadi 1904–1962* (Cairo: Palm Press, 1994).
60. Ali Mubarak cites 400 privately owned carriages and 486 passenger carriages in 1875. Mubarak, *khiṭaṭ*, vol. 1, 103; Wilkinson, *Handbook*, 113. The omnibus had been in use since the mid–19th century; however, the small number of wide roads had limited its use.
61. Ehud Toledano,*State and Society in mid–19th Century Egypt* (Cambridge: Cambridge University Press, 1990), 166–67.
62. Previously, the use of horses was limited to the [male] mamluk aristocracy. Fay, "Women and Households," 128–29; Lane, *Manners*, vol. 1, 262; Gaston Wiet, *Cairo: City of Art & Commerce* (Norman: University of Oklahoma Press, 1964), 82–83; Baedecker, *Egypt*, xviii.
63. Tamraz, *Cairene Houses*, 71.
64. Cecil, *Leisure*, 122.
65. André Raymond, "Essai de Géographie des Quartiers de Résidence Aristocratique au Caire au XVIIIème siècle," *Journal of the Economic and Social History of the Orient* VI (1963), 31.
66. The old houses did not cease to exist. Many were given to family members, high bureaucrats, and European advisors. Doris Behrens-Abouseif, *Azbakiyya and its Environs from Azbak to Ismail, 1476–1879* (Cairo: IFAO, 1985), 82–88; Abu-Lughod, *Cairo*, 94; Fay, "Women and Households," 104–08; Hunter, *Khedives*, 100–01. See also Göçek, *Bourgeoisie*, 43; Tamraz, *Cairene Houses*, 24–25.
67. Toledano, *State and Society*, 57. See also Gabriel Baer, "Slavery and its Abolition," in his *Studies in the Social History of Modern Egypt* (Chicago: University of Chicago Press, 1969), 167.
68. On abolition, see Ehud Toledano, *Slavery and Abolition in the Ottoman Middle East* (Seattle: University of Washington Press, 1998). On the African slave trade, see Eve Troutt Powell, *A Different Shade of Colonialism*, 136–41.
69. See Russell, "Modernity, National Identity, and Consumerism: Visions of the Egyptian Home, 1805–1922," in Relli Shechter, ed., Transitions in Domestic Consumptions and Family Life in the Modern Middle East: *Houses in Motion* (New York: Palgrave, 2003), 37–62.

70. Fay, "Women and Households," 166–71; Demetra Vaka, *Haremlik* (Boston: Houghton Mifflin, 1909), 73. See also Nelly Hanna, *Habiter au Caire* (Cairo: IFAO, 1991).
71. Fay, "Women and Households," 217–18, 295; Afaf Marsot, "The Revolutionary Gentlewomen in Egypt," in Beck and Keddie, eds., *Women in the Muslim World* (Cambridge: Harvard University Press, 1978), 265–66, 275. See also her *Women and Men*. Edward Lane, on the other hand, reports that "in most families the husband alone attends to the household expenses," although he also points out that women are in charge of domestic affairs. See Lane, *Manners*, vol. 1, 259–60.
72. See Russell, "Modernity." See also Nancy Reynolds, "*Sharikat al-Bayt al-Maṣri*: Domesticating Commerce in Egypt, 1931–1956," *Arab Studies Journal* (Fall 1999/Spring 2000): 26–51.
73. Lane, *Manners*, vol. 1, 265; Sophia Lane Poole, *The Englishwoman in Egypt: Letters from Cairo, Written During Residence There in 1842* (London: Charles Knight and Co., 1844), vol. 2, 18. Compare these accounts to Huda Shaarawi, *Harem Years: The Memoirs of an Egyptian Feminist*, edited, translated, and introduced by Margot Badran (New York: The Feminist Press, 1987), 68–69.
74. Match-making and gossip were two other functions of the *dallalas*. Lane, *Manners*, vol. 1, 216; Elizabeth Cooper, *Women of Egypt*, 236; see also Judith Tucker, *Women in Nineteenth-Century Egypt* (Cambridge: Cambridge University Press, 1985), 82; André Raymond, *Artisans et Commerçants au Caire au XVIIIème* siècle (Damascus: IFAO, 1973–74), vol. 1, 274–75.
75. See e.g., Volney, *Voyage en Syrie et en Egypte Pendant les Années 1783, 1784, 1785* (Paris: Chez Dugour et Durand, 1799), 95; Walter Tyndale, *An Artist in Egypt* (London: Hodder and Stoughton, 1912), 41; Peter Gran, *Islamic Roots of Capitalism* (Austin: University of Texas Press, 1979), 18, 20.
76. "The Woman and Expenses of the House," *al-muqtaṭaf* 26, 7 (1901): 689.
77. Robert Tignor, *Modernization and British Colonial Rule in Egypt, 1882–1914* (Princeton: Princeton University Press, 1966), 381–82.
78. Tignor, *Modernization*, 381; Advertisement for the phone company, *anis al-jalis* 1, 5 (1898). This advertisement also appears in 1904, 1905, and 1906.
79. See e.g., Mary Whately, *Among the Huts in Egypt: Scenes from Real Life* (London: Seeley, Jackson, & Halliday, 1871), 174–75.
80. Edwin de Leon, *The Khedive's Egypt* (London: Samson Lew, Marston, Seale, & Rivington, [1877] 1882), 27. See also Taylor, *Egypt*, 26.
81. Muḥammad al-Muwayliḥi, *ḥadith ᶜIsa ibn Ḥisham aw fatra min zaman* (Cairo: Dar al-Qawmiya al-Tafaa wal-Nashr, 1964; fourth edition), 4–5.
82. Muwayliḥi, *ḥadith*, 36.
83. Mitchell, *Colonising*, 116.
84. Lady Baggot, "Ladies' Fashion," *al-muqtaṭaf* 8, 1 (1883): 53–54. For other articles on the corset, see e.g., "The Eastern Young Woman at the End of the Nineteenth Century," *al-hilal* 6, 5 (1897): 169–74; "The Corset," *al-muqtaṭaf* 19, 8 (1895): 598–600; "Wisdom for Women of Fashion," *al-muqtaṭaf* 43, 6 (1913): 588–89.
85. "The Tyranny of Fashion," *al-muqtaṭaf* 33, 6 (1908): 518–19 . See also "Women's Expense on Their Clothing," *al-muqtaṭaf* 38, 1 (1911): 82–83; "The Extravagence of Americans and Easterners," *al-muqtaṭaf* 39, 4 (1911): 392–294; "The Absolutism of Fashion," *al-muqtaṭaf* 39, 5 (1911): 498–99; and "The Woman's Fashion and Thrift," *al-hilal* 9, 11 (1901): 332–35.
86. "Winter Clothes and Taking off the Overcoat," *al-muqtaṭaf* 15, 5 (1891): 338–39.

87. ᶜAbd al-Fataḥ ᶜUbbad, "Women and the Creation of Fashion Among the Arabs in Islamic History," *al-hilal* 31, 9 (1923), 908.
88. See e.g., "Fashion," *al-hilal* 30, 2 (1921): 155–57.
89. *al-laṭa'if al-muṣawwara* (July 21, 1919): 3.
90. *al-laṭa'if al-muṣawwara* (March 31, 1919): 5.
91. *Muwaylihi, ḥadith*, 21.
92. *al-laṭa'if al-muṣawwara* (June 12, 1922): 5; see also (May 9, 1921): 5. Jirousek notes that during times of transition a "hybridization" takes places in which "features of the disappearing and emerging dress" occur at the same time. See her "Transition," 204. Ironically, what was disappearing had been the "new, reformed" dress in the previous century.
93. "Powder," *al-muqtaṭaf* 6, 5 (1881): 301; "Water and Soap is not Rouge and Cremes," *al-muqtaṭaf* 6, 8 (1881): 457–59. According to Kathy Peiss, turn-of-the-century American beauty culturists did not approve of make-up. Instead, they stressed breathing, exercise, diet, and bathing. Kathy Peiss, "Making Faces: The Cosmetics Industry and the Cultural Construction of Gender, 1890–1930," *Genders* 7 (Spring 1990); 147. See also her *Hope in a Jar* (New York: Metropolitan Books, 1998).
94. Elizabeth Frierson, "Cheap and Easy: The Creation of Consumer Culture in Late Ottoman Society," in Donald Quataert, ed., *Consumption Studies*, 254.
95. *al-laṭa 'if al-muṣawwara* (November 6, 1922): 12.
96. Muwaylihi, *ḥadith*, 109–14.
97. M. de Chabrol, "Etat Moderne, Essai sur les Moeurs des Habitants Modernes de l'Egypte," in *Description de l'Egypte* (Paris: Imprimerie Royale, 1822), vol. 2, 119.
98. Tugay reports an instance of a slave in Ismail's *ḥarim* and a physician falling in love. Ismail spoke to both the patient and the doctor, and then he arranged a marriage between the two. Emine Foat Tugay, *Three Centuries: Family Chronicles of Turkey & Egypt* (London: Oxford University Press, 1963), 305.
99. For the Ottoman context, see Frierson, "Cheap and Easy," 253. For examples, see advertisement for the Banayatatu Sisters, in 1901 and 1902 in *anis al-jalis* or the advertisement for surgeon/obstetrician, Wadiᶜa Ṣidnawi, *al-saᶜada* 3, 1 (1904), inside cover.
100. Muwaylihi, *ḥadith*, 112–13.
101. I was reminded of Muwaylihi's words at a presentation by Joe Dumit, entitled "Drugs for Life: Pharmaceutical Grammars in the Age of DTC," Evocative Objects Seminar, MIT, March 3, 2003. Dumit's research focuses on the effects of direct to consumer advertising.
102. Muwaylihi, *ḥadith*, 205–11.
103. See e.g., "The Detriment of Tobacco Smoking," *al-muqtaṭaf* 3, 3 (1878): 84; "The Danger of Smoking," *al-muqtaṭaf* 6, 4 (1881): 241; "Health Advice for Girls," *al-tarbiya* 2, 5 (1906): 35–36; "The Smoking Woman," *anis al-jalis* 9, 9 (1906): 257–60.
104. "Economy is Economy" *al-muqtaṭaf* 50, 3 (1917): 282–83; "Alcohol," *majallat jamᶜiyat malaji' al-ᶜAbbasiyya* 9, 1 (1327[AH]): 29–31.
105. In general, turn-of-the-century magazines encouraged women to nurse their own children, or if unable, to seek women of good health and morals. See e.g., Dr. Maḥmud Sidqi, "The Danger of Wine," *al-tarbiya* 3, 2 (1908): 13–14; Muḥammad Zaki, "Europeanized Turkish Women," *anis al-jalis* 9, 7 (1906): 165–66. The home economics section of *al-muqtaṭaf* frequently ran articles on the benefits of breast-feeding, how to breast feed, and how to wean children. See e.g., "Care of Those Who Breastfeed," *al-muqtaṭaf* 14, 1 (1889): 59; "Health Measures," *al-muqtaṭaf* 19, 3 (1895): 218–19; "Breastfeeding," *al-muqtaṭaf* 30, 5 (1905): 388–89; "Breastfeeding," *al-muqtaṭaf* 39, 4 (1911): 394–96;

"Breastfeeding," *al-muqtaṭaf* 39, 5 (1911): 499–500. al-Ahram also waged a number of campaigns to encourage proper breastfeeding, hygiene for milk sterilization, and the utility of formula. See Yunan Labib Rizq, "al-Ahram: A Diwan of Contemporary Life," *al-Ahram Weekly*, October 7–13, 1999.

106. "In Morals and Customs," *al-ustadh* 1, 3 (September 6, 1892): 51–56. For an analysis of class-based responses to Westernization with respect to women, see Juan Cole, "Feminism, Class, and Islam in Turn-of-the-Century Egypt," *IJMES* 13 (1981): 384–407. See also, "Objection of a Simpleton," and "The Response," *al-ustadh* 1, 7 (October 4, 1892): 164–66. Nelly Hanna traces the roots of such criticism to an earlier period. See her *In Praise of Books* (Syracuse: Syracuse University Press, 2003), 54, 147, 172–73.
107. The story appears translated in Louis Awad, *The Literature of Ideas in Egypt*, part one (Atlanta: Scholars Press, 1986), 80–84.
108. Untitled cartoon, *al-laṭa'if al-muṣawwara* (September 15, 1919): 6. See also, Magda Baraka, *The Egyptian Upper Class*, 68–69.
109. Muwayliḥi *ḥadith*, 47; *al-laṭa'if al-muṣawwara* (March 31, 1919): 5 and (November 6, 1922): 12; "Economy is Economy," *al-muqtaṭaf* 50, 3 (1917): 282–83. An article in *al-hilal* highlights the invention of a man-powered tram that would be more effective and inexpensive for smaller cities like Tanta and Mansura. "The National Tramway," *al-hilal* 12, 1 (1903): 27–30. Ṭal^{c}at Ḥarb's critique of the Belgian-owned Cairo Tramway Company appeared in *al-ahram* throughout September ending on September 17, 1919, highlighting government support, excessive fares, and the high profit margin.
110. *al-laṭa'if al-muṣawwara* (March 19, 1917): 8.
111. Muwayliḥi, *ḥadith*, 195; 224; 231–32; 265–66; 273–74; Mitchell, *Colonising*, 116–17.
112. Muwayliḥi, *ḥadith*, 186–90; 269–72.
113. See e.g., *al-laṭa'if al-muṣawwara* (February 7, 1921): 5.
114. "Gaiety is not Expensive Furniture," *al-muqtaṭaf* 14, 7 (1890): 485; "Furnishings of the Home," *al-muqtaṭaf* 18, 2 (1893): 121–22; "The Absolutism of Fashion," *al-muqtaṭaf* 39, 5 (1911): 498–99.
115. Muwayliḥi, *ḥadith*, 100. See also 46–47.
116. Muwayliḥi, *ḥadith*, 163–64.
117. Muwayliḥi, *ḥadith*, 178.
118. Awad, *Literature*, 86–87.
119. "The Extravagence of Americans and Easterners," *al-muqtaṭaf* 39, 4 (1911): 392–94.
120. "The Reasons for Egyptians Competing With Western Manufactured Goods," *al-tarbiya* 2, 1/2 (1905): 2. Other articles critiqued the types of goods purchased in these stores. See e.g., "Girls' Education," *al-sa^{c}ada* 1, 10 (1902), 215.
121. "The Masculine Woman," *anis al-jalis* 4, 9 (1901), 789.
122. "Sewing," *al-muqtaṭaf* 8, 10 (1884): 587–88.
123. Muwayliḥi, *ḥadith*, 57; see also, 94.
124. Muwayliḥi, *ḥadith*, 47.
125. "The Eastern Young Woman at the End of the Nineteenth Century," *al-hilal* 6, 5 (1897), 173–74.
126. Muḥammad Zaki, "Europeanized Turkish Women," *anis al-jalis* 9, 7 (1906): 170–74; "Complaint of Mothers About the Upbringing of Girls," *al-muqtaṭaf* 28, 10 (1903): 874–78; "Reading Novels," *al-muqtaṭaf* 32, 8 (1907): 671–72.
127. Wadi^{c}a Effendi al-Khury, "The Woman's Rights," *al-muqtaṭaf* 7, 1 (1881): 17–22; "The Future of the Woman," *al-muqtaṭaf* 54, 1 (1919): 76–77.
128. "The Good Year," *al-sufur* 1, 1 (1915): 6–7 and 1, 2 (1915): 7–8.

4 ADVERTISING AND CONSUMER CULTURE IN EGYPT: CREATING *al-Sayyida al-Istihlakiyya*

1. Peter Burke, "*Res et Verba*: Conspicuous Consumption in the Early Modern World," in John Brewer and Roy Porter, eds. *Consumption and the World of Goods* (London: Routledge, 1993), 148–49. See also Rosalind Williams, *Dream Worlds* (Berkeley: University of California Press, 1982), 19–57.
2. Roger Owen, *The Middle East in the World Economy* (London: Methuen, 1993), xxi–xxii, 9. Charles Issawi, "Middle East Economic Development, 1815–1914: The General and the Specific," in M.A. Cook, ed., *Studies in the Economic History of the Middle East*, (Oxford: Oxford University Press, 1970), 395. An exception is Fatma Müge Göçek's *Rise of the Bourgeoisie, Demise of Empire* (New York: Oxford University Press, 1996), in which she examines the consumption of Western goods and ideas as a factor leading to the segmentation of the Ottoman bourgeoisie into bureaucratic and commercial factions over the course of the eighteenth and nineteenth centuries. The role of consumption has been the topic of two conferences, leading to two anthologies: Donald Quataert, ed., *Consumption Studies and the History of the Ottoman Empire, 1550–1922: An Introduction* (Albany: SUNY Press, 2000); Relli Shechter, ed., *Transitions in Domestic Consumption and Family Life in the Modern Middle East: Houses in Motion* (New York: Palgrave, 2003).
3. Grant McCracken, *Culture and Consumption* (Bloomington: Indiana University Press, 1990), 22; Burke, "*Res et Verba*," 155; Carole Shammas, "Changes in English and Anglo-American Consumption from 1550–1800," 178, 199, Sidney Mintz, "The Changing Roles of Food in the Study of Consumption," 263 and Jan de Vries, "Between Purchasing Power and the World of Goods: Understanding the Household Economy in Early Modern Europe," 107, 120, all three of which are in Brewer and Porter, *Consumption*.
4. Neil McKendrick, John Brewer, and J.H. Plumb, *The Birth of Consumer Society* (Bloomington: Indiana University Press, 1982), 1–11; McCracken, *Culture*, 22.
5. Raymond Williams, "Advertising the Magic System," in his *Problems in Materialism and Culture* (London: Verso Editions and New Left Books, 1980), 174; Gary Cross, *Time and Money* (London: Routledge, 1993), 156; James Norris, *Advertising and the Transformation of American Society* (New York: Greenwood Press, 1990), 1–4; Michael Miller, *The Bon Marché* (Princeton: Princeton University Press, 1989), 35–36, 45–46; William Leach, "Transformations in a Culture of Consumption: Women and Department Stores, 1890–1925," *Journal of American History* 71 (September 1984), 322; Hrant Pasdermadjian, *The Department Store, Its Origins, Evolution and Economics* (London: Newman Books, 1954), 1–2, 24.
6. Pasdermadjian, *Department Store*, 2, 10–12; John Ferry, *A History of the Department Store* (New York: The MacMillan Company, 1960), 2; Miller, *Bon Marché*, 25–27, 34–35. See also Robert Twyman, *A History of Marshall Field & Co.* (Philadelphia: University of Pennsylvania Press, 1954); Edward Hungerford, *The Romance of a Great Store* (New York: Robert McBride & Co., 1922); Sean Callery, *Harrods, Knightbridge: The Story of Society's Favourite Store* (London; Ebury Press, 1991); Au Bon Marché, *Souvenir of the Bon Marché* (Paris: E. Plon, 1891); William Lancaster, *The Department Store: A Social History* (London: Leicester University Press, 1995); and *Les Grands Magasins à Paris, à Berlin et en Amérique* (Paris: Berger-Levrault, 1913).
7. Susan Strasser, *Satisfaction Guaranteed* (New York: Pantheon, 1989), 67–69, 73, 204–05; Miller, *Bon Marché*, 24–25, 27, 48; Ferry, *History*, 3; Pasdermadjian, *Department Store*,

10; Joseph Appel, *Growing Up with Advertising* (New York: The Business Bourse, 1940), 53 and 60. On credit in the Ottoman context, see Elizabeth Frierson, "Cheap and Easy: The Creation of Consumer Culture in Late Ottoman Society," in Quataert, ed., *Consumption Studies*, 250–51.

8. Pasdermadjian, *Department Store*, 11, 25–26, 32; Strasser, *Satisfaction Guaranteed*, 206; Miller, *Bon Marché*, 45, 48–51, 167–74, 218; Appel, *Advertising*, 41; Leach, "Transformations," 323–26, 329; *Jordan Marsh Illustrated Catalog of 1891: An Unabridged Reprint* (Philadelphia: Athenaeum of Philadelphia, 1991). The monumental nature of these stores is documented in illustrations 15–18 of Williams, *Dream Worlds*. The main branch of the Sednaoui department store in Cairo still maintains its original elevators, positioned in the store by Gustave Eiffel. Cam McGrath, "Schindler's Lift," *Middle East* (October 2002), Issue 327.
9. McCracken, *Culture*, 29; T.J. Jackson Lears, "From Salvation to Self-Realization: Advertising and the Therapeutic Roots of the Consumer Culture, 1880–1930," in Richard Wightman and T.J. Jackson Lears, eds., *The Culture of Consumption*, (New York: Pantheon Books, 1983), 3; Jennifer Scanlon, *Inarticulate Longings* (New York: Routledge, 1995), 16; Stuart Ewen, *Captains of Consciousness* (New York: McGraw Hill, 1976), 54; Miller, *Bon Marché*, 182–83; Appel, *Advertising*, 62–63; Williams, "Advertising," 170–74; C.Y. Ferdinand, "Selling it to the Provinces: News and Commerce Round Eighteenth-Century Salisbury," in Brewer and Porter, *Consumption*, 397–98; Strasser, *Satisfaction Guaranteed*, 90.
10. Ferdinand, "Selling"; Jeremy Popkin, "The Business of Political Enlightenment in France, 1770–1800," in Brewer and Porter, *Consumption*, 7; Miller, *Bon Marché*, 38.
11. Helen Damon-Moore, *Gender and Commerce in the Ladies' Home Journal and the Saturday Evening Post, 1880–1910* (Albany: SUNY Press, 1994), 51; Norris, *Advertising*, 14, 99, 103.
12. Appel, *Advertising*, 78; Roland Marchand, *Advertising the American Dream: Making Way for Modernity* (Berkeley: University of California Press, 1985), 8; Norris, *Advertising*, 63; Kathy Peiss, "Making Faces: The Cosmetics Industry and the Cultural Construction of Gender, 1890-1930," *Genders* 7 (Spring 1990), 144–45. See also her *Hope in a Jar* (New York: Metropolitan Books, 1998).
13. Anne McClintock, *Imperial Leather* (New York: Routledge, 1995), 207, 210. She points out that by the 1890s Britons were consuming 260,000 tons of soap per year.
14. McClintock points out, that ritual and fetish also played a role. McClintock, *Imperial Leather*, 210–11. See also Timothy Burke, *Lifebouy Men, Lux Women* (Durham: Duke University Press, 1996).
15. Strasser, *Satisfaction Guaranteed*, 6–7; Norris, *Advertising*, 99.
16. Damon-Moore, *Gender and Commerce*, 24, 51; John Kenneth Galbraith, *Economics and Public Purpose* (Boston: Houghton Mifflin, 1973), 31–32; Norris, *Advertising*, 80–81.
17. Damon-Moore, *Gender and Commerce*, 100; McClintock, *Imperial Leather*, 209; Strasser, *Satisfaction Guaranteed*, 109.
18. Strasser, *Satisfaction Guaranteed*, 93; Williams, "Advertising," 178–79; Scanlon, *Inarticulate Longings*, 198–99; Marchand, *American Dream*, 33–35, 51. Egypt lacked indigenous agencies during this period. See Relli Shechter, "Press Advertising in Egypt: Business Realities and Local Meaning, 1882–1956," *Arab Studies Journal* 10, 2/11, 1 (Fall 2002/Spring 2003), 45–48, 50–52, 57.
19. Norris, *Advertising*, 62, 68–69; Peiss, "Making Faces," 150–51; Damon-Moore, *Gender and Commerce*, 179, 187; Scanlon, *Inarticulate Longings*, 32. See also Ruth S. Cowan, *More Work for Mother* (New York: Basic Books, 1983).

20. Scanlon, *Inarticulate Longings*, 32, 134–35, 170, 207, 219; Norris, *Advertising*, 74–77, 109; Marchand, *American Dream*, 18–20, 228–32; Ewen, *Captains*, 175; Williams, "Transformations," 188–89.
21. As quoted in Damon-Moore, *Gender and Commerce*, 24.
22. Henry Foster Adams, *Advertising and its Mental Laws* (New York: Macmillan, 1916), 317 as cited in Rachel Bowlby, "Soft Sell: Marketing Rhetoric in Feminist Criticism," in Victoria de Grazia and Ellen Furlough, eds., *The Sex of Things* (Berkeley: University of California Press, 1996), 381.
23. Christine Frederick, *Selling Mrs. Consumer* (New York: The Business Bourse, 1929), 12.
24. Damon-Moore, *Gender and Commerce*, 54. See also, Michael Schudson, *Advertising, the Uneasy Persuasion* (New York: Basic Books, Inc., 1984), 238.
25. Mary Ann Fay, "Women and Households: Gender, Power, and Culture in Eighteenth-Century Egypt" (Ph.D. diss., Georgetown University, 1993), 234; Owen, *Middle East*, 47–48; Peter Gran, *Islamic Roots of Capitalism, 1769–1840* (Austin: University of Texas Press, 1979), 5–8, 18, 21; Afaf Marsot, *Women and Men in Eighteenth-Century Egypt* (Austin: University of Texas Press, 1995), 104; F. Hasselquist, *Voyages and Travels in the Levant in the Years 1749, 1750, 1751, 1752* (trans.) (London, 1766) as cited in Owen, *Middle East*, 9.
26. Edward Lane, *An Account of the Manners and Customs of the Modern Egyptians* (New York: Dover Publications, 1973), 312–17.
27. André Raymond, *Artisans et Commerçants au Caire au XVIIIème siècle* (Damascus: IFAO, 1973/74), vol. 1, 204, vol. 507–14. See also Marsot, *Women and Men*, 99–103.
28. See e.g. Owen, *Middle East*; Charles Issawi, *The Economic History of the Middle East 1800–1914* (Chicago: University of Chicago Press, 1966); David Carr, *Foreign Investment and Development in Egypt* (New York: Praeger Publishers, 1979). See also M.A. Cook, *Studies*; A.L. Udovitch, ed., *The Islamic Middle East, 700–1900* (Princeton: Darwin Press, 1981).
29. Carr, *Foreign Investment*, 12; Owen, *Middle East*, 69–75; Charles Issawi, "The Economic Development of Egypt, 1800–1960," in his *Economic History*, 362; Ali al-Giritli, "The Commercial, Financial, and Industrial Policies of Muhammad Ali," in Issawi, ed., *Economic History*, 389.
30. John Bowring, "Report on Egypt and Candia," 80–81 as cited in David Landes, *Bankers and Pashas* (Cambridge: Harvard University Press, 1958), 87. I will include the *mutamaṣṣirun* when using the term indigenous entrepreneurs. On the *mutamaṣṣirun*, see Robert Vitalis, *When Capitalists Collide* (Berkeley: University of California Press, 1995), 12–15.
31. Toledano, *State and Society in Mid-Nineteenth-Century Egypt* (New York: Cambridge University Press, 1990), 126–32; 76–77; Hassan, *In the House of Muhammad Ali* (Cairo: AUC Press, 2000), 101–03; al-Rafa^{c}i, ^{c}*aṣr Isma*^{c}*il* (Cairo: Dar al-Ma^{c}arif, 1987 [1932]), vol. 1, 15, 18–21; Owen, *Middle East*, 123.
32. al-Rafa^{c}i, *Isma*^{c}*il*, vol. 1, 26–27; 33–34, 53, 62. On debt, see Owen, *Middle East*, 122–23.
33. On the Sednaoui family, see Jurji Zaidan, *tarajim mashahir al-sharq* (Cairo, 1922), vol. 1, 302–09; On the Chemla family, see Nancy Reynolds, "*Sharikat al-Bayt al-Miṣri*: Domesticating Commerce in Egypt, 1931–1956," *Arab Studies Journal* (Fall 1999/Spring 2000), 84–85.
34. These descriptions come entirely from Magda Baraka's *The Egyptian Upper Classes Between Revolutions, 1919–1952* (Reading: Ithaca, 1998), 117–20.
35. Egypt, *niẓarat al-maliyya, ta*^{c}*dad sukan al-qutr al-miṣri, 1897* [*Census of 1897*] (Cairo: al-Maṭba^{c}a al-Kubra al-Amiriyya bi Bulaq, 1898), 28; *niẓarat al-maliyya The Census of*

Egypt Taken in 1917 (Cairo: Government Press, 1920), 568–71; *Annual Report 1898*, 43; *Annual Report 1899*, 35; *Annual Report 1901*, 40–41; Beth Baron, *The Women's Awakening in Egypt* (New Haven: Yale University Press, 1994), 82–83, 89–92; Baraka, *The Egyptian Upper Class*, 65.

36. On visual culture and representation, see Nicholas Mirzoeff, *The Visual Culture Reader* (New York: Routledge, 1998).
37. Marchand, *American Dream*, xviii–xx.
38. For two blatant examples, see that of the Armour company in Madagascar and the Stork margerine company in Zimbabwe. Strasser, *Satisfaction Guaranteed*, 143; Burke, *Lifebouy Men, Lux Women*, 162.
39. Baron, *Women's Awakening*, 67–71. Cole also emphasizes the importance of subventions; however, he speculates that advertising revenues became more significant by the late 1870s, when government support for the press declined. Juan Cole, *Colonialism & Revolution in the Middle East* (Princeton: Princeton University Press, 1993), 128. Shechter found advertising to be quite limited before World War I. See his "Press Advertising," 45–48.
40. According to Ami Ayalon, the first advertisements appeared in this newspaper in the 1830s. See his *The Press in the Arab Middle East: A History* (New York: Oxford University Press, 1995), 203.
41. See e.g. *al-waqa*^{c}*i al-miṣriyya*, advertisement for the Egyptian Company, November 30, 1865; advertisement for sale of marble pillars by the Diwan of Imports, December 21, 1865; advertisement for sale of musical instruments by the Diwan of Imports, June 28, 1866.
42. See e.g. *al-waqa*^{c}*i al-miṣriyya*, advertisement for sale of a house in Abdin, January 11, 1866; advertisement for publication on *tawḥid*, February 1, 1866; advertisement for the sale of four *waqf* properties, February 8, 1866; advertisement for books by Bulaq Press, May 3, 1866.
43. Shechter, "Press Advertising," 46.
44. For example, as late as 1917, all but one of the advertisements in *al-manar* dealt with the magazine or the press itself. The single exception was a one-line advertisement for a medication that could be purchased through the magazine. Shechter emphasizes the close relationship between the press and advertising, pointing out that a number of big publishing interests opened their own advertising agencies in the interwar period. Shechter, "Press Advertising," 51.
45. Abbas Kelidar, "The Political Press in Egypt, 1882–1914," in *Contemporary Egypt: Through Egyptian Eyes: Essays in Honor of P. J. Vatikiotis* (London: Routledge, 1993), 1–9; "For History," *ummahat al-mustaqbal* 1, 1 (1930), 27; Ijlal Khalifa, *al-ḥaraka al-nisa'iyya al-ḥaditha: qissat al-mar'a al-*^{c}*arabiyya* ^{c}*ala arḍ Miṣr* (Cairo: al-Maṭba^{c}a al-^{c}Arabiyya al-Ḥaditha, 1973), chapter 3; Baron, *Women's Awakening*, 1.
46. Baron, *Women's Awakening*, 67–71.
47. "The Benefits of Advertisements," *al-hilal* 5, 11 (1897): 413–14; *al-hilal* 4, 9 (1896), 344; "Advertisements in *al-hilal*," *al-hilal* 10, 5 (1901): 151; "The Benefits of the Overlooked," *anis al-jalis* 6, 12 (1903), 1637 and 1639.
48. It is not clear who wrote the advertisement copy. In some cases, magazines resorted to format advertisements in which all advertisements followed the same pattern. For imported products, the advertising copy often came from the West. It is not clear what role, if any, indigenous women played in writing advertising copy. It should also be noted that there was skepticism on the part of local producers of goods and services with respect to the utility of advertising. Shechter, "Press Advertising," 45–46.
49. Advertisements for stores, e.g., provided information on the range of goods available, the arrival of new goods, and the store's location. Sometimes stores might claim to have a

greater variety than their competitors or that their goods came from the best companies in Europe.

50. Frierson, "Cheap and Easy," 247.
51. See e.g., advertisement for Vin Mariani that appeared in all 1901 issues of *anis al-jalis*, or that of Vin Nourry in *anis al-jalis* in late 1902–04, which also ran in *al-mu'ayyad*.
52. See e.g. advertisement for Banks Pills, *al-ahram* (March 14, 1900) and (April 31, 1900), *anis al-jalis* 4, 3 (1901), back cover; advertisement for Hemagene Tailleur, *al-ahram* (January 30, 1904). On the effects of Victorian medicine, see Hibba Abugideiri, "Egyptian Women and the Science Question: Gender in the Making of Colonized Medicine, 1893–1929" (Ph.D. diss., Georgetown University, 2001), 410–70.
53. Compare the aforementioned products to advertisements for Lydia Pinkham's Vegetable compound and Dr. Pierce's Favorite Prescription, in Bob Perlongo, *Early American Advertising*, 17 and 43, respectively.
54. Frierson, "Cheap and Easy," 248–49.
55. The full range of Doan's advertisements appear in *anis al-jalis* from 1903 to 1906. Doan's also bought advertising space in *al-ahram*, *al-hilal*, and *al-liwa'*.
56. A full range of Scott's Emulsion advertisements appeared in *anis al-jalis* from 1903–06. Scott's Emulsion also bought advertising space in *al-ahram*.
57. Health Oil advertisement, *al-sa^{c}ada*, appears several times in 1902; Mahmud Kamil's Tooth Remedy advertisement, *anis al-jalis*, appears several times during 1900; advertisement for hair restoration medication, *anis al-jalis* 5, 6 (1902), 1105. My own research on the 1922–52 period, as well as that of Relli Shechter, suggests that in the interwar period, these small, local competitors were no longer able to afford advertising after the arrival of multinationals, e.g. Bayer and Colgate. "Press Advertising," 55.
58. See e.g. advertisement for Adamantine hair restorer, *al-mu'ayyad* (January 7, 1902), 6; Hazeline Snow advertisement, *al-mu'ayyad* (March 1, 1914), 7; Alaska Hair Creme, *anis al-jalis* 1, 5 (1898), back cover.
59. *al-mu'ayyad* 8, 2065 (1897), 4.
60. I compared a random week's advertisements in the daily *al-mu'ayyad* during the years 1893, 1897, 1902, 1906, 1910, and 1914 to all the advertisements from the monthly *anis al-jalis* from 1898–1906. Regarding the mainstream press, Marilyn Booth refers to it as the *malestream* press in order to "signif[y] the close association between the predominant daily newspapers and monthly magazines on the one hand, and male culture, direction, and assumptions about male power in the sphere of public discourse and political action on the other." See her "Men and the Women's Press," *IJMES* 33, 2 (2001), 171, 193n2.
61. Nearly one-fifth of *al-mu'ayyad*'s advertising was dedicated to government sales of land, employment opportunities, or court announcements. See, e.g. *al-mu'ayyad* 1, 37 (1890), 4; *al-mu'ayyad* 1, 38 (1890), 3.
62. Specialty stores represent about 25 percent of the advertising in *anis al-jalis*, and about 15 percent in *al-mu'ayyad*. Department store advertising in *anis al-jalis* outnumbers *al-mu'ayyad* by more than four times, representing 13 percent and 3 percent, respectively.
63. *Anis al-jalis* contained no advertisements for dentists or lawyers; however a number of doctors, mostly those specializing in the care of women and children, advertised, representing about two percent of all advertisements. There was a greater range of specialists advertising in *al-mu'ayyad*, although a great many who advertised were specialists in the care of women and children. Urban professionals represented about 10.5 percent of the advertisements in *al-mu'ayyad*.
64. See, e.g., advertisement for G.H. Mumm & Co., distributors of fine champagne, *anis al-jalis* 1, 2 (1898), back cover; Vin Mariani, *anis al-jalis* 4, 1 (1901), inside cover; Vin Nourry, *anis al-jalis* 5, 12 (1902), back cover; advertisement for Vin Norry [Nourry],

al-mu'ayyad (January 4, 1902), 3. More of the patent medicines that advertised probably had alcohol, but of these only Vin Mariani and Vin Nourry had "wine" specifically in their names and descriptions.

65. Nevertheless, it was not unknown, particularly among non-Muslim editors. See e.g., advertisements for Canadian Club Whiskey and Crown Beer in *al-muqaṭṭam*, January 18, 1897 and April 14, 1900, resp.
66. Shechter, "Press Advertising," 55. See also my "Commodifying Identity: Women and Egyptian Advertising 1922–52," paper presented at MESA and the AHA, November 2002 and January 2003, resp.
67. *al-sa^{c}ada* 1, 1 (1902), 17, 18; 1, 3 (1902), 64, 70, 71; 1, 14 (1903), 2.
68. See e.g., advertisement for the ^{c}Abbas Hotel, *al-sa^{c}ada* 1, 15 (1903), inside cover; advertisement for Niccola Madur & Co., 2, 4 (1903), 505.
69. Russell, "Commodifying Identity"; see also Shechter, "Press Advertising," 44–57.
70. "Benefit of *al-laṭa'if* Advertisements," *al-laṭa'if al-muṣawwara* (November 23, 1920), 9. An advertisement from the following year guarantees benefits and encourages potential advertisers to try it just once. *al-laṭa'if al-muṣawwara* (March 14, 1921), 10.
71. Advertisement for *al-laṭa'if* agent in Brazil, *al-laṭa'if al-muṣawwara* (December 25, 1922), 3. This circulation figure is probably close to double the actual figure. Nevertheless, accounting for reading aloud and re-circulating individual issues makes compilation of statistics difficult. For circulation figures, see Ami Ayalon, *Press*, 148–51.
72. These advertisements include a hair dye, complexion creme, weight loss product, and "Eastern" pills guaranteed to give a woman the bust of a goddess. The company naively assumed a universal representation of beauty, and their failure was easily measured since customers were to respond by mail to a company in France. See *al-muqaṭṭam* (April–May 1892).
73. See e.g., advertisement for the Barrere hernia belt, *al-liwa'* (January 6, 1903), 3.
74. Compare a 1906 advertisement for Creme Simon and one from 1917. *al-mu'ayyad* (October 31, 1906), 7; *al-laṭa'if al-muṣawwara* (November 5, 1917), 9.
75. See e.g, *al-laṭa'if al-muṣawwara* (January 8, 15, 22, and February 26, 1917).
76. Makhazin Chamla advertisement, *al-laṭa'if al-muṣawwara* (April 5, 1915), 4; Nadko dye advertisement, *al-laṭa'if al-muṣawwara* (July 24, 1922); De Ricoles advertisement, *al-laṭa'if al-muṣawwara* (August 27, 1917), 10. See also advertisement for Creme Minerva that opens, "Oh beautiful women." *al-laṭa'if al-muṣawwara* (August 22, 1922), 6.
77. These advertisements are similar to those run contemporaneously for a Western company, Webber & Company, except that they are larger, and the picture of the stylish man changes, whereas the Webber ad remains the same. Advertisements for the Egyptian Clothing Company, *al-laṭa'if al-muṣawwara* (December 4, 11, and 25, 1922), 15.
78. Regarding the cigarette, see Shechter, "The Egyptian Cigarette: A Study of the Interaction Between Consumption, Production, and Marketing in Egypt, 1850–1956," (Harvard University, 1999), 41–42. Regarding the *tarbush*, during this period there is little marketing of this all-important product. As the class of *effendiyya* expanded in the post–World War I era, marketing intensified and became nationalistic in nature. See Shechter, "Press Advertising," 49. See also Russell, "National Identity and Egyptian Advertising in the Liberal Era, 1922–52," paper presented at the Middle East Center, University of Pennsylvania, October 2002.
79. Although the text would change with the season or arrival of goods, this picture remained the same in *al-laṭa'if al-muṣawwara*'s advertising between 1915 and 1917. Note the remarkable similarity to the advertising for Au Bon Marché in Paris, documented in Miller, *Bon Marché*, 177.
80. See her "Cheap and Easy," 249–50.

81. See, e.g., advertisement for the stores of Yusif and Aḥmad al-Gammal, *al-muqtaṭaf* 54, 5 (1919), back cover, and advertisement for Mauardi, *al-laṭa'if al-muṣawwara* (January 31, 1921), 11.
82. Photographic images in advertising were rare during this period. This campaign ran between 1921 and 1922 in *al-laṭa'if al-muṣawwara.*
83. See e.g., Westinghouse advertisement, *al-mu'ayyad* (February 26, 1914), 6; Hazeline Snow advertisement, *al-mu'ayyad* (March 1, 1914), 7; Lipton tea advertisement *al-mu'ayyad* (February 26, 1914), 6; advertisement for the Egyptian Wheat Company (with the registered wheat leaf trademark), *al-laṭa'if al-muṣawwara,* ran throughout 1917; advertisement for the Ẓirafa Company (with the registered giraffe trademark), *al-laṭa'if al-muṣawwara,* ran throughout 1919. Relli Shechter argues that prior to World War I, most products were unbranded and sold in bulk, and that there were only limited legal mechanisms to protect brand names. "Press Advertising," 45–46.
84. See e.g., Grape-Nuts advertisement that ran throughout 1922 in *al-laṭa'if al-muṣawwara.*
85. See e.g. the aforementioned Wadi^c^a al-Hawawini campaign in *al-laṭa'if al-muṣawwara,* 1922; the Kodak catalog offer, *al-laṭa'if al-muṣawwara* 1921–22.
86. Advertisement for Au Petit Tailleur Egyptien, *al-laṭa'if al-muṣawwara* (February 21, 1916), 9; advertisement for Optometrists, *al-laṭa'if al-muṣawwara,* ran frequently in 1921 and 1922; advertisement for Muḥammad Kamil & Co. Grocer, Hazbin Brothers Manufacturers, Ramsis Cigarette Company, al-Tarḥib Pharmacy, and the Abu Hol Trading Company, *al-laṭa'if al-muṣawwara* (April 24, 1922), 15.
87. *al-laṭa'if al-muṣawwara* (February 23, 1920), 5. Another campaign that resembled a general-interest story is one for Gargoyle Motor Oil, entitled "This is What is of Interest to Every Ford Owner," *al-laṭa'if al-muṣawwara* (December 25, 1922), 15.
88. Advertisement for White Rose Patisserie, *al-laṭa'if al-muṣawwara,* ad ran throughout 1920.
89. For the Ottoman context, see Frierson, "Cheap and Easy," 251–52.
90. See e.g., François Levernay, *Guide Générale d'Egypte* (Alexandria: Imprimerie Nouvelle, 1868), advertisements; Mary Broderick *A Handbook for Travellers in Lower and Upper Egypt,* (London: John Murray, 1896), advertisements; Hotel Windsor advertisement, *anis al-jalis* 5, 12 (1902), back cover; ^c^Abbas Hotel advertisement, *al-sa^c^ada* 1, 15 (1903), inside cover; al-Ḥayat Hotels advertisement, *al-muqtaṭaf* 46, 3 (1915). Interestingly enough, *al-liwa'* carried an advertisement for a Paris hotel. Advertisement for Hotel Beaujon in Paris (November 3, 1902), 4.
91. Advertisement for the Marin hotel, *al-laṭa'if al-muṣawwara* (July 3, 1922), 5; advertisement for the Lebanon Vacations Company, *al-laṭa'if al-muṣawwara* (July 24, 1922), 14. Baraka describes Ras al-Bar as a location "for families and for freedom from the restrictions of formal dress and the bustle of the city," while she describes Lebanon as a destination for those who were "neither too squanderous nor too thrifty." See her *The Egyptian Upper Classes,* 205.
92. Before World War I, only an elite of mostly foreign workers received paid vacation. Even by the 1930s, Beinin and Lockman argue that few workers enjoyed paid vacations. See their *Workers on the Nile* (Princeton: Princeton University Press, 1987), 40, 45, 123.
93. Ferry, *History,* 4. In her study of London's West End, Erika Rappaport notes changes and accommodations that had to take place in mid–late nineteenth-century London, e.g. providing places where women could, eat, "rest," and socialize. See her *Shopping for Pleasure* (Princeton: Princeton University Press, 2000), 74–107. Thus, accommodating women is not unique to Middle Eastern culture.

94. One finds the terms *al-sayyidat al-muwaṭiniyyat* or *min hurum al-muslimin*. The latter term signifies religious distinction amongst those who practice segregation, while the former term translates into female citizens or national ladies.
95. *Anis al-jalis*, with its small, localized readership had a large number of advertisements for this potential group of consumers. See e.g., advertisement for G.B. Zola American Ice-Creamery, advertised throughout 1901; advertisement for Reiser & Binder Photography, ran regularly from 1900–06; advertisement for the medical practice of the sisters Banayutatu, ran in 1901 and 1902; advertisement for Dick & Co., ran throughout 1901; Grand Magasins du Printemps Nouveautés advertisement, ran from 1901–06. According to Baron, the Cairo-based *fatat al-sharq* also had advertising geared toward the secluded shopper. Baron, *Women's Awakening*, 94.
96. Advertisement for Madame Massert, *anis al-jalis*, ran from late 1900 through 1901; advertisement for Maison Stein, ran from 1900 to 1905.
97. Huda Shaarawi, *Harem Years: The Memoirs of an Egyptian Feminist*, translated and introduced by Margot Badran (New York: The Feminist Press, 1987), 68–69.
98. See e.g., Grace Thompson Seton, *A Woman Tenderfoot in Egypt* (New York: Dodd, Mead, and Company, 1923), 51.
99. A small one-line advertisement for the National Soap Laboratory appeared in *al-ᶜa'ila* in 1904, and in a Creme Simon skin whitener advertisement, the instructions for the product read "use Creme Simon every day with Creme Simon soap"; however, the advertisement was not for soap. Creme Simon advertisement, *al-mu'ayyad* (October 31, 1906), 7; Palmolive advertisement, *al-laṭa'if al-muṣawwara* (January 2, 1922), 10. A single advertisement for laundry detergent also appears in 1922. Zahrat Miṣr advertisement, *al- laṭa'if al-muṣawwara* (July 3, 1922), 15. According to the British Chamber of Commerce, there were three modern oil and soap companies in 1901; however, by 1911, there are none. *List of Financial, Manufacturing and Transport Companies Established in Egypt* (Alexandria, 1901[3rd edition]), 526–27 as cited in Owen, *Middle East*, 236.
100. *al-laṭa'if al-muṣawwara* (March 27, 1922), 6.
101. Nestle's, Allenburys', and Glaxo were all frequent advertisers during this period.
102. The literacy rate of unmarried women aged 10–29 in the three most advanced governates of the delta, reached 32 percent by 1917. *Census of 1917*, 569.
103. During the Ottoman period Egypt imported large quantities of Nabulsi soap, amounting to roughly 3/4 of the city's production. Beshara Doumani, *Rediscovering Palestine: Merchants and Peasants in Jabal Nablus, 1700–1900* (Berkeley: University of California Press, 1995), 24, 71–72, 280. In the interwar period soap advertising grew tremendously, among foreign multinational competitors, e.g. Lever Brothers and Colgate-Palmolive, traditional Nabulsi competitors, and new Egyptian firms backed by both foreign and domestic capital.
104. See e.g., Judith Tucker, "Muftis and Matrimony: Islamic Law and Gender in Ottoman Syria and Palestine," *Islamic Law and Society* 1, 3 (1994), 285.
105. Although advertisements for soap greatly increased during this period, there are few depictions of the targeted consumer actually doing the work. Compare e.g., two soap [laundry] advertisements from 1949. In one, the consumer is clad in an apron and is arranging a stack of clean clothing, while in the other the consumer is marveling at her servant's ability to get a tablecloth clean. Dabas soap advertisement, *al-ithnayn wa dunya* (April 4, 1949), 43; Sunlight soap advertisement, *al-ithnayn wa dunya* (October 17, 1949), 24.
106. Yunan Labib Rizq, "al-Ahram: Diwan of Contemporary Life," *al-Ahram Weekly*, October 7–13 1999; Hibba Abugideiri, "Colonized Medicine," 429.
107. *al-laṭa'if al-muṣawwara*, February 13, 1922, 15.

108. According to Roger Owen, at the time that Volney visited Cairo in the mid–eighteenth century, he could find no one to repair his watch. See his *Middle East*, 46. Specialized stores for clocks and watches, as well as jewelers selling clocks and watches, were frequent advertisers in both the mainstream and women's press. See e.g., advertisement for Sussman, *al-mu'ayyad* 4, 875 (1893), 4; Anṭun Effendi Jalaḥ, *al-ᶜa'ila* 3, 2 (1904). Singer and authorized Singer agents were also frequent advertisers, buying space in *anis al-jalis, al-mu'ayyad, al-muqtaṭaf, and al-ahram.* To aid in the promotion of its product, Singer offered free demontrations and lessons in its stores, just as it did in the United States. For other advertisements for home furnishings, see e.g., Maison Vrana advertisement, *anis al-jalis* 1, 1 (1898), front cover; Hugo Hacktt advertisement, *anis al-jalis* 3, 8 (1900), 320; Levi, Pezzi et Palaggi advertisement, *anis al-jalis* 4, 1 (1901), back cover; advertisement for A. Beer, *anis al-jalis* 4, 1 (1901), back cover; advertisement for Westinghouse, *al-mu'ayyad* (February 26, 1914), 4; advertisement for Ilyas ᶜAḍḍad's furniture store, *al-la ṭa'if al-muṣawwara* (October 16, 1922), 15; advertisement for the Edison Store's agent, *anis al-jalis* 4, 7 (1901), back cover.
109. As Frierson points out in the Ottoman context, such calls were especially resonant in which the health of children was concerned. See "Cheap and Easy," 253–54.
110. See e.g., advertisement for Canadian Club Whiskey by Walker & Co., *al-muqaṭṭam* (January 18, 1897), 3; advertisement for Crown Brewery, *al-muqaṭṭam* (April 14, 1900), 4; advertisement for G.H. Mumm & Co., *anis al-jalis* 1, 2 (1898), back cover; advertisement for Estis & Co. [false teeth], *al-mu'ayyad* 1, 12 (1889), 3; advertisement for Dr. Tawfiq ᶜAzmi, *al-saᶜada* 1, 3 (1902), 69; advertisement for Dr. Niccola Ḥabib, *al-laṭa'if al-muṣawwara* (March 6, 1922), 10; advertisement for store producing surgical instruments and metal works, *al-laṭa'if al-muṣawwara* (May 8, 1916), 6.
111. Nancy Mickelwright, "London, Paris, Istanbul, and Cairo: Fashion and International Trade in the 19th Century," *New Perspectives on Turkey* 7 (Spring 1992), 126–29. See also Charlotte Jirousek, "The Transition to Mass Fashion System Dress in the Later Ottoman Empire," in Quataert, ed., *Consumption Studies*, 201–42.
112. See e.g., advertisement for Madame Bonafanitura, *anis al-jalis* 3, 10 (1900), 399; advertisement for J. Barki, *anis al-jalis* 3, 11 (1900), 436; advertisement for E. Ashton, *anis al-jalis* 3, 8 (1900), 320; advertisement for Grand Magasins Chalon, *anis al-jalis* 3, 11 (1900), 438; advertisement for Magasins Victorie, *anis al-jalis* 3, 11 (1900), 437; advertisement for Maison Stein, *anis al-jalis* 3, 11 (1900), 438; advertisement for Ḥamṣy & Najjar, *al-saᶜada* 1, 1 (1902), 17; advertisement for Jurji Ṣaliḥ, *al-saᶜada* 1, 1 (1902), 18; advertisement for Ilyas al-Ṭawil, *al-saᶜada* 1, 14 (1903), 2; advertisement for Ḥasan Bey Madkur, *al-saᶜada* 1, 3 (1902), 69; advertisement for Sednaoui, *al-saᶜada* 1, 14 (1903), 1.
113. According to Graham-Brown, photography spread more rapidly in the Middle East than any other region outside the United States and Europe, with the possible exception of India, due to the strong Western presence and the growth of the tourist trade. Graham-Brown, *Images of Women* (London: Quartert Books, 1988), 38. Both advertisments ran frequently in *al-laṭa'if al-muṣawwara* in 1922. See also Kodak advertisement, *al-laṭa'if al-muṣawwara* (March 20, 1922), 15. Compare to American counterparts, e.g. 1891 and 1898 Kodak advertisements from Edgar R. Jones, *Those Were the Good Old Days: A Happy Look at American Advertising, 1880–1930* (New York: Simon and Schuster, 1959).
114. The "Take Kodak with you" advertisement ran frequently in *al-laṭa'if al-muṣawwara* during 192[illegible] while the "Brownie" advertisement ran occasionally in *al-laṭa'if al-muṣawwara*

in 1922. Compare these advertisements to their American counterparts between 1905 and 1915, see e.g., Strasser, *Satisfaction Guaranteed*, 103–06 and Marchand, *American Dream*, 134. Advertisements with the indigenous model began running in *al-laṭa'if al-muṣawwara* in December of 1921 and continued throughout 1922. Apparently, even Queen Nazli took up photography. See Hassan, *In the House of Muhammad Ali*, photograph 32.

115. Jordan Goodman, *Tobacco in History: The Cultures of Dependence* (London: Routledge, 1993), 47; Norris, *Advertising*, 129; Marchand, *American Dream*, 97; Shechter, "Egyptian Cigarette," 93–94.
116. On elite female smoking, see Mary Eliza Rogers, *Domestic Life in Palestine* (London: Kegan Paul, 1989), 11, 101. See also Fanny Davis, *Ottoman Lady* and Emine Foat Tugay, *Family Chronicles*. On women generally, see Shechter, "Egyptian Cigarette," 23–25. See also the protagonist's discussion of smoking in Bahaa' Taher's *Aunt Safiyya and the Monastery*, translated and edited by Barbara Romaine (Berkeley: University of California Press, 1996), 67–68.
117. Shechter, "Egyptian Cigarette," 139–43.
118. This series of advertisements ran throughout 1922 in *al-laṭa'if al-muṣawwara*. These advertisements appear at the same time that skilled cigarette rollers were organizing under the threat of extinction due to the spread of mechanization in the factories. See Beinin and Lockman, *Workers on the Nile*, 49–57 and 125–26. It should also be noted that Dr. Bustany was one to change with the times. During the wave of nationalist sentiment just after the Anglo-Egyptian Treaty of 1936, he advertised his line of Cherif Cigarettes as "Egyptian," emblazened with the tri-star Crescent, and "rolled by the hands of an Egyptian worker." Still seeking female consumers, this advertisement appeared in *fatat al-sharq* (October 1937).
119. See e.g., advertisement for J. Barki, *anis al-jalis* 3, 11 (1900), 436; advertisement for E. Ashton, *anis al-jalis* 3, 8 (1900), 320; advertisement for Walker & Meimarachi, *al-sa*ᶜ*ada* 1, 1 (1902), 20; advertisement for Ḥasan Bey Madkur, *al-sa*ᶜ*ada* 1, 3 (1902), 69; advertisement for Sednaoui, *al-sa*ᶜ*ada* 1, 14 (1903), 1; advertisement for ᶜAkawi & Ward, *al-sa*ᶜ*ada* 1, 2 (1902), 47; advertisement for Demitri & Anṭun al-Ṣalaḥani, *al-sa*ᶜ*ada* 1, 1 (1902), 18–19.
120. See e.g., advertisement for Sednaoui, *al-laṭa'if al-muṣawwara* (March 29, 1915), 3.
121. Advertisement for Sagrestani, *anis al-jalis*, ran throughout 1901; advertisement for L. Kramer & Co., *al-*ᶜ*a'ila* 3, 2 (1904), 16.
122. Abbas Hilmi II, *The Last Khedive of Egypt: Memoirs of Abbas Hilmi II*, translated and edited by Amira Sonbol (Reading: Ithaca, 1998), 56.
123. *al-sa*ᶜ*ada* 1, 3 (1902), 69. Hasan Bey Madkur also advertised in *al-*ᶜ*a'ila*.
124. *al-sa*ᶜ*ada* 1, 1 (1902), 20.
125. Advertisement for Aḥmad Kamil's store, *al-sufur* 1, 7 (1915), 7; advertisement for Muḥammad ᶜAmir's store, *al-laṭa'if al-muṣawwara* (February 14, 1921), 10; advertisement for White Rose Patisserie, *al-laṭa'if al-muṣawwara*, ran throughout 1920; Egyptian Clothing Company advertisements, *al-laṭa'if al-muṣawwara*, ran between 1921 and 1922; advertisement for Ilyas ᶜAḍḍad's furniture store, *al-laṭa'if al-muṣawwara* (October 16, 1922), 15; free movie offer, *al-laṭa'if al-muṣawwara* (April 24, 1922).
126. Frierson, "Cheap and Easy," 246.
127. According to Frierson, by imperial decree, Muslim women were forbidden from shopping in Christian establishments. "Cheap and Easy," 251.
128. "Egypt," Flags of the World website, http://www.grey-net.com/fotw/flags/eg.html (12/30/1999). Originally, the flag may have been red, and it is uncertain when green

was adopted as the color. A black and white photograph (dated February 22, 1922) of Safiyya Zaghlul draped in the flag, describes it as the "Red and White Flag of Egypt." See Seton, *A Woman Tenderfoot in Egypt*, 20.

129. Use of the word foreigner was not uncommon in turn-of-the-century advertising, including references to individuals from Syria. Lactagol advertisement, *al-laṭa'if al-muṣawwara*, ran throughout 1922. Compare to a 1915 American advertisement for Royal Baking Powder that appears in *Inarticulate Longings*, 135.
130. In political cartoons of the 1919–22 period, Egypt was frequently depicted as a female in pharaonaic garb. See Beth Baron, "Nationalist Iconography: Egypt as a Woman," in James Jankowski and Israel Gershoni, eds., *Rethinking Nationalism in the Arab Middle East*, (New York: Columbia University Press, 1997): 105–24; Pollard, "Nurturing the Nation: The Family Politics of the 1919 Revolution" (Ph.D. diss., University of California at Berkeley, 1997), 236–49.
131. *al-laṭa'if al-muṣawwara*, ad ran throughout 1922; Strasser, *Satisfaction Guaranteed*, 118; Marchand, *American Dream*, 223.
132. Robert Tignor, "Bank Misr and Foreign Capitalism," *IJMES* 8 (1977), 181.
133. See e.g., *al-laṭa'if al-muṣawwara*, March 12 and April 9, 1923. In one ad, the wife of King Tutankhamun praises the shoes produced by her sons; while in the other, three women ranging in dress from Western to modified indigenous share a love for the Egyptian shoe company because of an on-going sale, its products in conformity with Egyptian tastes, and its value for price. Nevertheless, the magazine also used a pharaonic motif in its 1927 campaign for Ovaltine.
134. See variations throughout 1923 in *al-laṭa'if al-muṣawwara.*
135. Endorsers include local traders, employees, doctors, and even a Turkish officer. See *al-laṭa'if al-muṣawwara* 1923.
136. *shajarat al-durr*, July 10, 1922; see also December 28, 1922.
137. Advertisement for the al-Ahram wal-Ibrahimiyya al-Miṣriyya factories, *majalat nashr al-^{c}ilanat*, July 1, 1929, 19.
138. See e.g., advertisement for the stores of Muḥammad and Sa^{c}id Shanatawi, *ruz al-yusif* 184 (August 5, 1930), 35; or advertisement for the stores of Aḥmad Isma^{c}il al-Miṣri, *al-ithnayn wal-dunya* (June 11, 1951), 36.
139. For a complete discussion of nineteenth-century educational policy, see Aḥmad ^{c}Izzat ^{c}Abd al-Karim, *tarikh al-ta^{c}lim fi ^{c}aṣr Muḥammad ^{c}Ali* (Cairo: Maṭba^{c}at al-Nahḍa al-Miṣriyya, 1938) and his *tarikh al-ta^{c}lim fi Miṣr min nihayat Muḥammad ^{c}Ali ila awa'il ḥukm Tawfiq, 1848–1882* (Cairo: Maṭba^{c}at al-Naṣr, 1945).
140. Salama, *tarikh*, 33–93.
141. For a small sampling of the range of articles, see e.g., untitled article on the opening of the Siyufia school, *al-waqa^{c}i al-miṣriyya* (May 20, 1873): 2; "Minister of Public Instruction Attends a Foreign Girls' School Examination," *al-waqa^{c}i al-miṣriyya* (March 10, 1874): 1; "The American Mission Girls' School," *al-muqtaṭaf* 10, 1 (1885): 55; "Household Duties and Women's Education,"*al-laṭa'if* 2, 8 (1888): 422–38; "National Life" [on the importance of teaching the national language], *al-ustadh* 1, 2 (August 1892): 25–41; "The Khedive's Visit to Egyptian Schools," *al-ustadh* 1, 14 (November 1892): 313–15; "Thanks for Support" [to Princess Zubayda for a donation to a charitable school], *al-ustadh* 1, 29 (March 1893): 702–03; "Morals Education," *al-muqtaṭaf* 18, 1 (1893): 37–38; "Girls' Education," *anis al-jalis* 1, 7 (1898): 192–97; "The National School," *anis al-jalis* 4, 6 (1901): 713–14; "The Ministry of Public Instruction," *al-liwa'* (February 9, 1904): 1–2; "The History of Education in Egypt From the Most Ancient Times to the Present," *al-hilal* 15, 3 (1906): 131–52; "The Interference of the Occupation in the Plan for the Egyptian

University," *al-tarbiya* 3, 3 (1908): 1–3; "Muslims at Christian Schools," *al-manar* 12, 1 (February 12, 1909): 18–26; "Colonel Roosevelt's Speech" [at the American College for Girls], *al-jins al-laṭif* 2, 10 (1910): 273–78; "Girls' Education: A Dialogue Between a Man and a Woman," *al-muqtaṭaf* 41, 1 (1912): 81–83; "Who is More Worthy of Education First, Fathers and Mothers or Boys and Girls," *al-mu'ayyad* (February 1, 1914): 2; "The Egyptian Schools and the Course of Education," *al-muqtaṭaf* 44, 2 (1914): 113–17; "The Teachers' School at Bulaq," *al-muqtaṭaf* 46, 4 (1915): 395–96; Ceza Nabaraoi, "L'Enseignement secondaire féminin en Egypte," *L'Egyptienne* (November 1927): 5–10.

142. For example, *al-hilal, al-muqtaṭaf* and *al-muqaṭṭam* frequently covered the opening and events of Coptic, Greek, and American Mission schools, while *al-ustadh, al-tarbiya, al-liwa'*, and *al-mu'ayyad* gave more coverage to Muslim charitable associations and their schools. Nevertheless, the lines were not hard and fast since all publications encouraged more widespread education.
143. See e.g., advertisement for Mademoiselle Steiner Wilchelm Heino, *anis al-jalis* 4, 11 (1901), 881; advertisement for piano teacher, *anis al-jalis* 3, 10 (1900), 399; advertisement for Katrin Isṭafan's National School for Girls, 2, 6 (1899), 244.
144. In her *Egypt and Cromer*, Marsot repeatedly refers to *al-muqaṭṭam* as the "voice of the Agency." See pages 96, 111, 113, 171. Nevertheless, its Anglophile leanings varied according to subject. Goldschmidt argues that its pro-British leanings were partly attributable to its editors' desire to balance the view presented by *al-ahram*, which was avowedly pro-French, perhaps owing to the French Mission education of the newspaper's Greek Catholic founders. See his *Modern Egypt: The Formation of a Nation State* (Boulder: Westview Press, 1988), 46. Marsot views the founding of *al-mu'ayyad* in 1889 as a nationalist, Islamic balance to the two leading papers.
145. Compare e.g., the advertisement for St. Mary's Mission School [for boys and girls], *al-muqaṭṭam* (October 1, 1896), 4 to the advertisement for the Bab al-Luq Girls' School, *al-muqaṭṭam* (October 1, 1896) 1.
146. For details, see Goldschmidt, *Modern Egypt*, 49–50 or Marsot *Short History*, 78–79.
147. Advertisement for the Kamal school, *al-liwa'* (November 30, 1902), 3; advertisement for the Hussayniyya School, *al-liwa'* (January 10, 1903), 3.
148. Advertisement for the Shaykha Ismahan, *al-liwa'* (February 8, 1904), 3.
149. We can speculate that a paper, e.g. *al-liwa'*, with such a distinct political platform, received funding from a variety of sources including the Khedive Abbas II. Thus, it was not as dependent upon advertising revenue and thus its rates were more affordable.
150. See e.g., advertisement run by the widow of Ya[c]qub [c]Aṭallah, *al-liwa'* (February 8, 1904), 3; advertisement run by the widow of Dr. Ḥasan Muḥammad Pasha, *al-mu'ayyad* (October 28, 1906), 6.
151. Advertisement by Zaynab [c]Abd al-Raḥman, *al-mu'ayyad* (January 15, 1893), 4.
152. Advertisement by [c]Alish [c]Abd al-Ra'uf, *al-mu'ayyad* (January 3, 1897), 3.
153. During this era the "New Woman" or "New Man" was targeted in advertisements, and part of the role of the New Woman was purchasing the right items for her family, which focused upon health and nutrition. In the era following independence, there would be more advertising that targeted the "New Family," with holiday/occasion advertising campaigns [[c]Id, New Year, back to school, etc.], eating establishments that cater to couples and families, and depictions of children in advertisements. See my "National Identity," and "Commodifying Identity."

5 *al-Sayyida al-Istihlakiyya* AND THE "NEW WOMAN"

1. Marilyn Booth, "*Woman in Islam*: Men and the Women's Press in Turn-of-the-20th-Century Egypt," *IJMES* 33 (2001): 171; Lisa Pollard, "Nurturing the Nation" (Ph.D. diss., Berkeley, 1997), 160–71; Pollard, "Patriarchy Under Construction: 'Fatherhood' in the Revolutionary Era," paper presented at MESA, November 2001. See also the striking similarities between the essays on Turkey, Iran, and Egypt written by Deniz Kandiyoti, Afsaneh Najmabadeh, and Margot Badran, resp. in *Women, Islam, and the State*, Deniz Kandiyoti, ed. (Philadelphia: Temple University Press, 1991), 22–47, 48–76, 201–36, resp.
2. Russell, "Commodifying Identity: Women and Egyptian Advertising, 1922–1952," paper presented at the annual meeting of the MESA and the AHA, November 2002 and January 2003, resp. "National Identity and Egyptian Advertising in the Liberal Era, 1922–1952," paper presented at the Middle East Center, University of Pennsylvania, October 2002.
3. The single biggest complaint regarding the *Ladies' Home Journal*, according to a survey done by the J. Walter Thompson agency, was that it lacked coverage of current events. Jennifer Scanlon, *Inarticulate Longings* (New York: Routledge, 1995), 1, 4, 6–7, 8, 21–48, 200, 227. See also Helen Damon-Moore, *Gender and Commerce in the Ladies' Home Journal and the Saturday Evening Post, 1880–1910* (Albany: SUNY Press, 1994).
4. Mary Ann Fay, "International Feminism and the Women's Movement in Egypt, 1904–23: A Reappraisal of Categories and Legacies," paper presented at the conference on Institutions, Ideologies and Agencies: Changing Family Life in the Middle East, UNC-Chapel Hill, April 2003.
5. Leila Ahmed, *Women and Gender in Islam: Historical Roots of a Modern Debate* (New Haven: Yale University Press, 1992), 162.
6. The titles of these books appeared in the new publications section of *al-hilal*, *al-manar*, and *al-tarbiya* between 1894 and 1918.
7. Booth, "Men and the Women's Press," 177–78. See also Pollard, "Nurturing," 160–71.
8. Naguib Ḥagg, "The Eastern Woman and the Western Woman," *anis al-jalis* 4, 5 (1901), 658.
9. See e.g., "The Building of a House and Its Happiness," *al-muqtaṭaf* 6, 6 (1881): 368–69; "The Distinction of the Woman," *anis al-jalis* 5, 1 (1902): 915-19; "Paradise of the Woman," *anis al-jalis* 5, 3 (1902): 978–82; Muḥammad Muṣṭafa ^{c}Agizi, "The Nation is Reformed Only with the Reform of Families," *anis al-jalis* 6, 9 (1903): 1558–59; "Advice from a Mother to her Daughter on Marital and Household Matters," *al-sa^{c}ada* 1, 8 (1902): 169–70; Ḥabib Ma^{c}ushy, "The Woman's Dominion over the World," *anis al-jalis* 7, 4 (1904): 1773–83; Naguib ^{c}Awwad, "The Life of the Married Couple," *al-sa^{c}ada* 2, 3 (1903): 476–79 and 3, 9/10 (1904): 593–96; "Knowledge and the Woman," *al-sa^{c}ada* 2, 9/10(1904): 596–604; "The Man and the Woman," *anis al-jalis* 9, 7 (1906): 165–66; "Characteristics of the Woman" *anis al-jalis* 9, 9 (1906): 270–72; "For Whom is the Leadership of the Family," *al-muqtaṭaf* 32, 7 (1907): 571–73; "Quranic Commentary [on the Equality of Men and Women]," *al-manar* 12, 5 (1909): 331–32; An anonymous Egyptian (male) doctor, "Education of the Egyptian," *al-mu'ayyad* (February 19, 1914): 2; "The New Woman in the East and the West," *al-hilal* 30, 3 (1921): 222–31; "The Man's Love and the Woman's Love," *al-hilal* 31, 5 (1923): 486–89; Muḥammad Zaki ^{c}Abd al-Qadir, "Where is Happiness?," *ummahat al-mustaqbal* 1, 5 (1930): 161–65.
10. Judith Tucker, *In the House of Law: Gender and Islamic Law in Ottoman Syria and Palestine* (Berkeley: University of CA Press, 1998), 38; 46. See also her "The Arab Family in

History: 'Otherness' and the Study of the Family," in her *Arab Women: Old Boundaries, New Frontiers* (Bloomington: Indiana University Press, 1993): 195–207.

11. See Jane Hathaway, *The Politics of Households in Ottoman Egypt* (Cambridge: Cambridge University Press, 1997), chapter 6, 109–24. See also Mary Ann Fay, "Women and Households: Gender, Power, and Culture in Eighteenth-Century Egypt" (Ph.D. diss., Georgetown University, 1993).
12. Fay, "International Feminism."
13. We might even speculate that she had been part of a household that educated female slaves. She had been raised in an Ottoman-Egyptian household and was given as a present to Sultan Pasha.
14. Margot Badran, *Feminists, Islam, and the State* (Princeton: Princeton University Press, 1995), 32–38. See also Mervat Hatem, "Through Each Other's Eyes: The Impact on the Colonial Encounter of the Images of Egyptian, Levantine-Egyptian, and European Women, 1862–1920," in *Western Women and Imperialism: Complicity and Resistance* (Bloomington: Indiana University Press, 1992), 38–43.
15. See anecdote in Samia Serageldin's semiautobiographical novel, *The Cairo House* (Syracuse: Syracuse University Press, 2000), 37. Contemporary estimates on the rate of first cousin marriage (either parent) range from 28 to 35%, with the rate in upper Egypt being as high as 50%.
16. Qasim Amin dedicated *The New Woman* to Zaghlul, citing the latter's marriage as an inspiration for his writing. Amin, *The Liberation of Women* and *The New Woman*, Samiha Peterson, trans. (Cairo: AUC Press, 2000), 113. For information on Safiyya's upbringing, see Badran, *Feminists*, 80. Regarding the canonization of their marriage as exemplary, see Booth, *May her Likes be Multiplied* (Berkeley: University of California Press, 2001), 218. This type of marriage was not anomylous and grew more common in the early-twentieth century. See e.g., Leila Ahmed, *A Border Passage* (New York: Penguin Books, 1999), 41–46; Magda Baraka, *The Egyptian Upper Class Between Revolutions, 1919–1952* (Reading: Ithaca, 1998), 143.
17. Cynthia Nelson, *Doria Shafik, Egyptian Feminist: A Woman Apart* (Gainesville: University of Florida Press, 1996), 7–10. Nelson does not state when the marriage took place. Presumably it was shortly after 1900, since Shafik was born in 1909 and had two elder siblings.
18. Baraka, *The Egyptian Upper Class*, 222, 170.
19. Baraka, *The Egyptian Upper Class*, 173–74. On male memoirs in the late Ottoman context, see Selçuk Akşin Somel, *The Modernization of Public Education in the Ottoman Empire, 1839–1908* (Leiden: Brill, 2001), 248–49.
20. Booth, *May*, 210.
21. Shaun Lopez, "The Culture/Gender Wars: Margaret Fahmy and the Shaping of Sexuality in 1920s Egypt," paper presented at MESA, November 2002.
22. With the demise of slavery and the decline of polygamy, female underlings/employees (foreign and domestic) could be prime targets for wanted and unwanted male attention. Cartoons in the post-independence era frequently contain a motif of servants and secretaries receiving such attention from their bosses. See my "Commodifying Identity." Regarding liaisons and even secret marriages between elite men and European women, see Baraka, *The Egyptian Upper Class*, 172. Prince Hassan Hassan was the product of a marriage between a Spanish girl of distinctly humble origins and his father Prince Aziz, a founding member of the Wafd who met his wife while in exile. Upon the death of his father, Hassan and his siblings were removed from his mother's ("unsuitable") guardianship and placed in the care of his great Aunt Nimet Ismail. See his *In the House of Muhammad Ali* (Cairo: AUC Press, 2000), 1, 34.

23. Hatem, "Through Each Others' Eyes," 42.
24. Tucker, *In the House of Law*, 45 and 113–47, 125, 139. Maturity for males came when they could dress, groom, and toilet themselves, while for females it meant outward signs of physical maturity.
25. See e.g., "The Woman's Rights," *al-muqtaṭaf* 7, 1 (1882): 17–22; Maryum Nimr Makarius, "Raising Children," *al-laṭa'if* 3, 3 (1888): 97–104; Girgis Effendi Ḥanna, "The Status of the Mother," *al-muqtaṭaf* 14, 6 (1890): 404–08; Tawfiq ^{c}Aziz, "Is the Upbringing of Children Dependent on the Mother or the Father," *al-hilal* 1, 5 (1893): 213–14; John and Niqula Ḥaddad, "Is the Upbringing of Children More Dependent on the Mother or the Father," *al-hilal* 1, 7 (1893): 322–24; "Household Organization," *anis al-jalis* 2, 3 (1899): 110–12; An anonymous female writer, "Knowledge and the Woman," *anis al-jalis* 2, 4 (1899): 142–45; Muḥammad Muṣṭafa ^{c}Agizi, "The Nation is Reformed Only with the Reform of Families," *anis al-jalis* 6, 9 (1903): 1558–59; "Complaint of Mothers About Raising Daughters," *al-muqtaṭaf* 28, 10 (1903): 874–78; "Knowledge and Women," *al-sa^{c}ada* 2, 3 (1903): 480–83, continued in 2, 7/8 (1904): 561–64 and 2, 9/10 (1904): 596–04; "The Woman's Education," *al-sa^{c}ada* 2, 7/8 (1904): 566–67; "The Woman, the Conscience, and Upbringing," *anis al-jalis* 6, 3 (1903): 1355–1359; "The Wife's Beauty and the Mother's Beauty," *al-^{c}a'ila* 3, 9 (July 4, 1904): 65–67; "The Shame of an Ignorant Mother," *al-tarbiya* 1, 2 (1905): 13; "The Nation [*al-umma*] is a Fabric of Mothers, So We Must Educate Daughters," *al-hilal* 15, 4 (1908): 139–43; "Duties of the Woman," *al-jins al-laṭif* 1, 3 (1908): 87; T. Ḥanayn [female student], "The Ignorance of Mothers in Proper Education," *al-jins al-laṭif* 1, 4 (1908): 110–14; "The Woman, Between Prostitution and the Veil," *al-hilal* 19, 2 (1910): 106–09; Labiba Hashim, "Upbringing," [speech given at Egyptian University] reprinted in *al-muqtaṭaf* 38, 1 (1911): 274–76; "Who is More Worthy of Education First, Fathers and Mothers, or Boys and Girls," *al-mu'ayyad* (February 1, 1914): 2.
26. al-Zahra, "The Cornerstone," *al-sufur* (December 29, 1916): 7.
27. Omnia Shakry, "Schooled Mothers and Structured Play: Child Rearing in Turn-of-the-Century Egypt," in *Remaking Women*, Lila Abu-Lughod, ed. (Princeton: Princeton University Press, 1998): 126–70. Both *al-muqtaṭaf* and *al-hilal* contained women's columns, the former with its regular "*bab tadbir al-manzil*" section, and the latter, with its frequently recurring "*hadith al-ma'ida*" column.
28. See e.g., "Decorating the Table," *al-muqtaṭaf* 6, 12 (1882): 750–51; "Household Duties and Women's Education," *al-laṭa'if* 3, 10 (1888): 422–38; "Organization of the House," *al-muqtaṭaf* 23, 3 (1899): 217–18; "The Administration of the Mistress of the House," *al-muqtaṭaf* 23, 4 (1899): 296; "Household Organization," *anis al-jalis* 2, 3 (1899): 110–112; "Household Organization," *anis al-jalis* 2, 4 (1899): 155–57; "Household Organization: The Interior of the House," *anis al-jalis* 2, 5 (1899): 195–99; "Household Organization: The Conduct of Servants," *anis al-jalis* 2, 7 (1899): 277–80; "Household Servants and Ladies," *al-hilal* 9, 13 (1901): 393; "Advice from a Mother to her Daughter on Marital and Household Matters," *al-sa^{c}ada* 1, 8 (1902): 169–70; "On Household Organization and Its Duties," *al-sa^{c}ada* 1, 14 (1903): 423; Naguib ^{c}Awwad, "The Life of the Married Couple," *al-sa^{c}ada* 2, 3 (1903): 476–79; Ḥanna Ṣarah, "Teach the Girl," *anis al-jalis* 9, 1 (1906): 19–20; "Administration of the House," *al-muqtaṭaf* 32, 7 (1907): 576–77; ^{c}Ali, "Our Household Life," *al-sufur* (July 30, 1915): 1–2; Muḥammad Zaki ^{c}Abd al-Qadir, "Where is Happiness?," *ummahat al-mustaqbal* 1, 5 (1930): 161–65.
29. "Household Administration," *anis al-jalis* 2, 3 (1899): 110–12; "Household Administration," *anis al-jalis* 2, 4 (1899): 155–57; "Household Administration: The Interior of the House," *anis al-jalis* 2, 5 (1899): 195–99; "Household Administration: The Conduct of Servants," *anis al-jalis* 2, 7 (1899): 277–80.

30. By no means does this mean that multigenerational households disappeared. The nuclear family was merely becoming more of an ideal or model. See e.g., "The Family," *al-sufur* (January 9, 1917): 2.
31. Fay, "International Feminism."
32. *Bab tadbir al-manzil* originated in 1881 and continued beyond the period under study. Prior to 1881, household hints appeared as a semi-regular section. Although Nadia Farag has asserted that the Syrian Christian writers had little concern for Egyptian society and the Egyptian woman, I found that there are an overwhelming number of references to the contemporary situation in Egypt. Nadia Farag, "*al-Muqtaṭaf*, 1876–1900" (Ph.D. diss., Oxford, 1969), 173–96.
33. In examining the period between 1881, when the department begins, and 1922, when my study ends, I found 148 articles about women and their roles, 179 items relating to childcare, 45 items related to women's rights/education, 46 articles on interior decoration, 90 biographies or eulogies of Western and Eastern women, 28 items related to fashion, and 37 articles on economics/finance. There were also numerous recipes, household hints, and health/beauty items, which might only comprise one or two sentences. Many of these designations are somewhat arbitrary given that an article might relate to both childcare and health.
34. See e.g., "Home Furnishings," *al-muqtaṭaf* 18, 2 (1893): 121–22.
35. "Administration of the House," *al-muqtaṭaf* 32, 7 (1907): 576–77. See also, "Administration of the Mistress of the House,"*al-muqtaṭaf* 23, 4 (1899): 296.
36. "Heating Food," *al-muqtaṭaf* 33, 6 (1908): 514–15. See also, "Household Chemistry," *al-muqtaṭaf* 8, 3 (1883): 179–81; "The Leisure of the Mistress of the House," *al-muqtaṭaf* 14, 1 (1889): 57–58; "New Styles of Cooking," *al-muqtaṭaf* 18, 1 (1893): 38.
37. Booth, *May*, 173.
38. "Building a Home and its Happiness," *al-muqtaṭaf* 6, 6 (1881): 368–69; "Decorating the Table," *al-muqtaṭaf* 6, 12 (1882): 750–51; "Organization," *al-muqtaṭaf* 6, 12 (1882): 751–52; "Organization of the Salon," *al-muqtaṭaf* 13, 5 (1889): 329–31; "Happiness of the Home," *al-muqtaṭaf* 14, 6 (1890): 404; "Gaiety is not Expensive Furnishings,"*al-muqtaṭaf* 14, 7 (1890): 485–86; "Decorating the House," *al-muqtaṭaf* 16, 8 (1892): 564–65; "Home Furnishings," *al-muqtaṭaf* 18, 2 (1893): 121–22; "Furnishings of the House and their Organization," *al-muqtaṭaf* 21, 2 (1897): 137–38; "Organization of the House," *al-muqtaṭaf* 23, 3 (1899): 217–18; "The New Home," *al-muqtaṭaf* 23, 7 (1899): 543–45; "The First Principles of Household Organization," *al-muqtaṭaf* 32, 8 (1907): 668–69; "The Tasteful House and the Sitting Room," *al-muqtaṭaf* 55, 4 (1919): 430–31.
39. "Foreign Proverbs About Economy," *al-muqtaṭaf* 7, 8 (1883): 507; "Assessing the Expenses of the House," *al-muqtaṭaf* 14, 8 (1890): 557–58; "Spending Money," *al-muqtaṭaf* 14, 10 (1890): 703; "Economy in the Kitchen," *al-muqtaṭaf* 22, 11 (1898): 752–54; "Buying Necessities," *al-muqtaṭaf* 23, 5 (1899): 379; "The New Home," *al-muqtaṭaf* 23, 7 (1899): 543–45; "The Woman and the Expenses of the House," *al-muqtaṭaf* 26, 7 (1901): 689–91; "The First Principles of Household Organization," *al-muqtaṭaf* 32, 8 (1907): 668–69; "Economy of Expenses," *al-muqtaṭaf* 47, 6 (1915): 586.
40. See e.g., "*Dirhams* with Children," *al-muqtaṭaf* 13, 6 (1899): 412; "Spending Money," *al-muqtaṭaf* 14, 11 (1890): 703; "The Economy of the Woman in her Clothing," *al-muqtaṭaf* 60, 1 (1922): 84–85. See also, Shakry, "Schooled Mothers," 141–43.
41. "The Tyranny of Fashion," *al-muqtaṭaf* 33, 6 (1908): 518; "Women's Expense on Their Clothing," *al-muqtaṭaf* 38, 1 (1911): 82–83; "The Extravagance of Americans and Easterners," *al-muqtaṭaf* 39, 4 (1911): 392–94; "The Absolutism of Fashion," *al-muqtaṭaf* 39,

5 (1911): 498–99; "Women's Clothing," *al-muqtaṭaf* 47, 3 (1915): 296; "The Economics of Expenses," *al-muqtaṭaf* 47, 6 (1915): 586; "Economy is Economy," *al-muqtaṭaf* 50, 3 (1917): 282–83; "The Rise of the Cost of Living in Egypt," *al-muqtaṭaf* 51, 5 (1917): 497–500; "The Economy of the Woman in her Clothing," *al-muqtaṭaf* 60, 1 (1922): 84–85.

42. Margot Badran, *Feminists*, 48–52. See also, Afaf Marsot, "The Revolutionary Gentlewomen in Egypt," in Lois Beck and Nickie Keddie, eds., *Women in the Muslim World* (Cambridge: Harvard University Press, 1978), 261–76. Ellen Fleischmann, in her work on the "New Palestinian Woman" highlights the importance of charitable work in the nationalist struggle. While conceding the conservative orientation of these organizations, she notes their importance in fulfilling needs not provided by the mandate. Fleischmann, *The Nation and its 'New' Women: The Palestianian Women's Movement, 1920–1948* (Berkeley: University of California Press, 2003), 95–114.
43. Pollard, "Nurturing the Nation," 222–62.
44. Afaf Marsot, *Egypt Under Cromer* (New York: Praeger, 1969), 6–12; see also Arthur Goldschmidt, *Modern Egypt: The Formation of a Nation State* (Boulder: Westview Press, 1988), 34–35.
45. Marsot, *Egypt Under Cromer*, 10.
46. Quoted in Marsot, *Egypt Under Cromer*, 11 and Goldscmidt, *Modern Egypt*, 35.
47. Even the royal family circulates such stories. See Hassan, *In the House of Muhammad Ali*, 65.
48. Beth Baron, "Nationalist Iconography: Egypt as a Woman," in James Jankowski and Israel Gershoni, eds., *Rethinking Nationalism in the Arab Middle East* (New York: Columbia University Press, 1997): 105–24; Pollard, "Nurturing the Nation," 233–62.
49. Badran, *Feminists*, 74–78; ^{c}Abd al-Raḥman al-Rafa^{c}i, *thawrat 1919* (Cairo: Dar al-Ma^{c}arif, 1987), 209–14, 234–35. Images can be seen in *sijill hilal al-muṣawwar* (Cairo: Dar al-Hilal, 1992), vol. 1: 94–95, vol. 2: 1014–15; and Grace Thompson Seton, *A Woman Tenderfoot in Egypt* (New York: Dodd, Mead, and Co., 1923).
50. Baraka, *Egyptian Upper Class*, 71.
51. Quoted in Erez Manela, "The Wilsonian Moment and the Rise of Anticolonial Nationalism: The Case of Egypt," *Diplomacy and Statecraft* 12, 4 (December 2001), 109.
52. Badran, *Feminists*, 74–81; al-Rafa^{c}i, *1919*, 427.
53. See Booth, *May*, 148.
54. Badran, *Feminists*, 83.
55. Seton, *A Woman Tenderfoot in Egypt*, 29–30; Laṭifa al-Ziyat, *al-mar'a al-miṣriyya wal-taghayyur al-ijtima^{c}i 1919–1945* (Cairo: Dar al-Kutub, 1984), 31–32; Badran, *Feminists*, 83, 172–73; "Fresh Egyptian Proposals," *London Times* (January 23, 1922), 10; Shohdi Attia el-Shafei, *taṭawwar al-ḥaraka al-waṭaniyya al-miṣriyya 1882–1956* (Cairo, 1957), 50.
56. Seton, *A Woman Tenderfoot in Egypt*, 29–31; "Fresh Trouble in Egypt," *London Times* (January 25, 1922), 9; "Egypt's New Era," *London Times* (March 1, 1922), 9; Marsot, "Revolutionary Gentlewomen," 271–72.
57. Seton, *A Woman Tenderfoot in Egypt*, 30.
58. Badran, *Feminists*, 84.
59. Badran, *Feminists*, 83. For more information on the founding of Bank Misr, see Tignor, "Bank Misr and Foreign Capitalism," *IJMES 8* (1977): 161–81.
60. Badran, *Feminists*, 81; The New Woman Society actually preceded the WWCC, and it included many of the same women.
61. Fleischmann, *The Nation and Its New Women*, 130–31.

62. In September of 1990 I had the great fortune of interviewing this remarkable woman in Washington, DC.
63. For a discussion of the history of Egyptians in the field of archeology, see Donald M. Reid, *Whose Pharaohs? Archeology, Museums, and Egyptian National Identity in Egypt from Napoleon to World War I* (Berkeley: University of California Press, 2002).
64. Her publications include *George Sand, auteur dramatique* (Paris: E. Droz, 1934); *Chales Poncy, Poète-maçon, 1821–1891* (Paris: Les Presses Universitaires de France, 1934); and *L'histoire de France à travers la chanson* (Alexandria: Farouk 1st University, 1950). Fahmy also spoke to me about her work on the relationship between poetry and music, on Goethe and Islam, and on the Arabic spirit of the Spanish composer Albéniz (1860–1909).
65. Nelson, *Doria Shafik*, 11–13.
66. Nelson, *Doria Shafik*, 14–24. Interviews conducted by Magda Baraka support the view of both Shafik's sister and Fahmy's sister regarding women and work. See her *The Egyptian Upper Class*, 176.
67. Nelson, *Doria Shafik*, 25–36.
68. Doria Shafik, *L'Art pour l'art dans l'Egypte antique* (Paris: Paul Geuthner Press, 1940); Shafik, *La Femme et le droit religieux de l'Egypte contemporaine* (Paris: Paul Geuthner Press, 1940).
69. Princess Chivekiar was the first wife of King Fuad. Fuad, who grew up in exile and returned to Egypt in 1895 under the auspices of his nephew Abbas II, had little in the way of material resources. Chivekiar was the granddaughter of Ahmad Rifat, Fuad's uncle. She was quite wealthy and therefore seemed a logical choice. She gave birth to a son within the first year of the marriage; however, he died before his first birthday, and she bore him no further children. Her brother, Prince Ahmad Sayf al-Din made an attempt on Fuad's life in 1898; shortly thereafter Fuad divorced Chivekiar. Consequently, for the rest of her life rumors surfaced regarding her illwill toward Fuad and his progeny. Hanafi al-Maḥalawi, *ḥarim muluk miṣr min Muḥammad ᶜAli ila Faruq* (Cairo: Dar al-Ameen, 1993), 133–42; William Stadiem, *Too Rich: The High Life and Tragic Death of King Farouk* (New York: Carrol and Graf, 1991), 62, 63, 103–04, 105–06, 112, 181, 187, 189, 220, 231–32, 277–78, 372.
70. Nelson, *Doria Shafik*, 119–22.
71. Shaarawi's husband Ali was one of the founders of the Wafd party. Nevertheless, Shaarawi herself broke ranks with the Wafd in late 1924 when she resigned as president of the WWCC. Regardless, in comparison to Chivekiar, she did represent Egyptian party politics. Badran, *Feminists*, 80–87.
72. Nelson, *Doria Shafik*, 122–41; Badran, *Feminists*, 80–123; Fay, "International Feminism." Shafik continued her activism by storming parliament in 1951 demanding women's rights and the reform of personal status laws. After the revolution of 1952, she was an outspoken critic of the Nasserist regime, even carrying out a 1954 hunger strike to demand women's representation in government. Nasser countered her activism with the dissolution of her magazine and union, and he placed her under house arrest. Even after she was no longer watched by an armed guard, she remained in semi-seclusion for the rest of her life. In 1975, she fell from the balcony of her sixth-floor apartment, in what many believe was her last act of protest, suicide.
73. Polygamy is still legal in Egypt and only in January of 2000 have some modifications been made to personal status law that allow the woman the right to seek a judicial divorce from her husband by giving up claims on her deferred dower. For legislation from the 1920s, see Badran, *Feminists*, 94–95, 124–41. Regarding recent changes, see Diane Singerman, "Rewriting Divorce in Egypt: Reclaiming Islam, Legal Activism, and Coalition Politics,"

paper presented at the conference on Institutions, Ideologies and Agencies: Changing Family Life in the Middle East, UNC-Chapel Hill, April 2003.

74. In her study of biographies in the women's press, Booth points out that this responsibility belonged to women; however, when bad marriages were portrayed, it was usually the fault of the man. Since the biographies were about exemplary women, this is not surprising. Booth, *May*, 209.

6 Education: Creating Mothers, Wives, Workers, Believers, and Citizens

1. Education in this context does not include vocational education and apprenticeships.
2. Yacub Artin, *L'Instruction Publique en Egypte* (Paris, 1890), 124–25; Zaynab Farid, *ta^{c}lim al-mara' al-^{c}arabiyya fil-turath wa fil-mujtama^{c}at al-^{c}arabiyya al-mu^{c}aṣira* (Cairo: Maktabat al-Anglo-al-Miṣriyya, 1980), 29–39, 43; Jonathan Berkey, "Women and Islamic Education in the Mamluk Period," in Nikki Keddie and Beth Baron, eds., *Women in Middle Eastern History* (New Haven: Yale University Press, 1991): 143–57; Hind Abou Seoud Khattab and Aydad Grein el-Daeif, "Female Education in Egypt: Changing Attitudes over a Span of 100 Years," in Freda Hussein, ed., *Muslim Women* (London: Croom Helm, 1984), 170; Nagat al-Sanabary, "Comparative Study of the Disparities of Educational Opportunities for Girls in the Arab States" (Ph.D. diss., University of California—Berkeley, 1973), 228–29; Peter Gran, *Islamic Roots of Capitalism: Egypt, 1760–1840* (Austin: University of Texas Press, 1979), 129; Edward Lane, *An Account of the Manners and Customs of the Modern Egyptians* (London: M.A. Nattali, 1846), vol. 1, 88, 90; Nelly Hanna, *Making Big Money in 1600* (Syracuse: Syracuse University Press, 1998), 26–27, 181n11; James Heyworth-Dunne, *An Introduction to the History of Education in Modern Egypt* (London: Cass, 1968), 14–15, 86; Sa^{c}id Isma^{c}il ^{c}Ali, *tarikh al-tarbiya wa ta^{c}lim fi Miṣr* (Cairo: ^{c}Alim al-Kutub, 1985), 156–76.
3. Nadia Hijab defines the three determinants of women's work as need, opportunity, and ability, all of which can be seen at the level of the state and the locality. Nadia Hijab, *Womanpower* (Cambridge: Cambridge University Press, 1988); Afaf Marsot, *Egypt in the Reign of Muhammad Ali* (Cambridge: Cambridge University Press, 1984), 21; Aḥmad ^{c}Izzat ^{c}Abd al-Karim, *tarikh al-ta^{c}lim fi ^{c}aṣr Muḥammad ^{c}Ali* (Cairo: Maktabat al-Nahḍa al-Miṣriyya, 1938), 30–31.
4. Egypte, Ministre de l'Instruction Publique, *Régulations approuvées par le Ministre de l'Instruction Publique pour l'organisation des écoles sous Muhammad Ali* (Paris, n/d); ^{c}Abd al-Karim, *Muḥammad ^{c}Ali*, 27–28, 38–39, 43, 45; Aḥlam Ragab ^{c}Abd al-Ghaffar, *tarikh al-tarbiya wa niẓam al-ta^{c}lim fi Miṣr* (Cairo: Dar al-Thaqafa lil-Ṭiba^{c}a, 1991/92), 130–31; Selçuk Akşin Somel, *The Modernization of Public Education in the Ottoman Empire, 1839–1908* (Leiden: Brill, 2001), 28.
5. Hibba Abugideiri has argued that not only did medicine help to disseminate state authority, but that it helped to build it. See her "Egyptian Women and the Science Question: Gender in the Making of Colonized Medicine, 1893–1929" (Ph.D. diss., Georgetown University, 2001), chapter 1.
6. The work of *ḥakimas* has received considerable attention in recent years: Abugideiri, "Colonized Medicine"; Laverne Kuhnke, *Lives at Risk* (Los Angeles: University of California Press, 1990); Khaled Fahmy, "Women, Medicine, and Power in Nineteenth Century Egypt," in Lila Abu Lughod, ed., *Remaking Women* (Princeton: Princeton University

Press, 1998), 61; Mervat Hatem, "The Professionalization of Health and the Control of Women's Bodies as Modern Governmentalities in Nineteenth-Century Egypt," in Madeline Zilfi, ed., *Women in the Ottoman Empire* (New York: Brill, 1997); Amira Sonbol, *The Creation of a Medical Profession in Egypt, 1800–1922* (Syracuse: Syracuse University Press, 1991); Heather Sharkey, "Two Sudanese Midwives," *Sudanic Africa: A Journal of Historical Sources* 9 (1998); Elise Young, "Between Daya and Doctor, A History of the Impact of Modern Nation-State Building on Health East and West of the Jordan River" (Ph.D. diss., University of Massachusetts—Amherst, 1997); Mario Ruiz, "Virginity on Trial, Sex and Violence in Khedive Ismail's Egypt, 1863–1879," paper presented at MESA, November 2002. In the contemporary context, see the forthcoming MIT dissertation from Livia Wickham on midwifery and birthing practices in the occupied territories.

7. Antoine Clot, "La Création d'une école d'instruction médicale pour les femmes," *Cahiers d'Histoire Egyptienne* 1: 3 (1948), 245–46; Laverne Kuhnke, *Lives*, 123; Abugideiri, "Colonized Medicine," 94.
8. Clot, "Création," 246; ^{c}Abd al-Karim, *Muḥammad^{c}Ali*, 294–95, Kuhnke, *Lives*, 124. Some eunuchs were allowed to take the examinations, receiving a new rank upon graduation. Abugideiri, "Colonized Medicine," 327.
9. Clot, "Création," 247; clot, *Aperçu général sur l'Egypte*, vol. 2 (Paris: Fortin, 1840), 425; ^{c}Abd al-Karim, *Muḥammad^{c}Ali*, 297–99; 304–06; Abugideiri, "Colonized Medicine," 326.
10. Abugideiri, "Colonized Medicine," 323.
11. ^{c}Abd al-Karim, *Muḥammad^{c}Ali*, 300–301, 306–308; Clot, *Aperçu*, 427–28.
12. Abugideiri, "Colonized Medicine," 319–20, 368; Fahmy, "Women," 48–49.
13. Heyworth-Dunne, *Education*, 125; Donald Reid, "Education and Career Choices of Egyptian Students, 1882–1914," *IJMES* 8 (1977), 350; Yacub Artin, *L'Instruction*, 128–29; ^{c}Abd al-Karim, *Muḥammad ^{c}Ali*, 93–101.
14. Artin, *L'Instruction*, 129–30, 134; ^{c}Abd al-Karim, *Muḥammad^{c}Ali*, 673–74; J.H. Sislian, "Missionary Work in Egypt During the 19th Century," in Brian Holmes, ed., *Education and the Mission Schools* (New York: Humanities Press, 1967), 198–99; Emine Foat Tugay, *Three Centuries: Family Chronicles of Turkey and Egypt* (London: Oxford University Press, 1963), 123, 127; "Les Grandes Figures Féminine d'Egypte: S.A. La Princesse Zeinab," *L'Egyptienne* 1, 4 (May 1925), inside cover.
15. Huda Shaarawi, *Harem Years: The Memoirs of an Egyptian Feminist*, edited, translated, and introduced by Margot Badran (New York: The Feminist Press, 1987), 39–42, 62–63.
16. Juan Cole, "Feminism, Class, and Islam in Turn-of-the-Century Egypt," *IJMES* 13 (1981), 394; Margot Badran, *Feminists, Islam, and Nation* (Princeton: Princeton University Press, 1995), 80.
17. ^{c}Abd al-Raḥman al-Rafa^{c}i, *aṣr Isma^{c}il*, vol. 1 (Cairo: Dar al-Ma^{c}arif, 1987 [1932]), 21, 48. See also, James Williams, *Education in Egypt Before British Control* (Birmingham, 1937), 78–79.
18. C. von Malortie, *Egypt: Native Rulers and Foreign Interference* (London, 1882), 69.
19. Aḥmad ^{c}Izzat ^{c}Abd al-Karim, *tarikh al-ta^{c}lim fi Miṣr min nihayat ḥukm Muhammad ^{c}Ali ila awa'il ḥukm Tawfiq* (Cairo: Maṭba^{c}at al-Naṣr, 1945), vol. 1, 3–27, 169–90; ^{c}Abd al-Ghaffar, *tarikh*, 148–51; Heyworth-Dunne, *Education*, 288–307, 313–30.
20. For more information on this process, see the text of the Law of 10 Rajab 1284 (1867) reprinted in ^{c}Abd al-Karim, *tarikh*, vol. 3, 34–60.
21. *al-waqa^{c}i al-miṣriyya*, December 20, 1873, 1; Muḥammad Abu al-Aṣad, *siyasat al-ta^{c}lim fi Miṣr taḥt al-iḥtilal al-bariṭani, 1882–1922* (Cairo: Dar al-Nahḍa al-^{c}Arabiyya,

1982), 133–34; Amin Sami, *al-ta^{c}lim fi Miṣr fi sanatay 1914 wa 1915* (Cairo: Maṭba^{c}at al-Ma^{c}arif, 1917), 19.

22. *al-waqa^{c}i al-miṣriyya* (January 12, 1874), 1; James C. McCoan, *Egypt* (New York: Peter Fenelon Collier, 1898), 217–18;
23. Supporters include Edwin de Leon, *The Khedive's Egypt* (London: Sampson Lew, Marston, Seale, & Rivington, 1882 [1877]), 158; McCoan, *Egypt*, 103; Pierre Crabités, *Ismail the Maligned Khedive* (London: George Routledge and Sons, Ltd., 1933), 151. For critics see Blanchard Jerrold, *Egypt Under Ismail* (London: Samuel Tinsley & Co., 1879), 29; Theodore Rothstein, *Egypt's Ruin* (London: A.C. Fifield, 1910), 36.
24. Octave Sachot, *Rapport adressé à Son Excellence Monsieur Victor Duray Ministre de l'Instruction Publique sur l'Etat des Sciences, des Lettres et de l'Instruction Publique en Egypte dans la Population Indigène et dans la Population Européenne* (Paris, 1868), 20–22; DW, PI, Letter from Ismail to Stanton, box 12; DW, PI, Telegram from Ismail to Nubar, August 9, 1869, box 12; Letter from Ismail to Nubar, September 1, 1869, box 12.
25. Still others credit Ali Mubarak with the founding of the school. Yunan Labib Rizq, "The Schools of Prominent, Virtuous Women," *al-ahram* (March 30, 1995), 5; Ellen Chennells, *Recollections of an Egyptian Princess by her English Governess*, vol. 2, 24–25, 83; Zaynab Farid, "Education of Girls in Egypt," masters thesis and doctoral dissertation, ^{c}Ain Shams University, 1961 and 1966, resp., as cited in Ijlal Khalifa's *al-ḥaraka al-nisa'iyya al-ḥaditha* (Cairo: al-Maṭba^{c}a al-^{c}Arabiyya al-Ḥaditha, 1973), 106.
26. Emmaline Lott, *The English Governess in Egypt* (Philadelphia: T.B. Peterson & Brothers, 186–?), 108; Ḥanafi al-Maḥalawi, *ḥarim muluk Miṣr* (Cairo: Dar al-Ameen, 1993), 82–83; Artin, *L'Instruction*, 134; Abbas Hilmi II, *The Last Khedive of Egypt: Memoirs of Abbas Hilmi II*, edited and translated by Amira Sonbol (Reading: Ithaca, 1998), 40; *al-waqa^{c}i al-miṣriyya* (September 23, 1874), 1; DW, PI, article from *Le Moniteur Egyptien* (November 18, 1878), box 12.
27. *al-waqa^{c}i al-miṣriyya* (August 5, 1873), 1; Rizq, "Schools," 5; Chennells, *Recollections*, vol. 2, 88; McCoan, *Egypt*, 209–10.
28. McCoan, *Egypt*, 210; de Leon, *The Khedive's Egypt*, 163; Chennells, *Recollections*, 88–89; *al-waqa^{c}i al-miṣriyya* (May 20, 1873), 2; DW, PI, box 49, doss. 35/1, "Des écoles de filles," *Le Courrier de Port Said* (February 8, 1875); Rizq, "Schools," 5; Artin, *L'Instruction*, 134–35; DW, MW, NM, box A4, Yacub Artin, *Mémorandum sur l'Enseignement des Jeunes Filles, Soumis à S.A. le Khédive Abbas Pacha Helmy*, June 10, 1892 (Cairo: Imprimierie Centrale). ^{c}Abd al-Karim supports Artin's claims regarding the initial students, based upon the records of the *madaris al-^{c}arabi*. ^{c}Abd al-Karim, *tarikh*, vol. 2, 359.
29. Sachot, *Rapport*, 20–22.
30. According to ^{c}Abd al-Karim, French entered the curriculum in 1875 and piano in 1876. ^{c}Abd al-Karim, *tarikh*, vol. 2, 361–62; DW, PI, box 49, doss. 35/1, Dor Bey, "Ecoles Primaires Arabes Inspectées Dans Les Provinces et Governants," undated.
31. Ismail's educational advisors included Egyptians like Tahtawi who saw the need for civil education, and European advisors, e.g. Dor Bey who also saw a relationship between history, education, and national character. See *manahij al-albab al-miṣriyya fi mabahij al-adab al-^{c}aṣriyya*, 2nd edn. (Cairo: Maṭba^{c}at Shirkat al-Ragha'ib, 1912), 350–51 and *L'Instruction Publique en Egypte* (Paris: A. Lacroix, Verboeckhoven, & Co., 1872), 36–44, resp.
32. ^{c}Abd al-Karim, *tarikh*, vol. 2, 368; Chennells, *Recollections*, vol. 2, 89; McCoan, *Egypt*, 210, Dor Bey, "Ecoles Primaires."
33. Artin, *L'Instruction*, 189; DW, PI, box 12, Dor Bey, *Rapport*, December 25, 1875; Heyworth-Dunne, *Education*, 375.

34. Chennells, *Recollections*, 88–90.
35. Artin, *L'Instruction*, 135–36; McCoan, *Egypt*, 211.
36. Heyworth-Dunne, *Education*, 432; Sami, *al-ta*[c]*lim*, app. 2, 9; Dor Bey, *L'Instruction*, 226–27, 385.
37. Artin, *Mémorandum*, part one; Magda Baraka, *The Egyptian Upper Class between Revolutions, 1919–1952* (Reading: Ithaca, 1998), 175.
38. de Leon, *The Khedive's Egypt*, 164.
39. Artin, *Mémorandum*, introduction; Artin, *L'Instruction*, 135; Rizq, "Schools," 5.
40. DW, NM, box A/1/M, doss. 27; *al-ahram* (October 10, 1889) as cited by Rizq, "Schools," 5; DW, NM, box M6, Request from the *diwan al-awqaf* to the *majlis al-nuẓẓar* regarding an order to ameliorate the issue of what is necessary at the school for girls until the end of 1889, November 18, 1889.
41. DW, MW, NM, box M6, Note from the Ministry of Public Instruction to the *majlis al-nuẓẓar* regarding the request of Yusif Effendi Kanfan, July 19, 1887.
42. Artin, *Mémorandum*, introduction. See also Artin, *Considérations sur l'Instruction Publique en Egypte* (Cairo, 1894), 150.
43. [c]Abd al-Karim, *Muḥammad*[c]*Ali*, 670; [c]Abd al-Karim, *tarikh*, vol. 2, 354; Church of Scotland, *Home and Foreign Missionary Society* (Edinburgh, 1859), vol. XVI, 134 as cited by Sislian, "Missionary Work," 178; Brian Holmes, "British Imperial Policy and Mission Schools," in his *Education*, 30–31; Heyworth-Dunne, *Education*, 330; Sami, *al-ta*[c]*lim*, 16, 34.
44. Sislian, "Missionary Work," 175, 178, 180.
45. *Missionary Register* (1829), 308 as cited in Sislian, "Missionary Work," 193.
46. John Bowring, "Report on Egypt and Candia," Great Britain, House of Commons, *Sessional Papers*, 1840, vol. xxi, 138.
47. Bowring, "Report," 137–38; James Thayer Addison, *The Christian Approach to the Moslem* (New York: Columbia University Press, 1942), 141–42; Sislian, "Missionary Work," 187, 191–93, 195–96, 198, 200; Andrew Watson, *The American Mission in Egypt, 1854–1896* (Pittsburgh: United Presbyterian Board of Publications, 1898), 32; [c]Abd al-Karim, *Muḥammad* [c]*Ali*, 673–74.
48. Heyworth-Dunne, *Education*, 90, 275; Peter Gran, *Islamic Roots*, 3–75; Sami, *al-ta*[c]*lim*, 13; Sislian, "Missionary Work," 217.
49. Girgis Salama, *tarikh al-ta*[c]*lim al-ajnaby fi Miṣr* (Cairo: Wakil Madrasat al-Naṣr, 1963), 42; Sislian, "Missionary Work," 218–21; Sami, *al-ta*[c]*lim*, 13–14, 16.
50. Sislian, "Missionary Work," 218.
51. McCoan, *Egypt*, 224; Sislian, "Missionary Work, 202, 213; A. Watson, *American Mission*, 94–95.
52. Salama, *tarikh*, 46–47; Sislian, "Missionary Work," 207–08.
53. Nevertheless, the slave trade continued long after its official cessation in 1877. See Eve Troutt Powell, *A Different Shade of Colonialism* (Berkeley: University of California Press, 2003), 1–4.
54. Heyworth-Dunne, *Education*, 406–08; Khalifa, *al-ḥaraka*, 100; Sislian, Missionary Work," 221, 226–27; Dor Bey, *L'Instruction*, 276–79; Sami, *al-ta*[c]*lim*, 16.
55. McCoan, *Egypt*, 223–24; de Leon, *The Khedive's Egypt*, 163; DW, MW, NM, box A4, Letter from Scott Moncrieff to Nubar Pasha, May 13, no year given.
56. Mary Whately, *Ragged Life in Egypt* (London: Seeley, Jackson, and Halliday, 1863), 120, 123.
57. Whately, *Ragged Life*, 46–48.
58. Whately, *Ragged Life*, 49, 170.
59. Whately, *Ragged Life*, 49–52, 55.

60. Whately, *Ragged Life*, 105, 161–62; 169–70; Whately, *Among the Huts in Egypt: Scenes From Real Life* (London: Seeley, Jackson, & Halliday, 1871), 65, 115.
61. Whately, *Ragged Life*, 169–79; Whately, *Scenes*, 109.
62. Whately, *Scenes*, 113–14, 189.
63. McCoan, *Egypt*, 224; DW, MW, NM, box A4, letter from Aly Ibrahim to Riaz Pasha, May 1, 1880.
64. Whately, *Ragged Life*, 67–68; Whately, *Scenes*, 109, 123–24, 138, 284–85.
65. Whately, *Ragged Life*, 181.
66. Whately, *Ragged Life*, 52–53, 110; Whately, *Scenes*, 115; PA, Loretta Mitchell, "The Sorrow of Egypt" (Pittsburgh: Women's General Missionary Society [WGMS], n/d).
67. Mine Ener, "Petitions of the Poor," Paper delivered at MESA, November 1996. For a more detailed account, see her *Managing Egypt's Poor and the Politics of Benevolence, 1800–1952* (Princeton: Princeton University Press, 2003). For examples of subventions provided by the government, see DW, PI, doss. 35/3.
68. McCoan, *Egypt*, 224; DW, MW, NM, box A4, Letter from Scott Moncrief to Nubar Pasha, May 13, no year given; Letter from Aly Ibrahim to Riaz Pasha, May 1, 1880; and Report from Rogers Bey to the Council of Ministers, 3 Rajab 1298.
69. DW, MW, NM, box A4, series 178, Request to the Finance Committee, July 9, 1894.
70. Lane, *Manners*, vol. 1, 90. "Sewing," *al-muqtaṭaf* 8, 10 (1884): 587–88; Tucker, *Women*, in Nineteenth-century Egypt (Cambridge: Cambridge University Press, 1985), 86.
71. *al-ahram* (April 12, 1887; July 9, 1887; July 6, 1890) as cited by Rizq, "Schools," 5.
72. Helen Montgomery, *Western Women in Eastern Lands: An Outline of Fifty Years of Women's Work in Foreign Missions* (New York: MacMillan & Co., 1910), 86–87, 105–06.
73. Elizabeth Cooper, writing in 1914, places the number of converts at 200, most of whom were Copts. Elizabeth Cooper, *Women of Egypt* (New York: F.A. Stokes, 1914), 348; PA, *The Educational Work of the American Mission in Egypt* (n/p, n/d), 2.
74. Charles Watson, *Egypt and the Christian Crusade* (Philadelphia: United Presbyterian Church of North America, 1907), 223–24; A. Watson, *American Mission*, 435–36.
75. PA, "Carrie M. Buchanan Girl's Boarding School" (Pittsburgh: WGMS, n/d); PA Carrie Buchanon, "Broadening Horizons in Egypt" (Pittsburgh: WGMS, n/d).
76. Patricia Hill, *The World Their Household* (Ann Arbor: University of Michigan Press, 1985), 3, 134; Charles Forman, "The Americans," *International Bulletin of Missionary Research* (April 1982), 55.
77. Montgomery *Western Women*, 45, 52–54; L. Mitchell, "The Sorrow of Egypt."
78. Cuno, "Fate of Divorce," paper presented at the conference on Institutions, Ideologies and Agencies: Changing Family Life in the Middle East, UNC-Chapel Hill, April 2003.
79. Cooper, *The Women of Egypt*, 98; A. Watson, *American Mission*, 402; C. Watson, *Egypt*, 221–22; PA, Minnehaha Finney, "Kindergarten Schools in Egypt, the Vision," in *The Child in the Midst* (np/nd).
80. A. Watson, *American Mission*, 371; C. Watson, *Egypt*, 250; Finney, "Kindergarten;" PA, Sadie Thompson, "From Darkness Into Light" (Pittburgh: WGMS, n/d), 2; Sarah Graham-Brown, *Images of Women* (London: Quartert Books, 1988), 47.
81. Earl Elder, *Vindicating a Vision* (Philadelphia: The United Presbyterian Board of Foreign Missions, 1958), 136; *Educational Mission*, 18; Cooper, *The Women of Egypt*, 21; Dor, *L'Instruction*, 281–84.
82. A. Watson, *American Mission*, 95, 98, 124, 138, 288; *Educational Mission*, 4, 6; Heyworth-Dunne, *Education*, 333.

83. Heyworth-Dunne, *Eduction*, 410–11; A. Watson, *American Mission*, 94–95; 288–91; McCoan, *Egypt*, 223; Sami, *al-ta*[c]*lim*, 34.
84. A. Watson, *American Mission*, 448.
85. Elder, *Vindicating a Vision*, 137–38; A. Watson, *American Mission*, 265, 279, 302; McCoan, *Egypt*, 222–23. After visiting Egypt in 1922, Grace Thompson Seton indicated that the daughters of Pashas and Beys paid an additional fee at the American Mission school in Luxor. See her *A Woman Tenderfoot in Egypt* (New York: Dodd, Mead & Company, 1923), 100.
86. Seton, *A Woman Tenderfoot in Egypt*, 97; Addison, *Christian Approach*, 143–44. For detailed statistics on the numbers of students and schools, see A. Watson, *American Mission* and C. Watson, *Egypt*.
87. Dor, *L'Instruction*, 284; "Carrie M. Buchanan Girl's Boarding School"; *Educational Mission*, 5–6, 15, 16; PA, *Program of Studies for the Mission Schools for Girls in Egypt*; PA, Stella Robinson, "Fatma At School" (Pittsburgh: WGMS, n/d); Seton, *A Woman Tenderfoot in Egypt*, 100.
88. Montgomery, *Western Women*, 100–101.
89. Seton, *A Woman Tenderfoot in Egypt*, 100; Finney, "Kindergarten"; Omnia Shakry, "Schooled Mothers and Structured Play: Child Rearing in Turn-of-the-Century Egypt," in *Remaking Women*, 139–41.
90. Heyworth-Dunne, *Education*, 409–10.
91. A. Watson, *American Mission*, 261, 162–63, 205–06, 442–43; .
92. A. Watson, *American Mission*, 266; Sami, *al-ta*[c]*lim*, 34; McCoan, *Egypt*, 218–19; Dor, *L'Instruction*, 185–87.
93. Heyworth-Dunne, *Education*, 90, 91–92. For an account of traditional Jewish education in Egypt, see S.D. Goitein, *A Mediterranean Society* (Berkeley: University of California Press, 1988), vol. 5, *The Individual*, 415–96.
94. Jacob Landau, "The Beginnings of Modernization in Education: The Jewish Community in Egypt as a Case Study," in William Polk and Richard Chambers, eds., *The Beginnings of Modernization in the Middle East* (Chicago: University of Chicago Press, 1968), 299–312; A. Watson, *American Mission* 95, 137; Heyworth-Dunne, *Education*, 272–73, 422; McCoan, *Egypt*, 219–20.
95. Heyworth-Dunne, *Education*, 91, 272–75, 311, 334–36, 412–14; Montagne Fowler, *Christian Egypt* (London: Christian Newspaper Co., Ltd., 1901), 226–27; Salama, *tarikh*, 74, 78; Dor Bey, *L'Instruction*, 285–89; McCoan, *Egypt*, 220.
96. Salama, *tarikh*, 83, 85, 86–89; Heyworth-Dunne, *Education*, 336 360, 406, 414–15; Dor, *Statisque des ecoles civiles* (Cairo, 1875); McCoan, *Egypt*, 220.
97. See e.g., DW, PI, box 195, "Note sur la création d'un système générale d'enseignement primaire en Egypte," December 8, 1889.
98. Salama, *tarikh*, 130–31.
99. For general accounts of education under British occupation, see Abu al-Aṣad, *siyasat al-ta*[c]*lim* and Sa[c]id Isma[c]il [c]Ali, *dur al-ta*[c]*lim al-miṣri fil-niḍal al-waṭani* (Cairo: al-Hay'a al-Miṣriyya al-[c]Amma lil-Kitab, 1995).
100. Marsot, *Egypt Under Cromer* (New York: Praeger, 1968), 54–55. See also Abbas Hilmi II, *Memoirs*, 247–54.
101. Cromer to Gorst, March 12, 1908, The Cromer Papers, PRO, FO, 633/14 as cited in Robert Tignor, *Modernization and British Colonial Rule in Egypt, 1882–1914* (Princeton: Princeton University Press, 1966), 320.
102. Lord Macaulay, Speech given in the House of Commons on July 10, taken from Lady Trevelyan, ed., *The Works of Lord Macaulay, Complete* (London: Longman, Green, and Co., 1866), vol. 8, 141.

103. *Annual Report 1902*, 38.
104. DW, MW, NM, box 16, Note from Fakhry to *majlis al-nuẓẓar* regarding the increase in fees at government schools, June 5, 1905. Fakhry goes on to state that experience from the last 20 years indicates that increasing fees results in an appreciable increase in the moral level of the government schools.
105. DW, MW, NM, box 4B, doss. 59, Note to the Council of Ministers from Aly Mubarak regarding placement of students upon the termination of their studies, September 1889; *Annual Report 1898*, 40–41; DW, MW, NM, box A23, Note from the Higher Council of Public Instruction, October 1, 1901; "Opinion on the Issue of Education and the Assessment of Fee Levels in Government Schools," *al-mu'ayyad* (January 2, 1902), 2; *Annual Report 1902*, 54–55; *Annual Report 1905*, 86; *Annual Report 1906*, 110; *Annual Report 1909*, 49–50; DW, MW, box B23, Documents relating to the repeal of the primary certificate, December 28, 1915–January 6, 1916.
106. See e.g., DW, AT, box 236, Father Bizya, "The Crisis of Education," undated, but appears with material from 1913–1916.
107. DW, MW, NM, box 16, Note from Fakhry to *majlis al-nuẓẓar* regarding the increase in fees at government schools, June 5, 1905; *Annual Report 1907*, 31.
108. *Annual Report 1898*, 39–40.
109. *Annual Report 1905*, 83–84.
110. DW, MW, NM, box 16, Note from Saad Zaghlul to Council of Ministers regarding a law for free positions in the government schools, July 2, 1907; "Regulations Relating to the Admission of Non-paying Pupils to the Abbas School" [enacted by Ministerial Order No. 1325, June 25, 1908] published in Ministry of Public Instruction, *Regulations, 1914* (Cairo: Government Press, 1914); *Annual Report 1907*, 31–32; *Annual Report 1898*, 43; *Annual Report 1903*, 61; *Annual Report 1904*, 73–74. Given that the British limited the size of the Egyptian army, it seems likely that Cromer's main concern was young men avoiding work. For Zaghlul's tenure as Minister of Public Instruction, see Amil Fahmy Ḥana Shanuda, *Sa^{c}d Zaghlul naẓir al-ma^{c}arif* (Cairo: Dar al-Fikr al-^{c}Arabi, 1977).
111. DW, MW, NM, box A4, Note from Ali Mubarak to the *majlis al-nuẓẓar* regarding the return boys' and girls' elementary schools from the *waqf* administration to the Ministry of Public Instruction, July 5, 1888 and July 12, 1888; DW, PI, box 195, Adly Pacha, Note sur la création d'un système général d'enseignement primaire en Egypte, December 8, 1889; DW, MW, NM, box 2, Ali Mubarak, Report on the State of *Kuttabs*, March 10, 1890; DW, MW, box 2, Note to the Council of Ministers Regarding Regulations of the Kuttabs, June 1902; DW, MW, NM, box 2, Fakhry, Règlement Relatif aux Subventions Annuelles aux *Kuttabs*, December 9, 1897; *Annual Report 1898*, 43; *Annual Report 1901*, 40–41; *Annual Report 1902*, 53; *Annual Report 1904*, 73; *Annual Report 1905*, 87–88; *Annual Report 1906*, 113.
112. See e.g., untitled article on the Khedive's support of a free school, *al-waqa^{c}i al-miṣriyya* (January 12, 1874); "Thanks [for] Concern" [regarding the donation of Princess Zubayda to Madrasat al-Nil] *al-ustadh* 1, 29 (1893), 702; program of support from the princesses solicited by Muhammad Abdu discussed in Muḥammad Rashid Riḍa, *tarikh al-ustadh al-imam Muḥammad ^{c}Abduh* (Cairo, 1931), 895 as cited in Khalifa, *al-ḥaraka*, 110; "Organization of the Union to Educate Girls [Under the Patronage of the Queen Mother]," *al-hilal* 22, 6 (1914), 469.
113. Journalists were ardent supporters of these schools, and editors catalogued the activities of groups with whom they were affiliated. For example, Abdullah Nadim, chronicled the activities of the "Firm Bond Society" and other Islamic charitable organizations, while the editors of *al-hilal* and *al-muqtaṭaf* chronicled the activities of Coptic, Greek, and American organizations. See e.g., "The Firm Bond Society in Alexandria," *al-ustadh* 1,

16 (1892): 379–80; "The Nile Benevolent School," *al-ustadh* 1, 20 (1893): 478–81; "The American Mission Girls' School in Alexandria," *al-muqtaṭaf* 10, 1 (1885): 55; "New School for Girls," *al-muqtaṭaf* 12, 2 (1887): 123–24; "A School for Girls in Faggala," *al-muqtaṭaf* 12, 8 (1888): 513; "The Averoff Girls' School," *al-hilal* 2, 21 (1894): 669.

114. *Annual Report 1905*, 87; *Annual Report 1907*, 34; DW, MW, NM, box 17, contains two documents discussing the waiving of registration fees on land sold at half price to two individuals, as well as a listing of 20 societies and/or individuals benefiting from the program, April 27–July 9, 1909; *Annual Report 1906*, 90; *Annual Report 1908*, 41–42; *Annual Report 1902*, 55.
115. *Annual Report 1908*, 39; *Annual Report 1909*, 40–41; *Annual Report 1910*, 36–37; Sami, *al-ta^{c}lim*, 100–02; Shanuda, *Zaghlul*, 137–52.
116. See e.g., Joseph Szyliowicz, *Education and Modernization in the Middle East* (Ithaca: Cornell University Press, 1973), 130; Brian Holmes, "British Policy," 17–18; Tignor, *Modernization*, 342–43.
117. Lord Cromer, *Modern Egypt*, vol. 2, 155–57; 159; 539–42.
118. Karen Offen, "Liberty, Equality, and Justice for Women: The Theory and Practice of Feminism in Nineteenth-Century Europe," in Renate Bridenthal, Claudia Koontz, and Susan Stuard, eds., *Becoming Visible: Women in European History*, (Boston: Houghton Mifflin, 1987), 346.
119. Leila Ahmed, *Women and Gender in Islam* (New Haven: Yale University Press, 1992), 150–53.
120. *Annual Report 1898*, 43–44; *Annual Report 1902*, 56; *Annual Report 1904*, 77; *Annual Report 1907*, 34.
121. "Egyptian Schools and the Fate of Education," *al-muqtaṭaf* 44, 2 (1914), 114; *Annual Report 1898*, 44; *Annual Report 1899*, 36; *Annual Report 1901*, 40.
122. DW, PI, NM, box 195, Mohamed Zeki, "Règlement de l'Ecole de Médicine, de Pharmacie, et de l'Ecole médicale des Filles, 1892"; Sami, *al-ta^{c}lim*, app. 3, 15; Abugideiri, "Colonized Medicine," 358. The displacement of *ḥakimas* was becoming apparent in advertising, as new male graduates began advertising in the mainstream and women's press.
123. Ali Mubarak, *Cinquième Rapport à Son Altesse Le Khédive sur l'Enseignement Public en Egypte Année 1889* (Cairo: Imprimerie Nationale, 1890), 18–20; Higher Consultative Committee, minutes of the May 21, 1889 session as cited by Abu al-Aṣad, *siyasat al-ta^{c}lim*, 144; *al-ahram* (September 26, 1889) as cited by Rizq, "Schools," 5; Artin, *Mémorandum*, introduction.
124. Mrs. Yacub Sarruf, "'The Sania School,'" *al-muqtaṭaf* 14, 12 (1890): 836–38; *al-ahram* (October 20, 1890) as cited by Rizq, "Schools," 5.
125. Artin, *Mémorandum*, part 3.
126. DW, MW, box A4, Note from the Agent of the Ministry of Public Instruction Regarding Girls' Education, July 18, 1899.
127. DW, MW, NM, box A4, Alice (Elise?) Forbes [headmistress], Arabic translation of her Report on the Abbas School's Girls' Division, July 20, 1897.
128. DW, MW, NM, box 16, M. Fakhry, Note from the Ministry of Public Instruction to the *majlis al-nuẓẓar* Regarding the Increase in Fees at Government Schools, June 5, 1905. Both the boys' and girls' divisions of the Abbas school also maintained a number of free positions for children of railway workers.
129. DW, MW, NM, box 16, Note on What Has Resulted from School Fees in 1906; *Annual Report 1907*, 34; *Annual Report 1906*, 92.

130. Khalifa, *al-ḥaraka*, 107; *Annual Report 1911*, 27; Loi de 1913 portant sur la création d'une école d'Economie Domestique et l'agrément de l'exécution de cette loi promulguée par Arrête Ministeriel #1735 du Avril 1913 in *Regulations 1914*; DW, MW, NM, box A4, Adly Yeghen, Ministerial note regarding the implementation of Law #14 of 1916 relating to the creation of higher elementary schools for girls, June 6, 1916; DW, MW, NM, box H4, Adly Yeghen, Note to the Council of Ministers concerning changes in the program of study at boys' and girls' elementary schools, July 23, 1916; DW, MW, NM, box 17, Note to the Council of Ministers Regarding Non-Paying Students at the Abbas School for Girls, February 16, 1921. Although the first secondary school for girls did not open until 1920, there was an experimental program that allowed girls to continue studies at Sania without receiving teacher training. See *Annual Report 1910*, 55. On secondary education, see also Ceza Nabaraoui, "L'Enseignement secondaire féminin en Egypte," *L'Egyptienne* (November 1927), 5–10.
131. DW, PI, box 12, George Robb, *Educational Progress*, 5–6, 27; *Annual Report 1898*, 44; *Annual Report 1903*, 65; DW, MW, NM, box 2, Ahmed Mazloum, Note to the Council of Ministers Regarding Instructing Women to Teach in *Kuttabs*, June 2, 1903; Abbas Hilmi and Ahmed Hechmat, Law of February 8, 1913 Relating to Elementary Training Colleges for Women Teachers and Ministerial Order No. 1722 (March 3, 1913) Embodying Regulations to the Same Effect in *Regulations 1914*; Sami, *ta^{c}lim*, app. 3, 26–27, 29–31; "The School for Teachers at Bulaq," *al-muqtaṭaf* 46, 4 (1915), 395–96; Shanuda, *Zaghlul*, 142–43; *Annual Report 1908*, 44–45; Ministry of Education, *Report of the Elementary Education Committee and Draft Law* (Cairo: Government Press, 1919), 26; "From Where are the Teachers," *al-muqtaṭaf* 42, 6 (1913), 596; *Annual Report 1907*, 34; *Annual Report 1909*, 47; *Annual Report 1911*, 25–26; Sidney Low, *Egypt in Transition* (New York: The MacMillan Co., 1914), 307; DW, MW, NM, box B7, Correspondence regarding female students, August 18, 1908–July 23, 1916.
132. "Encouragement of Education in Egypt," *al-muqtaṭaf* 5, 7 (1880), 189; Reid, "Career Choices," 373–75; DW, MW, NM, box 16, Sa^{c}d Zaghlul, Response from the Ministry of Public Instruction to Observations made by the *majlis al-shura al-qawaniyya* on December 18, 1906, Relating to the Preparation of Teachers, Improving Their Condition such that Demands for Positions are Met, and Expanding the Scope of Religious Instruction, May 25, 1907; DW, AT, box 231, Sa^{c}d Zaghlul, Note on a Celebration to Honor *Kuttab* Teachers, November 29, 1909; DW, MW, NM, box H4 for materials on meeting the demand for Egyptian teachers; *Annual Report 1902*, 53; *Annual Report 1898*, 44; *Annual Report 1907*, 37; DW, MW, NM, box 16, Note from the Ministry of Public Instruction Regarding an Edict for Free Positions in Schools, July 2, 1907; *Report and Draft Law 1919*, 26; US Bureau of Education, *Bulletin 1919*, No. 42 (Washington DC: Government Printing Office, 1919), 97–99; DW, MW, NM, box 16, Gafar Waly, Note sur l'admission à titre gratuit à l'Ecole Normale Sultanieh de tous les étudiants qui se destinent à la carrière de l'enseignement, September 27, 1921; Ruth Woodsmall, *Moslem Women Enter a New World* (New York: Round Talk Press, 1936), 182; "Regulations of the Sanieh Training College [Enacted by Ministerial Order #1389], Dated June 20, 1905" in *Regulations 1914*.
133. Artin, *Mémorandum*, part one; DW, MW, NM, box 2, Ahmed Mazloum, Note to the Council of Ministers Regarding the Instruction of Women to Teach in *Kuttabs*, June 2, 1903; Ibrahim Maḥmud, "The New Teacher's Division," *anis al-jalis* 3, 10 (1900), 378–79.
134. Donald Reid, *Cairo University and the Making of Modern Egypt* (Cambridge: Cambridge University Press, 1990), 52; Nabawiyya Musa, "Dhikrayati," serialized in her *majallat al-fatah* as cited in Badran, *Feminists*, 53–54; DW, AT, box 233, Request for Newspapers

and Journals for the Egyptian University Collection, undated but with material from 1908–09.

135. Shaarawi, *Harem Years*, 93; Malak Hifni Nasif, "Speech of the Egyptian [Female] Speaker About Women," *al-manar* 12, 5 (1909): 353–71 (See also her *al-nisa'iyyat*, a compilation of her speeches and essays published in 1910); DW, AT, box 233, Announcement for Lecture at the Women's Section of the Egyptian University.
136. Reid, *Cairo University*, 53; DW, AT, box 233, Mlle. Couvreur, List of Suggested books, November 27, 1910; DW, AT, box 231, The Egyptian University: Administrative Council's Decision Plan for the Running of the University 1911–12; DW, AT, box 233, A. Couvreur, Note Regarding the Women's Section, May 1, 1911; Labiba Hashim, "Education," *al-muqtaṭaf* 38, 3 (1911): 274–81.
137. DW, AT, box 231, The Egyptian University Administrative Council's Decision Plan for the Running of the University 1911–12; DW, AT, box 230, Ministry of Public Instruction, *Secondary Certificate Examination, 1907: Statistics* (Cairo: National Printing Dept., 1907), 8–9; Sami, *al-ta^c lim*, app. 3, 54.
138. Reid, *Cairo University*, 55–56; Hagai Erlikh, *Students and the University in Twentieth Century Politics* (London: Cass, 1989), 39; Badran, *Feminists*, 54–55; Beth Baron, *The Women's Awakening in Egypt* (New Haven: Yale University Press, 1992), 132; For Mlle. Couvreur's response to the suppression of the women's section, see DW, AT, box 233, Note on Women's Section, July 9, 1912. Although Egyptian women no longer attended, there were a small number of European women who attended classes with men. DW, AT, box 236, The Egyptian University: Report of the Administrative Council, March 29, 1913.

7 The Discourse on Female Education

1. Peter Gran, "Tahtawi in Paris," *al-ahram weekly*, January 10–16 2002.
2. al-Ṭahṭawi, *murshid al-amin lil-binat wal-banin* (Cairo: Maṭba^c at al-Madaris al-Malakiyya, 1289[AH]), esp. 6, 32, 48–49, 66–68, 91, 101–06, 120–21, 134, 195–207, 215–56, 273–77, 372–73. According to Selçuk Akşin Somel, these discussions began in the 1840s and 1850s, and they continued through the Hamidian period. See his *The Modernization of Public Education in the Ottoman Empire, 1839–1908* (Leiden: Brill, 2001), 185.
3. Barak Salmoni, "Pedagogies of Patriotism: Teaching Socio-Political Community in Twentieth-Century Turkish and Egyptian Education" (Ph.D. diss., Harvard University 2002), 616.
4. Mrs. Salma Ṭanus, "Women's Education and Their Upbringing," *al-muqtaṭaf* 8, 4 (1884), 234–35.
5. Mrs. Maryam Jurji Ilyan, "The Rights of Women and the Necessity of Their Education," *al-muqtaṭaf* 8, 7 (1884): 358–60.
6. Mrs. Shams Shaḥadi, "The Right is the First That is Said," *al-muqtaṭaf* 8, 8 (1884): 491–94.
7. Peter Mansfield, *The British in Egypt* (London: Cox and Wyman, Ltd., 1971), 139–41.
8. Regarding education in general, see e.g., "Education," *al-muqtaṭaf* 7, 1 (1882): 111–12; "The Objective of the Educated," *al-mu'ayyad* 1, 5 (1889): 1; "National Defense: Decision of the Knowledgeable People," *al-ustadh* 1, 8 (1892): 184–91; "Teaching [Our] Sons," *al-ustadh* 1, 9 (1892): 202–08; Muḥi al-Din Effendi Ṭarabulsi, "Questions and Suggestions,"

al-hilal 2, 13 (1894): 401–02; "Where is Reform," *al-liwa'* (January 14, 1903): 1–2; "What is Beneficial From Education Which is Charged to the Nation [*umma*]," *al-tarbiya* 2, 5 (1906): 25–26; "Egyptian Government Schools and the Arabic Language," *al-hilal* 15, 7 (1908): 393–410; "Muslims in the Schools of Christian Organizations," *al-manar* 12, 1 (1909): 18–26; "The Life of Language in the Sciences," *al-manar* 12, 2 (1909): 108–12; "The Ottoman State," *al-manar* 16, 2 (1913): 107–12; Muḥammad Bayumi al-Ḥanid, "Who is Most Worthy of Education: Fathers and Mothers or Sons and Daughters," *al-mu'ayyad* (February 14, 1914): 2. This concern even extends to contemporary discussions of the history of education. See e.g., Salama, *tarikh*, 126–127; Abu al-Aṣad, *siyasat al-ta^{c}lim*, 223.

9. Even after English supplanted French in government schools, French continued to be important for the Mixed Courts and legal professions, commercial enterprises, among the royal family and the country's elite, the Masonic Lodges, department stores, Suez Canal Company, the press (including editors of the Arabic press), in the nascent cinema industry, hotels, the antiquities service, and even in high-class brothels. See quotation by Magdi Wahba translated by Magda Baraka in *The Egyptian Upper Class Between Revolutions, 1919–1952* (Reading: Ithaca, 1998), 135.
10. *Annual Report 1898*, 41; *Annual Report 1899*, 35; *Annual Report 1905*, 85; Douglas Dunlop, "Note With Reference to the Linguistic Basis of Instruction in Egyptian Government Schools," February 10, 1907 in *Annual Report 1906*, 108–15; Abbas Hilmi II, *The Last Khedive: Memoirs of Abbas Hilmi II*, translated and edited by Amira Sonbol (Reading: Ithaca, 1998), 174; "Letter from Professor Edouard Lambert" translated in Abbas Hilmi II, *Memoirs*, 183–87. See also Robert Tignor, *Modernization and British Colonial Rule in Egypt, 1882–1914* (Princeton: Princeton University Press, 1966), 348; Peter Mansfield, *The British in Egypt*, 144; John Marlowe, *Cromer in Egypt* (New York: Praeger, 1970), 292; Amira Sonbol, *The New Mamluks* (Syracuse: Syracuse University Press, 2000), 62.
11. Nina Nelson, *Shepheard's Hotel* (London: Barrie and Rockliff, 1960), 72; Abbas Hilmi II, *Memoirs*, 289; Sonbol, *The New Mamluks*, 114; Mansfield, *The British in Egypt*, 143; J.W.A. Young as cited by Judith Tucker, *Women in Nineteenth-Century Egypt* (Cambridge: Cambridge University Press, 1985), 123–24
12. al-Sayyid ^{c}Ali, "The Integrity of Education in Egypt," *al-tarbiya* 3, 1 (1908): 5–6. See also, Abu Ḥafs, "Education Policy," *al-tarbiya* 3, 2 (1908): 3–5 and al-Sayyid ^{c}Ali "Education Policy," *al-tarbiya* 3, 3 (1908): 9–11; Amil Fahmy H. Shanuda, *Sa^{c}d Zaghlul: naẓir al-ma^{c}arif* (Cairo: Dar al-Fikr al-^{c}Arabi, 1978), 79–106.
13. Abbas Hilmi II, *Memoirs*, 257–60.
14. By 1909, most European teachers in government schools had to pass an elementary Arabic examination before their appointment could be confirmed or before they could receive an increase in salary. *Annual Report 1907*, 32, 35.
15. DW, MW, NM, box A23, "Projet d'extension de l'enseignement religieux dans les écoles primaires," April 2, 1907; DW, MW, NM, box 16, "Response of the Ministry of Public Instructions to the observations made at the 18 December 1906 session of the *majlis al-shura al-qawaniyya* relating to the expansion of religious education," May 25, 1907; DW, MW, NM, box 16, "Note to the Finance Committee Concerning the Increase in Budgetary Expenses for 1910," June 1909; *Annual Report 1909*, 41.
16. This meeting, sponsored by the National Party, was held to apprise the European press of the consequences of the British occupation. Rifaat Wafik, "L'Instruction en Egypte," in *Oeuvres du Congrès National Egyptien* (Brussels, 1910), 143, 144, 160; Rifaat Wafik, "L'Angleterre et L'Instruction en Egypte," in *Oeuvres*, 391, 430–39.
17. Untitled cartoon, *al-laṭa'if al-muṣawwara* (August 7, 1922), 16.

18. See his "Pedagogies of Patriotism," 820.
19. Chamber of Deputies, August 2, 1926, 3190 as cited by Baraka, *The Egyptian Upper Class*, 271.
20. "His Majesty Sultan ᶜAbd al-Ḥamid," *anis al-jalis* 1, 1 (1898): 13–14; Katrin Isṭafan, "Education," *anis al-jalis* 1, 7 (1898): 168–72; "Young Women's Education," *anis al-jalis* 1, 7 (1898): 192–97; "Girls' Education," *anis al-jalis* 1, 8 (1898): 245–47; "Girls' Education," *anis al-jalis* 2, 2 (1899): 57–63; An anonymous female, "Knowledge and the Woman," *anis al-jalis* 2, 4 (1899): 142–45; Ibrahim Maḥmud, "Education and Upbringing," *anis al-jalis* 3, 7 (1900): 271–77; Naguib Ḥagg, "Girls' Schools and Their Education," *anis al-jalis* 4, 6 (1901): 691–97; "The Woman, the Mind, and Education," *anis al-jalis* 6, 3 (1903): 1355–59; "[What is] In Knowledge and Education with Respect to Health," *anis al-jalis* 7, 10/11/12 (1904): 1987–89; "Education of the Woman," *anis al-jalis* 7, 10/11/12 (1904): 1990–92; Yusif Effendi Ghanimat al-Baghdadi, "Reform of Female Education," *anis al-jalis* 7, 10/11/12 (1904): 2031–35; Ḥanna Ṣarah, "Teach the Young Woman," *anis al-jalis* 9, 1 (1906): 19–20.
21. See Beth Baron, *The Women's Awakening in Egypt* (New Haven: Yale University Press, 1994), 122–43.
22. Naguib Ḥagg, "The Eastern Woman and the [Female] Westerner," *anis al-jalis* 4, 5 (1901): 658–64; Naguib Ḥagg, "Girls' Schools and Their Education," *anis al-jalis* 4, 6 (1901): 691–97; "The Egyptian Conference: The Danger of Foreign Education, Especially for Girls," *al-manar* 14, 4 (1911): 287–95, esp. 294; ᶜAli Ḥasan Badir, "There is no Misdeed [Committed] Against Girls," *al-mu'ayyad* (February 26, 1914): 2.
23. See e.g., Maḥmud Ibrahim, "The New Teacher's Division," *anis al-jalis* 3, 10 (1900): 271–277; Muḥammad Zaki, "Europeanized Turkish Women," *anis al-jalis* 9, 6 (1906): 170–74.
24. Naguib Ḥagg, "Girls' Schools and Their Education," *anis al-jalis* 4, 6 (1901), 696.
25. "The Complaint of Mothers About Girls' Education," *al-muqtaṭaf* 28, 10 (1903), 877.
26. For example, according to Muḥammad Abu al-Aṣad, English remained the language of instruction at the Sania school until the time of the 1919 Revolution, when students complained. Arabic was gradually phased in thereafter. Muḥammad Abu al-Aṣad, *siyasat al-taᶜlim al-miṣri fil-niḍal al-waṭani* (Cairo: al-Hay' al-Miṣriyya al-ᶜAmma lil-Kitab, 1995), 233.
27. al-Faḍila, "Girls' and Women's Section," *al-tarbiya* 3, 3 (1908): 14–15.
28. See e.g., "Religious Education in Government Schools," *al-manar* 14, 3 (1911): 221–26. This article cites a report by the English headmistress of the Sania school highlighting the importance of religious instruction and morals. The author bemoans the fact that Dunlop ignored this woman's advice, and he replaced her on two different occasions. See also, Naguib Ḥagg, "Girls' Schools and Their Education," *anis al-jalis* 4, 6 (1901): 691–97; "The Woman's Education," *al-saᶜada* 2, 7/8 (1904): 566–67; "Knowledge and Women," *al-saᶜada* 2, 9/10 (1904): 596–604; ᶜAli Ḥasan Badir, "There is No Misdeed [Committed] Against Young Women," *al-mu'ayyad* (February 26, 1914): 2; Najiya Rashid, "The Danger of Foreign Schools," *tarqiyat al-mar'a* 1, 6 (1326): 88–93.
29. Thomas Philipp, *The Syrians in Egypt, 1775–1975* (Stuttgart: Steiner Verlag Weisbaden, 1985), 161.
30. Salmoni, "Pedagogies of Patriotism," 232.
31. J. ᶜA., "The Egyptian [Female] Student," *al-tarbiya* 1, 1 (1905): 6; See also, Salma, "Life or Ignorance," *al-tarbiya* 1, 2 (1905): 13; Untitled article in *qism al-banat wal-sayyidat, al-tarbiya* 3, 2 (1908), 13.
32. "The Egyptian Woman," *al-tarbiya* 1, 5 (1905), 36.
33. "Compulsary Food at Girls' Schools," *al-tarbiya* 3, 2 (1908): 22–23.

34. Muḥammad Bayumi al-Ḥanid, "Who is More Worthy of Education First, Fathers and Mothers or Sons and Daughters," *al-mu'ayyad* (February 1, 1914): 2.
35. M.Sh., "He Who Educates the Girl Closes the Prison," *al-mu'ayyad* (February 15, 1914): 2.
36. Writing on the period from independence to 1952, Salmoni as well found "nowhere did anyone speak out against female education or downplay its significance." See his "Pedagogies of Patriotism," 613–14.
37. "Women's Education," *al-manar* 2 (1899): 332–34.
38. Naguib Ḥagg, "Girls' Schools and Their Education," *anis al-jalis* 4, 6 (1901), 695–96.
39. Mrs. Yacub Sarruf, "The Sania School," *al-muqtaṭaf* 14, 12 (1890), 836–38. See also "Women's Education," *al-manar* 2 (1899): 332–34.
40. See e.g., "Children's Technical Schools," *al-muqtaṭaf* 35, 6 (1909): 1212–13. Tahtawi also addressed these issues. He believed that boys and girls of the lower and middle classes were entitled to a primary education consisting of technical/vocational education. al-Ṭahṭawi, *murshid*, 60–64.
41. "A School in Its Place," *al-muqtaṭaf* 35, 6 (1909), 1214–15. These views continued in the period beyond my study. See e.g., the comments of Aziz Abaza in the Chamber of Deputies regarding necessity of child labor in fields and factories, May 23, 1933, 1364 as cited by Magda Baraka, *The Egyptian Upper Class*, 275.
42. "The Woman's Education," *anis al-jalis* 7, 10/11/12 (1904), 1991. For a similar opinion, see Ṣ. Ilyas, *al-jins al-laṭif* 2, 5 (1909), 133–36.
43. "Girls' Education," *al-muqtaṭaf* 10, 4 (1885): 201–05.
44. "Girls' Education," *al-muqtaṭaf* 10, 4 (1885), 204.
45. See 187n46 of this work.
46. Ṭanus, "Women's Education," 233–34.
47. "Girls' Education: A Dialogue Between a Man and a Woman," *al-muqtaṭaf* 41, 1 (1912): 81–83.
48. "Household Duties and Women's Education," *al-laṭa'if* 3, 10 (1888): 432–38; "The Home, Hygiene, and Health," *al-laṭa'if* 2, 9 (1888): 385–92; Yusif Effendi Ghanimat al-Baghdadi, "Reform of Female Education," *anis al-jalis* 7, 10/11/12 (1904): 2035–36; Maḥmud Ibrahim, "Education and Upbringing," 3, 7 (1900): 271–77; Maḥmud Ibrahim, "The Future of Women in Egypt," *anis al-jalis* 3, 9 (1900): 345–49; "Girls' Education," *majallat jam^c iat al-malajy al-^{c} abbasiyya* 9, 2 (1327): 419–23; Aḥmad Abu Ḥashima, "Where is Girls' Education," *al-mu'ayyad* (February 26, 1914): 2. Malak Hifni Nasif provided a radical opposing view, asserting that women should have unrestricted freedom of education and be allowed to pursue careers if they so desire. "Speech of an Egyptian [Woman] About Women," *al-manar* 12, 5 (1909): 353–71.
49. *Annual Report 1905*, 88; Juan Ricardo Cole, "Feminism, Class, and Islam in Turn-of-the-Century Egypt," *IJMES* 13 (1981), 391, 396–99.
50. "Teach the Girl," *al-sa^{c}ada* 1, 4 (1902), 74. See also, "Upbringing and Education," *al-sa^{c}ada* 1, 1 (1902): 3–4; "Satisfaction is Part of Happiness," *al-sa^{c}ada* 1, 9 (1902): 189–92; "Girls' Education," *al-sa^{c}ada* 1, 10 (1902): 213–16; "Knowledge and Women," *al-sa^{c}ada* 2, 3 (1903): 480–83; Naguib ^{c}Awwad, "Knowledge is Necessary for Women," *al-sa^{c}ada*, 2, 5 (1903): 524–28; "Knowledge and Women," *al-sa^{c}ada* 2, 7/8 (1904): 561–64; "The Woman's Education," *al-sa^{c}ada* 2, 7/8 (1904): 566–67; "Knowledge and Women," *al-sa^{c}ada* 2, 9/10 (1904): 596–604.
51. Raḥma Sarruf, "The Shortage of Girls' Schools, Its Reform is Necessary," *al-muqtaṭaf* 35, 2 (1909): 793–95.
52. Since *al-sufur* was a magazine edited by men focusing on women's issues, one could certainly question the authenticity of its female anonymous writers, at a time when more

women were signing their full names in the press. "My Childhood and My Youth," *al-sufur* (December 1, 1916): 5.

53. Mrs. Yacub Sarruf, "The Sania School," 838.
54. DW, MW, NM, box A4, Alice (Elise?) Forbes, Arabic translation of her Report on the Abbas School's Girls' Division, July 20, 1897.
55. *Annual Report 1910*, 55.
56. *Egyptian Gazette* (May 28, 1913) as cited in Leslie Schmida, *Education in the Middle East* (1983), 40.
57. *Annual Report 1907*, 40; *Annual Report 1908*, 44; *Annual Report 1909*, 48.
58. *Annual Report 1910*, 60; *Annual Report 1911*, 27; Loi de 1913 portant sur la création d'une école d'Economie Domestique et l'agrément de l'exécution de cette loi promulguée par Arrête Ministeriel #1735 du Avril 1913 in *Regulations 1914*.
59. Ahmed Hechmat, "Regulations Relating to Primary Education Certificate for Girls Promulgated by Ministerial Order #1754, August 10, 1913" in *Regulations 1914*.
60. DW, MW, NM, box H4, Note from Adly Yeghen to the Council of Ministers Concerning Changes in the Program of Study at Boys' and Girls' Elementary Schools, July 23, 1916.
61. DW, MW, NM, box A4, Adly Yeghen, Note to the Council of Ministers Concerning the Law and the Order Pertaining to the Creation of Higher Elementary Schools for Girls, June 6, 1916.
62. DW, MW, NM, box A4, Law #14 for the Creation of Higher Elementary Schools for Girls and Ministerial Decision #1934, June 20, 1916.
63. DW, MW, NM, box A4, Changes in the Organization of Sania Teachers' College, July 20, 1921; DW, MW, NM, box A4, Letter from Gafar Waly to the President of the Council of Ministers Regarding the Sania Teachers' College, August 28, 1921.
64. DW, *Période Ismail*, box 12, George Robb, *Educational Progress in Egypt During the Period of 1882–1922*, June 29, 1922, 27–29.
65. Compare comment by Eldon Gorst in *Annual Report 1909*, 48 and Miss Forbes, a headmistress, in her "Report."
66. Salmoni, "Pedagogies of Patriotism," 626–30.
67. Cole, "Feminism," 398.
68. DW, MW, NM, box A23, Adly Yeghen, Note to the President of the Council of Ministers on Discontinuing the Primary Certificate Examination for Girls, May 25, 1915.
69. DW, MW, NM, box A4, Changes in the Organization of Sania Teachers' College, July 20, 1921; DW, MW, NM, box A4, Letter from Gafar Waly to the President of the Council of Ministers Regarding the Sania Teachers' College, August 28, 1921; Robb, *Educational Progress*, 29.
70. See e.g., *Annual Report 1902*, 54–55; *Annual Report 1903*, 61.
71. See e.g., "Elementary Schools or the College," *al-hilal* 14, 1 (1905): 18–22; "The College or Elementary Schools," *al-hilal* 14, 2 (1905): 117–18. For a similar discussion of private versus public education, see "How do I Become a Human Being," *al-tarbiya* 1, 2 (1905): 1–3.
72. Sami, *al-ta^{c}lim*, 84.
73. For statistics on the growth of foreign, community, and governmental schools, see Sami, *al-ta^{c}lim*, 32, app. 1, statistics for 1914 and 1915.
74. For a discussion of the discourse on the veil, see Leila Ahmed, *Women and Gender in Islam* (New Haven: Yale University Press, 1992, 144–68. See also Cole, "Feminism," 394–99.
75. Booth, *May Her Likes Be Multiplied*, 111, 149–50.

8 Textbooks: Defining Roles and Boundaries

1. Michael Apple and Linda K. Christian-Smith, "The Politics of the Textbook," in their *The Politics of the Textbook* (New York: Routledge, 1991), 1–3.
2. See e.g., Kenneth Teitalbaum, "Critical Lessons from our Past: Curricula of Socialist Sunday Schools," and Allan Luke, "The Secular Word: Catholic Reconstruction Dick and Jane," in Apple and Christian-Smith, *Politics*, 135–65 and 166–90, respectively.
3. See e.g., H. Lazarus-Yafeh, "An Inquiry into Arabic Textbooks," *Asian and African Studies* 8, 1 (1972): 1–19; Olivier Carré, *Enseignement islamique et idéal socialiste: Analyse conceptuelle des manuels d'instruction musulmane en Egypte* (Beyrouth: Dar El-Machreq, 1974); Michael W. Suleiman, "Values Expressed in Egyptian Children's Readers," *Journal of Cross-Cultural Psychology* 8, 3 (1977): 347–55; Avner Giladi, "Some Aspects of Social and National Contents in Egyptian Curricula and Textbooks," *Asian and African Studies* 19, 2 (1985): 157–86; Heather Behn, "The Portrayal of Gender Roles in Egyptian Primary School Textbooks," paper presented at MESA, November 1989.
4. With respect to the study of women and gender, the older studies tend to utilize methods of analysis based on numbers of representations in illustrations and in narratives, as well as the characteristics and functions of male and female characters.
5. See e.g., Barak Salmoni, "Pedagogies of Patriotism: Teaching Socio-Political Community in Twentieth-Century Turkish and Egyptian Education" (Ph.D. diss., Harvard University 2002); Betty Anderson, "Writing the Nation: Textbooks of the Hashemite Kingdom of Jordan," *Comparative Studies of South Asia, Africa, and the Middle East*, 21, 1/2 (2001): 5–14; Nathan Brown, "Democracy, History, and the Contest over Palestinian Curriculum," paper presented at Adam Institute Conference on "Attitudes Toward the Past in Conflict Resolution," Jerusalem, November 2001; Gregory Starett, *Putting Islam to Work: Education, Politics, and Religious Transformation in Egypt* (Berkeley: University of California Press, 1998).
6. Christine Sleeter and Carl Grant, "Race, Class, Gender, and Disability in Current Textbooks," in Apple and Christian-Smith, *Politics*, 79–80.
7. Robert Bocock, *Hegemony* (New York: Tavistock Publications, 1986), 37.
8. Gregory Starett's recent work on education and religious transformation in Egypt, particularly chapters 4 through 6, are useful for understanding the role of curricula, textbooks, methods of instruction, and the idiosyncracy/history of the individual teacher. See his *Putting Islam to Work*.
9. My research on textbooks was carried out at the documents office of the Ministry of Education, located in the Museum of Education. I am grateful to both Beth Baron and Raouf Abbas for making me aware of this fascinating cache of books. The oldest textbooks housed in the documents office, specifically for girls, were published between 1910 and 1920.
10. *Annual Report 1903*, 61; *Annual Report 1902*, 53; *Annual Report 1905*, 87–88; *Annual Report 1906*, 89–90; Ministry of Public Instruction, *Syllabus of the Primary and Secondary Courses of Study* (Cairo: National Printing Department, 1897), 14; Selçuk Akşin Somel, *The Modernization of Public Education in the Ottoman Empire, 1839–1908* (Leiden: Brill, 2001), 6; Chamber of Deputies, June 9, 1937, 1356–65 as cited by Magda Baraka, *The Egyptian Upper Class Between Revolutions, 1919–1952* (Reading: Ithaca, 1998), 275; Barak Salmoni, "Pedagogies of Patriotism," 586, 594. See also Benjamin C. Fortna, *Imperial Classroom* (Oxford: Oxford University Press, 2002).

11. Egypt, Ministry of Public Instruction, *Syllabuses of Hygiene for Various Schools* as promulgated by Ministerial Order No. 1756, August 10, 1913 in *Regulations 1914* (Cairo: Government Press, 1914).
12. Dr. Sarubyaq, *^{c}ilm al-ṣiḥa lil-makatib* and *^{c}ilm al-ṣiḥa lil-makatib lil-banat* (Cairo: Maṭba^{c}at al-Ma^{c}arif, 1918 [fifth printing]).
13. Anne McClintock. *Imperial Leather: Race, Gender and Sexuality in the Colonial Contest* (New York: Routledge, 1995), 207-08.
14. This literature dates back to the 17th and 18th centuries, and perhaps earlier. Some texts are dated from the 19th century, but were copied from earlier sources. See e.g., al-Shaykh al-^{c}Alama al-Salik al-Naṣiḥ Abi al-^{c}Abbas Aḥmad Ibn ^{c}Abdullah al-Gaza'i, *^{c}ilm al-tawḥid*, 1888.
15. See e.g., ^{c}Abdullah Nadim, "In Morals and Customs," *al-ustadh* 1, 3 (1892): 51–56; "Economy is Economy," *al-muqtaṭaf* 50, 3 (1917): 282–83; "Alcohol," *majallat jam^{c}iyat malaji' al-Abbasiyya* 9, 1 (1327): 29–31; Dr. Maḥmud Sidqi, "The Danger of Wine," *al-tarbiya* 3, 2 (1908): 13–14; Muḥammad Zaki, "Europeanized Turkish Women," *anis al-jalis* 9, 7 (1906): 165–66.
16. Mitchell, *Colonising Egypt* (Cambridge: Cambridge University Press, 1988), 114–22.
17. Muḥammad Rushdy, *al-tadbir al-^{c}amm fil-ṣḥa wal-maraḍ* (Cairo: Maṭba^{c}at al-^{c}Itimad, 1919 [1912]).
18. For more information on this relationship, see Pollard, "Nurturing."
19. *al-tarbiya al-awliyya wal-akhlaq*, part one, trans. by Ḥafiẓ Ibrahim (Cairo, 1913 [second printing]), introduction.
20. ^{c}Ali Effendi Fikry, *adab al-fatat* (Cairo: al-Handiyya, 1911 [sixth printing]), 2–4.
21. Francis Mikha'il, *al-tadbir al-manzili al-ḥadith* [*TMH1*], part one (Cairo: Maṭba^{c}at al-Ma^{c}arif, 1910), 4.
22. Anṭun al-Gamayyil, *al-fatat wal-bayt* [*FB*] (Cairo: Maṭba^{c}at al-Ma^{c}arif, 1916), 7.
23. al-Gamayyil, *FB*, 15–16.
24. Francis Mikha'il, *al-tadbir al-manzili al-ḥadith [TMH2]*, part 2 (Cairo: Maṭba^{c}at al-Ma^{c}arif, 1911), 3–4.
25. Mikha'il, *TMH1*, 3–4.
26. Mikha'il, *TMH1*, 43–45.
27. Francis Mikha'il, *al-niẓam al-manzili [NM]* (Cairo: Maṭba^{c}at al-Ma^{c}arif, 1913), 55–56.
28. Mikha'il, *TMH1*, 85–94, and 163–67.
29. al-Gamayyil, *FB*, 71–72.
30. Regarding servants, in *Household Organization*, Mikhail explains that he had discussed servants' policy in a previous book, and in the others he has no chapters or subsections pertaining to servants, although he occasionally makes reference to them. Gamayyil devotes 17 pages to the subject, encouraging the young woman to be a benevolent dictator over her servants. Mikha'il, *NM*, 85–86; Mikha'il, *TMH1*, 5–8, 12; al-Gamayyil, *FB*, 104–21.
31. According to Yacub Artin, between 1882 and 1907, house rents increased from a ratio of 1 to 2.5 and domestic servants' wages from 1 to 2.1. See the extract from his *Essai sur les causes de renchérissement de la vie materielle au Caire au courant du XIXe siècle* in "The Trend in Prices, 1800–1907," in Charles Issawi, ed. *The Economic History of the Middle East* (Chicago: University of Chicago Press, 1966): 450–51. Baraka reports that this trend continued after independence. See her *The Egyptian Upper Classes*, 178.
32. al-Gamayyil, *FB*, 164.
33. Mikha'il, *TMH1*, 163–67; 220–25.
34. Mikha'il, *TMH1*, 19.
35. al-Gamayyil, *FB*, 47–48.

36. Mikha'il, *TMH1*, 19–24; al-Gamayyil, *FB*, 47–50.
37. al-Gamayyil, *FB*, 47; Mikha'il, *TMH2*, 139–48; al-Gamayyil, *TMH1*, 19–24.
38. Mikha'il, *NM*, 9–12.
39. Mikha'il, *TMH1*, 28–30.
40. al-Gamayyil, *FB*, 51–53.
41. al-Gamayyil, *FB*, 73–74. He also has subsections entitled "Cleanliness and its Benefits" and "How to Clean the House" in another chapter. al-Gamayyil, *FB*, 50–59.
42. al-Gamayyil, *FB*, 33. According to Timothy Burke, similar concerns regarding servants and the correlation between physical dirt and "moral" filth were present in Rhodesian textbooks. See Jeannie Boggie, *A Husband and a Farm in Rhodesia* (np: Salisbury, 1939), 106 as cited by Burke, *Lifebouy Men, Luxe Women* (Durham: Duke University Press, 1996), 20.
43. Mikha'il, *NM*, 14–16.
44. Note that only in one of his textbooks were photographs widely used. In parts one and two of *tadbir al-manzili al-ḥadith*, he relied upon sketches. Mikha'il, *NM*, 12–14.
45. Mikha'il, *NM*, 12–14.
46. Mikha'il, *NM*, 66–85.
47. Mikha'il, *TMH1*, 36; Mikha'il, *NM*, 32–51; 66–85.
48. Mikha'il, *NM*, 21–31.
49. al-Gamayyil, *FB*, 65.
50. al-Gamayyil, *FB*, 11.
51. Mikha'il, *TMH1*, 14; Mikha'il, *TMH2*, 137–38.
52. al-Gamayyil, *FB*, 18, 35, 37.
53. al-Gamayyil, *FB*, 38–42; Mikha'il, *TMH1*, 17–18.
54. Salmoni, "Pedagogies of Patriotism," 630.
55. al-Gamayyil, *FB*, 43–46; Mikha'il, *TMH1*, 14–16; Mikha'il, *NM*, 69–70.
56. See e.g., Ministry of Public Instruction, *al-madaris al-ibtida'iyya al-darja al-ula* (Bulaq: Maṭba^{c}at al-ahliyya, 1885); Ministry of Public Instruction, *lycée: madrasat al-normal, qism al-mubtadiyan, brugramat*, (1887); Ministry of Public Instruction, *Syllabus 1892*; Ministry of Public Instruction, *Syllabus 1901* (Bulaq, 1901); Ministry of Public Instruction, *Syllabus of Secondary Courses of Study* (Cairo: National Printing Department, 1905); DW, MW, NM, box A23, Report on Curriculum in Primary Schools, June 7, 1897; DW, MW, NM, box A23, Changes in Secondary Curriculum, October 28, 1902; DW, PI, box 12, George Robb, *Educational Progress in Egypt During the Period of 1882–1922.*
57. *al-nafaḥat al-^{c}abbasiya fil-mabadi al-ḥisabiyya* (Cairo: Maṭba^{c}at al-Kubry al-Amiriyya, 1898), 76–82; ^{c}Abdullah Effendi Dhaki, *nuzhat al-albab fi ^{c}ilm al-ḥisab* (Cairo: Maṭba^{c}at al-Ma^{c}arif, 1900), 224–228
58. Note, not all textbooks eliminate the French conversion rate. Muḥammad Ḥamid, *mu^{c}ayyan al-ṭulab ^{c}ala al-ḥisab* (Maṭba^{c}at al-Amiriyya, 1891); *al-nafahat al-^{c}abbasiya fil-mabadi' al-ḥisabiyya* (Cairo: Maṭba^{c}at al-Kubry al-Amiriyya, 1898); Muḥammad Khalid Ḥasanayn, *kitab al-ḥisab lil-madaris al-ibtida'iyya*, part one (Cairo: Maṭba^{c}at al-Ma^{c}arif, 1926).
59. Robb, *Educational Progress*, 5–6, 13, 27–29; DW, AT, box 231, The Egyptian University: Administration Council's Plan for the Operation of the University for 1911–12.
60. ^{c}Ali al-Kilani, *al-ḥisab lil-aṭfal*, part one (Cairo: Maktabat al-Ahliyya).
61. See e.g., Dhaki, *ḥisab*; Ḥamid, *ḥisab*; Ḥasanayn, *ḥisab*; Committee from Employees of the Ministry of Public Instruction, *kitab al-ḥisab lil-makatib al-^{c}amma al-ilzamiyya*, part four (Cairo: Maṭba^{c}at al-Amiriyya, 1938).
62. al-Gamayyil, *FB*, 36–37; 86–90.

63. Mikha'il, *TMH1*, 139–156; Mikha'il, *TMH2*, 5–13; Mikha'il, *NM*, 64–66.
64. Mikha'il, *TMH1*, 175–78.
65. al-Gamayyil, *FB*, 38, 91–97.
66. According to Lane, in the 1820s/30s, people did not commonly change their clothes for sleep. Thus, pajamas were a recent innovation. Lane, *An Account of the Manners and the Customs of the Modern Egyptians* (London: M.A. Nattali, 1846), vol. 1, 210.
67. al-Gamayyil, *FB*, 79, 97; Mikha'il, *TMH1*, 94, 225–32, 232–37. On the sewing machine, see Uri Kupferschmidt, "The Social History of the Sewing Machine in the Middle East," unpublished paper presented at the Ben Gurion University Workshop on the history of consumption, March 2001.
68. Mikha'il, *TMH2*, 101–02.
69. Mikha'il, *TMH2*, 103–37.
70. al-Gamayyil, *FB*, 97–98.
71. al-Gamayyil, *FB*, 99–100.
72. Mikha'il, *TMH1*, 5–8; *TMH2*, 40–42, 62–100.
73. Magda Baraka, *The Egyptian Upper Class*, 177.
74. al-Gamayyil, *FB*, 37.
75. Mikha'il, *TMH1*, 26–28; 171–75.
76. al-Gamayyil, *FB*, 17.
77. al-Gamayyil, *FB*, 25, 168.
78. Mikha'il, *TMH2*, 168, 174.
79. Mikha'il, *TMH2*, 169–70.
80. Mikha'il, *TMH1*, 185–96.
81. al-Gamayyil, *FB*, 21–23,
82. Mikha'il, *TMH2*, 168, 174.
83. Mikha'il, *TMH2*, 173–74.
84. Baraka, *The Egyptian Upper Class*, 170.
85. Baron, *The Women's Awakening*, 20, 72, 156.
86. Biographical information on al-Gamayyil obtained from *al-laṭa'if al-muṣawwara*, July 28, 1941, 1 and *al-ithnayn wal-dunya*, January 26, 1948, 30.
87. The letter from Ismail Sabri Pasha was one that had been sent to the author, and the one from Mustafa Lutfi al-Manfaluti had been published in *al-ahram*.
88. According to A. Shanuda, after Saad Zaghlul's appointment as Minister of Public Instruction, more working class women enrolled in *kuttabs*, and increasingly larger numbers of middle class women entered public schools and teacher training colleges. See his *Sa^{c}d Zaghlul: naẓir al-ma^{c}arif* (Cairo: Dar al-Fikr al-^{c}Arabi, 1977), 142–43, 157–59.
89. Marilyn Booth argues that teaching did not contradict this role since teachers at the time were unmarried. Booth, *May Her Likes Be Multiplied: Biography and Gender Politics in Egypt* (Berkeley: University of California Press, 2001), 128. Nevertheless, even in receiving higher education and postponing marriage, teachers were challenging this construct of new womanhood.
90. Baron, *The Women's Awakening*, 41–42, 155–58, 164–67.
91. Cathlyn Mariscotti, "Egyptian Women's Differentiated Constructs of Gender Identity in the Early 20th Century," paper presented at MESA, November 1995.
92. Ministry of Public Instruction, *Code of Regulations Relating to School Organization and Discipline* (Cairo: National Printing Department, 1911), 18–19, 24, 35–36.
93. Historically, in the Middle East, the role of the teacher has been a powerful one. For a discussion of traditional Islamic pedagogical technique, see A.L. Tibawi, *Islamic Education Its Traditions and Its Modernization into the Arab National Systems* (London: Luzac, 1972), part one, chapter 3.

94. Muḥammad Aḥmad Rakha and Muḥammad Ḥamdi, *kitab al-akhlaq lil-banat* (Cairo: al-Maṭba^{c}at al-Handasiyya, 1918).
95. Rakha and Ḥamdi, *al-akhlaq*, 11–22.
96. Rakha and Ḥamdi, *al-akhlaq*, 23–60.
97. Rakha and Ḥamdi, *al-akhlaq*, 61–88.
98. Baraka, *The Egyptian Upper Classes*, 212–13.
99. Rakha and Ḥamdi, *al-akhlaq*, 89–93.
100. Rakha and Ḥamdi, *al-akhlaq*, 96–148.
101. In the late nineteenth century, two biographical dictionaries, written by women and about women, set the standard for the genre of biographies that emerged in the mainstream and women's presses in the early twentieth century. See Maryam al-Naḥḥas, *ma^{c} riḍ al-ḥasna' fi tarajim al-mashahir al-nisa'* (Alexandria: Maṭba^{c}at Jaridat Miṣr, 1879) and Zaynab Fawwaz, *al-durr al-manthur fi tabaqat rabbat al-khudur* (Cairo: al-Maṭba^{c}a al-Kubra al-Amiriyya bi-Bulaq, 1894). For a discussion of this genre, see Booth, *May*.
102. Rakha and Ḥamdi, *al-akhlaq*, 96–99.
103. Rakha and Ḥamdi, *al-akhlaq*, 99–101.
104. Rakha and Ḥamdi, *al-akhlaq*, 105–07.
105. Denise Spellberg, *Politics, Gender, and the Islamic Past* (New York: Columbia University Press, 1994), chapter 5.
106. Rakha and Ḥamdi, *al-akhlaq*, 107–09.
107. Rakha and Ḥamdi, *al-akhlaq*, 109–11.
108. Rakha and Ḥamdi, *al-akhlaq*, 111–13.
109. Rakha and Ḥamdi, *al-akhlaq*, 113–15.
110. Rakha and Ḥamdi, *al-akhlaq*, 115–16.
111. Rakha and Ḥamdi, *al-akhlaq*, 116–19.
112. Rakha and Ḥamdi, *al-akhlaq*, 119–22.
113. Rakha and Ḥamdi, *al-akhlaq*, 122–25.
114. Rakha and Ḥamdi, *al-akhlaq*, 125–28.
115. Rakha and Ḥamdi, *al-akhlaq*, 128–33.
116. For more information on Grace Darling, see Jessica Mitford, *Grace Had an English Heart* (New York: E.P. Dutton, 1988).
117. Rakha and Ḥamdi, *al-akhlaq*, 134–39.
118. Rakha and Ḥamdi, *al-akhlaq*, 140–43.
119. Rakha and Ḥamdi, *al-akhlaq*, 144–48.
120. As mentioned in chapter 7, Tahtawi enumerated a number of exemplary women in his *murshid al-amin lil-banat wal-banin*. The overlap between Tahtawi and Rakha and Hamdi includes Bilqis, Aisha, Shajarat al-Durr, and Elizabeth. Among the women that Tahtawi mentions, but that do not make their way into the Rakha and Hamdi text, are Maryam, Hatshepsut, Cleopatra, and Catherine the Great. Rifa^{c}at al-Rafi^{c} al-Ṭahṭawi, *murshid al-amin lil-binat wal-banin* (Cairo: Maṭba^{c}at al-Madaris al-Malakiyya, 1289), 32, 67, 105–06. Biographies on women from the classical Islamic period were often taken from early Islamic sources verbatim, and those for more recent women taken from the al-Nahhas and Fawwaz dictionaries with or without editing. Marilyn Booth, "Prescribing Lives for Women in Egypt," lecture given at Center for Middle East Studies, Harvard University, March 19, 1997.
121. Booth, *May*, 64.
122. This was a common feature of biographies in the women's press. See Booth, *May*, 172.
123. The "woman behind the man" was also a staple of turn-of-the-century biographies that appeared in the women's press. Booth, *May*, 174, 215.

124. According to Mervat Hatem, between 1927 and 1937 alone, the number of women in the labor force increased six-fold. See her "Egypt's Middle Class in Crisis: The Sexual Division of Labour," *Middle East Journal* 42 (1988), 412.
125. Ruth Woodsmall, *Study of the Role of Women in Lebanon, Egypt, Israel, Jordan, and Syria, 1954–1955* (New York: International Federation of Business and Professional Women, 1956), 26–33.
126. Egypt, Ministry of Public Instruction, *Syllabuses of Hygiene for Various Schools* as promulgated by Ministerial Order No. 1756, August 10, 1913 in *Regulations 1914.*
127. ^{c}Ali Mubarak, *^{c}alam al-din* (Alexandria: Maṭba^{c}at Jaridat al-Maḥrusa, 1882), 446–47, 816–18, 962–63 as cited in Timothy Mitchell, *Colonising Egypt*, 63–64.
128. Rifa^{c}at al-Rafi^{c} al-Ṭahṭawi, *al-^{c}amal al-kamila li Rifa^{c}at al-Rafi^{c} al-Ṭahṭawi* Muḥammad ^{c}Imara, ed. (Beirut: al-Mu'asasa al-^{c}Arabiyya lil-Dirasat wal-Nashr, 1973), 108–09, 114.
129. Ṭahṭawi, *al-^{c}amal al-kamila*, 117–19.

9 CONCLUSION

1. Joseph Sève came to work for Muhammad Ali some time after the fall of Napoleon. He later converted to Islam and changed his name to Suleiman al-Faransawi. His daughter married Muhammad Pasha Charif (Sharif).
2. This wording comes from an American visitor to Nazli's *ḥarim*. Grace Thompson Seton, *A Woman Tenderfoot in Egypt* (New York: Dodd, Mead and Company, 1923), 61.
3. Juan Cole, "Feminism, Class, and Islam in Turn-of-the-Century Egypt," *IJMES* 13 (1981), 387; Judith Gran, "Impact of the World Market on Egyptian Women," *MERIP Reports* 58 (June 1977), 4.
4. Cole, "Feminism," 391. This outlook continued after independence. See e.g., an article published in the magazine of the Muslim Brotherhood, delineating the "proper" education of girls and citing unneccessary subjects, including law, history, geography, physical and mathematical sciences, and foreign languages. "Mail Box—Girls' Education," *al-ikhwan al-muslimin* (April 4, 1945), 20.
5. An examination of two marriages from the late–1940s/early–1950s in the semi-autobiographical *The Cairo House* is telling. When Shamel, the father of the protagonist decides that he is ready for marriage, he leaves the matter to his elder sister and his eldest brother's wife, his only instructions being "no cousins . . . and none of these 'modern' girls." The author juxtaposes the durability of this marriage in the face of crisis to the short-lived marriage of Gina and Ali, who married for "love." Samia Serageldin, *The Cairo House* (Syracuse: Syracuse University Press, 2000), 23, 32, 40–42. Currently Hanan Kholoussy of New York University is conducting doctoral research on the issues of gender, marriage practices, and nationalism in early twentieth century Egypt.
6. For a discussion of the different types of messages within advertisements, see Roland Barthes, "The Rhetoric of the Image," in *The Visual Culture Reader*, Nicholas Mirzoeff, ed. (London: Routledge, 1998), 71–73.
7. Marshall McLuhan, "Woman in the Mirror," in *The Visual Culture Reader*, 131–32.

Index